THE
SIDNEY
FAMILY
ROMANCE

THE
SIDNEY
FAMILY
ROMANCE

MARY WROTH,
WILLIAM HERBERT,
AND
THE EARLY MODERN
CONSTRUCTION OF GENDER

GARY WALLER

WAYNE STATE UNIVERSITY PRESS   DETROIT

Library of Congress Cataloging-in-Publication Data

Waller, Gary F. (Gary Fredric), 1945–
    The Sidney family romance : Mary Wroth, William Herbert, and the early modern
construction of gender / Gary Waller.
        p. cm.
    Includes bibliographical references and index.
    ISBN 0-8143-2436-3 (alk. paper)
    1. Wroth, Mary, Lady, ca. 1586–ca. 1640.   2. Pembroke, William Herbert,
3d Earl of Pembroke, 1580–1630.   3. Authors, English—Early modern,
1500–1700—Biography.   4. Women and literature—England—History—17th
century.   5. Man-woman relationships in literature.   6. Psychoanalysis and
literature.   7. Authorship—Sex differences.   8. Sex role in literature.   9. Sidney
family.   I. Title.
    PR2399.W7Z95   1993
    823.9'003—dc20
    [B]   92-42532

Book design by Joanne E. Kinney

Jacket Art: Title page from *The Countess of Montgomeries Urania,* by Lady Mary
Wroth, 1621. By permission of the Folger Shakespeare Library.

FOR KATIE

CONTENTS

LIST OF ILLUSTRATIONS

PREFACE

Writing this book has not been as I expected. It has led me into many "adventures" (one of Mary Wroth's favorite words), few of which I anticipated. It started in 1987 as an excursion back to familiar landmarks: I planned to revisit Wroth's poems, which I had edited ten years before; reopen some early work on Philip, Mary, and Robert Sidney; and retrace some of the steps I had taken in *English Poetry of the Sixteenth Century*, especially the delightful but incomplete meanderings through Petrarchism. This would be my "big book" as A. C. Hamilton once advised me: it would summarize two decades of research on the Sidney circle and extend my project of bringing contemporary theory to bear on that work. It would persuade my literary history friends who thought I dabbled too much in theoretical name-dropping that I could "do history"; it would reassure those in theory who thought my fascination with the Sidneys was a retrogressive nostalgia for "literature." I would take it slowly. It would be fun, and, as it involved traveling back to familiar ground, it would be easy.

It was indeed fun. It was taken relatively slowly. I did revisit Wroth and the other Sidneys. But they, and I, and virtually everything else had changed. In 1987 I received a fellowship from the John Simon Guggenheim Foundation, giving me nine months in Cambridge. In 1990 the Newberry Library awarded me a fellowship to work on *Urania*, and so gave me a wonderful opportunity to discover the riches of its collection and superb working atmosphere. In 1991 I spent a similarly pleasant time at the Rosenbach Library. But I not only lived, and very intensely, with Wroth's and Pembroke's writings in congenial surroundings; I found I was reading them with very different commitments. As so often, the personal intervened as the book took shape: I married; my

11

wife and I conceived our first (and my third) Cambridge son; I decided to give up (for three years, as it turned out) being an administrator, finished a book of poems, and then watched with increasing excitement and apprehension as the first drafts of the Big Book started to sound as if I was walking, or stumbling, into new territory. It was not as easy as I had thought; but it was becoming more fun.

What I found were the inevitable contradictions of living in history. I intensified my passion for, and commitments to, both psychoanalysis and feminist theory; I brooded over how a materialist cultural politics might interact with these commitments. And, still finding myself fascinated by how actual human beings, not just "historical subjects," in the past and today, struggle within their histories and write themselves into poems, plays, letters, and prose stories, I was tagged by some of my colleagues with the supposedly odious label of "humanist"—and found myself objecting less and less. To help me through some of these contradictions, I turned to a group of recent studies that took my thinking and self-examination well beyond literary and cultural history: Klaus Theweleit's *Male Fantasies*, Louise Kaplan's *Female Perversions*, Jessica Benjamin's *Bonds of Love*, and—a work with which I have conducted a fascinated, indignant dialogue (or polylogue, since a number of the voices I hear in myself are involved)—Camille Paglia's *Sexual Personae*.

What I have above all discovered in writing this book was that in visiting my past work I was visiting not just books and manuscripts, but parts of myself, some long neglected, some formed back before I could remember—back even before my own fantasies of separation, autonomy, and mutuality, matters which loom very large here, were taking shape. One argument of this book is that both individually and as historical subjects formed by the complexities of gender, class, and ethnicity, we are tied to what we study and read and write about in more ways than we suspect. Another is that those ties (and the agency that knowing more about them should produce) ought to be part of our academic discourse. I have developed these arguments in chapter one, so I will not go over them further here.

There is no way I will be able to record all my debts to friends, old and new, who have played a part in the writing of this book. Some, however, do deserve special acknowledgement. Margaret McLaren, much of whose work on Mary Wroth lies unpublished (though it is widely quoted by all of us in the field), gave me the initial impetus to work on Wroth. Naomi Miller and I spent three years working on a volume of essays on Wroth, which we conceived over a Spenser Society luncheon and nurtured at many conferences, meetings, and not least by electronic mail. Janel Mueller invited me to write on the Sidney family romance for *Modern Philology* and then subjected my essay to the most rigorous and helpful critique since Lionel Knights worked over my doctoral dissertation twenty-five years ago. Josephine Roberts, ever gracious and supportive, gave me all kinds of help, especially with *Urania*. Mary Ellen Lamb helped me clarify some of my thinking on masculinism as we planned a joint Shakespeare Association seminar, and has, indeed, given me provocative support over many years. Bill Sessions has always counseled care, humility, and a search for wisdom, and provided not a little of all along the way. A number of my (now former) students worked on Wroth and Pembroke with me with an intensity which gave me new insights at crucial stages: I think particularly of Craig Dionne, Susan Rudy Dorscht, Stacia Nagel, and Michele Osherow. I have also benefited directly from personal or professional help from Elaine Beilin, Jonathan Dollimore, Heather Dubrow, Richard Dutton, Margaret Hannay, Janis Holm, Jean Howard, Coppélia Kahn, Michael Kahn, Peggy Knapp, Roger Kuin, Barbara Lewalski, Barbara Mowat, Carol Neely, Mary Beth Rose, Phyllis Rackin, Deborah Rubin, Ann Shaver, Alan Sinfield, Robert Stillman, Kris Straub, Heather Weidemann, Michael Wheeler, and Suzanne Woods. My new colleagues at the University of Hartford, especially Humphrey Tonkin and Jonathan Lawson, gave me the impetus to go through separation anxiety and finish the damn thing. Candy Grover was a very helpful research assistant. I am grateful for the enthusiasm of the Wayne State University Press, especially Lynn Trease and Sandra Williamson. My greatest debt is recorded in the dedication.

Earlier versions of parts of chapters one, three, and eight appeared in "Mother/Son, Father/Daughter, Brother/Sister, Cousins: The Sidney Family Romance," *Modern Philology*, 88 (1991); and "The Sidney Family Romance: Gender Construction in Early Modern England," in *Reading Mary Wroth: Representing Alternatives*, edited by Naomi Miller and Gary Waller (University of Tennessee Press, 1991). Other paragraphs and phrases have appeared in *English Poetry of the Sixteenth Century* (Longman, 1986), the second edition of which has been taking shape at the same time as this book was being revised for publication. A version of chapter two was presented at the Shakespeare Association of America conference in Kansas City in 1992, and I am grateful for the comments made by members of the seminar. Parts of chapter four were presented at conferences on "Sex and Sexuality in the Middle Ages and Renaissance" at the University of Toronto in 1991, and "The Practice and Representation of Reading in Britain" at Magdalene College, Cambridge, in 1992. A few paragraphs have surfaced in the *Sidney Newsletter*, to the editor of which, Gerald Rubio, I have been indebted over many years.

Quotations from the published writings of Pembroke and Wroth are taken from the following sources:

Pembroke, William Herbert, third earl of. *Poems Written by the Right Honorable William Earl of Pembroke, Lord Steward of his Majesties Household, Whereof Many of Which Are Answered by Way of Repartee, by Sir Benjamin Ruddier*. London: Matthew Inman, 1660. Cited in the text as as 1660.

Wroth, Lady Mary. *The Countess of Mountgomeries Urania*. London: John Marriott and John Grismand, 1621. Cited in the text as *Urania*.

———. *The Poems of Lady Mary Wroth*, ed. Josephine A. Roberts. Baton Rouge: Louisiana State University Press, 1983. Cited in the text as *Poems*.

———. *Lady Mary Wroth's Loves Victory: The Penshurst Manuscript*, ed. Michael Brennan. London: Roxburghe Club, 1988.

———. "The Countess of Montgomery's Urania." Newberry Library continuation (MS fY 1565. W 95), 2 volumes. Cited in the text as *N1* and *N2*.

In quoting from early modern texts, original spelling has been kept, but *i* and *v* have been regularized.

1

The Sidney Family Romance:
Breeching the Subject

If anyone is inclined to turn away in horror from this depravity of the childish heart or feels tempted, indeed, to dispute the possibility of such things, he should observe that these works of fiction, which seem so full of hostility, are none of them really so badly intended, and that they still preserve, under a slight disguise, the child's original affection for his parents.

Sigmund Freud

The crochet needle moves forward, steadily enlarging old patterns and creating new ones. In the process of creating something new, every so often at some crucial juncture the needle reaches back to pull in earlier stitches and patterns, integrating some facet of the old into a new pattern of organization. Whatever was created earlier can always be given new meaning, and some of what is created later will always bear the influence of earlier patterns.

Louise Kaplan[1]

n 1908, in his *Der Mythus von der Gerburt des Helden* (Myth of the Birth of the Hero), Otto Rank printed an essay by Freud, "Der Familienroman der Neurotiker" (The neurotic's family romance). Noting that "the liberation of an individual, as he [sic] grows up, from the authority of his parents is one of the most necessary though one of the most painful" events of life, Freud describes the symptoms of what he termed the "family romance." Each involves a person's desire to change his or her family circumstances—for instance, fantasies of having richer or more noble parents, or not having to share parental love with siblings. In Freud's account of the Oedipal crisis, as a boy comes to learn what appear to be the facts of sexuality, he develops feelings of hostility and envy towards his father, coupled with an intense desire to bring his mother—the subject, claims Freud, "of the most intense sexual curiosity"—into "situations of secret infidelity" with him. Other typical fantasies of the family romance may involve incestuous feelings for siblings, desires to return to either fancied or real conditions in early childhood when the child was unindividuated from the mother, and a child's "most intense and momentous" general wish, simply "to be big" like his or her parents. In children, such day-dreams, Freud argues, have aims that may have an immediate erotic focus, but are more generally ambitious—not only to seduce or emulate the parents, but simply to be free of their control. In adults, the symptoms of the family romance emerge in desires to discover or recapture a lost state of autonomy, a goal that may be projected, negatively or positively, upon love-objects— lover, spouse, child—who thereby become incorporated into the patterns of desire laid down in childhood.

Our "family romances," then, according to Freud, are the stories— enacted in fantasies or patterns of concrete behavior, or in the narratives of art—that we repeat throughout our lives to enact, relate, or explain these early patterns of desire and frustration generated within the dynamics of the family. The "innumerable peculiarities of the erotic life of human beings," writes Freud, "as well as the compulsive character

17

of the process of falling in love itself are quite unintelligible except by reference to childhood and as being residual effects of childhood."[2]

I shall have occasion to criticize quite radically Freud's formulation of the "family romance," but at this point it should be noted, not entirely in passing, that the phrase has broader connotations than its use within developmental psychology or psychoanalysis. Harold Bloom, for instance, has extended the concept of the family romance to incorporate his analysis of the "anxiety of influence" in literature. More vulgarly, the phrase, "family romance" might be used to refer to the melodramas, or (indeed) tragedies of proscribed erotic attraction between siblings or parents and children—the erotic entanglements of Nabokov's *Lolita* or *Ada*, for instance; or the *cris de coeur* of lovelorn "kissing cousins,"[3] as witness this extract from the "Ask Beth" column in the Boston *Globe* for 25 March, 1988:

> Dear Beth:
> My cousin is extremely precious to me, but killing me. She says she loves me. We have had intimate contact several times, but she also has sex with many boyfriends. She lives so far away I only see her a couple of times a month . . . every time I see her, I fall in love all over again.
>
> Far Gone in Heartache

On this occasion, "Beth"'s stern response was as follows:

> Your cousin is a "sexpot," and your attraction is strongly sexual . . . Intimate relations with first cousins aren't very healthy anyway. You'd be much better off developing real friendships closer to home with girls you can have dates with. When you've made a loving relationship, your awkward passion for your cousin will fade.

Part of my subject in this book is, indeed, a pair of first cousins, not only their "awkward passion," but the stories they both lived and wrote about; and, more broadly, how they (cousins and narratives alike) were constituted as gendered and familial subjects within their complex, early seventeenth-century family romances. William Herbert, third earl of Pembroke (1580–1630), was the son of Mary Sidney Herbert, countess of Pembroke, the sister of Sir Philip Sidney. His cousin, Mary Sidney Wroth (1587?–1653?), was the daughter of Philip and Mary's younger brother Robert, earl of Leicester, viscount de L'Isle, and his wife, Barbara Gamage. William Herbert, whom I shall usually designate by the title he inherited in 1601, Pembroke, was one of the Jacobean court's richest and—excluding James I's serial male favorites—most powerful courtiers and politicians. He was also an occasional poet of moderate talent, some of whose poems were collected and published in 1660 by John Donne, son of the poet and dean of St. Paul's. Mary Sidney Wroth was, for the first decade of the reign of James I, one of the court ladies in attendance on James's wife, Queen Anne; she was the wife—and for the last forty years of her life, the widow—of one of James's occasional hunting companions, Sir Robert Wroth. She was also the most accomplished woman writer in English before Aphra Behn (who may have been her granddaughter): she wrote the first Petrarchan sequence in English by a woman, *Pamphilia to Amphilanthus*, one of the first plays by a woman, *Love's Victory*, and a long and intriguing prose romance, *The Countess of Mountgomeries Urania*. The first part of *Urania* was published in 1621, along with *Pamphilia to Amphilanthus*, but none of Wroth's other writings were published in her lifetime. *Love's Victory* was first published in 1988, and the complete *Urania* is due to be published for the first time in 1994. Pembroke and Wroth were first cousins; many of Wroth's writings (though few, if any, of Pembroke's) refer to their relationship; and together they had, in circumstances that have to be pieced together largely from obscure family records and discrete references in letters and papers, two illegitimate children. Cousins, lovers, parents, and writers, their separate and conjoined histories make up a fascinating, multi-leveled family romance. Freud's concept may, as I shall suggest, need extension and revision, but it does more than provide us with a striking catchphrase. It draws attention to an intriguing psycho-cultural phenomenon that illuminates the lives of the Sidney cousins, and, beyond, the contradictory social, familial, and gendered discourses by which they were constructed, and which to a startling extent remain with us today.

An initial assumption of this study is that the texts of "literature" (in this case more than two hundred and fifty poems, a five-act play, and a prose romance over six hundred thousand words long), as well as (using the term more broadly) the "texts" of the Sidney cousins' everyday material practices, including about two hundred and fifty letters, as well as records of their participation in court entertainments and ceremonies—are all constituted within social practices. But they are not, as an older historicism would say, simply "reflections" of the social. That is, while we need to note the extent to which institutions like the court, the church, and the family are among a society's repressive (or dispersed) structures of determination and control—means by which "individuals" are constructed as "subjects"—we should not underestimate the extent to which particular subjects struggle to articulate themselves in discursive practices, including what has been, however variously, termed "literature."[4] It was in part by writing in self-consciously "literary" forms that the subjects of my study made their marks, however faint, upon the world that so powerfully marked and, in turn, "wrote" them. This relative autonomy of writing, and the residual power of literary forms like the Petrarchan lyric or the prose romance in both shaping and articulating a sense of being a "subject," will constitute an important part of my discussion. It is especially important in the case of Mary Wroth, since it was primarily through her writing that she was able to assert herself against the dominant forces of her culture. If the claim that a poem, play, or prose romance can constitute a disturbance in the ideologies of a culture makes me an ally of those who support the reading and enjoyment of what (as some say) we used to valorize as "literature," I make no apologies. "Pleasure," "insight," and "literature" may be terms that need radical demystification, but they have a long and complex place in the history of our attempts at self-understanding, and they should not be dismissed by a cavalier (or puritan) sneer. It is in the texts of our past, whether "canonical" or for various reasons marginalized, that we read, as Catherine Belsey puts it, "the struggles and transformations which brought into being the world we now inhabit." They also, she adds, "constitute an intervention in those struggles."[5]

The relative autonomy of literary forms, then, will be assumed in my argument. But today any reading of literary (and broader cultural) texts that come to us from the past must grapple with the methodological and wider political issues raised by a variety of revisionist historicisms, including so-called new historicism, cultural materialism, and feminism. Although, increasingly, much of the best scholarship on the early modern period is sufficiently eclectic to combine elements of all three approaches as well as others—so that to distinguish them may seem artificial—their different emphases are perhaps worthy of comment.

New historicism has tended to focus on texts as parts of a network of cultural forces, what Greenblatt terms "a shared code, a set of interlocking tropes and similitudes that function not only as the objects but as the conditions of representations."[6] In the new historicist view, a cultural formation is bound together, almost as in a conspiracy within which individual texts and individual subjects alike are both imprisoned and legitimated. Like the various versions of "old" historicism, which it wants to supplant or supplement, although asking a wider range of questions, including many originating in the concerns of the present, new historicism characteristically sees the past as "other" and resists, not always successfully (or in my view, always wisely), the appropriation of earlier texts by those concerns. It wants to put texts from the past back into the history of their original production. By contrast, cultural materialism's focus is more on growing points and contradictions within a culture, and therefore on the possibilities of historical change: it endeavors to see texts as reproduced in our history rather than simply produced in theirs. Cultural materialism has been especially concerned with resistances to institutions rather than, as is more characteristic of new historicism, with their recuperative power. It has looked especially to

emergent marginal groups—women, witches, the disenfranchised poor—
and to conflict among class factions that may generate social change. By
contrast, the primary concern of new historicism has been the dominant
groups of a culture—in the case of the early modern period, primarily
the monarch and the male aristocracy.

Cutting across both new historicism and cultural materialism—and
at times providing a powerful critique of both—recent feminist scholarship has also characteristically read the past as part of a project to change
the future, drawing attention to the neglected and vital force of gender
in the construction of subjectivity, and characteristically arguing that
gender assignments and relations between the sexes are not subsidiary to
class or race, but constitute "a primary aspect of social organization." Judith Newton notes that there has been, ironically, "much less resistance
(among men and women both)" in recent cultural history and theory "to
seeing class or economic development as a force in constructing gender"
than there has been to assigning gender an equivalent importance, especially outside the domestic and "private" spheres. What she calls "a
dirty secret of history" is that "politics, public institutions, and economic
development"—not to mention the sense of autonomy in the world
beyond the family enjoyed by or denied to individual men and women—
"have been significantly informed by gender, gender relations, the family,
and in particular by men's psychological and emotional investments in
and anxieties over women."[7] The Marxist tradition—which underpins
much cultural materialist work and maintains an important, if uneasy,
relationship with new historicism—has had particular difficulty in handling gender as a major historical determinant. Julia Swindells and Lisa
Jardine point out that the avoidance of the "specificity of women" by the
left occurs in part because such specificity raises the issue of how we live
within ideologies, not just collectively but individually, and so presents
the problem of how to represent subjectivity within a model of history
that has predominantly insisted on a collective determinism. They quote
Sally Alexander: "In speaking of the self and sexual difference feminism
is at its most disturbing. Sexuality, intimacy, divergent conceptions of
need are evoked and haunt the Marxist historian with the specter of
bourgeois individualism, gossip, and the crumbling of working class
unity . . . But if we are to pursue the history of women's experience . . .
there can be no retreat from a closer enquiry into subjectivity and
sexual identity."[8]

The impact of these new historicisms (the plural perhaps a more
accurate way of describing the variety and interactions of the current
ferment) makes me particularly concerned with two initial epistemological questions. The first (as my starting with a concept from Freud
would suggest) is the often uneasy confrontation of psychoanalysis and

historical studies. Jacqueline Rose suggests that what she terms the "return" to psychoanalysis in literary and cultural theory has come "from a dissatisfaction with certain accounts of the social, certain accounts of ideology," like those of Althusser or Macherey for whom the problems of "the subject" and "subjectivity" have been difficult ones to articulate. In his studies of patterns of post-Renaissance childrearing, Philip Greven has argued that without a concern for some kind of psychology, social and intellectual history will remain "curiously remote from the inner life" of the people being studied. What exerts influence in the minds and actions of men and women are not only what is visible, overt, and quantifiable: cognition and action are preceded and accompanied by emotional allegiances and desires that may not be fully conscious or made explicit in a period's documents.[9]

Juliet Mitchell argues that psychoanalysis provides a crucial ingredient of cultural analysis precisely because it concerns itself with such a problem, with "the material reality of ideas both within, and of, man's [sic] history . . . the ideas that people hold and live by." Since the turn of the century, psychoanalysis has tried, variously and contradictorily, to decipher and model the ways by which the habits and seeming laws of human societies have been internalized in what Freud ambiguously named as the unconscious. At the very least, its charting of "the borderline between the biological and the social"—not coincidentally the very terrain occupied by the family and its multiple romances—provides us with rich metaphors for the latent content behind compulsive patterns of individual and social behavior and for the ways recurring fantasies surface in language and other cultural practices. If, to adapt Deleuze and Guattari's formulation, "the unconscious is a desiring-machine and the body parts, components of that machine," cultural historians probing the textual manifestations of human behavior can usefully ponder both theoretical and clinical studies in psychoanalysis and related fields, including developmental psychology, family therapy, and psychotherapy. But they need to do so not only in the classic Freudian areas of the manifestation of desires in dreams and fantasies, or in the common second-generation Freudians' focus on patterns of separation/individuation and object relations, but in ordinary material details: in styles of social relations, attitudes towards work, modes of political or familial conflict, in habituated feelings, in short, in what are felt to be "individual" or "personal" desires and in the most everyday patterns of living. We might then be able to articulate what John Brenkman calls a "collective psychoanalysis" or "a socially grounded theory of subjectivity," which locates ideology, as Jane Gallop puts it, "in a desiring body," and thereby traces the narratives of history where we all experience them, in our bodily experiences as human subjects.[10]

And yet, as if unable to shake its origins in the European bourgeoisie of the late nineteenth century, mainstream psychoanalysis has remained an extraordinarily conservative discourse, often as repressive in its analyses as what it seeks to cure—not least in the reinforcement of bipolar gender stereotypes, the widespread reification of the nuclear family, and the focus on the autonomous "individual" as the object of a reified therapeutic "normalcy." As Eli Zaretsky notes, Freud "invented" psychoanalysis precisely at the point of Western history when the family was increasingly seen as a refuge from both the "economic" and the "social," and in the past seventy or so years Freud's reading of the family had to undergo radical rewriting. His assumption that the patterns of the late nineteenth-century bourgeois family provided the model for transhistorical psychic mechanisms is wildly inadequate. As Mark Poster argues, even if (for instance) we can speak of an Oedipal stage in the early modern family, we cannot assume it would have had the same meaning that it does for a child in Freud's time, or today. A boy's feelings of hostility towards his father may not have had "the same play of love against the body, without the same reliance on the father for support and identification, without the same value to the mother . . . without therefore needing to internalize the father as deeply."[11] So an initial caution about the use of psychoanalysis can be summarized in Fredric Jameson's warning: "Always historicize."[12] It is a warning that psychoanalytical criticism has not always heeded: historical concerns, indeed, have rarely entered psychoanalysis except in the most partial and idealist manner. While Freud's account of the family romance remains a classic articulation, it requires (as does much else in Freud) radical revision.

A second caution arises in relation to Freud's key concept of the "unconscious." His generally consistent assertions were that the human being was a monadic energy system, that an individual unconscious outside of historical and social determinants was inherent in that system, and would (Freud even speculated at times) eventually be located in the brain. In his discussion of the unconscious as a biological function of the human organism, Freud produced a scientific dead end, but he did bequeath us a dazzlingly powerful metaphor for how familial and broader cultural forces construct our behavior and assumptions. In this study I will use the term "unconscious" within a cultural constructivist model to point to the means by which (rather than the place where) social norms are internalized, legitimated, repressed, and reproduced. It is a process that operates within the family even before birth. As children, we are assigned subject positions within and outside the family by our society's ideologies, which are habituated and internalized *as* (a better way of putting it than *in*) the unconscious. As individuals accommodate to the contradictory ideological practices by which they are integrated into institutional structures, they are forced into self-division, what Freud termed "splitting": parts of the self become repressed, "id"-like, because, in David Lichtman's words, "they are cut off from continued growth of the conscious agent." As Mitchell puts it, "the unconscious mind is *the way in which* we acquire" (my emphasis) our roles within the conflicts that position us as subjects within a particular historical formation. Such a formulation of the unconscious (which owes much to recent feminist theory, as it does to the materialist psychoanalysis of Deleuze and Guattari) destabilizes the Freudian reification of a biologically based autonomous self and with it any notion of a fixed set of unconscious drives formed outside of social construction.[13] It also advances my goal of historicizing the unconscious: to show how the conscious and unconscious practices of the two subjects of this book were both constructed and acted within specific historical material conditions. Indeed, we can speak of "the" unconscious, implying some permanent feature of the psyche, only insofar as historically produced repressions become locked into recurring symptomatic patterns.

My use of psychoanalysis in this study is, however, somewhat different from the Lacanianism currently fashionable in many post-modern circles. As Daniel Dervin points out, "preferring one 'reading' of the psyche over others solves some problems, creates others,"[14] and since my investigations of psychoanalysis are unashamedly concerned with real historical subjects—people who desired, suffered, achieved, were confused, turned to each other and inside themselves for help—my affinities are therefore less with Lacanian psychoanalysis than with the more eclectic clinical and theoretical work of feminist psychoanalysts like Jessica Benjamin and Louise Kaplan, and behind them, the long clinical tradition of detailed case histories examined by Robert Stoller, D. W. Winnicott, Margaret Mahler, or Melanie Klein. As the British socialist analyst Michael Rustin puts it, Lacanian theory tends to be "elitist in its political implications, as well as academic in its practice"; further, he argues, it has a singular lack of attention . . . to the experience of human feeling and relationships." For all its striking insights, Lacanian psychoanalysis, in positing a unfixed subject, has disconnected cultural theory from what Rustin terms its "proper base in clinical work."[15] "Proper" here, like "real," is of course, a question-begging term: and what passes for "real" experience and "proper" perspective varies across time and cultures. But it is real men and women, not social structures, who are born, suffer, achieve, yearn, laugh, anguish over choices made by or for them. It is real people who are constructed as "subjects." My focus is unashamedly that of finding ways of describing how historically existent men and women become psycho-culturally constructed as gendered subjects—using as my evidence both their textual practices, their "writings," and their material, embodied lives.

The second methodological issue I want to accentuate is the place of the cultural historian in the history he or she constructs. This history of the Sidney cousins is, in what I hope is an untrivial sense, also *my* history. It is futile and at times disingenuous to disown one's own place and commitments within the history one writes. Each of us brings a distinctive, even if always changing, repertoire, conscious and unconscious, to our reading and interpretative experiences. This repertoire is derived from what Tony Bennett terms a "reading formation," a historically specific construction of the ideological struggles of our particular time and place. Our repertoires, therefore, are not purely "personal," simply the product of our "subjective" ego-identities or "individual" preferences, ambitions, or goals. And because it is *from* a distinctive place and *for* distinctive goals, reading has, implicitly or explicitly, a utopian (or distopian) dimension: ultimately it is our own visions of the future that determine how we view the past. The most engaging readers, I submit, are those who are most engaged with such a vision and who wrestle to make it a part of the stories they tell.

While not all of our particular repertoires—whether specifically "literary" or more general—are strictly relevant to a publicly articulated discussion in a scholarly study, it is, I believe, foolish to imagine that one's beliefs and hopes about ideologically charged issues of class, gender, race, or agency should (or even can) be excluded from discussion. In his recent study of manhood and the American Renaissance, David Leverenz has similarly noted how his readings are bound up with his own involvement with gender role reversals that called into question the dominant ideologies of American maleness. Jane Gallop has likewise recently affirmed her need to "make connections between my work" and "my memories, my sexuality, my dreams." In *Sexual Personae*, a book I continue to read with a mixture of anger and fascination and with which I argue throughout this study, Camille Paglia makes clear the connections between her ethnic background and her celebration of Western masculinism. Stephen Greenblatt's recent collection of essays, *Learning to Curse*, analyses the autobiographical impulses in his writing. And, in a moving preface to *The Country and the City*, Raymond Williams, whose words over many years have stirred my own conscience, speaks of finding himself caught on the boundaries between the contradictory worlds whose history is charted in his book. This study is likewise about its author's struggles with the issues, or at least their historical consequences, that its ostensible subjects contended with.[16]

The case history that is (or should be) the classic warning to any interpreters of other human subjects, especially to male interpreters of women is, of course, Freud's analysis of "Dora." Reading his patient as the sometimes helpless, sometimes duplicitous, victim of her own desires, Freud neglected to ask what part he himself played in her analysis. In view of his insistence on reading Dora's story against the grain, the analyst's seemingly neutral stance provokes not only the question he asked—where was Dora in all of this?—but rather: where was Freud? What is the stake of the observer, the analyst, the reader, the critic, in the analysis he or she offers?[17] In the case of both Pembroke and Wroth, I am trying to describe the cultural practices in which they were implicated, but my own commitments and, no doubt at times, contradictory positions in relation to the gender politics of my own period are not irrelevant. That is why a preliminary discussion of the place of the historian in the history he or she writes cannot, I believe, be confined to a coy paragraph or two in a preface, but must be set in the foreground. It is not simply part of my "approach" or "methodology," but part of my subject—what I am writing about, not merely what I am writing with. My own (though given my place and history they are not my "own") family romances are no doubt deeply involved in my writing about those of the Sidney cousins. Those who have been a part of them (and those who have listened patiently to my thinking aloud about them, or watched me, with irony, sympathy, or indignation, act them out), will at least recognize that I am trying to understand why they take the shape they do—and, further, that they are not "mine" alone, but have formed the material practices of generations of Western men, and not a few women.

I write, then, as a middle-aged white male, working in the late-twentieth century American academy, who brings to his studies a back-ground of the alienation and restlessness of the international academic—Britain and its late Empire (a distant part of which I was born and grew up in), as well as North America. Imperial power (of different kinds), gender and class contradictions, the deracination of the academic intel-lectual, even the repeated return-of-the-repressed all too characteristic of middle age, are parts of the repertoire which I bring to this study. Many of these factors are only of marginal relevance, but some are central. Roland Barthes remarks that we study what we love and hate: I am conscious of a fascination with Pembroke and Wroth for a variety of contradictory and intense reasons. I was born—"interpellated," as Althusserians (in this case, I think, with stunning accuracy) are wont to say—into the system of class, racial, and gender hierarchies that constituted the late British Empire. I thus acquired a seemingly instinctive colonial cringe before the very vestiges of the once dominant ideological apparatuses of monarchy, aristocracy, and class privilege which play such a large part in this book. My education gave me an inevitably contradictory and thankfully strong indoctrination in egalitarianism. In turn, that was countermanded yet further by what in the 1950s was termed "meritocracy," by which I increasingly gained privileged access to precisely those places and institutions which for hundreds of years had helped create the oppressive system into the lower orders of which I had, by class, been assigned, and against which I was increasingly determined (albeit, ironically, in the educational apparatuses themselves!) to struggle. Later I found myself—moved by, as it were, a mixture of chance and choice from an archaic to another, still emergent, empire— on "the American strand," as Pembroke's distant cousin George Herbert put it.[18] Add to that combination of contradictions a commitment to gender equality (its origin very heavily and involved with what looking back appears to be a comically but deep-rooted chivalric reverence for women, the historical and psychological origins of which are by no means irrelevant to this study), and the product is the common picture of an uneasy left-liberal academic, trying (more or less successfully) to drag his all too thoroughly interpellated unconscious and bodily actions into line with his intellectual aspirations and convictions. It is a picture, I suggest, both tragicomic and yet peculiarly positioned in relation to the histories that produced it to be able to offer some insights into the equally tragicomic, seemingly deterministic yet random, lurches of our shared history.

For these parenthetical paragraphs to be of more than therapeutic value, they need to articulate not a "subjective" but a broadly shared set of contradictions. From the amalgam of factors of race, class, gender and (at least would-be) agency that I have summarized, some are of particular significance. I am especially conscious in this study of writing as a male about a woman. While the focus of my study is the family and broader social relationships that surrounded and produced two subjects in crucial respects differently as a man and a woman, there is no question that my primary interests and allegiances are directed to Mary Wroth, not William Herbert, though in that I may, as one of my students once suggested to me, be deceiving myself. I have lived nearly half a century with the increasing conviction (born, as I hinted above, from early nurturing, first developmental and then intellectual) of the persuasiveness of feminist arguments about the history of gender oppression in Western history. It is no accident that many of my scholarly and other writings have concerned women writers or writings about women, but as R. W. Connell puts it in a similar prefatory confession to a study of sexual politics, for a man wishing to position his work and commitments in an appropriate relationship to feminism, there is a "fine line to tread between intruding on women's business and sharing the work of common problems."[19] I believe in the struggle for a society in which men and women would share equally in work opportunities and child rearing, where a multiplicity of gender roles would be celebrated, and where the encultured oppression of men and women alike would be much less pressing. I believe therefore that the attempt to write from one's place in the system of sexual politics must be a major priority for the scholar and teacher.

Within recent literary and cultural criticism, the debates on what has been termed "femmeninism," men reading as women, have focused on the questions of whether (and if so, how) men can read women's writing outside the seemingly gender-neutral but predominantly masculinist discourse of criticism and scholarship.[20] Commonsensically, there seems to be no reason why men cannot ask some of the same questions of a text as women ("how do I respond?", "what are the effects of this text on me?", "what particular powerful ideas are operating here?"). Yet one might counter: are such questions really the "same"? That is, are they asked from the "same" gendered position—that defined by having the body of a woman and having distinctive demands made on and on behalf of that body, or having the gender assignment of "woman" (these two categories are clearly not necessarily synonymous)? What part does gender play in reading? What repertoire of gendered reading strategies (as opposed to textual strategies) are operative within any particular reading situation, in the different matching of repertoires that occurs whenever we read? That "we," of course, constitutes a large part of the problem. Can a man—in early modern England, in America today, when and wherever—catch the grain of the voice, the intonation or syntax which would distinguish a woman's expression of the "same" concepts or concerns? And are such concerns of particular importance when dealing with women writers? These are hard questions, not just intellectually but experientially difficult. For those of us who are men, they challenge us to rethink many of the critical practices we may have comfortably taken for granted most of our professional—indeed, perhaps, for most of our personal—lives. Nor does being self-consciously part of an intellectual or critical avant-garde guarantee a willingness to rethink our gender conditioning. The sexual chauvinism of leftist male intellectuals in America is legendary. One of the most disturbing aspects of certain varieties of the new historicism has been, Carol Neely has argued, its indifference towards gender. Leverenz has called attention to its tendency to reinforce "the reigning American ideology of manhood, which orients the self toward power, not feelings."[21]

My engagement with Mary Wroth, then, is one aspect of this book affected by matters of gender; another is that I am one man writing about another. Notwithstanding the vast historical differences between Pembroke and me—articulated in substantial matters of class, privilege, upbringing, and outlook—is there, I question, a substratum, culturally produced but changing relatively little in four hundred years, of Western patriarchal male behavior that appalls me even while, at times, I find its echoes in my own inheritance, upbringing, and (too often) behavior? Klaus Theweleit's remarkable study, *Male Fantasies*, which analyzes the fiction, autobiographical writings, and fantasies of members of the *Freikorps*, the mercenary armies who later became the basis of the Nazi S. S., provides uncanny insights not only into the socially produced unconscious fantasies of white, right-wing German males of the 1920s, but the main patterns of Western male behavior.[22] Closely attending to language and structure, and underlining the closeness of psychoanalyst and literary critic, Theweleit looked especially closely at his subjects' attitudes towards women, to the dualistic categories of "white" virgin and "red" whore—the designations not without political application— in terms that find echoes back to Petrarchism (and earlier) and forward to the pop culture of our own time. To read such material as a man can be a deeply disturbing experience, especially if one acknowledges one's interpellation into (and often ineffective struggles against) not dissimilar assumptions. It helps underline the calls made by many contemporary feminists for male critics to study the construction of their own gendered assumptions before presuming to invade territory properly belonging to women. In this study I hope to show ways by which we can, indeed, recuperate something of the history of being interpellated as a man. In writing *The Sidney Family Romance*, I am hoping to read those family romances of our own time, which at more times than I sometimes care to acknowledge, reflect upon my own. In particular, I will return more than occasionally to the ideology of gender polarity into which we are so deeply and destructively interpellated by our history. As fundamental as class or race in fixing the subjectivity of early modern England, it remains deeply embedded not only in what Kaplan terms the "dichotomous and caricatured gender ideals of childhood," but the institutional and socializing structures of today, including the family.[23] Part of my agenda is to open repressed or forgotten parts of our history to show both how we became enslaved to such an infantile model of gender and the means by which its lived contradictions started to call it into question, even more than three hundred years ago.

Three great concepts, or "key words," to use Williams's useful term, recur throughout this study. In unguarded moments they may seem absolutes, givens (and to some people, even indispensable preservers) of our culture. They are, in fact, reverberating registers of cultural contra- diction and historical change. Within the current scholarly excitement in early modern studies, two of them, "family" and "gender," have become highly controversial. The third, "romance," has long been of interest, but it too is currently being rewritten in intriguing and controversial ways. Intense pressure has especially been brought to bear upon "family" in the early modern period—through, for instance, the controversies involving Lawrence Stone, Alan MacFarlane, Peter Laslett, Susan Amussen, and other social historians, including the French Annaliste school—and upon "gender" from the extraordinary variety of feminisms, theoretical, scholarly, and practical, Anglo-American and European. "Romance," a staple of traditional genre scholarship, is also being newly scrutinized by a variety of feminists and cultural historians.[24] Behind many of these revaluations stand, inevitably, the figures of Freud and Marx, their insights (and errors) written over and over into later discourses. Marx's readings of family and gender are still suggestive, while the Marxist reading of history has been repeatedly, and differently, rewritten as a never-ending romance. Freud's models of family and gender are the more obviously pervasive; they remain, at the very least, powerful irritants and often magnificently suggestive. But they, too, have been radically rewritten in powerful ways—by Kleinians, object relationists, Lacanians, and various kinds of feminists.[25] And among these swirling currents those of us who grew up through our schooling to revere what we once completely unselfconsciously termed the "literature" of early modern England have learned, sometimes through great anguish, to reread texts which we so long took for granted—by Shakespeare, Spenser, Donne, others, together with texts by writers hitherto marginalized by class, race, or gender. It is a fascinating, if at times anguished, time in which to be at work in the early modern period.

I will now introduce these key words and hope that the trails on which they will lead in subsequent chapters will prove as productive in elucidating the Sidney family romance as they are currently controversial. First, to *family*. Every society develops a range of what Gayle Rubin terms "systematic ways to deal with sex, gender and babies . . . a set of arrangements by which a society transforms biological sexuality into products of human activity, and in which these transformed sexual needs are satisfied."[26] Since the early modern period, even more directly than the church, state, and various educational apparatuses, the family has been the main agent of enculturation in Western history, the earliest structure through which society imprints its distinctive ideological patterns upon its children, and so eventually upon its adults. Yet to write "the family" is immediately to introduce a major ideological blurring. In the age of what San Francisco's Board of Supervisors in 1989, closely followed by other municipal authorities, designated the "domestic partnership," it no longer seems quite so natural to say "the family" as if there were a primitive underlying structure against which we could measure historical deviations. The various founding fathers of modern family history—Engels, Le Play, and Freud—all assumed, for different reasons, that there was both an "original" nuclear family structure and a single, evolutionary history of the family. Poster defines the family as a "social space where generations confront each other directly and where the two sexes define their differences and power relations," but what has been considered the natural "social space" has clearly varied too greatly across cultures, and historically within particular cultures, to make even such a general definition particularly useful.[27]

Even if there is no "original" or "natural" family structure, nonetheless it is clear that there has been a remarkable continuity in the ideology and the material practices of family life from the early modern period until perhaps as recently as the 1980s and still, predominantly today. The concern with family psychodynamics among feminist theorists, including Chodorow, Dinnerstein, and Kaplan, has been a major phenomenon in the past twenty years, such that were it to make headway in the popular handbooks and material practices of our society, it might be giving voice to the first major break in the ideology and practices of child rearing and domestic partnerships in the past five or six hundred years. It might start to subvert, from within, the fearful dualisms that have so distorted the human possibilities of our history. That remains to be seen. Notwithstanding the much publicized breakdown of the so-called nuclear family, and the welcome, if slow and piecemeal, liberalization of the definition of contractual partnership, over the past four hundred years the dominant family relationships have remained relatively constant, even if the significances assigned to them have changed. As Laslett puts it, "normative change" in family history has been an "inch-by-inch operation," even in periods of rapid social or technological change.[28] This continuity may be a matter for regret: those of us who see the recognition and empowerment of multiple domestic partnership arrangements and the restructuring of child care responsibilities as important political goals can see how very little has changed, even recently, since the early modern period. Throughout this period, the predominant familial relationships have been those between a man and a female spouse over whose body, property, and movements he had legal or quasi-legal (and to a large extent, practical) control, between a child and a mother and/or mother substitute, and between the child and parents, especially the father, as the embodiment of familial and wider socially sanctioned authority. Other relatively constant aspects of the dominant ideology of the family have been the preference for a relationship (though by no means universally reflected in practice) between a child's conception and upbringing with parental marriage and, perhaps most stable and important of all, a varying but almost universally enforced period of learning and apprenticeship for the adult

31

roles that children must undertake. Part of that apprenticeship involves the internalization of gender expectations: what constitutes "men" and "women" in a particular social formation is communicated through ordinary aspects of family experience—what Althusser called "the forms of family ideology (the ideology of paternity-maternity-conjugality-infancy and their interactions)"[29]—that, notwithstanding variations, largely by class, have changed relatively slowly in the past four hundred years.

With such a degree of continuity in both the dominant ideologies of the family and many of its material practices, it is with some confidence that many historians of the early modern period have used contemporary studies, both theoretical and clinically based, of what Greven terms the "inner life" of families. His work on early New England child rearing patterns and David Hunt's on the psychology of family life in early modern France are exemplary for how modern developmental studies—in their cases, the work of Erikson and Winnicott—may be used in relation to data produced by social historians. Likewise, Theweleit's work in a later period, with its astounding, and perhaps overly ambitious, amalgamation of material detail and speculative framework, is enormously suggestive for any attempt to create a meaningful dialogue of psychoanalysis and cultural history. In *The Sidney Family Romance* I am not attempting so ambitious a study as Greven's or Hunt's, let alone Theweleit's. I am concerned primarily with gender assignment, not the whole complex of the changing ideologies of family structures and interrelations. But, like them, I am commited to finding ways of analyzing the "inner lives" of my subjects, in the (obvious) absence of direct evidence and with a paucity of documentation. Hence I have used evidence from, on the one hand, historical documents—including the writings of the two cousins—and recent historical researches, along with, on the other hand, contemporary studies of family interactions and gender construction, and detailed case histories drawn from nearly a century of clinical and therapeutic studies.[30]

Gender, to which my preliminary discussion will now move, is not a characteristic with which one is born; nor, indeed, is it a stable mode of categorization, either across history or even within the life of an individual subject. Kaplan's metaphor of the crochet pattern for human development, which I quoted at the start of this chapter, involves both the successive re-seeing of the past from the perspective of an always moving present and the predicting of the future in terms of these successive revisionings of the past. The dominant ideologies of a society try to fix patterns by which individual subjects live their lives (it is, in a sense, their job to try to do this). In doing so they inevitably produce tensions and contradictions within and against which we spend our lives defining ourselves, often with enormous pain and confusion. A child is born and raised not only to biological parents (and, in the aristocracy of early modern England, into a support system of surrogate caretakers), but into an ideological matrix of assumptions, expectations, and hopes, articulated (even before birth) in parental and familial fantasies, preparations, and (immediately after birth) in the earliest practices by which the child is nurtured. One of the goals of this process is to fix the child's gender assignment. As the child grows, its polymorphous desires are directed into a myriad gendered behaviors, laying the basis for later patterns that may often be compulsively repeated across a variety of activities which may seem unrelated to their apparent origins in infancy.

By "gender," then, I mean, following Joan Wallach Scott, a "socially constructed, not inherent, organization of social difference." It is a primary, not a subsidiary aspect of social organization, a fundamental system of assigning meanings and defining what passes as "knowledge" to individual subjects. An especially crucial issue is the categorization of gender assignments. We are so used to the reified binary opposition of "man" and "woman"—"that great fatal divide" in France Morrow's phrase—that we may even see those categories as more "natural" than "family." We may "know" that being gendered as male is not simply the recognition of a child's "real" nature, some primeval essence of maleness deterministically wired to the genetic code. Masculinity, as Connell puts it, is not the "consequence of XY chromosomes, or even the possession on which discussions of masculinity have so lovingly dwelt, the penis. The physical sense of maleness grows through a personal history of social practice, a life-history-in-society."[31] But the ideology of gender in the early modern period was, indeed, that being gendered as male followed from being visibly sexed as male, and that being male meant the assignment of a superior place within a multitude of social apparatuses, including the family. The common monarchist analogy between the family and the state, advanced by James I himself and later in the century, Robert Filmer, saw the patriarchal family principles of gender differentiation and hierarchy as a microcosm of the order of creation. As Coppélia Kahn points out, as the monarchy consolidated its power it encouraged obedience to the paterfamilias in the home, according to the traditional analogy between state and family, king and father. James I stated, "Kings are compared to fathers in families: for a king is truly *parens patriae*, the politic father of his people." What Stone terms the "internalized sense of obligation to the absolute king as father of his people" is paralleled and reinforced in the family by an ideology of absolute obedience to the husband and father.[32]

In recent years, Mahler's work on separation and individuation has become very influential in explaining the tensions and contradictions of early childhood. A "landmark in the theory of the self," in

Benjamin's words, her work has offered a persuasive genealogy of the conflicts and anxieties associated with a child's growing independence. Her work traces a characteristic transition from a sense of primal oneness with initial caregivers (historically, predominantly the mother) from the second half of the second year. Unfortunately, her work (like that of Freud) downplays the social construction of the personality and ends in reinforcing the Freudian concept of the family as a closed system.[33] The family may be the initial locus of desire, a major place of libidinal production, but the shape taken by the libido is produced within the broader social struggles, not merely (as Freud repeatedly argued) within the relationships of individual fantasy life. The uneasy split between "private" and "public" life that was starting to take shape in the early modern period perhaps reaches its climax in Freud, to the detriment of discussions of child rearing and family dynamics into our own time. Only recently has there been a serious attempt in the psychoanalytical tradition to locate the formation of "individual" psyches in a wider social context.

Mahler's main point, however, is acceptable: gradually—the length of the period may be shorter or longer than she claimed—a child becomes aware of itself as the contradictory subject of both its own strivings and others' demands and expectations. Within this process, a key discovery is gender assignment. As Amussen's *An Ordered Society* shows, gender is a category that structured early modern social and political experience in crucial ways. The family was a vital economic unit, the basis for political and social order, an arena where wider social struggles, such as opposition to unjust power and resistance to tyranny, were fought out. Relations between those assigned as "men" and "women" were overwhelmingly structured in terms of domination and submission; men were accorded a natural, God-given power over lesser beings, who included women, at least of their own or lower classes. The rare exception of a female monarch like Elizabeth I does not challenge the general rule, though her example did serve, as I shall show with reference to *Urania* in chapter seven, as a tempting fantasy for women. The nature of a woman's assigned position in the hierarchy of gender was a traditional topic for theological, moral, rhetorical, and poetical disputation. Ruth Kelso showed long ago that the nature and scope of the court lady, in particular, was a recurring topic in courtly handbooks, and, as Kathleen McLuskie comments, such works were designed to instruct women "not only in virtue but in subordination." While there are many writers who praise women's noble or gentle or decorative qualities—and are no less sexist in doing so than women's detractors—almost never is the hierarchy of the two sexes challenged.[34] It has taken some four hundred years to shake, even partially, the hold of this complex of dualisms and hierarchies, and those of us who believe that we are largely free of them may often find them returning in unexamined thoughts or actions, unsettling reminders of a world some of us, at least, thought we had lost.

The hierarchy and polarization of gender assignments was dependent on a variety of surveillance and enforcement structures, but gender differentiation was not usually, in Althusser's terminology, a "repressive" so much as an "ideological" apparatus, articulated in a myriad everyday assumptions and practices—costume, gesture, posture, patterns of upbringing, modes of address, legal rights, manners—so that it seemed to be part of the natural order.[35] We can trace something of the deep-rooted mechanisms by which the family inculcated gender roles from the manuals on child rearing practices written in the early modern period. Such works are useful not only for reconstructing actual child rearing practices but also for their underlying assumptions. The issues of anality and sexuality that today we see as crucial to the development of a gendered psychological profile—including bowel habits and toilet training, separation and individuation, sex play, masturbation, Oedipal behavior—are often absent, but they may be implied and are sometimes surprisingly frankly mentioned. Swaddling is much commented upon and was a virtually universal process for all children during infancy. It certainly reduced bodily contact between children and adults, and it was possibly, as some developmental psychologists insist, a crucial factor in the development of sensual awareness and the capacity for tenderness— capacities that many recent readings of Shakespeare's *Coriolanus* have seen as a concern of that play.[36]

The handbooks deal in most detail with patterns of discipline and socialization. Their consistent assumption is that authority is the basic principle of child rearing, and, since child rearing is part of a family's dynastic and moral, even theological, responsibilities, the father acts as the ultimate authority. Silence, patience, and reverence constitute desirable behavior for children. Rudeness, disobedience, noisiness, and talkativeness are usually mentioned as a child's main vices, and rigid corporal punishment is recommended to enforce obedience. Greven's studies of early New England child rearing show that the crucial issue for those parents was the taming of a child's will. Both supposedly "natural" corruption and any potential rebellion had to be repressed and punished; this resulted, he argues, in the development of children who were significantly alienated from their own bodies, possessed an "intense hostility toward their own innermost natures," and who eventually developed into adults with strongly authoritarian temperaments.[37]

There are unmistakable indications in the lives of both Sidney cousins of the inculcation of such ideals. Some readers of the Sidney family letters suggest, however, that there was also an unusual degree of affection between Robert Sidney and his family, even though he was absent much of their childhoods. Likewise, young William Herbert may have grown up at Wilton in a far less rigid intellectual atmosphere than Greven's categories allow for. Boyd Berry has suggested that Pembroke's was among the first generations of English children brought up with "pleasure" as one of the goals of child rearing. In 1579, in what amounts to one of the earliest works of pediatrics, John Jones argued that the "natural gifts of body and mind that are in the child"—especially the "first pleasures," such as eating, secreting, and "emptying"—should be given greater attention by child raisers. Is it coincidental that such an opinion was being put forward at the time that Pembroke's maternal uncle Philip was advocating pleasure as one of the major goals of poetry? Just as humanism was concerned with learning through what Sidney termed "delight," child raising manuals were starting to suggest that children might learn effectively by means of pleasure and games rather than coercion: even "the first infusion of children in learning and religion," wrote William Perkins, "must be so ordered that they may take it with delight." Does such advice point to a sign of what in discussing marriage Stone calls "affective individualism" in early modern child rearing practices?[38] A number of his contemporaries comment on Pembroke's unusual degree of emotional warmth and, with some disapproval, on the extent to which his self-indulgence stood in the way of his achieving political greatness.

Hunt's study of family life in early modern France likewise provides some clues to contradictory developmental patterns—another aspect perhaps of what I called some years ago the "matching of contraries" in the Sidney circle—that may have been at work in the upbringing of the Sidney cousins.[39] Using Erikson's model of psychological development as a series of stages in conjunction with data from Philippe Aries and the *Annaliste* school of social history, Hunt examined the upbringing of the future Louis XIII, as recorded in the diaries of the royal physician, Jean Héroard. The diaries depict a regimen of repression and violent punishment designed to control the will of the child: "beating, whipping, abusing and scolding" were commonplace, and generally, Hunt argues, "the adults were not at all sympathetic to the child's emerging autonomy." If the case of the prince is typical, the relationships between a child and its parents, even its mother, were not close. But there was a more diffused affection afforded a royal or aristocratic child by the many care givers and servants, including the wet nurse, and there were some distinctive areas of laxity. Sexuality, for instance, was more open than in the later bourgeois family: Héroard records with evident amusement the young prince's masturbation, exhibitionism, and sexual games with the servants, and his awareness from a very early age of adult sexual interactions.[40]

If, as Kaplan puts it, "the earliest images of the parents [and care-givers] from the infantile period of life" remain factors in adult rela-tionships, can we say, even in general terms, what the effects of such a pattern of upbringing upon early gender assignments might be? For a boy, the age of seven would be a crucial landmark, since boys and girls were dressed similarly until about then, at which point the boys would be put into breeches, "breeched," and thus have their aspirations to their father's authority and autonomy at least visibly acknowledged. Greven, Hunt, and Poster all identify the issue of authority and au-tonomy as the crucial question in an early modern child's upbringing. Critiquing the assumed universality of the Freudian pattern of oral, anal, and genital stages of development, Poster indicates that the central factor in the formation of the sense of self in the early modern family was the parents' inability to deal with the infant's striving for sepa-ration/individuation. When authority was challenged, it was met with force, he notes: "the issue in the bourgeois home was toilet training; the issue in the chateau was obedience to authority." The early modern equivalent to the Oedipal phase probably centered not so much on parental sexuality as parental power.[41]

I have, once again, introduced into the discussion a seemingly gender-neutral term, "child." Children are, however, not gender neutral. If, as Nancy Hartsock puts it, men and women "grow up with personalities affected by different boundary conditions, differently constructed and experienced inner and outer worlds," then these differences are at least in part, perhaps predominantly, constructed in early childhood.[42] The two cousins would have shared a common pattern of upbringing in many material details, including clothing, but there would have been two crucial differences. The first, which unfortunately remains a dominant pattern in the West today, concerns the influence of predominantly same-sex care givers on the psychological development of the infant. A sense of identity, however differently it may be encoded historically, is initially mirrored for a girl in the mother and mother-surrogate care givers. A variety of modern developmental experts suggests that being gendered like the mother may cause a blurring of boundaries—especially in a social formation that stratifies the relative power of men and women—that will reinforce distinctive patterns of ego development and gender discrimination. For a girl in such a society, the body and the family, rather than the world outside, become the primary environments in which ego and social development occur, and insofar as the world outside the family is a permitted area of exploration, it will primarily be one provided or approved by the family.

Genital differences between boys and girls would not cause, but they might well reinforce, such tendencies: the boy's penis is a location of assertion and display, directed out at others as well as being unavoidably available to himself, as Héroard observes of young Louis with some amusement; by contrast, the girl's genitals as the source of identification and direct stimulation are likely to be less accessible. As Doris Bernstein notes, the defining experience of the body is "different for the girl in the midst of the same psychic development. Her eyes, her hands, her genitals, do not provide clearly defined boundaries. In attempting to form a mental image of herself and her experiences, she repeats, from within, her own body, the non-specific generalized, undifferentiated psychic experience of earlier stages." Beneath his apparently gender-neutral clothes, the unbreeched male child is anatomically prepared for and ideologically inserted into an earlier and more absolute differentiation process meant to encourage both autonomy and the promise of future authority. One repeated effect will be that in times of crisis, the ideology of being male directs him outside, whereas the girl's gender coded body experience "leads her inward and back to a more diffuse, undifferentiated state."[43]

Thus the second difference between the cousins' upbringing was that for Mary Sidney, as a girl, the desire to emulate a man's power and the autonomy that accompanied it might never be realized in any satisfying and consistent way. With a male of Pembroke's class, part of his assumed authority and eventual sense of autonomy derived from the advantages and obligations of belonging to a powerful family. The Sidneys and Herberts brought up their children to think of themselves as intimately obligated for their privileges to their kin, dead as well as alive. In the earl of Surrey's epitaph on Clere—"Norfolk sprang thee, Lambeth holds thee dead"—the deceased man's name is syntactically subordinated to the family estate, Surrey making "even his death an obliging act of deference towards the family." The authority of ancestors in the consciousness of the children of such families must have been striking. As the inheritor of the father's role, the embodiment of the family's future with its past, the eldest son was the major conduit of authority in the family. Well before he was an adult, pressures to arrange a dynastically advantageous marriage would increase, though—as Pembroke's own marriage indicates—there is some evidence that eldest sons were assuming an increasing degree of choice, or at least a veto power over their parents' preferences. After rejecting a number of possible brides, following the death of his father Pembroke conducted his own marriage negotiations with the Talbot family—where two previous earls of Pembroke had turned before him for wives. But even acting with some independence, he was still subordinating any tendencies towards Stone's "affective individualism"[44] to the careful cementing of a liaison of property and influence.

In the case of his cousin, personal wishes were far more ruthlessly subordinated to the family. In such a family as the Sidneys, a daughter could have few expectations concerning her autonomy. Her exchange value was dubious—at worst she was an embarrassing financial burden, at best a means by which political alliances might be cemented. Thus in 1626 the rivalry between Pembroke and Buckingham was patched over by a proposed alliance between Pembroke's niece and Buckingham's son, both of whom were still infants (in fact, after Buckingham's assassination two years later, the betrothal was never consummated). In Mary's case, while the marriage alliance with the Sidneys provided the Wroths with influential court connections, what Robert Sidney gained was largely the relief of marrying off a daughter. For Mary, marriage was simply one step in what was assumed to be a smooth transition from girlhood and dependence on her father's family to dependence within her husband's. To reject such a destiny was almost impossible, and repeated rejection of proposed marriages would have put most women in an economically and even physically vulnerable position. Shakespeare's Angelo simultaneously beseeches and threatens Isabella: "Be that you are, / That is, a woman; if you be more, you are none" (*Measure for Measure*, 2. 4. 134–35). To attempt to be "more" would be to call into question the assignment of being a woman.

To argue that the behavioral patterns and fantasies of the Sidney cousins' family romances centered on matters of authority, autonomy, and agency may make them sound, at first hearing, not unlike Freud's. But Freud's description of the family romance needs to be reinterpreted on two main grounds: first, his seeing family romances as individual fantasies produced within the family rather than by historically specific contradictions within the culture; and second, his almost total elision of gender. I therefore turn now to outlining an alternative, historically rooted, model of the family romance.

Where Freud did speak of influences outside the individual psyche, he focused almost exclusively on either immediate family circumstances or, more generally, abstractions like the quasi-anthropological and ahistorical "civilization." A more satisfactory model of the family romance is that formulated by Deleuze and Guattari. For them the incestuous family romance as outlined by Freud is not even a primary, let alone biological, desire, but rather a form that desire assumes because of the repression to which it is inevitably subject by particular social formations. The unrealizability of infantile desires, they argue, forces us back into the family as the site where we strive, inevitably imperfectly, to realize some equivalent for them. The struggle to impose one's fantasies upon the world does not simply arise from a sense of hostility towards one's dependence; it arises specifically from our increasing awareness of, and our attempts to reach out to, the world.[45] This is a process that starts as soon as a child becomes aware of himself or herself as separate from parents, especially the mother: in short, from the onset of Mahler's separation/individuation process. Frustration experienced in the world—where we might realize our sense of being a separate self and also acknowledge chosen commitments of allegiance or community—forces us back, either literally, or in terms of projected and transferential fantasies, upon the family. The family seems to have been there first; it seemed to give us us both the impetus to become separate and the temptation to return; when the world does not reward our desires, it is the family to which we may all too readily return. In this model our family romances are played out in the family, because at first it seems as if only in the protection and familiarity of the family can we find opportunities for displaying them.

We want to see our desires take shape in the world. In what Mahler calls the rapprochement phase, we learn, however imperfectly, to settle for what we can get, and our lifelong struggles to accept such a compromise (ending only, as Freud in his gloomier moods put it, in the stasis of death) produce characteristic strategies of adaptation. Perhaps the most important of these are our fantasies, the narrativizations of our desires, expressed in stories we construct in our heads, sometimes tell to others, and write down or recognize in others' tellings and writings. These stories—perhaps another name for them is "scripts," since we assign parts in them to ourselves and other real or imagined characters, often using pre-set and long familiar roles and scenarios—include what are rather loosely called "perversions."

"Perversity" and "perversion" will play important roles in this study, and it is important to pause briefly over the terms. Jonathan Dollimore has eloquently argued for a rejection of the sexological basis of categorizing "perversion" and for a return to "theological" accounts, in order to develop a theory of dissidence and insurrection. He especially rejects the Freudian account whereby, as we grow to adulthood, the polymorphous perversity of childhood is transformed through repression and sublimation into socially acceptable expressions of our energies. But Freud also argued that "perverse" behavior does not disappear; in fact, it is so widespread that it is, paradoxically, "normal." What is more objectionable is the popular sense of "perversions" as morally reprehensible (yet pruriently fascinating), "kinky" sexual practices, which are, of course, strategies that any person may use, randomly or systematically, to enhance sexual excitement. In her recent feminist psychoanalyst study, *Female Perversions*, Kaplan uses the term "perverse strategy" to refer to the ways in which adult adaptive behavior may reenact infantile strategies or scripts of adaption, and in doing so acquire a compulsive

40

character. Above all, she argues, this compulsive reenactment of infantile coping strategies—which may be expressed in a variety of practices, some "kinky," others very commonplace (and what is regarded as "normal" or "deviant" is, of course highly specific to different cultures, classes, and social groups)—bears a direct relation to the stereotypes of gender assignment that from our earliest years have molded our desires and fantasies. In the case of men, the characteristic patterns enlist gender stereotypes of virility, domination, and independence; in the case of women, stereotypes of self-punishment and renunciation. Contrary to Freud's predominant assertion, such patterns, she explains, are not somehow inherent in our being biologically "men" and "women," but are directly related to our socialization within the gender ideologies of particular societies.[46]

Such an emphasis on the culturally produced nature of our psychological strategies and the way they may acquire a "perverse" caste by compulsion is a major breakthrough from much of the dominant psychoanalytical tradition, both Freud's and that of the second-generation Freudians like Mahler and Klein. What Kaplan's work brings into play is not only a wealth of clinical studies but feminist theory. Mahler, like Freud before her, assumed that the differences between boys and girls were not culturally produced but somehow represented inherent differences. Writing to Fliess, Freud acknowledged that the family romance might have a gendered aspect when he described "the revenge-and-exoneration romances which my hysterics compose about their mothers if they are boys." But there is little indication that he considered the fantasy structures of girls as separate from boys, at least in more than the most general terms: in remarks in "Creative Writing and Daydreaming," he asserted that the typical fantasies of boys were focused on ambition, those of girls those on love.[47] Women remained a mystery to Freud all his life, as he often noted, though the remark is true in more ways than he knew.

Throughout this book, in discussing the Sidney cousins, I will raise what I believe to be a fundamental question: are there discernibly different gendered, historically specific, patterns of fantasy? Particularly, what is the woman's version of the family romance? And do the answers to that question vary historically? Freud argued that beneath the (male) child's desires for autonomy and control may lie a chronic insecurity that dates back to the peculiar path of (male) ego formation. "Childhood love," he observed, his model always, if usually unstated, male, "is boundless; it demands exclusive possession, it is not content with less than all." Further, he goes on, "it has . . . no aim and is incapable of obtaining complete satisfaction; and principally for that reason it is doomed to end in disappointment." How far is that an inherently human characteristic? Or inherently male? Culturally as opposed to biologically produced? This personality characteristic that Freud essentializes has contributed materially (and some would add, tragically) to the emergence in the early modern period of what Jessica Benjamin terms the "one-sided autonomy" that "permeates the Western notion of the individual as thinking subject, as explorer of the world" and as aggressive authority figure, restlessly searching for proofs of his autonomy. Do we hear echoes in Freud's words of Hamlet's "boundless ambition"? How does the (male) ego come to terms with limitation, the awareness that he is "bounded in a nutshell"? As I will suggest in chapter two, when replicated as an epistemology, the virtues of the Renaissance hero, however eulogized by moralists and educators, lead to a world, as Hartsock puts it, "inhabited by a number of fundamentally hostile others whom one comes to know by means of opposition (even death struggle)."[48]

A recurring feature of the male family romance in the early modern period, and perhaps subsequently, is a desire for autonomy that grows from a primary dependence on and then rejection of the mother—a figure that would encompass both the biological mother and female care givers—and the consequent aspiration to the father's authority and power. "Boys discover," writes Benjamin, echoing the central Freudian developmental article of faith on Oedipal development, "that they cannot grow up to *become* [the mother]; they can only *have* her."[49] Then, more important, they discover that they cannot have *her*. This is less an anguish over sexuality than a contradictory response involving, simultaneously, loss of and desire for what the possession of the mother represents—the mythical wholeness and oneness lost in the separation/individuation process. It produces a distinctively fragile personality structure, one that looks to authorities outside the family to provide an alternative to the coherence seemingly lost. This contradiction—at once striving for independence and desiring a return to an undifferentiated state—is the basis of all too many male family romances, and it may continue the whole of a man's life, as the world repeatedly resists the imposition of individual desires, and he returns to the patterns of fantasy and fulfillment he once found (or yearned to find) within the family.[50] It is a cliché that men turn to or as they sometimes put it, "need" women to be trustworthy sources of stability, mother figures whom they can both reject and return to, and that women are socialized to likewise "need" men who will give them access to wider experiences, "adventures." As depressing and as prevalent as that dual pattern may be, it is even more so when we note that a man's drive to autonomy is so often achieved, and his accompanying insecurity overcome (however unsatisfactorily) by means of the domination of women, who are (of course) often blamed as the disappearing object at the same time as they

42

are yearned for as the cure for anxiety. Male domination often assumes a particularly curious form, moreover: in an agonal model of gender relations, whether gender politics operate by subtle or explicit coercion, masculine domination is all too often accompanied by the idealization of the objects of that coercion. The mixture of restless, unsatisfied self-assertion and recurrent boredom is a recurring male characteristic in our history. In a society that makes sexual conquest even a temporary guarantee of coherence and integration, the conquest of women may easily come to represent the most intense way of preserving the illusion of integration that the family, and most especially the mother, once offered the child. If Paglia is right, it is the rare man who can see "the abyss from which most men shrink: the infantilism in all male heterosexuality."[51] Such insight certainly never surfaces in Pembroke's writings, however clearly aspects of his life may display such a pattern. But it does underlie both the life and writings of his cousin.

Recent work on male sexual and relational behavior suggests, then, that the core of the dominant heterosexual culture's male family romances is built upon a contradictory encodement of gender identity. At once men want to be independent and autonomous, and to be reabsorbed into the mother. Seeking to fulfill that contradictory gender assignment may take various forms, including what I have referred to as "perversions." It will inevitably involve a man's assigning (or casting) members of the family within the scripts of his fantasies. It also involves what may remain a lifelong problem, how to assign roles to what Shakespeare called "the woman's part" (*Cymbeline*, 2. 5. 20) in himself. By contrast, the characteristic fantasies of the female family romance are, I will argue, predominantly two: fantasies of emulation of men's apparently desirable autonomy and (not usually found in the male version) fantasies of mutuality. The desire of emulation focuses on the male's apparent ease of achieving independence, his possession of paternal power: "not simply," Benjamin argues, "because he *has* a phallus, but because he (with his phallus) represents freedom from dependency on the powerful mother of early infancy." What is really wanted by a girl, Benjamin goes on, "is recognition . . . that one *is* a subject of desire, an agent who can will things and make them happen." Mahler argues that boys acquire this sense by their inherently greater "motor-mindedness" and by turning, as part of the family romance, to a model other than the mother, conventionally the father—or to someone who is the embodiment of the father's power and autonomy. Within the Freudian bourgeois family model, this fantasy conventionally includes the desire for the mother, as the favored object of the father's desire within the family. This playing out of Oedipus in the early modern period seems to be present to some extent but in a more diffuse form, and it was probably subordinate to the desire for autonomy and authority. As for the girl, no less than the boy, she too wishes her desire to be given recognition. The father's power over her derives not only from the fact that he is "big," as Freud put it, but because he represents an apparent solution to her inner conflicts. What she finds missing as an outcome of her increasing socialization into her gender assignment of being a woman is her identification with the phallus. She will never be her father. She is encouraged to bond with him as the object of his, not the subject of her own, desires.[52]

Hence, in the bimodal, heterosexual model that has been so dominant in our culture, at least since the early modern period, just as those coded as men learn to disguise their forbidden "feminine" wishes behind a stereotype of male virility, writes Kaplan, "so women learn to disguise their forbidden masculine wishes behind a stereotype of female innocence, weakness and self-sacrifice." In short, the female child proceeds with her "investigations" into the ways her fantasies fit the world in a pattern that may start out fundamentally similar to the male child's, but "she endows her discoveries with fantasies that pertain mainly to female development."[53] This is why Wroth's *Urania* is full of stories of a woman's desire directed to heroes (most notably Pamphilia towards Amphilanthus) such as she herself would be—a fantasy typically accompanied by the woman's adulation of the hero, regardless of his worthiness, specifically his independence and agency. In its most extreme form, this fantasy takes the form of expecting rejection, even abuse— what Wroth terms in both her poems and her romance, "molestation": she "submits to and adores an other who is what she cannot be." As I will show in chapter eight, *Urania* enacts this fantasy over and over, in story after story, with the heroine finding or putting herself in situations where she is humiliated, molested, or denied her desires, and receiving, in a measure, some perverse comfort that her expectations are thus fulfilled. This is the pattern she has been brought up to expect, and it embodies a destructive and perverse hope that in such surrender she will find her elusive own self. What a woman wants, to answer Freud's infamous question, is not a penis as such, but to go out into the world, leave home, make decisions of her own, have her daydreams acquire validity in the world beyond the family. As Bernstein comments, such demands are "commonly . . . understood as penis envy," but the "latent content is surely, 'Men can separate, individuate,' become separate human beings, whereas women often are not able to achieve this degree of autonomy, nor is it expected of them." Nor, in early modern England, was it barely possible.[54]

One of the most influential, and controversial, arguments in feminist psychoanalysis in recent years has been Chodorow's suggestion that women characteristically achieve their self-identity through relationships rather than autonomy. Mahler's separation/individuation model of development offers a brilliant account of the anxieties involved in becoming independent, but, like Freud, she focuses too exclusively on human beings as monadic energy systems and accepts too readily his masculinist insistence that, as Benjamin puts it, we "grow out of relationships rather than becoming more active and sovereign within them." Chodorow's argument provides an alternative to Mahler's exclusive focus on autonomy. But the fantasy of mutuality, of becoming "sovereign" alongside another or with others, has never been accorded primacy in the Western tradition, at least since the Renaissance, because it has never been valorized as a dominant male pattern. Within the dominant ideology of gender assignments, what men have seemed to embody, and women wanted to emulate, has been the dream of autonomy. The intersubjective, communal selves we might dream of have been denigrated because men have regarded such claims as threatening to their cherished autonomy and because generations of women have seen any desire for mutuality as involving a sacrifice of their own strivings for autonomy. "Why," asks Benjamin, must a search for recognition culminate in "submission, instead of a relationship of mutuality?"[55] That, I will suggest, is a question that occasionally surfaces in Wroth's writings, as it does in Shakespeare's, Donne's, and elsewhere in men's writings in the early modern period. Clearly, the answer lies not primarily in biological conditioning, but in the dominant gender ideologies of our history.

In chapters two and three I will discuss these different versions of the family romance in the context of Pembroke's and Wroth's lives, and in subsequent chapters trace them in their writings. It is a complex story, and not merely a dichotomy of unchanging male hegemony and female subordination. In a period in which the family was increasingly taking over from the church the major institutional function of reinforcing of gender roles, it was also the family that contained, as Natalie Davis puts it, "apertures"[56] for the development of women's agency. In Wroth's case, I will argue, these include sexuality and writing. Sexual self-assertion was conventionally part of the male prerogative, and writing, too, was traditionally a world dominated by male assumptions as well as male practitioners. Making his statement, leaving his mark on the world (it is often argued), is the goal of the male. The son comes to identify his own with the father's power, which includes possessing the right to these two areas of power and differentiation; by contrast, the daughter is asked to identify with the mother as the one who lacks this power. But, as I will suggest, writing and sexuality were also areas of possibility for a woman like Wroth, whose story is far more heartening than this initial discussion may suggest, not least because it shows the emergence into our cultural history of the possibility of more liberating practices. The Sidney family romance helps us to elucidate a small corner of an enormous psychological and cultural space in which we all still wander.

The other great "key word" of this study is *romance*. It is a word redolent, not to say overstuffed, with cultural and, not least, gendered contradictions. Here I want to focus on a few of the overlappings and contradictions in the vast scholarship on the term—which has been used to refer to a literary genre, a fictional mode, a narrative of personal or cultural history, or (more contentiously) what John Stevens terms "a special experience (or, rather, a set of experiences) of fundamental and continuing importance to western man." The last word takes on a particular irony when one considers that the predominant focus and audience for romance (in a number of senses) has been women. For Pembroke, Wroth, and their circle, "romance" referred primarily to a body of literature, derived variously from ancient Greece and medieval Europe, in England reaching its high point in Sidney's *Arcadia* and Spenser's *Faerie Queene*. Its subject matter was the loves, wars, and other adventures of idealized, high-born heroes and heroines (love, war, and adventure "for the very best people," as Stevens not entirely unironically puts it).[57] Anthropological and literary scholarship in the past century has dramatically broadened the term. Until recently, the dominant literary critical use of the term was that devised by Northrop Frye, who linked romance, as a narrative mode, to recurrent "myths" of questing, usually centered on a heroic male figure who journeys through an allegorical landscape in which moral, even cosmic, dramas are played out. More recent work by feminist critics studying prose fiction from the eighteenth century to the present has drawn attention to the ways in which these forms of romances have embodied and, to an extent, created the fantasies of their predominantly female audiences, by means of which temporary solutions are offered for the material contradictions of women's lives. For Frye the appeal of romance is built upon the eternal search of the libido, the desiring self, for a fulfillment found in the contemplation of a universal esthetic realm beyond the wasteland of the reader's present frustration. For many feminist critics, it is rooted in the material contradictions of the lives of the readers of romances: in political oppression, class inequality, family entrapment, and hierarchical gender relations.[58]

What links these different approaches to romance is the importance of desire and fantasy as the basis for its appeal. When Freud used the term in the essay which gives this study its title, he was joining, with a little irony, the two dominant senses of the word: romance as wishfulfillment and romance as narrative. The family romance is a narrative of desire. It takes its shape in relation to desires seemingly generated within the family, and it is articulated in narrative patterns that seem to account for and provide solutions to those desires. In our adult lives we carry around what Paglia terms "an incestuous constellation of sexual personae," so that "every encounter with friend or foe, every clash with or submission to authority bears the perverse traces of family romance."[59] In the case of the Sidney cousins, the recurring, even obsessive, subject of their family romances is the struggle for autonomy and agency in relation to gendered and, to an extent, class assignments. The written narrative forms in which these stories are embodied are the prose heroic romance, Petrarchan poetry, and pastoral drama. But also not to be overlooked as "romance" are their living narratives, the patterns in which their desires were enacted, displaced, or repressed in their lives. In chapters four to eight I will examine Pembroke's poems and letters, and Wroth's poems, letters, play and prose. In chapters two and three (and, to the extent of dealing with the two cousins' participation in the court drama, chapter seven), I will be concerned with how they lived out very differently gendered versions of the family romance. In this final section of this introduction, I will locate both the written and the enacted family romances of the two Sidney cousins in the intensely material settings in which they took shape.

The Sidney family romances not only had characters and plots, but settings. These became part of and helped give shape to the narratives of the cousins' separate and mutual desires, which were played out in the courts, great houses, and countryside of Elizabethan and Jacobean England. Places are never ideologically neutral. Not merely backgrounds where individual desires arise and develop, houses, palaces, and estates are in their turn already shaped by personal and family desires and by the broader cultural conflicts that layer them; in turn they help determine the shape and quality of the desires and conflicts of individual men and women. Where medieval space, as Foucault suggests, was epitomized by the courtyard, an enclosed square designed to immure, display, and regulate the activities within it, and to exclude alternatives, the Renaissance sense of space oscillates between the continuing medieval model and two contradictory impulses: a reinvention of the local and private and a desire to expand, even (in the new infinite universe of Bruno, Brahe, and Galileo) to infinity. The family houses of the new aristocracy, including those of the Sidneys and Herberts, show this contradiction in very material ways. The windows of medieval castles predominantly faced into the central courtyard. By the time the Sidney cousins were growing up, the outside walls of great houses like theirs were acquiring large external windows, while, internally, they were being divided into increasingly small, private rooms—what Mark Girouard terms "a constant series of retreats" of privy chambers, private dining and reception rooms—

thus reflecting and helping to create a desire for both expansiveness and privacy.[60] As my discussion of Wroth will suggest, the new availability of private space, which today most middle-class families in the developed world take for granted, was only gradually evolving, especially for women, in the early modern period.

Such material details deeply influence the developing patterns of a person's "inner life." As a child grows up, physical surroundings provide part of the shaping of experience that will have long lasting, seemingly "natural" effects on him or her. Even the notion of "childhood" itself— today manifested in special rooms, furniture, clothes, play areas, or parental concern to live in a safe neighborhood or a house rather than an apartment—is also a relatively new (or newly emergent) concept in the period. As I noted, no less than "family," "childhood" is a socially constructed concept; likewise, the spaces and buildings where "family" and "childhood" are articulated: however convenient and "natural" we may think a four-bedroom house in the suburbs or separate bedrooms for parents and children (it is curious how "nursery," with its archaic associations of Victorian gentility, has made a recent comeback in catalogs and stores) they are not inherently so, but derive from broader cultural patterns. But all patterns, including our own today, have deep developmental and psychological effects on a child and therefore on his or her adult behavior.

Families like the Sidneys and Herberts provided their members with continual reminders of their responsibilities and powers by the very presence of the houses in which they "dwelt," to use Jonson's phrase in "To Penshurst." Even today these houses—in their actuality or absence— provide tantalizing links between the modern scholar and the past which he or she wrestles to make sense of. In describing the "places" of the Sidney family romance, I find myself captured or, to use one of Mary Wroth's favorite metaphors, "molested"—since it is far more visceral than a mental temptation—by a laughably contradictory mixture of discourses. I try to visualize my two long-dead subjects simultaneously with the eyes of a modern tourist, a cultural historian, a male feminist, a reader of literature, a teacher, a child, a lover, a husband, a parent. All of these different and conflicting layerings have gone into this book, but they are often in contention, and at certain points the contradictions become present more forcibly. At times the primitive desire to know what-it-was-*really*-like comes upon all of us, and for me it is the case with the houses in which Mary Wroth and her cousin grew up, met, quarreled, wrote, made love, visited, parted, were (as we say, the cultural historian struggling to reassert himself) constituted as subjects. From such sentiments, nostalgia is easily born; and often from nostalgia a particularly repulsive brand of sentimental historicism. But the urge to find the signs of the human uses of places is a real and valuable one, and we should not ignore it.

I have often, for instance, been moved to reread Williams's introduction to *The Country and the City*, in which he acknowledges that while his book "often and necessarily follows impersonal procedures," there lies behind it a "personal pressure and commitment" to explore his own history—his own felt contradictions, caught as he felt himself to be, within a "history active and continuous . . . moving and present" in relation to the two great key words that are his subject.[61] I have felt like ambivalence visiting the sites of the Sidney family romance. I recall the bewilderment and inexplicable anger (and envy?) with which I once watched a helicopter bring what I learnt later was a bevy of Beautiful Young People down from London to what had been the site of Ivychurch Park, on the Wilton estate, and which had recently become part of the estate of a heavily guarded country house belonging to a London speculator. Or the frustration of finding what I (mistakenly) thought must be the approximate site of Baynard's Castle near what had, until a few years previously, been an elegant Victorian London tube station—that too swept away into the detritus of history. And then some years later, walking with a companion with whom many of my own family romances have been played out into the shooting of a movie scene involving both romance and violence—and then realizing that it was "there," where Baynard's Castle "really" did stand . . . At such times, the sonorous generalizations of imperium of the strains of Gray's "Elegy" beckon all too easily. History is a record of the barbarism that is civilization, and we should not sentimentalize the horrors of the history that have been perpetrated, too often, on behalf of families like those with which I am so fascinated. We need to acknowledge, too, how the past continues to manipulate us as subjects of regimes and ideologies seemingly dead or archaic.

Five dwellings played a crucial part in Wroth's and Pembroke's lives—and have played parts in the construction of this book. The layerings of history, mainly dating from the nineteenth century, have covered the Wroth estates. Today, the train from Cambridge to London clatters through the Lea Valley, past industrial ponds and Victorian terraces built on lands once hunted upon by Robert Wroth and King James. Their houses, Loughton and Durance, have long been demolished, leaving only a street name or two. Baynard's Castle was destroyed in the eighteenth century. But Wilton House and Penshurst Place remain, much visited by tourists, most of whom are willingly, and unwittingly, interpellated into reassuring reverence for the residue of the two families' power. In the late sixteenth century Wilton House was at once a sophisticated center of political and dynastic power and an isolated rural retreat from the court;

today, it is a charming monument to three hundred years of accumulated privilege and mediocrity, the power of its owners peaking precisely at the period of history at which we are looking. It was founded on confiscated religious lands and then consolidated by the family's ruthless accumulation of further lands, mainly in Wiltshire itself and farther west, in Wales, which had traditionally been the family's political base. When the second earl took Mary Sidney as his third wife, Wilton became what one of her acolytes, Nicholas Breton, termed a "little court," a seedbed of literary and religious studies centered on the Sidneian ideals of public service and Protestant piety. For Philip Sidney and his circle, Wilton was a cultural oasis, a retreat from what they often felt were the corruption and political compromises of the court. But, as Williams pointed out, the relations between court, city, and country are not only relations "of ideas and experiences, but of rent and interest, of situation and power." We should not forget, he continues, "that Sidney's *Arcadia*, which gives a continuing title to English neo-pastoral, was written in a park which had been made by enclosing a whole village and evicting the tenants."[62] I sometimes dream a communal, if not a family, romance of my own, that the Beautiful Young People in their chopper were descendants of the Pembrokes' evicted tenants. The return—socially, not individually— of the repressed.

Don Wayne has analyzed equivalent cultural contradictions in the Sidney family seat, Penshurst Place. Focusing on Jonson's "To Penshurst" about which I shall have more to say in chapter three, he displays both the poem's and the house's complex ideological functions, how they simultaneously affirm a set of values while putting them in question. Jonson celebrates the Sidneys' aristocratic status but hints also at gradually emergent bourgeois values, such as individual merit, property, and a degree of family affection that is in conflict with the strict aristocratic concern with kin and dynasty. He finds an equivalent ambivalence in the lives of the Sidneys and in the architectural improvements Robert Sidney was undertaking in the first decade of the seventeenth century. What the poem points to is a growing split in the whole family that connects, as subsequent chapters will show, with attitudes towards sexuality, writing and gender.[63]

Finally, perhaps the most intriguing of these houses is, as I noted above, one that a tourist (or voyeur) tracking down these sites of personal confrontation and cultural contradictions cannot see, which no doubt adds to its fascination. That is Baynard's Castle. It was located on the north bank of the Thames, near Blackfriars, and close to the Blackfriars theater. In 1546 Henry VIII had granted the keepship of the castle to the first earl of Pembroke; it became the main London residence of the Herbert family. As a Protestant faction developed in the court of Elizabeth during the 1570s and 1580s, it also became a major focus of oppositional political factions. In November 1579, a few months before Pembroke's birth, Baynard's was the site of intense discussions among the Sidneys, Herberts, and the earl of Leicester over Elizabeth's apparent intention to marry Alençon, and in 1615 it was the venue for one of the most important dinner parties in British political history, when Pembroke and others plotted to replace James I's current "minion" with George Villiers, later duke of Buckingham.[64] For the next century it remained the London base for both families. It is where the Sidneys and Mary Wroth stayed for most of their London visits. It was the place where she would have most often met her cousin. It is where some of *Urania* was written. It is to the lives, writings, and intertwinings and co(u)sinings of these two that I shall now turn.

2

"A FREE MAN":
THE GENDERING OF WILLIAM HERBERT,
EARL OF PEMBROKE

I cannot forbear telling of you that yet I endure a very grievous imprisonment . . .
For do you account him a free man that is restrained from coming where he
most desires to be, and debarred from enjoying that comfort in respect of which
all earthly joys seem miseries, though he have a whole world else to work in?

Pembroke to Cecil, 1602

In considering the so-far unending history made by men of the warrior caste,
it may be helpful to recall that it is not only that men make wars, but that
wars make men. For the warrior caste, war is not only death production, but a
means of reproduction; each war deforms the human spirit and guarantees that
the survivors—or some of them—will remain warriors.

Barbara Ehrenreich[1]

he subject of men in the patriarchal system, notes Stanley Kojnacki, "sounds like a tautology, but gender, and the family, marriage, and sex are things of men as much as of women."[2] This is a timely reminder. When I started to investigate the social and psychological mechanisms within early modern culture that served to differentiate Pembroke's and Wroth's gender assignments—upbringing, marital arrangements, careers at court, family responsibilities, economic independence—I found, despite the relative lack of public records from the early period relating to women's activities, that it seemed much easier to discuss Wroth than her more prominent cousin. Unquestionably, this is in part because of the persuasiveness with which contemporary feminism has developed a lexicon to differentiate women's gender assignments from the seemingly "natural" enculturation of a male in our history. But it has to do as well with the deeply ingrained assumption—even for someone committed, as I am, to a non-hierarchical gender politics— that men's cultural assignments still represent the default position. Our dominant gender ideologies make it difficult to think outside the binarism of Western gender assignments and even within that binarism, to conceive of women except in relation to men, not only as different but subsidiary. As a number of feminists have ironically suggested, one means of combating this deeply ingrained sexism is to recognize that it is about time that the decidedly *un*natural, or at least no less constructed, subject positions occupied by men, as men, within our cultural history should be given more attention.

My discussion of Pembroke in this chapter is designed, therefore, not so much to provide a detailed survey (as Andreas Gebauer has recently done) of his career as nobleman, courtier, politician, patron, and writer. My discussion makes no claim to be a biography of Pembroke; that somewhat archaic function, in the sense of summarizing existing documents and producing a chronological survey of his lordship's life, has been performed by Gebauer and J. R. Briley. My essay may rather have implications for a history of the ideologies of gender in that it focuses on the narratives which have been constructed around a particular individual subject within that history. It also contains, not incidentally, something of my own narratives. For as I ponder Pembroke's life, and especially his court activities—on the surface a fairly typical catalog of participation in tournaments, masques, and political intrigues—I ask myself: Why am I intrigued by this figure? What aspects of my own repertoire match (and mismatch) with his? Or, more accurately: what affinities and alienations are there between our positions in what is often, in traditional literary study, constructed as a "common" history and inheritance? In an age where most middle-class, educated males are increasingly sensitive to issues of gender, class and race—certainly more (we like to think) than were Pembroke and his friends and relations—why do I (since I should personalize the matter) find him such an interesting figure? Are there more "universal," or at least relatively stable, trans-historical aspects of our gender assignments than I wish to acknowledge? Are there, indeed, greater continuities within patriarchy in male behavior? Can we detect in many men today a nostalgia for the seeming autonomy and control as well as the apparently unfettered access to women in Pembroke's life? Is there a wistfulness, which many men might not want to acknowledge, for a level of unquestioned authority, even a level of violence, that would, despite our intellectual commitments, make us much more secure? Is that why Paglia's *Sexual Personae*, with its celebration of the heroic if doomed male struggle against the "harsh" chthonian "reality of female nature" as the "black maw that had spat him forth and would devour him anew," so intrigued male reviewers when it was published in 1990?[3] Why am I so angry when I reread it? Or why is the sweaty Jungianism of Robert Bly's search for master narratives of male history so appealing to (at least, to other) men? Questions, as Falstaff doesn't quite put it, that must be asked.

William Herbert, later third earl of Pembroke, was born on 8 April, 1579/80, at Wilton House.[4] He was the first child of the forty-six-year-old second earl, Henry Herbert, and Mary Sidney, his nineteen-year-old wife. Like the Sidneys, the Herberts were a relatively newly ennobled family, coming to political prominence and being granted the Pembroke title under Henry VIII. They had, however, risen more rapidly to power and riches than the Sidneys. Henry Herbert, the first earl of the Henrician creation built Wilton House and carried out a ruthless policy of land enclosures. Within a generation, the Pembrokes had become the most powerful family in the west of England. Visiting Wilton for the birth of the child who would become the third earl—or more precisely staying nearby at Ivychurch, one of the family's recently acquired estates—was the countess's brother Philip. He had spent much of the last months of his sister's pregnancy writing what would become *The Countess of Pembrokes Arcadia*, sending (so the story goes) new pages to Wilton

House each day for the amusement of his sister and the other "fair ladies" he addresses directly in the first version of the work, the so-called "Old" *Arcadia.* A century later, John Aubrey would record (or invent) gossip that "there was so great love between" Sidney "and his faire sister that I have heard old gentlemen say that they lay together, and it was thought the first Philip Earle of Pembroke," born in 1584, "was begat by him." William's parentage has not been attributed to his uncle—although it has been attributed to Shakespeare:

in one of the more bizarre offshoots of the Shakespeare sonnets industry, Rudolf Holzapfel asserted in *Shakespeare's Secret* that the sonnets are addressed to his son William Herbert, the issue of the "fact" that "the vivacious Mary Sidney, sister of Sir Philip Sidney" had been, at eighteen, the mistress of the fifteen-year-old Shakespeare. Less spectacularly melodramatic, though still in the realm of the fanciful and unprovable, are the speculations on whether Pembroke was the so-called Mr. W. H. of Shakespeare's sonnets. First proposed in 1832, and ranking second only in popularity to the argument in favor of Henry Wriothesley, Earl of Southampton, the argument for Pembroke rests, somewhat precariously, to put it mildly, on his initials, W. H., the dedication to him and his brother of the first Folio (1623), and unsuccessful marriage negotiations on his behalf in the 1590s, which are presumed to be the pretext for Shakespeare's first seventeen sonnets. In the past century, John Dover Wilson is the most respectable scholar arguing what there is of Pembroke's case; the most extensive recent argument is that of the psychiatrist John Padel, who has combined his case with a radical reordering of the sonnets that turns them into a single confessional narrative. In Appendix I to his edition of the sonnets, Stephen Booth provides a conveniently brief summary of what he terms the sporadic "outbreaks" of such inferential biography, dryly noting that the topic has "evoked some notoriously creative scholarship." Even if we were to be convinced that there really was a fair youth who lived, breathed, and (maybe) patronized Shakespeare, and that he was Mr. W. H., there is no substantial evidence that Pembroke was "it." No definite connection has been established between Pembroke and Shakespeare around the time in which the sonnets were written.[5]

Moving rapidly out of the realm of quasi-scholarly fantasy of a later period, we can find a number of more useful contemporary comments on Pembroke. Lucy Harington, countess of Bedford, wrote in 1625 that he was the "only honest hearted man imployed [at court] that I know now left to God and his cuntrie." Another court lady, Mary Erskine, called him "one of the most agreeable Men of his Time . . . He had prodigious quick Eyes, and a pleasing Countenance. He was a graceful and eloquent Speaker on all Subjects, having not only Wit and

Learning, but Judgment to apply them properly." In his *History of the Rebellion*, Clarendon likewise distinguished Pembroke from the bulk of Stuart nobles and statesmen in that he had "fame and reputation with all men, being the most universally beloved and esteemed of any of that age, and despite having a great office in the Court, he made the Court itself better esteemed, and more reverenced in the country." Clarendon stressed Pembroke's integrity, his equally high reputation in Court and country: "never man," he asserts, "was planted in a Court, that was fitter for that soil, or brought better qualities with him to purify the air." Then, with a magisterial period, Clarendon interrupts his panegyric with one of the most intriguing qualifications in his notoriously contradictory *History*. Pembroke's memory, he acknowledges, "must not be flattered." He was "not without some allay of vice": he indulged in "pleasures of all kinds, almost in all excesses." He then points to one particular "vice" to which, he asserts, Pembroke "was immoderately given up." Without naming names, it was, he asserts, to "women" that "he sacrificed himself, his precious time, and much of his fortune." Moreover, he continues, "some, who were nearest his trust and friendship, were not without apprehension, that his natural vivacity and vigour of mind began to lessen and decline by those excessive indulgences."[6]

Looking back, four hundred years later, to what do these moralizing but opaque comments point? What can they tell us—even through the filter of Clarendon's own complicated personal and political allegiances—not just of Pembroke's moral strengths or weaknesses, but of the questions I am pursuing here, the even murkier patterns of gender identity, class, familial, and broader cultural patterns? What kind of cultural biography of Pembroke do such comments help us construct? What was it for him to be born and socialized into assumptions and practices that were labeled as male? What did it mean to be interpellated as a male subject, in the Herbert and Sidney families, in England, in the late sixteenth century?

As I noted in chapter one, gender roles can theoretically be organized by any number of categories: the assignments of "man," "male," "son," "husband," and "father" are not absolute but are all constituted by custom, routine, repetition, and the distribution of power, even though in many societies they may be identified with the presence or absence of supposedly fixed biological characteristics. Seemingly inevitably, however, the social mechanisms by which gender roles are constructed tend to be mystified, as if they were "natural" categories. This was the case in early modern England, and most particularly in the upper orders of society, where there were powerful ideological forces constructing seemingly fixed roles for men and women. But—and this is a major strand of my argument about both the Sidney cousins—every society is heterogeneous, an unstable site of struggling relations and processes through which its dominant ideology is continually being constituted and contested. In Pembroke's life we can trace some of the contradictions that were (and, some would argue, are) inherent in being constructed as a man.

In her pioneering study of masculine patterns in Shakespeare's plays, *Man's Estate*, Kahn drew on Mahler, Winnicott, and especially Erikson, to construct a model of early modern masculinity in which gender assignment was based on "a destructively narrow and brittle foundation of identification with the father to the exclusion or repression of identification with the mother." She sees the period's dominant sense of male identity exemplified in the Shakespeare canon, his plays depicting a series of transitions from one strategy to another in a search for some stable identity. What she terms "a second birth into manhood," a conception akin to Mahler's "psychological birth," is solved, tragically narrowly she argues, by the boy's identification with the father, who offers him a model by which his fantasies of autonomy and power may be realized. His identity is constructed by being integrated into a male fellowship, with the feminine in himself and in the women with whom he interacts, necessarily marginalized, bypassed, or (as in the case of *Othello's* murder of Desdemona) killed. Achieving "manhood" depends on a fantasy of independence and mastery coupled with dependence on women (and blame for them if men find their cherished autonomy challenged). Shakespeare dramatizes, Kahn argues, the terrifying, destructive fantasy that male bonding, violence, and control of women will provide men with the stable and reassuring sense of themselves they lost as children. Only in the late plays does an alternative fantasy structure surface: through pain and loss men may learn to find themselves in relationships within the family. The male dilemma of reuniting with the "woman's part" is not solved; its "stubborn continuance" is seemingly inevitable. But a fantasy of belated rapprochement is seen as possible. It is an alluring argument, even if the Eriksonian model slightly flattens out the plays and dehistoricizes the pattern of male development somewhat. But it does touch on an uncanny number of the developmental patterns and fantasies of men in the period. Pembroke's life and writings display many of them, and Kahn's brilliantly clear exposition is one that is useful to have in the background of this exploration of his life.[7]

Curiously, apart from the accounts of his first twenty-five or so years by advocates for Pembroke as Shakespeare's Mr. W. H. (none of which have produced convincing arguments or even documentable connections with Shakespeare), there have been surprisingly few modern biographies of Pembroke: two valuable dissertations, by Briley (1961) and Brian O'Farrell (1966), and the single published account by Gebauer (1987). As their exhaustive documentation makes clear, there are detailed records of Pembroke's public activities extant. Born in 1580 at Wilton, his birth and christening are recorded in St. Mary's Church, Broad Street, in the village of Wilton that was part of the Pembrokes' family estates. His uncle Philip stood proxy for the queen at the christening. He grew up at Wilton House and may have visited London only once, for his uncle Philip's funeral, before he left, at the age of twelve, to attend Oxford. From such details—seemingly so innocent in their "no-nonsense" recitation in the *DNB*, somewhat more euphorically marshalled in earlier panegyrics by Wood or Lodge, and verging on the conspiratorial in the work of the (not always amateur) Shakespeareans mad in pursuit of the mysterious and likely mythical Mr. W. H.—we can read off something of his cultural situatedness.

What do we know of Pembroke's childhood? In order to answer that question adequately, we need both a typical developmental model for early modern aristocratic male childhood and, where possible, detailed historical records. As is the case for almost any person before the twentieth century, much must necessarily be speculative. We are lucky that not only are there many references to Pembroke in public documents throughout his life, but almost two hundred and fifty letters written by him. While many of them, especially from late in his career, deal with matters of state and administration, many contain personal revelations; those written in what was a particularly trying period in his early twenties—following the disclosure that Mary Fitton, a maid of honor with whom he was having an affair, was pregnant—are intensely revealing about the values he had acquired by the time he was in his early twenties. Further, as I indicated in chapter one, we can construct something of the personality conflicts typical of a boy given an upbringing like Pembroke's.[8] In speculating upon Pembroke's "inner life," therefore, we can not only consult what modern theory suggests about the construction of the male psyche, but test those insights against what we can locate in both sixteenth-century records and what can be constructed as a typical profile of an elder son growing up in an aggressive and powerful aristocratic family in that period.

Before he was sent to Oxford, the young William Herbert seems to have spent most of his early youth deep in the country at Wilton— perhaps, the modern urban cynic might be excused for adding parenthetically, one cause of his later great distaste for being in the country, which he expressed most vehemently in letters written when he was exiled to Wilton after the Fitton affair. The dominant figure at Wilton was not his father, who spent much of the time in Wales or at court, but his mother. Life in what Breton termed his mother's "little court" provided the young William Herbert with an intense and contradictory set of values that clearly left their mark upon him. It is relatively easy to reconstruct something of what Greven calls the "outer life"[9] of Wilton House during these early years of Pembroke's life, but it is possible too, to speculate with some likelihood how the experiences there would have affected him on more lasting levels. From the time of his mother's marriage in 1577 until she was widowed in 1601, the cultural life of Wilton was dominated by what is usually termed the "Sidney Circle." This was a loosely connected group of associates and friends of the countess and her brother, including those writers and seekers of patronage Mary Ellen Lamb has termed the countess's "bear whelps,"[10] who shared deeply held political, religious, and literary ideals that, at least in their own eyes, Wilton came to epitomize. In 1623 Walter Sweeper reminded Pembroke and his brother that their "famous Wilton house", had been "a little Universitie," renowned for its supporting, among others, the famous divine, "great Hugh Sanford," who was one of William's tutors.[11] In 1579 and 1580 Philip Sidney himself was at Wilton, formulating or writing not only the *Old Arcadia*, but what became *The Defence of Poesie*, *Certain Sonnets*, and probably at least the beginnings of *Astrophil and Stella*. It was to Wilton that he retired in a sulk after being scolded by the queen for quarreling with the Earl of Oxford, and making his unwelcome intervention on behalf of the Leicester faction's cause against a possible French marriage. To Wilton, too, came a number of Sidney's friends and associates to help create, in the isolation of the English countryside, the equivalent of what they admired in the noble houses and academies of France and Italy.

The emotional peculiarities of Pembroke's mother's relationship with her brother—another Sidney family romance which I have pursued elsewhere[12]—were mediated through a series of contradictions that may well have left their impact on the young William Herbert. Pious, intelligent, probably unhappy in her marriage, Mary Sidney (as she habitually called herself) was devoted to furthering her brother's ideals. Breton revealingly described Wilton thus:

> under heaven it was my greatest happiness . . . to light into the courtlike house of a right worthy honourable Lady . . . Her house being in a maner or kinde of a little Court, her Lorde in place of no meane commaund, her person no lesse than worthily and honourablie attended, as well as with Gentlewomen of excellent spirits, as divers Gentlemen of fine carriage . . . where first, God daily served, religion truly preached . . . honor kindly entertained, vertue highly esteemed, service well rewarded, and the poore blessedly relieved.

Elsewhere Breton focuses his praise by comparing Wilton to Urbino: "Who hathe redde of the Duchess of Urbina, may saie, the Italians wrote wel: but who knowes the Countesse of Pembroke, I think hath cause to write better."[13] Two ideological worlds collide in Breton's praise. The Protestant piety of Wilton—hardly a characteristic one would associate with Urbino—is attested by many observers, and Margaret Hannay has detailed Mary Sidney's strong support for the Protestant cause in her writings and patronage. But there was also the courtly, even hedonistic, side of Wilton. We can turn to Abraham Fraunce's pastorals for an undoubtedly equally idealized picture of the countess, presiding as Pembrokiana, "the Matchles Lady regent," in Ivychurch Park, where Sidney frequently stayed. In his poem, *The Countess of Pembrokes Ivychurch*, a hunt in Tasso's tale of Amyntas is adapted to the rural pleasures of Wiltshire, "that sweetest parck" of "prety Yvychurch," where Mary Sidney is shown giving "grace and life to the pastime[s]" of her courtly followers.[14] Piety and courtliness, Calvin and Castiglione: William was brought up within the peculiar mixture of neo-chivalry and Protestant militancy of Wilton House. These contradictions in the Wilton circle point outward and inward—outward to the cultural contradictions of the whole Sidneian ethos, and inward to how those contradictions were internalized.

What were the effects of growing up in such an atmosphere? What can we reconstruct of William Herbert's upbringing that might have determined the particular desires he sought to fulfill in his own family romances? Let us start with his parents and immediate caregivers. Lamb suggests that the early modern period evinces a particularly intensified version of the pattern of upbringing underlying Kahn's account of child/mother relations in the period. As argued by Chodorow, the boy's earliest identification is with female caretakers, including the mother, creating in him an uneasiness about his own "feminine" tendencies which increasingly threaten his developing sense of masculinity. The fear of women becomes a crucial part of his enculturation, and it is characteristically dealt with by over-compensatory idealization and accompanying denigration of women. Particularly is this the case when external gender differentiation, Lamb notes, "emerged with sudden force" at about seven when the boy was breeched: when a boy reaches the age of seven, advises Thomas Elyot, he should be removed from the company of women, in order that the potential for voluptuousness be discouraged. The separation/individuation process would be accelerated strikingly, perhaps with the external manifestations of potential male autonomy catching up with a rush to the internalized and repressed sense of being gendered male.

The distance of the father from the family also intensified this process. Fathers of aristocratic families like the Herberts and Sidneys spent much of their time apart from the family unit. In the case of William Herbert, too, his father was far older than his mother. Such age discrepancy was not atypical: many aristocratic mothers were far closer in age to their children than their husbands, and, as the children grew older, these women probably drew from them some of the emotional sustenance that they may have lacked from their husbands. It is clear from records and letters in the Sidney papers that the dominant figure in William's upbringing was his mother. She was active, keen on education and poetry, and dedicated to the memory and ideals of her brother. Her husband, thirty years older, by repute gruff and ill-tempered, increasingly ill and often incapacitated, especially from the late 1580's on, spent much of the first decade of his son's life on official business as lord president of Wales or at court. Mary Herbert was "sensitive, intelligent, and (one imagines) more than a little lonely," Briley notes, so that her son, especially in the first four years of his life, before his younger brother Philip was born, probably had more than usual attention from his mother.[15] Indeed, as I noted in chapter one, there are suggestions that his upbringing, while probably a strict one, and certainly concerned with the reinforcing of male privilege and authority, may well have had aspects that were unusually indulgent.

If William's father remained a distant, and at times hostile, figure to his son—one whom, as Briley suggests, he sought in later years to replace by his uncle Robert[16]—it is the figure of his other, dead, increasingly mythologized uncle, Sir Philip Sidney, that may be a crucial key to understanding him.[17] In his survey of the Pembroke family's patronage, Michael Brennan argues that Pembroke was explicitly educated to be the heir to his mother's dead brother. Thomas Moffett's *Nobilis* (1593) seems to have been written at the request of his mother to impress upon the young William Herbert that he, as yet a "growing shoot," was born to become a "flower of the Sidneys." When he was old enough, and therefore a potential source of financial support, he was continually reminded by aspiring writers that he was "Nephew to Sidney (rare worth's richest pearl)": Francis Davison, dedicating *A Poetical Rhapsody* to the newly created third earl in 1603, reminded him that he was both a "worthy son, unto a peerless mother" and "nephew to great Sidney of renown."[18] The presence of the near-mythical figure of the shepherd knight in Pembroke's family romance set forth for him a model of expectations and assignments regarding what it was to be a man.

What was it, indeed, to be a "man" in such a family and in such a time? In the 1620s the dramatist Philip Massinger—whose father Arthur had been Pembroke's steward at Wilton, and who had been given the distinctive family first name—wrote a series of plays the heroes of which embody an ideal of benevolent aristocracy. Margot Heinemann argues that in these plays Massinger "saw the world in terms of a noble order of patrons and aristocratic rulers, as he had experienced it in his youth" on the Wilton estates.[19] If that is so, the gender politics of that order are blatant: aristocratic males embody the society's most heroic values, which emerge as assertiveness, military courage, courtly gallantry towards decorative and subservient women, and the seemingly inborn assumption of the responsibilities of rank and birth. By the 1620s, Massinger's values are increasingly nostalgic, but they clearly embody residual commonplaces, designed to please his patrons, who included both Pembroke and his brother, to whom *The Bondman* (1623) is dedicated. They certainly provide us with clues to the ideology of masculinism upon which Pembroke's upbringing was built.

The most obvious assumption is the naturalness, indeed the virtue, of masculine dominance and aggression, most obviously seen in, though by no means confined to, military aggression. Here we must stand back, and contemplate one of the most banal and most destructive cultural metaphors of Western (some would say human, others patriarchal) culture. I will initiate this discussion, which will be one of my continuing concerns, with a safe cliché: that the link between the Western male psyche and ideologies of virility and domination has historically been very intimate. Paglia both essentializes and celebrates this link, seeing the "testing and purification of the male will" through struggle, control, and the violent imposition of intellect upon nature, especially as (literally) embodied in the female, as the core experience of Western civilization. This seems unsupportable nonsense, but it may be persuasive to some, since the assumption that men are more naturally aggressive is so deeply rooted in our culture. How "naturally" aggressive are we? And do we count as "aggression" basic survival behaviors which restrict or threaten the survival of others? Are we, as some bio-grammarians argue, "wired" for aggression and the destruction of others, even of ourselves? Freud claimed in *Civilization and Its Discontents* that an "inclination to aggression" was "an indestructible feature of human nature: *Homo homini lupus* . . . man [is] a savage beast to whom consideration towards his own kind is something alien."[20] His observations are probably at once too optimistic and too pessimistic: over-pessimistic in that he read a predominant Western cultural pattern as basic biological and psychic grammar, but over-optimistic in that he saw it as a matter of the "individual" psyche rather than of a whole culture's dominant ideology, and the product of historical processes in that culture.

A corrective to Freud's essentialism—and one of the most suggestive treatments in recent years of the structures, metaphors, and practices of the ideologies of Western masculinism is Theweleit's *Male Fantasies*. In this often impassioned, sometimes rambling mixture of brilliant speculation and minute textual analysis of the writings and fantasy world of the *Freikorps*, the proto-fascist mercenaries hired to put down incipient socialist revolution in Germany following the First World War, Theweleit denies constructing a history of Western patriarchial fantasies. Nevertheless, his study is full of fascinating and frequently disturbing detours into the history of Western art, literature, and military and erotic history. It leaves no doubt that the fascist personality is not merely an aberration of twentieth-century European history. The importance of *Male Fantasies* for my study of the Sidneys is both methodological and highly specific. In his quest to "find the desires and anxieties that are at the core" of the "mystique of war and violence," Theweleit moves provocatively between historical specificity and the broader claims of psychoanalysis, voicing (as I do) unsureness whether the seeming naturalness of male violence is rooted in culturally produced factors, or has biological or some other level of permanence. In this kind of speculative psycho-cultural analysis, it is certainly crucial to take the conjunction in "psycho-history" seriously: what Theweleit, following Deleuze and Guattari, terms "the desiring-production of the unconscious" is cathected upon historically specific patterns, codes, and conjunctions; and historical specifics must always be the locus for the playing out of patterns of human behavior, whether they are the products of culture or biology or a combination of the two.[21] This is an extraordinarily complex debate: to what extent do matters of relative size, shape, and hormonal constitution which seem more or less biological givens determine cultural meanings? Do they rather acquire meanings within culturally produced structures such as attitudes to "proper" or appropriate activities, privileging certain postures, movements, or even particular physical skills, games, and pastimes? Regardless of origins and causes, the assignment of what is "natural" to each gender articulates the characteristic metaphors of a culture, and these metaphors are observable in our distinctive gender choices and patterns.

Surveying the militaristic inheritance of the *Freikorps*, Theweleit regrets that recent historians have "rejected the conventional history of 'kings and battles' for the 'hidden history' of everyday life, almost to the point of forgetting how much of everyday life has, century after century, been shaped by battles and dominated by kings or warrior elites," and specifically by the ideologies that underpinned such elites.[22] In early modern England there was a multitude of cultural practices in which male aggression was reified as a seemingly "natural" process for the dominant classes, not only in the most obvious manifestations of war and politics. The structuring of a vast range of experience by a pattern of rivalry, struggle, and conquest points to the dominant ideology from which, of course, we are hardly immune today. At the time the young William Herbert was brought up, young noblemen, especially eldest sons, were educated to be soldiers within a peculiar, belated phase of chivalry. The longevity of chivalry's rituals, long after its military and political relevance were gone, has been widely commented upon by cultural historians. During the sixteenth century, English political organization and military technology altered drastically, rendering most of the specifically military aspects of chivalry obsolete; yet throughout the late Renaissance, the trappings of chivalry, most visibly in the form of such tournaments as the annual Accession Day tilts in which Pembroke took part, intensified.[23] Tournaments became the major institution to display what was seen as the essence of nobility, the ritualized expression of violence in the service of an ideal cause. The death of Philip Sidney in 1586 acted as a spur to the revival: Sidney was mourned as a self-sacrificing chivalric hero. By the time Pembroke was taking part in tournaments they had become rituals that at once asserted a nobleman's commitment to martial violence and allowed him to display himself to advantage within the usually less overtly physical aggression of the court's political and social rivalries. In *The Booke of Honor and Armes* (1590), Sir William Segar noted both the change and the continued centrality of at least the ideology of chivalric combat: "each particular Gentleman or other person professing Honor and Armes, ought sufficientlie bee moued thereunto for defence of his owne particular reputation." As Richard McCoy points out, by the time Segar is writing the goal is clearly "the regulation and containment of violence," so that the tourney became a form of "conflict negotiation." But the underlying ideology of masculinity as aggression remained untouched. When an embassy from England visited the Landgrave of Hesse in 1596, a combat "betwixt jest and earnest" was arranged, with the knights of Hesse announcing that they desired "not to make devises, but to show their manhood."[24]

Oddly enough, the first book dedicated to Pembroke, Robert Barret's *The Theorike and Practice of Modern Warres* (1598), points to the massive cultural conflicts in the continuation of chivalry. The work was dedicated to him, as well as to his father, the second earl, "in respect of your own vertues (resembling altogether that Noble Earle of Pembroke, your Grandfather, and that worthie Sir Phillip Sidney your Uncle)." Addressing the eighteen-year-old William's father, Barret specifically recommended his book for his son and heir "as a matter befitting his lordship, as well for the Martial matters already shining in him, as for the sympathie that his honorable birth and Nobilitie hath with this subject which we treat of, being warre and armes." Barret's advice echoes that given by Philip Sidney to his own brother Robert less than twenty years earlier.[25] Yet the book is pragmatically anti-chivalric, advocating far more up-to-date military technologies.

In his study of some of the modern descendants of this tradition, Theweleit extends his analysis of the *Freikorps* texts by a miscellany of pictorial images, including portraits, cartoons, and drawings. A number of Sidney and Pembroke family portraits can likewise help us here, especially since, as Jonathan Goldberg notes, portraits of families from this period "function as part of the apparatus and discourse of power": they are part of a dominant ideology's self-presentation, although not necessarily a mirror of "the actuality of family life."[26]

The chivalric ideal of the Sidneys is probably best epitomized in the Penshurst portrait of Philip Sidney, dressed in partial armor, one hand on hip, the other holding a sword, the essential heroic figure, "untrammeled," as Maureen Quilligan points out, "by any social context," as if the values he represents were absolute, unalterable by historical accident or even death. He exhibits what Paglia terms the "male exoskeleton," the ideology of (though Paglia would not accept that distancing phrase) "the hardness of western will." By contrast—apart from a Hilliard miniature of about 1595 which shows him as a melancholy noble youth—the numerous representations we have of Pembroke, including a number of paintings by members of the school of Van Dyke, show him not as a chivalric hero, but as a political and court officeholder. There is a half-length portrait by Abraham van Blijenberch, probably painted around 1618; another by Marcus Gheraerts the Younger from 1628; one by Van Dyke himself, painted in the late 1620s, in which Pembroke is wearing a black court dress, with the blue ribbon of the Garter around his neck, and the gold key of the office of lord steward hanging from his belt. There is a portrait by Mytons at Wilton, with copies at Audley End and elsewhere, which resembles the Van Dyke, as does an engraving by Simon de Passe, who also designed the elaborate titlepage to Wroth's *Urania*. Another portrait at Wilton of the school of Mytons shows Pembroke in a bedroom in what was probably meant to be his London lodgings, a tantalizing glimpse of what may have been Baynard's Castle. Another Van Dyke at Wilton, painted posthumously from the statue outside the Bodleian Library, is perhaps, iconographically, the most interesting of all, stressing as it does family continuity and allegiance. Painted about 1635, it inserts a representation of the late earl (who had died in 1630) alongside portraits of the fourth earl, his brother Philip, King Charles, and Queen Henrietta Maria.[27] None of these representations of Pembroke show him as a military hero. All indicate, at least on the surface, a major cultural transition in the family portrait: despite his upbringing Pembroke had become the family's first court bureaucrat, a far more successful politician than his uncles, inhabiting the space between chivalry and the politics of the bourgeois state. His career demonstrates how the ideology of masculine authority and dominance was being adapted to a new social formation.

Another useful gloss on both continuity and transition in the masculine ideals of the period can be seen in two family portraits of the Sidneys and Pembrokes. The first is of Robert Sidney's family, still hanging at Penshurst, which includes the earliest known portrait of Mary. Painted about 1597, the portrait centers on her brother, the seven-year-old William Sidney. Born in 1590, about four years after Mary, he was the oldest male child. In the portrait his mother rests her hand on his shoulder, as if pressing him forward for the approval of his father, the presumed viewer of the portrait. He thus takes his place in the family dynasty as the future patriarch. As Quilligan points out, he stands not only in the posture of son and heir, but specifically "in the Sidney posture," reflecting the inheritance that was presumably put upon both the eldest sons of the dead heroes' siblings, William Sidney and William Herbert. Portrayed about the time he would have been officially "breeched," the boy is clearly a male in transition, still wearing skirts as stiff and voluminous as his sister's, but starting to be differentiated from his four sisters by his "masculine" accouterments, which include a sword and buckler and a plumed hat. He is entering a domain of assigned maleness in which women figure in subordinate roles. His sword, that role's visible symbol, is placed so as to "constrain" Mary's body, as Quilligan puts it. Presented as the future authoritative male, he is the innocent and idealistic boy just entering his apprenticeship, and he will go forward to tournaments, jousts, playing at tilt, all parts of the ritual of transformation to male adulthood. The sword is the embodiment of future male power. The instruments of what Theweleit terms the "pain principle"—the masculine characteristics of domination, aggression, and penetration—are parallel, the penis hidden, the sword the external announcement of gender assignment. The father and his phallus, notes Benjamin, "come to symbolize the child's whole sense of difference between himself and adults, as well as between men and women."[28]

By contrast, and to convey both the ideological transition I am observing in the Sidney/Pembroke families, as well as the underlying continuation of gender hierarchies, we can jump ahead almost forty years—in fact to a few years after Pembroke's death in 1630—to the imposing painting by Van Dyke at Wilton House of Pembroke's brother Philip, fourth earl of Pembroke and his family. It provides a rich combination of striking poses and gestures that carry rich ideological significance. The painting includes background cherubs representing children who had died young, as if to stress the domestic rather than the military continuity of the family ideals. Yet despite the absence of the chivalric, the underlying gender ideology remains the same: the women are less prominently displayed than the men; they are more static and contained, decorative receptacles of domestic security; the men look attentive, peer eagerly forward, as if prepared for some action. Though the lack of an explicit military caste to the portrait is evident, reflecting the new domestication of the aristocracy as well as (more particularly) the insulated peace of the 1630s, nevertheless the gender politics that sustain the Pembroke family remain obvious.[29] The seemingly innocent details of these pieces show how deeply-ingrained gender assignments were lived out in material, physical details—literally in the body and the body's placements. It is in such material details of a culture that ideology operates. Ordinariness is also metaphor: dress and posture reflect the children's gender assignment, conveying very explicit messages as to what is expected of a child's sense of its gender. As Bernstein puts it, such "messages weave their way into the contents of the superego as well as the formation of the ego," structuring the apprehensions of anatomical or "body ego" differences.[30]

Theweleit's key category to describe the members of the *Freikorps*, derived from Mahler, is "the not-fully-born." In her work with children, Mahler isolated those who "never attained the security of body boundaries libidinally" and having little sense of body boundaries of their own, are never able to fully individuate. As they come to adulthood, she observed, they achieve ego stability only in relation to the demands of outside authorities. They are violent and frequently destructive, and what impels their violence and destruction—however it may be transferred into socially approved activities—is this childhood failure to fully differentiate, and a consequent "fear and longing for fusion" with some greater, authoritative power that might prevent their fragmentation. Such children, Mahler argues, develop a sense of self that is only "borrowed, painfully drilled into and fused onto the individual." The not-fully-born characteristically live out fantasies in which their incompletely formed egos have never adequately entered into object relations between a whole ego and a whole other. At times of stress, conflict, and regression, such a personality has to fall back on fantasies of incorporation into larger bodies for its stability. These bodies are mother surrogates, idealized authority figures who represent the mothering figures they want both to return to and separate from. In such circumstances, "the boy does not merely disidentify with the mother, he repudiates her and all her feminine attributes. The incipient split between mother as source of goodness and father as model for individuation is hardened into a polarity in which her goodness is redefined as a seductive threat to autonomy." The boy who seeks his sense of autonomy "must separate himself in the outside world from the mother's female body and in his inside world from his own already formed primary identification with femaleness and femininity. This great task is often not complete." The child "seeks (its whole life long, if need be) its unification" with maternal bodies or maternal substitutes, by means of which it can become whole. Theweleit extends Mahler's concept into a tool of cultural analysis, suggesting that the "not-fully-born" include the majority of Western men, and that, even in the twentieth century, "only a handful of men . . . had the good fortune to be in some sense fully born." Whether men with such characteristics become psychotic to the extent that members of the *Freikorps* demonstrate is presumably dependent upon the particular social formation in which they find themselves born and exercise their roles as males. Chivalry and the monarchistic state clearly provided such a structure for aristocratic men in early modern England.[31]

Theweleit suggests that in asking the question, "what was it to be a man?", we cannot neglect another, "what was it to "be a woman?"—and ask it from both a man's and a woman's point of view. In particular, what were (and perhaps still are) the "male fantasies" by which men in early modern England dealt with the women in their lives? They were, as we have seen, constructed in relation to the ideologies of gender produced within the family, as boys and girls oriented themselves to their gender assignments. In the case of a male child that process involved the development of a dichotomous "identification with the father to the exclusion or repression of identification with the mother," to repeat Kahn's formulation.[32] Just as women learn to disguise their forbidden masculine wishes behind a stereotype of female innocence, weakness and self-sacrifice, so men learn to disguise their forbidden feminine wishes behind a stereotype of male virility. In a society where gender assignments are strictly polarized, no intermediate or flexible roles—which, today, we would acknowledge, even celebrate, that most of us occupy—are permitted. The fiercely institutionalized binarism of the period produced what Dollimore describes as "a profound separation identification between identification and desire . . . Thus the male is required to identify with other males but he is not allowed to desire them." By contrast, he is supposed to desire women, but he is discouraged from both identifying with them and, at least as important, with what is identified as the "woman's part" in himself. The "qualities found in a real man," to use Machiavelli's revealing phrase, involve the affirmation of an aggressive selfhood: "nothing," however, "is more contemptible or more dangerous for a man [than] to be like a woman." When a boy's own "femininity" has to be repudiated, then his adult attitudes towards women may easily be primarily ones of fear, mastery, and distaste, attitudes which express a need but which seem unable to recognize women as different but like subjects. In a bipolar gender ideology, Kaplan notes, "all too often," a boy's "independence is founded on an infantile ideal of what a real man should be. He has very little opportunity to integrate the feminine and masculine aspects of his identity."[33]

Such a process would be reinforced by two recurrent patterns in a family such as William Herbert's. He had a remote father, and he was brought up by a number of attendant female caregivers. These would have included his mother, though it is highly unlikely that she fed him herself; the mothering functions would be shared among wet-nurses, servants, other female relations, and his mother. The consequence of such a pattern—a privileged male surrounded by doting, attentive, and predominantly subservient women—can easily be the early idealization of women as all-powerful objects to whom the boy looks for nurture and protection at the same time as he is being trained to differentiate himself from them and as he becomes aware that what supposedly constitutes him as a man involves rejecting the "woman's part" in himself. In adult life, a pattern may easily be established whereby he continually tries to recreate this primitive maternal bond while at the same time he seeks to break from it: "what boys seem to need most from the mother and continue to need and, as lovers and husbands, go on to get from other women is an all-present but unobtrusive Mother who is willing to stand by in the wings ready to rescue the mighty acrobat as he recklessly hurls his body through the open spaces." Thus he becomes one of Paglia's "questing knights, isolated against empty panoramas," compulsively re-playing what in her view is the male's primitive struggle to tame (female) nature. Such a bipolar gender ideology is not "true," any more than any other ideological construct. Dollimore, in fact, has made a compelling case for a more fluid system of gender roles to be implied even in the early modern period. But his is a perspective made possible only by later historical developments. The dominant gender ideologies of the period are overwhelmingly dichotomous; they predominantly produce male versions of the family romance, projecting early desires for simulta-neous dependence and independence upon adult relationships, which are satisfying to the extent that they seem to satisfy these contradictory de-sires. As Paglia puts it—seeing bipolarism as "fact" not ideology—"men know they are sexual exiles. They wander the earth seeking satisfaction, craving and despising, never content. There is nothing in that anguished motion to envy." But that tragic, noble calling to be a male is arguably a destructive product of the very ideology of patriarchy that it is designed to uphold. As Judith Butler observes, gender systems like those of the early modern period (and beyond) prescribe "normative sexual posi-tions that are intrinsically impossible to embody" without "inevitable comedy"—though the history of gender politics would suggest that the waste and distortion of "inevitable tragedy" is perhaps more accurate. The ideology of gender was no less crucial to the upholding of social, even cosmic order than the ideologies of class or race.[34] Its distortions remain with us.

69

Whether inherently male as Paglia insists, or culturally produced, this widespread and self-defeating pattern may haunt men in all their adult relationships: a man may choose the sexual objects nearest to those from which he both derived his earliest experiences of satisfaction and rejected in order to separate and individuate himself. It is not simply, as Freud noted, that "the finding of an object" is "a refinding of it," but within this pattern of repudiation and return, a man's search for that ambivalent lost object will frequently be "represented by an endless series of substitutive objects none of which, however, brings full satisfaction." When a man finds himself torn between sexual objects, between, as Freud put it,—unself-consciously assuming the hierarchical categorizations of Western patriarchy—a wife and mistress, what satisfactions are being served, what family romances acted out? Along with the desire to return to a mythologized primitive oneness, a man may be acting out a desire to recreate in adult relationships an early, real or fantasized, mother-child relationship that retains its hold over him even as an adult. But despite the plethora of such case histories recorded in the literature of psychotherapy, there can be no predictable formula; such patterns are always over-determined. A child may grow up in a household where the mother was sexually unfulfilled, or where, as in the case of Pembroke's mother, the husband was significantly older, often absent or ill, or where the marriage was—as was the case with most marriages of Pembroke's class—primarily political, familial, or dynastic. The man may desire a wife to fulfill needs for stability and nurture, and one or more mistresses who will represent the erotic mother he never had—frequently they will be younger, and therefore, in a society where male economic and physical coercive powers are assumed, more easily available to embody his fantasies. Such a pattern is related to one aspect of the "neurotic's family romance," the daydreaming that persists, as Freud notes, into puberty, serving not only as a fulfillment of wishes, but "as a correction of actual life," and invoked specifically to reject the parents "of whom he now has a low opinion and of replacing them by others."[35]

Of course, as I cautioned earlier, however many and detailed modern case studies there may be, we have no equally detailed cases from the early modern period to confirm or modify such patterns. We do, however, have a great deal of indirect evidence. Deborah Rubin has drawn attention to a particular mother/son relationship within the Herbert family itself, pointing to the ways Magdalen Herbert is written into her son George Herbert's *Memoriae Matris Sacrum*. These memorial poems, Rubin notes, are especially revealing for the ways the son wishes to repossess his dead mother. Like the nourishing/devouring women who appear in the fantasies of Theweleit's twentieth-century subjects, Magdalen Herbert appears, in her son's devotions to her memory, as a receptacle of his desires and fears. In one of the poems Herbert records the public praise accorded to her by others, but, as her son, his own desire is to climb back into her, to simultaneously possess and be possessed by her body, and he cries: "Hihine matris urna clausa est unico" (To me alone is my mother's urn shut up). He prays to Phoebus: "Sitque omnis motis nescia tanta quies" (And if there is such an unknown repose of all motion), he wishes to seek it out where he originated, inside his mother. He describes her dual motherhood of him, bringing him into this and the next world, in metaphors of the secret garden of erotic poetry: "Quare domus Dominaesit, gravitate docent". In one poem he wishes to appropriate her mothering function: he vows that his own body will swell up and give birth to her praises. In the next, he blames her spirit for removing her body and leaving him gaping for nourishment, so that he is heavy with tears, not with the milk with which she nourished him. Unlike her fruitful garden, his tiny garden is almost overgrown ("brevisque hortus, cuius cum vellere florum"); he is like an overturned tree, a polyp (Polypus) clinging to her side, and his whole world seems overwhelmed by floods.[36]

Such metaphors are conventional enough, but it is precisely in the recurrence of conventional metaphors that the assumptions of an ideology can invariably be located. Herbert's descriptions of his mother are uncannily like those of the *Freikorps* males depicting the nurturing, but potentially overwhelming and smothering, functions of women as registered in the fantasies of a son. Are these contradictions, as Paglia would argue, inherent in being male? Or in being male within a patriarchal society? At the very least there seems to be such endurance in Western history in the male fantasies about women that we can observe that the conjunctions of attraction/repulsion, fascination/abhorrence and dependence/dominance have an uncanny historical continuance. As Freud put it in his essay on the Mona Lisa, men fear women's sexuality as "ruthlessly demanding—consuming men as if they were alien beings."[37] Much of the eroticization of women in the Renaissance court—its caste of erotic titillation, the language of Petrarchism, the expression of political rituals in terms of the erotic—can be linked to this pattern of fascination for and fear of women. As I shall suggest in discussing both Pembroke's and Wroth's poetry in later chapters, the discourse of Sidneian Petrarchism in which they both wrote offered them all too accessible subject positions which reinforced these roles.

What psychological benefits does a man gain from his conscious or unconscious participation in this combination of idealization and domination and, more generally from the long history of misogyny of which it is a part? On a commonplace level this question is easy to answer. There is the security of belonging to a dominant majority, which produces an elevation of self-esteem over the supposed deficiencies of what can be conveniently be categorized as an "other" gender group. But beyond this there is an especially grotesque aspect to the tradition of misogyny: the most important motive for embracing it may lie in men's needs to reduce their irrational fears of women. Especially where the rational is privileged over the instinctive, any loss of rational control may be blamed upon women. The fear of women's sexual power also has deep roots in the supposed facts of women's bodies and male imaginings of them. In societies with only rudimentary awareness of sexual physiology, a woman's bodily processes may seem enigmatic and threatening: above all, as I suggested with George Herbert's poems on his mother, the fact that men come from a woman's body. Within such an ideology, the objects of men's love are finally, Julia Kristeva claims, "the primal mother" who is the "inexhaustible source of excitement" at the same time as she is "an impossible object."[38]

I will move next to seeing how far we might be able to construct a narrative of Pembroke's career that will be illuminated by some of the material I have sketched. However tentative we must be in applying modern case studies and theories of gender construction, two general patterns are incontrovertible: the contradictions within the chivalric male ideals by which young aristocrats were educated, and the distinctive place of women within that ideology and its attendant fantasy structures. Both constitute aspects of the Sidney family romance that can be located in detail in the lives and writings of the Sidney cousins.

Our main source of much useful gossip about the young William Herbert's activities at court before he inherited the Pembroke title in 1601 is the correspondence of Rowland Whyte, who lived, Lodge claims, "on terms of the strictest intimacy which the distinctions of ranks could allow, with the Earl of Pembroke, in whose house at Baynard's Castle he usually resided." Whyte was, in fact, employed by Mary's father, Robert Sidney, as his agent at court, but he had lodgings at Baynard's Castle, from where he wrote to Robert Sidney several times a week, especially in the latter half of the 1590s when Sidney was so often in the Low Countries. Young William is mentioned first in 1595 in connection with marriage negotiations. There are no records of his activities for 1596, though Hannay speculates that, at the age of sixteen, he may have accompanied Essex to the attack on Cadiz. By 1597 he is at court, and for the next few years he is frequently mentioned by Whyte. In 1598 Sidney was told that he was coming to live in London, somewhat against his father's will: "My lord Herbert hath with much ado brought his Father to consent that he may live at London." By 1599 he was established among the most fashionable young lords, "swagering yt," as Whyte puts it, "amongest the Men of Warre." Yet Whyte's observations of Herbert are tinged with anxiety. The young lord had, Whyte reported, frequent migraine headaches, finding "no Manner of Ease, but by taking of tobacco." Whyte also worried that Herbert was pursuing his advancement at court in a "cold and weake Maner"; he was concerned that there "is a want of Spirit and Courage laid to his Charge." Something of this tension might be seen in the young lord's attempts to break with his parents: he repeatedly demanded that they not attend him at court, and in 1600 they remained, at their son's insistence, at Wilton.[39] At last, he "resolves," wrote Whyte in some relief in September 1600, "to show hymself a Man at Armes," although Whyte worried that William has hired his former tutor Hugh Sanford to make him "some excellent Devise" in a tourney, which Whyte fears will be "some pedantike Invention." He reports a month later, however, with more satisfaction: Herbert "is practicing at *Greenwich* . . . he leapes, he dawnces, he singes, he gives Counterbuffes, he makes his Horse runne with more Speede; he thanckes me, and meanes to be exceeding merry with you this Winter in *Baynards* Castell, where you must take Phisicke." The special occasion of this outburst of glee is worth noting: Whyte had just told Herbert that Robert and his daughter Mary would soon be coming to Baynard's Castle. Herbert courted both the Cecil and Essex factions (playing tennis with Essex), and, like every other aspiring courtier, repeatedly expressed his devotion to and asked favors of the aging queen. In 1600 Whyte noted that he "is at court, and very discreetly follows his course of making love to" the queen.[40]

The court, of course, is a major cultural site of metaphorical, and therefore cultural, contradiction in the period. Later in the century, in the same work in which he gave his enigmatic assessment of Pembroke, Clarendon looked back at the institution where, like his subject, he had spent so much of his adult life. The court, he wrote, was where, "as in a mirror, we may best see the face of that time, and the affections and temper of the people in general," for, he continued, "the Court measured the temper and affection of the country." Ambitious men and women "swarmed" to the court, seeking titles, preferment, gain, glory, favors, rewards: it was, in Gabriel Harvey's words, the "only mart of preferment and honour." For members of Pembroke's class, the court was one of the key apparatuses beyond the family that reached into the very grain of what constitutes an individual, into his or her actions and attitudes, discourses, learning processes, the material details of everyday life. To be outside, so it seemed, was, in Donne's phrase, to be "not in the world."[41] Certainly, when banished to Wilton after the disgrace of his affair with Mary Fitton, Pembroke's immediate response was to fret about being exiled from court. "I have not yet been a day in the country, and I am as weary of it as if I had been prisoner there seven year," he complains:

"if the Queen continue her displeasure a little longer, undoubtedly I shall turn clown, for justice of peace I can by no means come unto, and one of the two a man that lives in the country must needs be . . . I have as little to do here as any man living."[42] From a different class, but exiled for a not unrelated misdemeanor and voicing similar anxieties, John Donne similarly expressed frustration at his immobility while the business of the bustling court moved on without him. He confessed to his friend Sir Henry Goodyere that he still retained "the same desires" as "when I went with the tyde" of court preferment, and he expressed continual anxiety that he was forced to suffer the "tediousness of my life" in exile. In 1604, while Pembroke was once again enjoying the status of a "free man," the still ostracized Donne wrote a verse letter to another friend, Sir Henry Wotton, "at his going Ambassador to *Venice*," which contains these bitter lines:

> 'Tis therefore well your spirits now are plac'd
> In their last Furnace, in activity;
> Which fits them (Schooles and Courts and Warres o'rpast)
> To touch and test in any best degree.[43]

"Activity" is the crucial term for the ambitious young male, needing to prove himself in the presence of his peers, and anxious to test the self that has been constructed not to be passive and wait, but to be in perpetual movement. In Donne's case, the result of inactivity is not just restlessness, but a deeper insecurity, which he articulated to Goodyere in 1608:

> Every Tuesday I make account that I turn a great hour-glass and consider that a week's life is run out since I went. But if I ask myself what I have done in the last watch, or would do in the next, I can say nothing; If I say that I have passed it without hurting any, so may the spider in my window . . . I would fain do something, but that I cannot tell what is no wonder . . . to be no part of anybody is to be nothing.

The last phrase speaks, I suggest, for far more men than Donne. It articulates not so much what Greenblatt termed a self-fashioning, but a helplessness before the fashioned nature of the self, the idea that, in Mahler's phrase, the "not-fully-born" needs a degree of self-definition that can come only from forces and institutions outside the self.[44]

Whyte commented more than once that his employer's nephew was "a melancholy young man." The "melancholy" about which he was anxious, and upon which Pembroke himself commented, is clearly related to the fashionable melancholy of the late Elizabethan period. In 1586 Timothy Bright published his widely read *A Treatise of Melancholy*; the first edition was sold out in six months. There, and in Burton's

Anatomy of Melancholy, the melancholic condition was associated with fashionable young aristocrats. If William Herbert perhaps reminds one of Shakespeare's Prince Hal in his initial reluctance to attend to his prescribed duties at court and in his rejection of his father, he is perhaps like Hamlet in his fashionable melancholy. In 1601 he wrote to Cecil to "assist me with your best means to get leave to go into some other land, that the change of climate may purge me of melancholy: for else I shall never be fit for any civil society." Steven R. Brown suggests that the typical child rearing patterns of the age contributed to the prevalence of melancholy, and that it was often combined with feelings of guilt caused by falling short of parents' expectations. What William Herbert's condition demonstrates are the typical traits of a narcissistic personality, characterized by emptiness and boredom, a continuous search for gratification, and serious deficiencies in the capacity to love and care for others. Familial and wider cultural structures, clearly historically locatable, produced this behavior in him. His was, indeed, a society designed to produce narcissism: a child in his position would be brought up to view the world through a series of dualisms of ideal and real; its unreasonable ego ideals such dichotomies produced were reinforced by authoritarian disciplinary patterns. As Otto Kernberg puts it in his study of borderline conditions, such a society produces a personality type with an unusual degree of self-obsession, "a great need to be loved and admired by others and a curious apparent contradiction between a very inflated concept of themselves and an inordinate need for tribute from others." Kristeva remarks pertinently that such a personality "has no internality" and that the love partners of such a person are merely "markers." While he may desire them, he does not cathect them as autonomous objects but rather as stages of his own construction.[45]

In his reading of the many comments in the Sidney letters concerning the young William Herbert, Briley infers that as soon as he came to court, Robert Sidney started to play the role of a substitute father for him. Sidney was, he observes, the one male in Pembroke's whole life for whom he ever expressed close feelings. Brought up with the chivalric ideal of his dead uncle Philip, the gallant, over-idealized soldier, patriot, Protestant, poet hanging over him, and with a dyspeptic, aging, and ill father, the one man who was at once family member, friend, and increasingly his dependent, was his uncle, "the only person he could truly trust, the only person who could truly orient him in this jungle of court intrigue in which he suddenly found himself." Whyte repeatedly encouraged Sidney to see his young, but soon to be enormously rich and powerful, nephew as a son, correctly perceiving the future earl not only as a potential ally, but a means for Sidney's own advancement. "Some Jealosy I had that you were sent away," he confides to Sidney in 1599, "because you should be here to advise and Cownsell him in a Matter of such Greatnes; for surely it wold be to your good to see him a Favorit." A few months later, in similar vein, he reminds Sidney that he was "greatly beholding unto him, and truly I hope, that by him you shall find a Ladder to goe up to that Honor you are worthy of." In 1599, he wrote to Sidney that "9000 [Lord Herbert] is highly favored by 1500 [the Queen] . . . but he greatly wants Advise, and extremely longs for you here," adding on another occasion that he again needed advice, not finding "whom he may trust in a matter of such moment." On other occasions he uses similar language to urge Sidney back to London to be near Herbert: "He exceedingly wishes you here because he is alone . . . not trusting anybody with the favours he receives."[46]

How can we explain this family romance centered on the substitute father figure, who possessed some authority, but who also posed no threat? From Sidney's perspective, especially as urged by Whyte, the young man represented an important future ally. That he had Herbert's good will is indicated by the young man trying (however unsuccessfully) to obtain one of his father's offices, the lord presidency of Wales, for Sidney before the old earl died. William often stayed at Penshurst, and the closeness between the two cousins may have been developing by the turn of the century, when William was twenty and Mary thirteen. But certainly there was a close bond with her father. A recent study of Tudor child rearing observes the striking prevalence of a search for "a dominant figure who will grant the love and redemption denied by depriving parents."[47] As he grew into early maturity, Pembroke may well have felt thwarted by both his own inaccessible and alien father and the shadow of the family's most famous male figure, from whom he was perceived to have inherited much of his intelligence, literary intents, and talents. We can observe here the classic aspects of the family romance—the imaginary construction of an alternative family and, in particular, an alternative paternal authority figure whose power he could both emulate and surpass. But there is a second, less obvious, sense in which Robert Sidney may have been cast in the role of fantasy father. In the classic Oedipal pattern, the son is defeated in his desire to possess the mother by the superiority of the father and instead turns to other women, to other fathers' daughters. What Robert Sidney gave him was a father figure over whom he could feel superior and score victories—not least sexual victories. The daughter of his fantasy father was his cousin Mary: "if the sister is not one's mother's child," remarks Freud, "one is relieved of all blame." At some point did Pembroke's relationship with Sidney's daughter become, consciously or unconsciously, part of the cost of Pembroke's support? Recent psychotherapeutic studies of sibling sexuality have some bearing on the family romance that Pembroke's relationship with his uncle and cousin set up. Michael Kahn has shown how the monolithic Freudian oedipal pattern, which puts such emphasis on the desire for the sister as a substitute, or "understudy" for the mother, needs to be rethought. When emotional warmth in the parent-child relations are lacking, when one or more parents are marginally available emotionally, children may turn to each other for their dependency and erotic needs. As the psychoanalyst Luciano Santiago puts it: "What initially seems to be the 'second best' love object may turn out to be 'even better' than the original." Kahn's reading of Freud's "wolf-man" study, dealing with the traumas of brother/sister relationships, likewise suggests that the emotional absence of parents can intensify the mutual dependency and sexual activities of high-access siblings and cousins, creating the possibility of a "family affair."[48]

We are perhaps now in a position to offer some explanation of Clarendon's remark that Pembroke was "immoderately given" to women. In his essay, "A Special Type of Object Choice," Freud describes four characteristics of erotic attraction that seem to fit Pembroke uncannily. The first is that only women who are "the possession of another" are desirable, a condition almost universally satisfied in the early modern period, especially in the sense that, as Theseus explains to Hermia, women (and many men) had to "fit their fancies to a father's will" (*A Midsummer Night's Dream* 1. 1. 118). The second is, as Freud quaintly puts it, that the desired woman should be "in some way or other of bad repute sexually, whose fidelity and reliability are open to some doubt." This, he explains, may include even "the faint breath of scandal," a condition easily satisfied within the Jacobean court. Third, there is the repetition of such attachments in, as Stephen Heath notes, "the compulsive cycle: encounter, act, verification; endlessly repeated, woman after woman." Such repetitions occur, Freud notes, "again and again in the lives of men of this type . . . The love objects may replace one another so frequently that a long series of them is formed." The supposed natural polygamy of the male was the occasion of some serious theological debate in the seventeenth century, and it has reappeared in Paglia's *Sexual Personae*, where much is made of the burden of men's sexual helplessness: "Male sex is repetition/ compulsion: whatever a man writes in the commentary of his phallic projections must be rewritten again and again." Such a pattern certainly has a distinctive material base in a society in which men are more mobile, have access to a multiplicity of places and social groups, and possess the relative freedom of political power and financial independence. Whether it is a permanent part of maleness, as Paglia claims, is dubious in the extreme. The fourth characteristic Freud notes is the chivalric posture of needing to "rescue" the woman whom one loves. Again, the social rituals of the early modern

77

court embody a classic family romance pattern, the maiden trapped in the tower, waiting for rescue by the handsome prince. We shall see some fascinating variations on these patterns when, in later chapters, we look in more detail at the lives of the Sidney cousins and at their writings.[49]

The first intensively documented event in Pembroke's life intriguingly illustrates Freud's categories. In 1600–1, Herbert became involved with a young court lady named Mary Fitton. She was the ward of Sir Francis Knollys, in whose house she dwelt and to whose amorous advances she had already been subject. Knollys's diary gives us an amusing sidelight on her affair with Pembroke. On discovering the liaison, he complained "that wch I had layed upp in my hart to be my comffort shold become my greatest discomfort." Knollys's judgment on his rival was that his lordship was a "man of synne," who "in the night sewed tares emongst the good corne both the true husbandman was beguiled and the good ground abused." That she certainly fancied Herbert to rescue her from the unwelcome attentions of the elderly Knollys is evident from the story of her dressing "as though she had bene a man" to "marche" through the streets of London to visit his lordship in his rooms. By 18 January, Herbert was writing to Cecil that "there were many false and scandalous reports forged of me," and by late January, it was found that Mary was pregnant. On 5 February, Pembroke was arrested and questioned on the matter. Cecil wrote to Sir George Carew of the "misfortune" that had occurred to Mary Fitton: she is, he wrote, "proved with child, and the Earl of Pembroke being examined confesseth a fact, but utterly renounceth all marriage. I fear they will both dwell in the Tower a while, for the Queen hath vowed to send them thither." Pembroke spent some time in the Fleet prison, but the baby died at birth, and both mother and father were released. Pembroke was exiled to the country, and from Wilton he sent frequent letters to Cecil and others bewailing his fate, petitioning to be able to return to court or be allowed to go abroad.[50]

Why was Cecil the recipient of most of these letters? Because the discovery of the affair coincided with the most momentous event of William Herbert's life so far—his becoming, on his father's death in February 1600/1, third earl of Pembroke, but remaining, for the eleven weeks before his twenty-first birthday, a ward of Cecil. In moments of crisis in our adult lives, we may tend to fall back on infantile patterns of reaction. In such cases, Kaplan notes, what we may become are adults who have achieved physical maturity "while retaining the dichotomies and caricatured gender ideals of childhood." Briley comments that "the facts we have indicate William Herbert was raised in the little world of Wilton and its adjoining estates as one of God's very special creatures," and in his letters to Cecil Pembroke is suddenly the petulant boy whose autonomy is threatened. He finds himself being treated not as a man but

78

like a woman: imprisoned, kept at home, watched. "I cannot forbear telling of you," he writes to the man who had suddenly assumed the power of the father over him, that "I endure a very grievous imprisonment. For do you account him a free man that is restrained from coming where he most desires to be . . ." He especially protests that "in this vile case," he is "most miserable . . . to be banished from the sight of her in whose favor" his hopes lie. The "her" he refers to is, of course, not Mary Fitton, but to yet another parental figure, the queen.[51]

Pembroke continued to fret under the restrictions of his exile: by the end of 1602, however, he wrote to thank Cecil for permission to travel abroad, and by July of 1603 he was back at Baynard's Castle. By the beginning of the reign of James, he was ready to resume his rightful life at court, hymned by his mother's secretary, John Davies of Hereford:

Pembrooke to Court (to which thou wert made strange)
Goe, doe thine homage to thy Soveraigne,
Weepe, and rejoyce, for this sadd-joyfull Change;
Then weepe for joy, thou needst not teares to faine
Sith late thine Eies did nought els entertaine.

The Fitton family petitioned in vain for Pembroke to pay compensation for Mary's disgrace. Her father wrote to Cecil in May 1601:

I can saye nothinge of the Erle but my daughter is confydent in her cleame before god and wishes my Lo: and she might meet before indifferent hearers. but for myself I expect no good from hyme that in all this tyme hath not showed any kindness, I count my daughter as good a gentlewoman as my Lord, though the dignity of honour be greater onlye in him wch hathe beguiled her, I feare, except my Lo^s honesty bee the greater vertues.[52]

Some compensation to the Fittons was arranged, including Pembroke's loss of the revenues of the Forrest of Dean for some years.

Freed from the restrictions imposed on him by his father and the authority vested in the power of Cecil and the old queen, Pembroke seems to have completed his break with parental figures in a dramatic severing of relations with his mother, a major episode in his life barely mentioned by Hannay, her most recent biographer. There is a remarkable letter written by the countess in 1604, which Briley terms "the most intriguing piece of correspondence" from this period of Pembroke's life, referring to a mysterious falling out between the two. She describes "a monster as hath divided myne owne from me, he that was held deerest part of me." She does not say who or what the "monster" was or the occasion. Briley speculates that it refers to some sexual peccadillo of hers that Pembroke has discovered, but there is no evidence for that. It might more easily refer to his mother's discovery of a liaison between her son and his cousin, a speculation that gains some plausibility from the anxiety expressed by Mary's father over his new son-in-law's displeasure shortly after the marriage, a matter that I shall take up in the next chapter. In a letter to his wife a few months later, Robert implies that Pembroke will be happy to visit Penshurst only so long as his mother will not be there, and it is clear that he made no attempt to heal the breach for some ten years.[53]

About the same time, as part of this belated assertion of his independence, Pembroke initiated his own marriage negotiations. Some attempts to arrange an appropriate match had been undertaken by his parents in the 1590s, since if his father had died before Herbert was married, his wardship might have passed out of the family's control. Whyte noted to Sidney, however, that he could not "find any disposition in this gallant young lord to marry," despite both his mother and father's trying to arrange matches, in 1595 with Elizabeth Carey, the granddaughter of Lord Hunsden, the lord chamberlain, and in 1597 and 1598 with Bridget Vere, daughter of the earl of Oxford, granddaughter of Cecil. By 1604, however, Pembroke was sufficiently in control of his own destiny to want matters to go very differently, and after some detailed, even ruthless, negotiations, he married Mary Talbot, the daughter of Gilbert, earl of Shrewsbury and granddaughter of Elizabeth Talbot (widely known as Bess of Hardwick), countess of Shrewsbury.

The marriage seems to have been entirely a dynastic matter. Clarendon noted Pembroke's "want" of "domestic content and delight (in which he was most unhappy, for he paid much too dear for his wife's fortune)."[54] What is interesting is not that the marriage was arranged, since that was normal for Pembroke's class; what is significant is that his discontent about a conventional arrangement was so obvious that Clarendon commented upon it. Certainly there is evidence for Pembroke's dissatisfaction (or disinterest) from the start. In the first two or three months of the marriage, Whyte writes repeatedly to the bride's father to assure him of the suitability and happiness of the match, so frequently that it is clear her family was both nervous and suspicious. On 15 February 1604, he assures Shrewsbury that William Herbert "surely is as honourable a kind husband as any is in Great Britain." A month later he assures him again that his daughter is "much beloved, much respected here," and six weeks later, on both 26 and 27 April, he writes the same sentiments: "Let me assure your Honours," he writes, "that my Lady Pembroke is very much respected by all her Lords." It may be, he admits, "the indiscretion of some that love tattling may buzz out the contrary, which occasions this protestation of mine to your Honour." Two weeks later, however, he admits that while Lady Pembroke is "a most noble worthy lady," she is unfortunately "no good courtier." Time will, he suggests ominously, "teach her to tread the path which her friends have done before." Thereafter there is little mention of her in either the Sidney letters or Pembroke's own correspondence. Like the Wroths, Pembroke and his wife produced no children for many years. Margaret Cavendish, duchess of Newcastle, commented upon the delay, noting of Pembroke's wife: "(some eighteen years after her marriage) she had one son, who died young"; this referring to Henry, who died in infancy in 1621. In fact, they had another son, James, who died at birth in 1616.[55]

Marriage clearly took a subordinate place within the activities of the ambitious young Jacobean nobleman. In the early years of the new reign, Pembroke slowly found an increasingly powerful place in James's court. Whyte's initial anxiety that Hugh Sanford's pedantic influence might lessen Pembroke's impact at the tilts was quickly relieved. Pembroke knew what he termed in a letter to Cecil "the disadvantage of absence" from court. "Absence is an enemy to preferment," Whyte likewise observed. There are records of Pembroke taking part in every King's Day (24 March) tilt from 1603 through 1615, and in 1606 Whyte was able to report a current rhyme with some satisfaction to Sidney: "The Herberts every cockpit day / Do carry away / The gold and glory of the day." In 1607 Pembroke took one of the four parts in a poetic challenge written by John Ford, *Honour Triumphant*, defending the proposition, "Fair Lady was never False." In 1611, Chamberlain noted, the Herbert brothers stood out at tilting and the barriers as "rich and dainty."[56] Never a royal favorite—unlike his more dashing and more boorish brother Philip and the succession of glittering young men who dazzled James—Pembroke nonetheless remained one of the most important political figures in the court, becoming lord chamberlain in 1616 and, handing that position to his brother in 1627, lord controller until his death in 1630.

In discussing Pembroke's career, I am less interested in a chronology of political events and accomplishments and more in the underlying patterns of gender assignment. In chapter one I suggested that the characteristic male fantasy of autonomy was embodied in countless material details: religious and political practices, culturally sanctioned images, commonplace turns of phrase and metaphors, leisure activities, codes of clothing, etiquette, and modes of address. One of the crucial material practices of the period which expresses the power of gender stereotypes concerns men's supposed "natural" mobility. Today, we regard social mobility as commonplace, but geographical mobility is a crucial material reality as well and, in early modern England, one that was built upon significant gender difference. For most men and women, travel beyond the family home was indicative of a degree of autonomy that most modern people take for granted. But for Pembroke and other members of the court, it seems to have been an obsession. The court itself seemed to be in perpetual motion. "The ebb and flow of the sea here are no more regular than the changes" in courtiers, wrote the Venetian ambassador in 1624, "those involving action are always doubtful; those already taken may always be changed." "The Rising unto *Place* is Laborious," wrote Bacon, and behind his metaphor of upward movement, "rising," is the residual moral disapproval which his own career (among many) served to transgress. Unlike Bacon, or Donne, Pembroke did not have to move upward, but he too was a man in continual movement, to oversee, control, gather support, reward, and in so many ways leave his mark upon men and women who were "his." From state records and Pembroke's letters, Briley has constructed his public movements, almost day by day, for thirty years of his public career. Never still, it seems, he moves from London to Wilton, follows the king hunting to Royston or to Sir Robert Wroth's (and his cousin's) estate nearby at Loughton, to Penshurst, back to Baynard's Castle, always circling around London or wherever the king was located.[57] For an age whose dominant ideology stressed stasis, it was an extraordinarily peripatetic existence. A whole history of mobility and its psychosocial effects waits to be written, and one of the most important differentiating factors, in this period at least, will prove to be gender. While women are confined, usually to spaces controlled by men, men are relatively free to move. The mixture of restless, unsatisfied self-assertion and periodic boredom is a recurring male characteristic in our history, and, in a society that makes sexual conquest even a temporary guarantee of coherence and integration, it may very easily be the conquest of women that comes to represent the most intense way of preserving an illusion of integration.

If movement and volatility are hallmarks of the Jacobean male aristocrat, a sense of belonging to a small, family-like community was another. We should not forget how small and closely knit a group the Jacobean aristocracy was. Pembroke's social superiors could be counted on perhaps two hands; the members of his circle of acquaintances were continually hunting, singing, flirting, and quarreling with each other. Their daily lives consisted of a succession of interlocking games and sports, tournaments, visits, dinners, negotiating dynastic marriages and the acquisition of land and political power. Their family romances are not merely those generated within their biological families, but those of the "family" of the Jacobean aristocracy. Many of them were, in fact, related. Reading accounts of, and from, members about the Jacobean court the behavior of the noblemen, one is reminded, at times, of Freud's myth of the primal horde. Taking up Darwin's conjecture that the primitive form of human society was that of a horde ruled over despotically by a powerful male, Freud speculated that "the fortunes of this horde have left indestructible traces upon the history of human descent." The "primal father," says Freud, had not yet been declared immortal, as he was to become later by the process of ritual deification. He controlled his sons and other subordinate males by regulating their desires and forcing them into emotional ties with him and, subordinately, to each other. Such reluctance reflects the power of the system's wider patriarchal assumptions. Just as God and the monarch (usually male) ruled over the created world and the nation, so authority over families, households, professions, guilds, and callings was exercised by minor sovereigns, dispensers of employment. This authority was almost universally vested in powerful, mostly older male figures, who exercised it over properly deferential inferiors. The younger males both bonded together and were rivals for the affection and favors of the king, one of whose prerogatives was the control of access to the young women of the tribe. The males fought for place, for agency within their allotted sphere, and to become king themselves (in the Jacobean court, to become a royal favorite). To prosper in such an atmosphere meant that in addition to "natural" attributes of strength, riches, and nearness to the monarch, one needed a perpetually aggressive stance towards one's peers.[58]

Among the males fighting for place and agency in the primal horde of the Jacobean court, Pembroke's reputation has been a curious one. It sets him aside from most fellow Jacobean aristocrats by its relative pacificity. The early years of James's reign saw an enormous surge of conspicuous consumption by the aristocracy and what was widely commented upon as lavish self-indulgence and looseness. Sir John Harington's description of the vulgar drunkenness at the entertainment for the king of Denmark is well-known. In not dissimilar fashion, Dudley Carleton writes to Winwood that at the nuptial of Pembroke's brother Philip and Susan Vere in 1605, "the King in his shirt and nightgown gave them a *Reveille Matin* before they were up and spent a good time in or upon the bed, choose which you will." It is perhaps a comment on the nature of his own less favored position at court as well as on his own marriage that Pembroke's wedding had no such festive romps, although there is a revealingly candid letter to his father-in-law about the time of his wedding which contains the remark: "You must pardon my short writing, for I am half drunk tonight."[59] Pembroke's letters, in fact, contain a number of such revealing personal asides. They make him seem less the consummately cool politician and more a contradictory personality, beset, if never seriously disconcerted by, conflicting desires and ambitions. Yet he was aware that the self-presentation that would gain him power and security in the court involved seizing every opportunity to display himself before the gazes of his peers and superiors.

83

One incident in which a residue of chivalry may be seen is his quarrel with Sir George Wharton, "one," noted John Nichols in his *Progresses of the Reign of King James*, "of the numerous court-feuds of the Reign."[60] From Prince Hal to Hamlet to Touchstone's quarrelsome Knight: according to the most detailed of many accounts—found in a letter from Thomas Coke to the Countess of Shrewsbury—Pembroke and Wharton quarreled first over cards, then over Wharton's striking one of Pembroke's pages; they came briefly to blows; then Wharton challenged Pembroke; the king intervened; both threatened to disobey the king's injunction, but finally both agreed to patch up a peace. However, apart from this episode, the general view of historians has been that Pembroke was never involved in the more blatantly violent male self-display of the court. In the nineteenth century, Samuel Gardner's view of Pembroke's relative pacifism was dismissive, like a hockey commentator on a player who is reluctant to fight: throughout his career, he concluded, Pembroke "had no force of character" to enable him to control events. His objectivity, praised so highly by Clarendon, was to Gardner "merely that of a wealthy man with nothing to seek for himself, and who was happy in the possession of an affable and unruffled disposition." Quoting Bacon—"for his person," observed that incisive observer of the Jacobean age, he was "not effectual"—Gardner comments that "with an intelligence greater than his power of will"; he was merely "the Hamlet" of the court. According to historians of this persuasion, his allegiances were largely elsewhere: in Clarendon's view, given to pleasure and self-indulgence, to Gardner, private pursuits of an apolitical kind. To such robust observers, Pembroke is an effeminate dilettante, rich enough to indulge himself without serious self-exertion. "As he spent and lived upon his own fortune, so he stood up on his own feet," Clarendon claimed. Not far from the surface of such evaluations is a disapproval that in some ways Pembroke marks a falling off from earlier heroic ideals or some essential male ideal. He was not, in a sense shared by Clarendon in the seventeenth century and Gardner in the nineteenth, fully a man.[61]

But there is no question that Pembroke was an effective politician. Patronage was the major means by which a powerful nobleman could exercise what at times appeared, even to contemporaries, as a determinative degree of coercion. However suspect in our own time (and the pejorative associations of "patronizing" are a register of the change), patronage was one of the major apparatuses of cultural control in pre-industrial Europe. It was a way by which the great and powerful registered their authority. Its impact was not only economic but ideological, affecting the most detailed material conditions and the "inner lives" of men and women. As Robert C. Evans notes, it was "a psychological system, in the sense that the assumptions behind a patronage culture inevitably affected how people thought about themselves, others, and their mutual interactions." Benefiting from the system meant being under continual surveillance and privileging hierarchical rather than equal relationships. Writers like Donne or Jonson might make claims for "friendship" as a way of leveling the hierarchy; there might be, as in the works of Shakespeare or the poems of Donne, assertions that love may introduce a world of mutual interaction between lovers in place of a hierarchical system. But the dominant structures of the age are those that emphasized hierarchy and subordination within an unabashedly patriarchal structure of coercion. As Evans comments, "literary patronage was not an isolated or peculiar arrangement, precisely because it reflected and replicated in one sphere the patterns of thinking and behavior dominant in society at large."[62] Gebauer's and Brennan's accounts of Pembroke's patronage show his systematic use of rank, power, position, and money to further his family's political and intellectual ends. Like Sidney's before him, Pembroke's patronage heavily favored anti-Catholic, anti-Spanish and pro-Protestant causes.

But—and this should be starting to emerge as a characteristic swerve in Pembroke's life—he does seem to have been unusual in his warmth towards poets and dramatists. His literary patronage, in fact, represent one of the last bastions of the older system that many writers looked back to and with which the Sidneys were nostalgically identified. "Gentle Sir Philip Sidney," wrote Thomas Nashe, "thou knewest what belonged to a scollar, thou knewest what paines, what toyle, what travel, conduct to perfection." Pembroke, in this at least, took the inheritance from his uncle seriously. Samuel Daniel, who had been his tutor, dedicated his *Defense of Poesie* (1602) to Pembroke, claiming that living at Wilton had inspired his poetry, and he continued to benefit from Pembroke's patronage during the first decades of the century. Other poets who dedicated works to William Herbert and frequently benefited financially from him were Browne, Wither, Sylvester, Chapman, May, Davies of Hereford (who may also have tutored William Herbert as a boy), Florio, Massinger, Donne, and Jonson.[63]

The most intimate connection Pembroke had with any major literary figure was with Ben Jonson, who noted in his conversations with William Drummond that "every first day of the new year he had 20lb sent him from the Earl of Pembrok to buy books."[64] As part of his idealization of (and ingratiation with) the Sidneys, Jonson dedicated a number of works to Pembroke, including *Catiline*, in which he voiced the commonplace of Pembroke's incorruptibility and recalled the golden age of his uncle Philip. Jonson's *Works* (1616) opens with the dedication of the Epigrams to Pembroke, and the collection includes an impressive tribute to Pembroke, followed by poems to Mary Wroth and the countess of Montgomery. Jonson's relations with the wider Sidney family, and his poem to Sir Robert Wroth in particular, will be discussed in some detail in chapter three. With Jonson's sometime partner and rival, Inigo Jones, Pembroke's relations were also cordial. From as early as 1597, he employed Jones to collect works of European art. Jones was given his own quarters at Wilton, and probably oversaw the rebuilding there after a fire in the early 1620s. He was hired by Pembroke's brother Philip, when he became the fourth earl, to draw up plans for remodeling Wilton House, which were carried out after his death. Jones also supervised the refurbishing of Houghton House in Bedfordshire about 1620 for Pembroke's mother.

However generous to poets Pembroke may have been, the cries of poets for support from noble patrons were usually heeded only if they furthered the political ambitions of the patron. In the 1620s, when Pembroke was one of the leaders of the anti-Spanish Protestant parliamentarians, he used his patronage as part of the machinery by which he accumulated parliamentary political power. Thomas Middleton's play, *A Game at Chess*, the "nine-days wonder" of 1624 which ridiculed the Spanish ambassador Gondomar, may have been part of a carefully managed propaganda campaign that involved Pembroke as lord chamberlain, his cousin Sir Henry Herbert as the master of the revels, and the increasingly militant Puritan and anti-Spanish faction in the court. Heinemann notes that "his financial and business interests tended to bring him into contact and sympathy with rising merchants, 'improving' landowners and capitalist entrepreneurs, many of them with Puritan sympathies." As the leader of the anti-Spanish group, Pembroke was continuing, in more practical ways, many of the political ideals Philip Sidney had bequeathed to the family. He was associated with the Virginia Company and was an incorporator of both the North West Passage Company in 1612 and the East India Company in 1615. He supported a number of openly Puritan propagandists and preachers—for instance, Cornelius Burges (who dedicated *The Fire of the Sanctuary newly uncovered* [1625] to him), John Preston, Thomas Scott, Samuel Heron, and Thomas Chaffinger, the Puritan who preached his funeral sermon. The Venetian ambassador referred to Pembroke as the "head of the Puritans." As Daniel Featley, the Puritan theologian, observed to him, of "our faith, you and your family have always been a principal defender and protector."[65]

Power and privilege rest on access to the economic base of production—and in early modern Britain that meant land.[66] After the king, Pembroke was perhaps the richest man in England, which, given the expenses his position (and if Clarendon is to be believed, his degree of self-indulgence) demanded, was just as well. The widespread struggles of the Jacobean aristocracy to maintain their economic position had material consequences, not just on Pembroke's life-style or sense of himself, but upon countless others lower in the social hierarchy. Some were men in positions like Donne's, dependent always on the whims of the rich for employment. Others were the many small landholders and tenants whose land the Pembrokes and the Sidneys (and, on a lesser scale, the Wroths) exploited or enclosed. Their successes were built upon the assimilation into the aristocracy of the developing entrepreneurism that was to maintain the English aristocracy's political power well into the nineteenth century and however archaically, beyond. Yet, like many of his class, Pembroke was probably land-poor. Hence he continually sought new offices and land, through lawsuits and by manipulating for reversions of court and local offices, especially in Wiltshire and the West country, Kent, and southwest of London—the latter areas also a sphere of influence of the Sidneys. Thus, as soon as James settled into his reign— Pembroke at his first meeting, said a Venetian correspondent, "actually kissed his Majesty's face, whereupon the King laughed and gave him a little cuff"[67]—Pembroke petitioned for the reversion of Clarendon Park near Wilton, forests in Somerset, Wiltshire, and Berkshire, along with many of the offices held by his father, the second earl. In 1603 Queen Anne—who seems to have been especially attached to him, just as she was to his cousin, Mary—gave him the rangership of the forest of Gillingham, and in 1604 he acquired the stewardship of the Duchy of Cornwall, later becoming lord lieutenant, which gave him access to fees and revenues from the growing tin mining industry. In 1608 he regained control of the Forest of Dean, another of his father's perquisites, but one he had temporarily lost over the Mary Fitton affair. This pattern of opportunistic acquisition continued throughout the first decade of the reign. It was by such means that the Jacobean aristocracy, especially the more powerful families—those, for example, represented in the Privy Council, which Pembroke joined in 1610—gradually started to represent an economic power that collectively grew to rival that of the monarchy. Over the long run, the monarchy was losing power not merely politically, but in its direct hold over the wealth of the country, even though in the short run—in the first three decades of the century—the monarch's power seemed to grow rather than slacken, not least because of the factiousness in the aristocracy.

Politically, Pembroke was invariably shrewd in his political dealings. The state papers and parliamentary records show an immensely detailed and patient building up of political power over the first decade of James's reign, followed by fourteen years of more or less successfully holding his own against the growing power of Buckingham, whose fortune Pembroke, ironically, had helped to make; then, finally, after the assassination of Buckingham, two years of relative inactivity, as if he had earned his rest. In the first decade of his career at court, the dominant faction was that of the Howard family, who regarded the rise of the Herberts with some envy. Pembroke's younger brother Philip—named after their uncle but characterized by his second wife Lady Anne Clifford as no scholar—was created earl of Montgomery in 1605, and was an early favorite of King James. He married Susan de Vere, daughter of the earl of Oxford, in one of the most spectacular marriages of the early reign. Their estates, just north of London, were near those of the Wroths—and it was to her that Mary Wroth dedicated *Urania*.

Pembroke's rise to favor was less spectacular than his younger brother's. Instead of cultivating the king's personal affection, he built up parliamentary support. In James's first parliament, he had at least thirteen members beholden to him. In 1604 he himself attended most of the sessions of the Lords and sat on a number of committees. By 1610, when he was first appointed to the Privy Council, he was attending the Lords regularly, but most of the early years of the reign he was concerned with consolidating his lands, his marriage, and friendships of various kinds. He was content to let the public world take its way while the Howards gained influence and while he was building the base of his political power, particularly in Wales, Wiltshire, and Cornwall. With Cecil dead and the Howards in ascendance, Pembroke became part of an anti-Spanish faction in the Privy Council that included Archbishop Abbot, Lord Chancellor Ellesmore, and Principal Secretary Winwood. In 1612 he had been rejected for the post of the Mastership of Horse, and in 1614 for the lord chamberlain's post, which went to the Howard family's candidate, the earl of Somerset, not least because Northampton, the leading member of the Howard faction, begged on his deathbed that neither Robert Sidney nor Pembroke, to whom he referred as the "Welsh juggler," be given it.[68] In 1614, seemingly resigned to a minor political role, Pembroke held one of the most significant factional supper meetings in British politics at Baynard's Castle. Pembroke, Abbott, Winwood, and Sir Thomas Lake decided to provide James with a new favorite to supplant Carr. The bait was Sir George Villiers, a Lancashire knight—handsome, sparkling, and superficial. James immediately fell in love; Somerset was upset; James tried to pacify him by an astonishingly frank letter, full of hurt and jealousy. Abbott and Pembroke, with the connivance of the queen, procured a knighthood for Villiers, who was made a gentleman of the Bedchamber. Then in 1615 came the news of the murder of Overbury, the arrest of Somerset and his countess and, in the disgrace, the end of the Howards' ascendancy. From the sidelines, James was very relieved that at the trial Somerset said nothing to involve him.[69] It is ironical, given the history of the next fifty years, that the fall of Carr would have occurred without Pembroke's promotion of Villiers. James's intimate favorite ("Christ has his John, and I have my George"), Charles's bosom friend, the arrogant, increasingly powerful upstart who, increasingly unpopular with the older aristocracy and the Puritans, was assassinated in 1628, helping to trigger ten years of extra-parliamentary rule and the Civil War. As Briley comments, "had Pembroke waited for a year, who can say how much the history of the next fifty years might have been affected."[70] Certainly for the next fifteen years the impact of Buckingham on English court life and politics was immense.

One immediate fallout was Pembroke's becoming lord chancellor in 1615. He thus became the supervisor of the royal "above stairs" activities and the king's expenditure. His pension of £3600 was supplemented by additional perquisites that brought it to nearly £5,000, one of the highest incomes of any royal official. He was responsible for the efficient operation of the court's activities, both at Westminster and on progress. He controlled the access of suitors and embassies to the king. He had direct supervision of almost two thousand people—the king's guards, armory and ordinance, the mint and wardrobe, the chaplaincy of the royal chapel, the office of the works. He supervised, too, the master of the revels, and so oversaw the court plays and musicians.[71] In 1621 he became lord lieutenant of Wiltshire and Somerset, and thus further increased his hold over the appointment of justices of the peace and members of Parliament. Yet as a political manager his agenda was usually one of moderation. He was continually looking for ways of reconciling king with Parliament: in 1614 he had wanted impositions to "be maturely considered by their Lordships, not doubting but if that might be accommodated, the rest would be easy enough." Frequently, he would oppose the king's dissatisfaction with Parliament and then loyally support the royal will; in 1624, after fighting the dissolution of Parliament, he nonetheless advised the Lords that they had come not to debate but to vote, since "the King has declared his will."[72] These years following his appointment as lord chamberlain were, however, marked by rivalry with Buckingham. While the Pembroke faction moved slowly into key positions in the State—in 1617 Pembroke, Montgomery, and Robert Sidney were rumored to be getting more key posts—Buckingham's more personal hold on the King increased rapidly. Pembroke and Buckingham clashed over such habitual matters as patronage, the appointment to minor offices invariably being demonstrations of power and prestige. The favorite's flamboyant personality and pro-Spanish interests clashed with Pembroke's more moderate style and pro-Protestant attitudes. While Pembroke was prepared always to back the king in the long run, he quarreled with Buckingham's pro-Spanish policy.

In 1625 James died, at Theobald's Castle, in Pembroke's arms. As the new reign took shape, Charles supported the truce between Pembroke and Buckingham. In the 1625 and 1626 parliaments the relative strengths of the two became evident. Buckingham could rely on his position as intimate and favorite of the king and queen. But Charles, like his father, needed the financial support of Parliament, and it was there that Pembroke's political strength lay. In the 1625 and 1626 parliaments, Pembroke commanded a solid bloc of thirty-two members of the Commons, including Sir Benjamin Rudyerd (whose activities as a poet will be mentioned in chapter five), along with a number of secretaries and other servants of Pembroke. As well he had at least thirteen supporters in the Lords. Buckingham, quite rightly, suspected Pembroke of plotting against him and trying to control key elements in the Commons. There is a remarkable letter in the state papers to Buckingham from one of his agents, Sir James Bagg, warning of Pembroke's power, popularity, and influence. He warns Buckingham not merely of the number of Pembroke's supporters, but his tactic of appearing "publiquely by strangers" and drawing even those not directly beholden to him onto his side, including the increasingly vocal Sir John Eliot. The rivalry between the two turned personal when Pembroke snubbed Buckingham and the king by visiting the disgraced earl of Bristol in 1625. There was some reconciliation, but as the impetus to impeach Buckingham grew in the Commons, the rivalry became more public.[73]

It is tempting to view this political rivalry between Pembroke and Buckingham in the homosocial terms I have mentioned in discussing some of the manifestations of male display in the court: two strong males, the stronger one once the protegé of the other, wrestling for the love of the king, the primal male. Each had different strengths and constituencies, but essentially they were fighting over the same territory, battling for something deep in the nature of patriarchy. Another, less essentialist interpretation would be to see the rivalry in terms of the contradictions of ideological struggle. Buckingham was the upstart, catapulted to social and political preeminence from the country gentry. He was wrestling with (though he owed his initial power to) a representative of the last vestiges of an increasingly archaic aristocratic power. Yet, paradoxically, Buckingham became the last politically powerful royal favorite, his role if not his origins, a holdover from an age of feudal absolutism. By comparison, Pembroke represented old money and land, yet it was his actions that gave voice to the emergent forces for property-owning (if not representational) democracy.

The Buckingham/Pembroke rivalry did not survive three years of the new reign. The clamor for Buckingham's impeachment grew, with Pembroke lending his implicit support. There was a temporary truce, probably at the initiative of Buckingham, as he sensed that he might benefit from the support of his rival. Pembroke probably set the terms. In 1626, a rapprochement between the two former allies was arranged; Pembroke became lord steward, his brother Philip lord chamberlain, and a marriage arrangement between Pembroke's nephew and Buckingham's four-year-old daughter Mary was drawn up, with Pembroke guaranteeing a generous dowry of £10,000 in addition to £2,000 from Montgomery. Peace seemed to be at hand. Pembroke wrote that "the King our master begins to shine . . . and I hope this next session [of Parliament] to see a happy agreement between him and his people." Then events swept over all of these hopes of peace.[74] Buckingham's 1627 attack on La Rochelle was a disaster, and only Pembroke's support would have prevented impeachment had a new Parliament been called. Yet there were forces in Parliament—including many of Pembroke's supporters—who were prepared to take matters forward, as an independent opposition was developing. The Petition of Right, acceded to by the king, was followed by a Remonstrance to remove Buckingham from the King's ouncil. Charles prorogued Parliament—and then came the assassination of Buckingham.

What from Pembroke's viewpoint was a fortuitous end to the rivalry seems to have coincided with his growing indifference to political power. His letters sound detached from what he might have experienced as a triumphant, if unforeseeable, event. He was increasingly ill and, at forty-eight, was, as one letter puts it, "busy . . . about settling the clock, as our old master was wont to term it."[75] There were rumors he would be given a dukedom and sign his court place over to his brother. He maintained his place, however, adding the chancellorship of the University of Oxford, and the vice-admiralship of South Wales to his honors but for all practical purposes, he was being bypassed by history. On 9 April, 1630, the family records note, "this noble lord . . . supped at Fishes Folly without Aldgate with the Lady Lucy Countess of Bedford, Countess of Devonshire, Mrs Murray with Severall other Lord[s] and Ladyes." The following day he went back to Baynard's Castle, complained of not feeling well, and later that day was found dead by servants, "suddenly," as the Venetian ambassador put it, "to the great sorrow of the whole court owing to his great qualities." True to his pleasures to the end, and characteristically indulging himself with women friends, Pembroke also uncannily fulfilled the prophecy of Richard Allen, Queen Elizabeth's astrologer (echoed by Pembroke's tutor Hugh Sanford and, in the 1620s, the prophetess Lady Eleanor Davies) that he would die by his fiftieth birthday, 10 April, 1630.[76]

In a sermon preached at his funeral at Baynard's Castle, one of Pembroke's chaplains, Thomas Chaffinger, drew the attention of Philip, now the fourth earl, to the aristocratic legacy he was inheriting. Like his dead brother, the preacher affirmed, he should see himself not only as "an Æneas to your Brother," but as "so famous and valiant a *Hector*" to Sir Philip Sidney; like his brother, the new earl was now being called to act in "the Theaters and Scaffolds of the greatest eminence," in "a glorious Court." He spoke of Pembroke—"our dear Master that's now lost to us"—not only as a man of "sweet and angelical conversation," but as a "just" man in a corrupt court, and concluded with an intriguing comment that deserves to stand alongside Clarendon's: "though I call him just, yet I dare not say he was perfect; though righteous, not without sinne . . . he knew that the way to heaven by innocency was long sithence blocked up, and therefore he tooke another course, and our hope is, he is arriv'd there by way of penitence."[77] One wonders if the congregation included the woman—another Sidney, in a sense now doubly a widow, and also a mother and a writer—to whom I shall next turn.

3

"BE THAT YOU ARE":
THE GENDERING OF MARY SIDNEY,
LADY WROTH

Cousin Germans have more reason to know one anothers Tempers and Humors from their dayly converse, and Education oftentimes together . . . for the Images of the Common Parents being not worn out of those who are not so nearly related to them, and it is a kind of incest for them to mix.

The Marriages of Cousin Germans, 1673

A female's *forbidden* masculine wishes have the same disastrous impact on her life as the analogous forbidden feminine wishes have on the life of a male. What adult women and men want is to regain access to the parts of themselves that they have learned to distrust and fear in the course of growing up from childhood to adulthood.

Louise Kaplan[1]

nlike Freud's, Deleuze and Guattari's reading of the family romance does not consider the repetition compulsion of fantasies generated in the family as the articulation of a primary desire; the family romance is rather a form that a subject's desire is forced to assume because of the repression to which society inevitably subjects it. The unrealizability of our desires within a repressive or restrictive society forces us, they argue, back into the family as the only site where we can struggle, inevitably imperfectly, to realize some equivalent for them. Yet the family is not only an apparatus for the institutionalizing of socially produced neurosis; it can also be an arena in which social contradictions battle, not least over the assignments of gender. As Kaplan notes, "One of the most effective and powerful instruments of socialization is gender conformity. The social order impresses its structures on its citizens through its ideals of femininity and masculinity. Fortunately, the family is not without its power to resist what seems inimical to its more personal interests."[2] For a woman born into the early modern aristocracy—perhaps for the vast majority of women, and even most men within patriarchal societies—such a reading of the family romance rings more true than Freud's biologically determinist version. It suggests how family romances are connected to both "personal" subject formation and broader social structures. The narratives of the family romance are responses to the process of separation and individuation that begins not long after birth and with which we all struggle as children, perhaps for much or all of our adult lives. But they are also our responses to being socially and historically constructed beings who struggle for some agency, often with enormous difficulty, in relation to forces outside the family. The ideologies of gender assignment play crucial parts in the process of the construction of our sense of self and our fantasies and narratives about how that "self" expresses itself. In an attempt to engender the Sidney family romance and provide some account of Mary Wroth's part in its complex infoldings, I want in this chapter to produce a narrative parallel to the one I constructed for Pembroke.

The core of the patriarchal male family romance, insofar as it is directed towards women, is the desire to possess (or repossess) women, initially in the family—mother, sisters, daughters—and then, once we venture out into the world beyond the family, "belonging" to other men. This pattern, to return to Freud's formulation, may be seen in relation to a child's desire to be "big" like "his parents": within this dominant bipolar ideology of gender, men are conditioned to exercise their authority and autonomy by acting like their fathers and father surrogates in their authority over and right of access to women. But what, within this depressing and destructive ideology, do (as Freud notoriously put it) or even can "women want"? What of the woman's version of the family romance? When Shakespeare's Angelo pleads to Isabella, "be that you are / That is a woman," the question that needs to be asked is, What did it mean to "be" a woman?

First, to historicize the question: to what extent can one speak of "women" in this period? Does such a category not elide differences of class, not to mention race? Sara Mendelson has argued that despite vast social differences of rank or class, and despite an overwhelmingly dominant ideology decreeing that a woman's family or class allegiances took precedence over those of gender, women in this period did share a distinctive female *mentalité*.[3] Its basis was that of being subordinate to men and male authority. Whether we read the family romance within Freud's or a revisionist model, a woman's place within the early modern family is overwhelmingly determined by her relations to the relative autonomy and power of men. Having the body of a woman—again, we should note that "possession" was almost exclusively accorded to men—made for differently constructed inner and outer worlds from those of men. For Wroth the contradictions of being a Sidney woman not only included being born into specific kin and class obligations; it meant that any struggles for agency or equality took specific shape in relation to her gender assignment and the relative autonomy and power of the Sidney men. As my survey of her life will show, it was her father who clearly played the dominant role in her early life—entering her life infrequently in person, yet supervising her education, deciding upon her marriage, and negotiating her dowry (needing, ironically, substantial financial help from Pembroke!). As she grew to adulthood and married, it was her husband's and cousin's authority against which she had to assert herself. And behind all the male authority figures within the family stood the self-proclaimed father of the realm, the king, in whose court/family Sidney, Pembroke, and Wroth all had obligations and duties.

With the major transitions of her life managed by and in the interests of men, Mary Wroth's life and writings predictably show a consistent struggle to come to terms with the multiple-yet-same figure of the

Lady Mary Wroth with an archlute, Penshurst Place.
Reproduced by permission of Viscount De L'Isle from his
private collection at Penshurst Place.

authoritative male under whose control her desires were constructed. The father, as the Freudian (and Lacanian) commonplace has it, is powerful because he represents the girl's desired freedom from dependency on the family. She seeks to realize her desires in relation to another who seems to have the power not only of realizing his own, but giving or denying hers as well. As Benjamin puts it, the belief that men will provide access to a world that is otherwise closed to her is one of the greatest motives in settling a woman into her gender assignment. Behind such acceptance, within a hierarchical gender system, lies "the fact that the mother is not the active subject of desire and that the father is that subject, the liberator."[4] The idealization of the father is, therefore, though in subtly different ways, an early fantasy in the patriarchal family romances for both genders: he is seen as the imaginary solution to many real and seemingly unsolvable conflicts and deprivations for both men and women. A familiar version of the family romance, which we can see in Wroth's idealization and attempted rejection of the father figure—a fascinating reversal of Pembroke's idealization and fear of the mother— involves casting him in the role of the glamorous or permissive hero who rescues her from the humdrum and oppressive; another version casts him in the role of the censor and inhibitor who drives her back to culturally predetermined roles, against which she must somehow struggle to assert herself. These two figures—in Hélène Deutsch's phrase, the idealized "day father" and the threatening "night father" who brings "all the dangers of cruelty and seduction in his train and mobilizes anxious nightmares"—lie behind the male figures in Wroth's poems and *Urania*, just as she seems to have projected them upon the three dominating male figures in her life: her "real" father, her husband, and her cousin.

In studying the patterns that structure Wroth's life and her writings, we need to ask how women's desires become, as Benjamin puts it, "alienated into forms of submission and dependency." If potentially we all have qualities that our society defines as "masculine" and "feminine," how is it that "femininity becomes inextricably linked to passivity, even to masochism, or that women seek their desire in another, hope to have it recognized and recognizable through the subjectivity of an other?"[5] But lest those questions sound too thoroughly deterministic, we should ask whether there are areas of agency that can "be characterized as feminine or female," as Nancy Hartsock puts it. What collective fantasies can we cite as evidence of emergent aspirations or practices in women's lives? And to what extent were women's desires acted upon: did they make material differences? What, for instance, was the force of such matters as the degree of women's identification with the family, the advantages and disadvantages of women's separation from most "public" events, the impact of the female life cycle, risky and frequent childbirth, aging, the lack of adequate contraception or medical knowledge, and the possibilities of developing special networks and alliances among women themselves? And if we tackle head on another area in which Freudian essentialism has been singularly unhelpful, another crucial area is surely the largely silenced power of women's own sexuality. Finally, of course, there is the increasing importance, to a striking extent in Wroth's case, of writing as an area of agency. What difference did her writing make to Wroth's sense of self? How did it bind her to or liberate her from her family? We cannot merely observe, as it is conventionally put, that Wroth's father "encouraged" her or that her aunt simply was a "model" or "mentor" for her: we need to ask more penetrating questions. What psychological and ideological dynamics were involved in being a writing woman? Was it emulation? rivalry? the conscious or unconscious rejection of the mother in favor of the power of the father?[6]

Then, what did it mean to be a woman in relation to men's fantasies? To be, for instance, interpellated into the fantasy world of late chivalry that was so central to the Sidney family and (as I suggested in the previous chapter) to Pembroke's upbringing, with its gender ideology of masculine heroism and male ostentation centered upon the authority of the warrior-prince, the courtier, the patriarch? In the multitude of the period's poems, plays, modes of address, and handbooks of behavior, there is certainly impressive evidence that, well into the early modern period, aristocratic women continued to occupy essential parts in the male rituals of chivalry—if not as homebodies, as in later bourgeois myths, let us say, at least as "great house" bodies. They were required to be chaste, decorative, inspiring, and (a term that acquires multiple ironies in Wroth's writings) constant—moving but unmoved, in multiple senses. In *Urania* the men are, like Pembroke in his own political career, in continual movement, pursuing adventures in an expansive, half real, half fantastic, landscape; the women are mostly expected to wait at home, however restless or trapped they appear, or—should they rebel against their restrictions—be put at risk for their boldness or, as Ann Shaver argues in connection with the punished heroines of Urania, their outspokenness. Even Pamphilia, though a queen, is made unhappy by her responsibilities, and when her husband dies, she returns home to her father.[7]

In a society in which the dominant ideology of gender relations is built on glaring discrepancies of autonomy, a recurring fantasy for the underprivileged class is to aspire to the power of the privileged. The disguising of women as men in Shakespeare's comedies enacts, in what must have been very complex ways (and quite different for conventionally gendered men and women), the power of such fantasies. When in *As You Like It*, Rosalind disguises herself as a man and takes on male roles—protecting "his" sister, negotiating property purchases, and courting a not particularly perceptive beloved—she acts with the boldness of a Mary Fitton dressing in men's clothes and visiting the no doubt delighted William Herbert in his chambers, possibly at Baynard's Castle itself. In real life such behavior was highly risky for a woman, and the consequences Mary Fitton suffered were, despite Pembroke's petulance, far more severe than the temporary disruptions to his lordship's career and pleasures. In the same way, the later life of Penelope Rich—years before, in some sense the "Stella" of Philip Sidney's *Astrophil and Stella*, and therefore occupying a prominent place in various Sidney family romances—would have been caution enough. Both Robert and Barbara Sidney kept in contact with her, and, at the age of forty, she was one of the few older women asked to dance at court. But she was hounded to penury and death by King James and his judiciary for not only pursuing the man she loved but then marrying him: "outstanding in beauty, gifted in every quality of mind and body except for chastity," pronounced a (male) contemporary, she "contracted an unfortunate union . . . violated the sacred and proper law of matrimony and caused havoc in a most noble family."[8]

That a recurring fantasy for women in the period is built on emulating men's relative autonomy is supported by recent scholarly work on how "errant women" and the figure of the amazon became demonized in the dominant (male) ideology. Vagrants and "masterless men" constituted a major social problem, not only because of theft or other crimes, but because they were outside the hierarchies of control and surveillance; all the more disturbing, as Dollimore points out, were the real or imagined "masterless, wandering women, perversely straying and inviting others to do the same." Likewise, the figure of the amazon was often ambivalent or demonic (Sidney's Cleophila is an exception, but "she" is Pyrocles in disguise). Fascination with the woman as armed warrior embodies, Simon Shepherd suggests, male fears of women's potential refusal of obedience to their assigned gender roles. Amazons are threatening because they represent a deviant alternative to the bipolar gender ideology. They, too, do not belong to men: they are "unassigned, masculinized females who roam unstructured out in open (male) cultural terrain." In such momentary breaks with the dominant, we can see the emergence of possible areas of agency, alluring fantasies that would not have been simply "individual" aberrations, but belonged to a whole gender group. As Shepherd notes, if "someone somewhere must have been doing some feminist thinking between the 'courtly' love of the early Renaissance and the female remonstration of the Revolution," it can be seen indirectly emerging in such demonized figures. Also relevant perhaps are the strong women characters in many Jacobean tragedies:

The Duchess of Malfi, The White Devil, The Revenge of Bussy d'Ambois, Macbeth, The Second Maiden's Tragedy. All these plays involve strong women characters in corrupt or disintegrating societies who struggle for political or sexual power (sometimes both) and who temporarily carve out for themselves a discourse of defiance, a temporary space of self-indulgence or self-assertion. All are defeated, as if the fascinating but demonic powers represented in the strong woman must be controlled and purged. Yet their oppositional strivings for autonomy and space are being given voice. They are Davis's "women on top," challenging patriarchy by attempting to appropriate men's autonomy.[9] Even in fiction, such a fantasy could only temporarily focus women's dreams of autonomy—the ending of *As You Like It* rewards men for their tolerance by restoring the patriarchal control of both father and husband over Rosalind, now appropriately dressed as a virgin bride, her frank desires tamed to their uses. It is well that we learn of Orlando's prowess in killing the lioness and overthrowing Duke Frederick's wrestler; otherwise we might wonder about his power to control the raging passions of his eager wife, whose boldness and autonomy we have been asked to admire.

At this point I find myself caught in a dilemma that is more than simply one of scholarly emphasis. Writing as a male, do I compound the problem by taking Wroth's marginality for granted? Am I imposing a dominant reading of history centered on activities predominantly coded "male" and ignoring her place in an alternative, subversive, history which would take as its landmarks activities more associated with women? In conventional historical terms, Wroth's life was certainly incidental to the main events of Jacobean history. She played no great part in politics; her forays into the law and commerce were desultory and largely conducted through male intermediaries; her sexual life was proscribed by demands of kinship and alliance; her writings were either not widely known, unpublished, or reviled, and have rarely received more than a passing mention in standard literary histories. But in recording those judgments on what conventionally are taken as spheres of significant activity, am I simply displaying residual masculinist prejudices? Are the categories of public visibility—political, social, or literary activities—adequate? Are there alternative ways of constructing a history of women in this period that do not simply append women to an existing history? And what might I, as a man, have to offer to such a project? How relevant to the project is the stake I have in it? Indeed, how sure am I that I know what that stake is? As I confessed in the first chapter, these are not easy questions to answer. It may be that the best way of tackling both the question of Wroth's apparent marginality and my own involvement in the argument I am developing is to ask: What are the areas which women have historically carved out for themselves in defiance or independence of male domination and the cult of heroic violence—whether wrestling, lion-killing, or politics? In trying to answer this question, I feel I am somewhat like Freud's listener to the primal scene in which "things heard by children at a very early age" are "only understood later" at the point at which the listener discovers that he or she is also involved in the witnessed but puzzling scene. As it has taken shape, my argument has come to call into question both my understanding of what recent feminist theory has termed "womanspace" and—not a trivial discovery—my own construction as a man.[10]

Joan Kelly-Gadol's well-known observation that the "renaissance" applied very differently to women from men has taught us to look for alternative readings of women's history, and in particular for possible areas of autonomy for women in which a different mode of relationship from the domination/submission pattern might be found. While the early modern period sees major shifts in the economy and new patterns of marriage, at least in the upper classes, there is certainly little evidence for the dissolution of the dominant ideology of sexual authority or gender identity. Yet in the greater range of practises— and fantasizing itself is a powerful social practise—we can sense an emergent fluidity in the ways gender assignments might, spasmodically or on the margins, be lived out. Constance Jordan argues that during the Renaissance traditional sex-based absolutism starts to be challenged by a wide range of alternatives, some of which underline the fact that gender roles are socially constucted, not natural. She sees Sidney's *Arcadia* as a pivotal register of what she terms this "feminist critique of patriarchy," and she accumulates a number of instances of breaks with the residual misogynist tradition.[11] Jordan's formulation applies to possibilities; just how far they were realized in the lives, inner or outer, of actual women is dubious. The opening up of discursive spaces for a variety of subject positions does not mean those positions will be actually occupied.

But there is certainly no question that we can sense signs of an emergent counter-history. Kelly-Gadol's observation regarding the lack of a Renaissance for women asks feminist historians to recast the terms of the debate and look to signs of women's activities that lie outside the categories of conventional history. Among these is the solidarity and sense of community among women: in groups, alliances, friendships, and female relations within the family, especially between mothers and daughters, which might provide strength and a measure of independence to women by excluding or circumventing men. Such a category draws not only on historical evidence, but arises from contemporary feminist psychoanalytical considerations of the construction of women in patriarchal society. Julia Kristeva speaks eloquently of women's "inner solitude" as a woman's first move towards such autonomy. Benjamin, perhaps the most

102

eloquent advocate in contemporary feminist psychoanalysis for a concept of "womanspace" that is not based on a reification of some biological determinism, argues that "the significance of the spatial metaphor for a woman is likely to be just this discovery of her own, inner desire, without fear of impingements, intrusions, or violation." Donna Bassin's 1982 paper, "Woman's Images of Inner Space," surveys the idea from Freud onward, illustrating it with a variety of contemporary women poets. The Freudian tradition has tended to see the fantasy of a productive inner space rooted in women's bodily organization and "instinctual needs." In a highly controversial treatment, Erickson wrote of the female genitals as a "natural" basis for the metaphor of inner space, a concept Bassin argues is "grounded in early vaginal sensations, [and self-]explorations of female genitals." Males, she argues, are by contrast "focused on what can be seen externally and less involved with what lies inside." Paglia's concurring view is, predictably, emphatic: "Woman's body is a secret, sacred space. It is a *temenos* or ritual precinct." Bassin suggests that the metaphorical power of "women's productive inner space has been constricted to a large degree to procreation," and she contends that it is necessary to expand the creative possibilities of what has been presented overwhelmingly in gender ideology as "nothing but an empty void" waiting to be filled. She argues that the metaphor of a woman's inner space should be regarded as equivalent to—though, historically, it has never attained the dominant position of—"phallic activity and its representations." An important part of women's fantasy life in patriarchal culture has been, as Benjamin puts it, "for a holding other whose presence does not violate one's space but permits the experience of one's own desire."[12]

Regardless of the extent to which there is a biological basis for such a concept, material considerations have clearly played a part in women's desires for private space, Virginia Woolf's "room of their own." As I noted in chapter one, it is precisely in the early modern period that architectural changes in the houses of the aristocracy start to allow for such a possibility. There are recurring scenes in *Urania* and *Pamphilia to Amphilanthus* of inner spaces, private chambers and gardens, as fervently desired and protected places for women's self-contemplation without onlookers, especially without other members of the family. Sometimes these private spaces may be shared with an intimate friend: *Urania* is full of private meetings, conversations and exchanges of stories of love and chivalry, confessions, and gossip, "sad but loving discourse passing those dark hours" (*Urania*, p. 123) between intimate friends, usually women, in such spaces. Private space, it seems, is not incompatible with a sense of autonomy if it is shared with a chosen friend, especially another woman. Both *Urania* and *Pamphilia to Amphilanthus* are replete with discussions of and references to networks of women friends. Friendships between women provide spaces in which the more brutal aspects of hegemonic male power might be escaped. Particularly important for Wroth in her life were the friendships she had with other members of the extended Sidney-Herbert families, notably with Pembroke's sister-in-law, Susan, countess of Montgomery, to whom *Urania* was dedicated.[13]

Another "inner space" is that afforded by fantasy and story telling. "Story" and the sharing of stories are crucial in Wroth's writings, especially in *Urania*, as I shall show in chapter eight. Lamb points out tellingly that in Sidney's *New Arcadia*, while men sometimes tell stories, they are characteristically brief, linear, monophonic accounts of heroic action, as if Sidney were recording an "ambivalence towards what is now called fiction as an activity appropriate for active males"; by comparison, in *Urania* it is predominantly the women who tell stories, usually to other women; in all cases, Lamb argues, they tell them "as women," thereby affirming their gendered solidarity across class lines and independence from men.[14] In *Love's Victory*, the women sit and gossip, sometimes with men, but they are invariably the initiators. I use the term "gossip" advisedly. It is a term that has long been labeled with patronizing hostility by men as a woman's weakness, but Miranda Chaytor has argued that it might more productively be seen as referring to the politics of the disenfranchised, and so provide us with a source for unraveling the connections between women's individual collusion or resistance and the system that assigned them restrictive gender roles. While much women's gossip in the period was no doubt, as she suggests, "used to reaffirm male-dominated hierarchies and not to undermine them," we should pause over the unease expressed by Lord Falkland to Secretary Conway, that "women . . . be no fit solicitors of state affairs; for though it sometimes happens that they have good wits, it commonly falls out that they have over-busy natures withall."[15] Men's dismissal of women's gossip may betray a fear that women have found a way of avoiding patriarchal control.

In the gossip, stories, shared fantasies, and wish-fulfillments that occupy the women characters in *Urania*, especially in the absence of men, we can see in small ways the makings of spaces in which an oppositional subculture centered on women's privacy and autonomy might develop. They are not merely the trivial products of women's exclusion from "superior" public male activities, but rather contain the seeds of an alternative "potential space." Another "womanspace," one specifically associated with the regulation or withholding of women's reproductive capacities from men, is mothering. Chodorow and Jane Flax (and within a different tradition, Kristeva) are among many contemporary feminists who have argued that mothering has either historically afforded—or even inherently constitutes—such a potential space. Do, as Kristeva argues, women's reproductive capacities and (if activated) motherhood provide a pre-cultural given that can play a determinative, trans-historical role in women's lives? In *Tales of Love*, Kristeva views motherhood as a central part of the "collective imagery" of Western women, affirming pregnancy as an entry into an extra-symbolic order that cuts across the linearity of male history. Likewise, in what she terms her "feminist formulation of the life-force," Haunani-Kay Trask writes of a counterbalance to male domination in women's "erotic/reproductive roles of biological and emotional mothering of children, men, and other women." This is, of course, a difficult argument for a man to make. Mothering, as constructed by gender conservatives, all too often turns out to be disempowering, answering not to women's but rather to men's needs as articulated through some simplistic gender stereotype of femininity. And, as Kristeva notes, at a time when "feminism demands a new representation of femininity," an argument praising mothering from any source, not least from a man, may seem to identify it with an "idealized misconception" and so circumvent "the real experience that fantasy overshadows."[16]

The history of reproductive politics—brought home to us in the United States today by the institutionalized backlash against the option of abortion—means we need carefully to examine the class, gender, or racial factors at work in particular historical formations. In this case, perhaps, we should distinguish between the patriarchal institution of motherhood and the historically specific though changing experiences of childbearing and mothering. In the early modern period the frequency and danger of childbearing were major factors in the social coercion of women. Childbearing was rarely an option for women—it was seen primarily as a natural function for which all women were born. But in Wroth's case it is possible to view her childbearing as an affirmation of her sexuality, a defiance of the patriarchal system in which her upbringing and marriage had placed her. Evidence would include not only her belated bearing of her one (presumably) legitimate child, but, once she was widowed, her two illegitimate children; more indirect but nonetheless telling evidence is found in *Urania*'s positive treatment of illegitimacy. Childbearing was, for her at least, something much more complex than an acceptance of her assigned role within dynastic politics. The desire to express herself as a sexual being may well have entered into her actions, which thereby became part of a gendered rewriting of the family romance, an attempt to project her own desires upon a repressive world.

Childbearing, and, to a lesser extent, mothering bring up the question of sexuality as an area of self-assertion, another "private space."

One of the great missing histories of our culture is that of women's (and to a lesser extent, men's) sexuality. Only in the past century have we had an even marginally acceptable discourse within which to think about it. Like gender, "sex" is a historically variable construction, with every society trying to enlist the polymorphous desires of its young to preserve its dominant economic, political and conceptual structures. What Benjamin terms woman's "search for her own desire" goes well beyond what we normally think of as "sexual," yet the sexual may at certain times in history be precisely where that search is concentrated and also where the potential agency it may promise is persecuted. The elision of women's right to and even possibility of having orgasms for perhaps almost two hundred years is one of the most remarkable, and appalling, examples of the ideological construction of sexuality in our history.[17] The early modern period produced remarkably frank discussions of women's sexual capacity as well as, more ominously, widespread references to the need to control women's "unruly" sexual desires. Certainly, much of what we can see of Wroth's sexuality was certainly assigned to her—in particular the submission to familial aggrandizement betokened by her marriage. As Edward Shorter notes, in this world we have with some relief lost, there was almost no sex outside of marriage save forcible sex, and, one would add, much that was forcible inside it. A woman was created to marry, and any suggestion that the aristocracy of the period was acknowledging greater freedom in spousal choice is certainly over-optimistic in relation to women. Furthermore, it was assumed that she would provide her husband with children, in particular, a male heir. And quickly: demographic studies suggest there was an average of sixteen months from a wedding until the birth of the first child.[18] In Wroth's case it was over ten years.

In the typical circumstances of the period a woman's sexuality could be seen to be predominantly under male domination. But what of those aspects of her sexual activities where male control could be avoided? Childbearing requires, at least at the outset, some male contribution, and its pain and danger can be moralized and idealized—as it has been so overwhelmingly in the Christian tradition—as a punishment for women, while a refusal or an inability to bear children, especially sons, might also be laid at a woman's charge. Sexuality is clearly an area of a woman's experience that is not entirely given or controllable, and yet—this is particularly threatening to patriarchal control—it includes pleasures and powers that can at least in part be claimed by a woman through her own actions. At once the site of instruction, repression, and control, sex is also the place of individual exploration, pleasure, and agency; orgasm is something from which men can be excluded, and even when men are intimately involved, what was widely believed to be the potential insatiability of female sexual desire was a traditional topic for men's fears, fantasies, stories, and (one should add) gossip. When they touch on female desire, the handbooks in Kelso's survey of Renaissance women, overwhelmingly written by men, warn even married women against lasciviousness and offering themselves to their husbands like prostitutes. The virulent attacks on women in the so-called "woman controversy" of the first decades of the seventeenth century articulate a growing unease not just with women's autonomy, but specifically their sexual demands and capabilities.[19] One of the charges Lord Denny throws at Mary Wroth over the publication of *Urania*, as I shall explain in detail below, is that of sexual insatiability, a charge intensified by the common assumption that women who write and speak out are unchaste.[20]

Of course, we do not know, except indirectly, what place sexual pleasure played in Wroth's affair with Pembroke or any other relationships. Wroth's marriage clearly had major difficulties from the start, but it is difficult, if not impossible, to assess the intensity, commitment, or continuity of the relationship with Pembroke. Was it already under way when she married? Was it some intense but discontinuous dalliance between adolescent cousins that was occasionally renewed? Was it a belated version of *droit de seigneur* or a deep and abiding mutual passion that for some years left both deeply frustrated? We can perhaps tell something from certain recurring, contradictory patterns in her writing. The first is one of male observation and a woman's consciousness of herself as a sexual being for (male) others. When a woman's every act is scrutinized and constrained for its sexual potential, as was so widely the case in the early modern period, the result is inevitably a heightened sense of one's own sexualization. The degree to which, as Denise Riley observes, women actually "live in the flesh distinctively of women, as it were," varies by historical circumstances, gender ideology, and day to day living: early modern society was one in which, at least among the aristocracy, there seems to have been an intensified inclusion of the details of a woman's existence as sexual, and therefore needing to be under male scrutiny and control. In classic texts of sadistic pornography, like the writings of the Marquis de Sade or *L' Histoire d'O*, we are used to the pattern of obsessive surveillance and regulation of dress, posture, diet, language, and bodily functions; but, however extreme and all too common (and, for many men, compulsive) a male fantasy such surveillance may appear to most of us, it would have been highly familiar to a woman of Wroth's society and class. Male writers frequently commented on the social and sexual appropriateness of women's clothing and demeanor, concentrating, as Peter Stallybrass notes, especially "upon three specific areas: the mouth, chastity, the threshold of the house."[21] A woman is most vulnerable, and therefore threatening, in her orifices of speech, sexuality, and potential escape from her husband's observation and control. In many of Wroth's poems, this level of surveillance is taken for granted; in others, more interestingly and almost uniquely in the period, it is felt as "molestation," a word that recurs throughout her writings. Rarely but strikingly, it may provoke a defiant and canny response in which the woman chooses to present a deceptive image to the onlooker and preserve her "real," or at least a different, self, but more frequently, it makes her feel trapped and abused.

The second pattern of sexuality we can observe in Wroth's writings is one in which the insistent male sexualization of women is paradoxically and calculatedly accepted by the woman as a potential strength. Lamb has pointed out how early modern women were sexualized not just as women but as writers and readers: "the sexualization of women's words—in their reading, their speech, their writing—represented a formidable obstacle to authorship which, while it did not prevent a woman's writing, affected what they could write." She suggests Wroth capitalizes upon this assignment, acknowledging "the sexuality permeating her writing to defend it, even to heroize it."[22] Her argument deserves to be extended from writing to more general sexual practices. *Urania* has many women characters who dare to make sexual choices, often—indeed, almost inevitably—suffering from doing so, but nonetheless repeatedly insisting on making them. As she enacted her version of the family romance, was Wroth, as Benjamin puts it, "drawn to ideal love as a second chance, an opportunity to attain, at long last, a satisfying father-daughter" relationship, one that was paradoxically both outside and inside the family? From the fact that there were two children, there may have been a continuing or at least intermittent relationship with Pembroke. The poems and the romance both tell us something, at least on the level of fantasy or displacement. There are also many concrete references in Robert Sidney's letters to interactions between Pembroke and his daughter. The Sidneys had stayed at Baynard's Castle frequently during Mary's childhood, and the closeness of the young Pembroke to his uncle has been commented upon in the previous chapter. It was Pembroke who helped provide Mary's dowry, and who found her a pet dog soon after the marriage. One set of events mentioned in the family letters is especially tantalizing. In September 1608, Wroth was seriously ill at Loughton, but his wife remained in town at Baynard's Castle until 19 September, when she seems to have left with Pembroke for Loughton. Robert Sidney wrote to his wife that Mary had been at Baynard's Castle "till now, but this afternoon doth go to Loughton." On 20 September, Robert further reports to his wife that Pembroke had been visiting Mary: "My Lord Pembroke told me yesternight that he had left my daughter that morning." By early October she had returned to

Baynard's Castle where she met again with her father, who accompanied her back to Loughton. He then notes that Lady Wroth was leaving Loughton immediately, probably going back to Baynard's Castle.[23]

Whatever its nature, it was probably only through her relationship with her cousin that she achieved some sense of her own desires. It was sufficiently stable, or at least recurrent, to produce two children. In her writing Wroth accepted and reveled in the sexualization of women's writing; it may be that an analogous point might be made about her sexual choices. Paradoxically, perhaps, by contracting a relationship close to a forbidden degree of consanguinity, she could both defy convention and enfold herself back into the family romance. Whatever psychosexual dimensions her long "adventure"—to borrow a recurring word in her romance—with her cousin may have had, it constitutes a distinctive breach with conventional gender assignments in early seventeenth-century society.

Wroth's sexual defiance, then—ironically afforded by the family, but also a striking re-gendering of the dominant male pattern of the family romance—is the second "womanspace" in which she strove to assert herself. The third was her writing. Wroth is the first woman writer in English in whose work a habitually submerged, historically specific, but distinctively female discourse starts to emerge. She wrote the first substantial collection of Petrarchan poetry in English by a woman, the first long work of prose fiction by a woman, and one of the first plays by a woman. And as important as these landmark achievements were, the assertions of self involved in the very act of writing—her defiance of literary and social conventions and her battles for both publication and privacy—mark her writing as an area in which, however tentatively and with whatever opposition, resistance to patriarchy can be sensed, and moreover an area in which she was carving out a space not just for herself but for subsequent women.

Traditionally the role of women in writing had been as a figure in discourse produced by men. The prefaces and dedications of the few books written by Renaissance women are full of a revealing contradiction—on the one hand, they are predominantly apologies for intervening in an activity forbidden to or at least unsuitable for women; on the other hand, they often express satisfaction that women were making their marks in an activity supposedly more natural to men. In this latter respect, *Urania*, in particular, is a cultural document of primary importance. Following its publication, Denny advised her to follow the lead of her aunt, Pembroke's mother, and, if she must write at all, to dedicate herself to pious writing, not scandalous romance. His hostility is a response not merely to what he felt were satires on his family, but to something much deeper. *Urania* is, as Denny sensed, an act of sexual defiance; it accepts the age's sexualization of women and turns it into an affirmation, not just on behalf of herself but women generally. For its author, *Urania* may have constituted at least in part an enacted daydream in which she imagines, within the residual, masculinist terms of chivalric romance, what her life as her cousin's "truest wife" might "really" be like (*Newberry 2*, fol. 26). As in her own life, fantasizing and storymaking—the writing of poetry, withdrawing from society to write or sing one's inner thoughts, the sharing of gossip, tale or anecdote—all play central roles in the fiction. But, as I shall show in chapter eight, the multiple adventures of *Urania* are not a purely personal romance. If they constitute Pamphilia's—and to an extent her creator's—"adventures," like all daydreams they are articulated within narrative forms and ideological contradictions produced by their culture. Their projections of unachieved, even unachievable, agency compulsively repeat yearnings for autonomy and transcendence that are at once private and intimate and at the same time historical and collective. Whatever our embarrassment, we would all recognize our own fantasies and daydreams as the products, in part, of the common narrative structures and commonplace motifs of our own culture which are placed within and provided with language by patterns of culturally produced discourses that name and layer our unconscious.

The marginalized classes of any society often do not leave records or even themselves know their most vital statistics. Readers of Frederick Douglass's autobiography will recall that, unlike the white children in nineteenth-century Maryland, he did not know his birthday. It may have been noted that in my sketch of Wroth's life in the opening paragraphs of the first chapter there are no definite years for either her birth or death. On 18 October, 1596, Rowland Whyte writes from Penshurst that "this is the birthday of Mistress Mary Sidney, which keepes me heare, and soe till Monday, when I will to court again." So we know her birthday, but not the year of her birth, although it was most probably 1587. The Gerhaerts portrait of 1596, which I discussed in chapter two, displays Mary to the right of her mother, her auburn hair dressed with feathers, and wearing a silvery gown, trimmed in coral, with a lace ruff. Margaret McLaren suggests that the costume displays the "two most important influences in Mary's life, that of the family and of the court." At about nine, she appears to be a tall girl. As Whyte reported to her father: "Mis Mary is grown so tall and goodly of her years, as your lordship cannot believe yet, unless you saw it; and surely will prove an excellent creature."[24] As I indicated in chapter one, Robert Sidney's letters have many affectionate references to "little Mall," or "Malkin." Yet Mary saw little of him: she was probably with her mother on Barbara Sidney's occasional visits to the Low Countries—for six months in 1590, between April and December 1592, and again in 1597. Before he was able to take more time away from his duties in the Low Countries in the last years of Elizabeth's reign, Robert Sidney spent much of his time in England at court. However he protested his reluctance to leave Penshurst and his family, as many of his letters assert, he was also anxious to protect his interests, feelings Whyte frequently echoed with some anxiety. As a child, Mary had spent part of most winters in London. When visiting London during Mary's childhood, the Sidney family—not as rich or politically important as the Pembrokes—usually stayed at Baynard's Castle, where they were given "all the rooms upon the waterside," although in 1595–6 they rented Alderman Catcher's house on Broad Street.[25]

The earliest area of experience in which the fantasies of the family romance develop for a woman is in the awareness of and control of access to her body. In the traditional family, both awareness and access play out differently with her parents, primarily in relation to the bond of gender she has with her mother and the authority of her father. It is probably not coincidental that *Urania* has many stories of violence and compulsion directed by fathers towards their unmarried daughters, especially with relation to their control over other men's access to their bodies. We hear repeatedly of the "cruel & tirannical power" of fathers over their children, arranging marriages for their daughters to "dull piece[s] of flesh," (*Urania*, pp. 35, 474). Educated to be a court lady— "she is very forward in her learning, writing, and other exercises she is put to, as dancing and the virginals," Whyte proudly reported to her father—Mary had little choice as to her role in family aggrandizement.[26] At the age of eight, she was told by the Lord Admiral that "she is already a fitt mayd for the Queen." In 1598 she was to stay with Lady Huntingdon while the rest of the family went to the Low Countries, but, still only nine, she was clearly upset by the prospect of being left behind. Whyte wrote to her father:

> Your lordship Wrytt into my lady to leave here the 3 greater behynd her, but I never saw one take yt so unkyndly as Mrs. Mary doth, who every tyme she thinkes of yt doth fall a weeping, and my lady when she perceves by doth beare her company. Mrs. Mary came to me and prayed me to wryte to you for leave to come over to see your Lordship, and that she was yet too yong to part from her mother.[27]

What Kahn has termed "the absent mother" is a perplexing aspect of Mary Wroth's life. Kahn's work on the "maternal subtext" in Shake-speare's plays focuses on "the imprint of mothering" on the male psyche; how do we construct a woman's version of the family romance that might stress, whether positively or negatively, Wroth's relation with the "maternal subtext" of her upbringing? Kahane argues that "unmediated access to maternal fullness" may be a "rescue fantasy in which the writer/daughter becomes the mother of her mother, a female version of the family romance in which the daughter gives birth to the mother she always wanted and constitutes this idealized mother as the essence of female difference." The mother Wroth desired may have been one who had a voice of her own that could be heard outside the domestic and dynastic, outside, that is, the traditional space permitted to a woman. Her father strongly reprimanded his wife for quarreling with their sons' tutor, warning her that she should continue to supervise their daughters' upbringing, but that he himself was the better judge of the education that was appropriate for his sons, "laying before her the want of education in her self, and [that she] therefore could not judge of it in others."[28] In Wroth's early development the relatively ineffectual influence of her mother is hinted at, briefly but perhaps tellingly, in such remarks. Lady Huntingdon seems to have agreed with Lady Sidney's concerns over her daughter's unreadiness for the life of a court lady, telling White that "little Mall" was too young for the life of the court. By 1602, however, when Mary was fifteen, she had been—the metaphor describing Ophelia's role as bait for Hamlet seems appropriate—"loosed" into the court. Whyte wrote from Baynard's Castle that "Mistress Mary on St Stevens day in the after noone dawnced before the Queen two galliards with one Mr. Palmer, the admirablest dawncer of this tyme; both were comended by her Majestie: then she dawnced with him a corante."[29]

As early as 1599, when she was probably twelve, negotiations for a marriage were started. Marriage to the eldest daughter of Sir Robert Sidney, a middle-level figure in the late Elizabethan court, one whose name and connections were more substantial than his fortunes, would not have been especially advantageous for a noble family like the Pembrokes. But it was an especially choice possibility for a family that was economically secure but lacked status and connections at court. In 1599, the Kentish knight Sir Thomas Mansfield unsuccessfully proposed a marriage between Mary and his eldest son, aged fifteen, and by 1603 negotiations were under way with the elderly country squire and parliamentarian, Sir Robert Wroth (1540–1606), for a marriage between Mary and his son. Like the Mansfields, the Wroths were wealthy, rising landowners, knights of the shire without courtly connections to match their ambitions. The Wroth family had prospered, like the Sidneys, from Henry VIII's dissolution of the monasteries. They had some minor noble connections: they were related by marriage to the first Lord Rich and also had connections with Thomas, Lord Cromwell. They were also loyal Protestants. Although one of those who proclaimed Mary queen in 1554, Sir Thomas Wroth had eventually become a Marian exile. He had returned under Queen Elizabeth and entered Parliament, where his greatest achievement was attempting to bring in a bill to enforce the shilling fine for willful absence from divine service. The Wroths were, in fact, regular members of Parliament: except in 1571, there was a member of the family sitting in every parliament from 1545 to 1604.[30] Unlike the Sidneys, however, the Wroths did not pursue connections at court or by marriage into the nobility. The elder Robert Wroth's correspondence reveals him to be a man primarily occupied with hunting, supporting the Reformed religion, and acquiring property. By the turn of the century the family owned extensive estates in Essex—especially in the Roding Valley, including Luxborough in Chigwell, Chigwell-cum-West Latch, Loughton, and Theydon Bois. Today these are still names on the outlying pages of the *London A to Z*; in the sixteenth century, today's ponds, pubs, and the industrial marshes of the Lee as it winds through the Roding Valley and an untidy sprawl of Victorian and later suburbia was all open country, rivers, and forest, including part of the Forest of Essex. Wroth seems to have lived well: there are letters from 1603 and 1604 inviting his neighbor Sir Michael Hickes to join him for some "verye good oysters," further enticing him with half a doe; and on 18 and 19 July, 1605, Sir Robert achieved the ultimate in country entertaining by being host to the king, who was hunting in nearby Waltham Forest. Following this prestigious visit, Wroth boasted to his neighbor Sir Michael of having sent "a brace of Buckes" to Robert Cecil, newly created earl of Salisbury:

> . . . from a true hart to him were, desyring you to be my presenter of them, not as a flatanabundus, but from him that soe loved and honored that pereles father of his . . . And I am semper idem, devoted long since, as you know, unto his ho[use]; in despight of all sicafants and other factious persons that desyre ye contrary.[31]

It may strike readers of Shakespeare's *2 Henry IV* that these remarks bring us uncannily close to the world of Justice Shallow—except that southwest Essex was rather closer to London and therefore the more likely for royalty, rather than a mere fat knight, to drop in for a couple of days hunting. Despite royal favor, however, as a good bluff countryman Wroth remained conventionally suspicious of the court: another letter to Hickes expresses relief of "the court being sumthinge remote" and so being afforded "tyme for yourselfe among yor friends." Six months or so later, on 28 January, 1605/6, he died, leaving most of his land to his eldest son Robert, and some recently acquired manors in Essex to his younger sons John, Henry, and Thomas. Robert and his bride of just over a year therefore inherited substantial properties, including the manor of Durance, which had been in the Wroth family since the fifteenth century. Between 1609 and 1612 Wroth had a new manor built at Loughton after his wife wrote to the Queen offering to make the land available for the king's hunting.[32]

What Mary brought to the marriage was, clearly, not wealth but precisely the advantage of such connections. She also brought a degree of court sophistication that the Wroth family had previously shunned. The Wroths, it might seem, were poised to do what the Sidneys themselves had done two generations previously—use marriage and court connections to enter higher circles of power. The marriage, however, was clouded in difficulties from the start. It was arranged with some financial difficulty. The Sidneys had prospered but, like many families whose political ambitions had increased their prestige, they were land-poor. Mary's dowry was arranged by her father only with the help of Pembroke, who, Sidney reported to his wife on 14 July, 1604, "with much kindness, told me that if he could take up £1000 we should have it." The marriage was delayed until the autumn because of dowry negotiations. In August William Browne, one of Robert's lieutenants in the Low Countries, wrote to him that the officers of the garrison had subscribed £200, so Robert used this money to pay for the wedding and as the first part of the dowry. But in more substantial ways, however advantageous to the families, the marriage seems not to have been either an immediate or long-term success. Some years later Ben Jonson told Drummond of Hawthornden that Mary Wroth was—Drummond's word is "is," but the conversation took place after Wroth's death—"unworthily married to a jealous husband." Only two weeks after the wedding there are two letters from Robert to his wife, referring to "words of grief" which she had put "in the end of a letter" written while the newly married couple were with her at Penshurst. Sidney refers cryptically to "that which you tolde me somewhat of the morning when I came away. "If it be so," he goes on, "I must confess it a great misfortune to us all, and yet I see no reason why we may not have hope of ammendment of it. But for the time it is very necessary that it be very secret kept and that by no circumstance it be discovered." That last clause makes whatever the "secret" is sound very embarrassing indeed, and seems to refer to something other than finance, the usual cause of discontent in such a marriage. The day after, Robert again replied to his wife, this time explicitly mentioning Robert Wroth's "discontent:"

> I finde by him that there was some what that doth discontent him: but the particulars I could not get out from him: onely that hee protests that hee cannot take any exceptions to his wife, nor her carriage towards him. It were very soon for any unkindness to begin; and therefore whatsoever the matters bee, I pray you let all things be carried in the best maner til wee all doe meet. For mine ennimies would be very glad for such an occasion to make themselves merry at me.

To what is he referring? McLaren speculates that the two letters refer to the "possible non-consummation of the Wroths' marriage"; Josephine

Roberts suggests that it may refer to a discovery of a previous contract between Mary and her cousin Pembroke, who, as I noted in the previous chapter, was concluding a marriage that was clearly even more uncongenial and, about the same time, was refusing to be in the same house as his mother. There is, however, no evidence for such a contract; nothing is more than circumstantial. It is only later in the marriage that more substantial evidence for her relationship with her cousin surfaces.[33]

Regardless of any exotic diversions or rumors that might have constituted specific "discontentment," the Sidney/Wroth marriage seems to have brought together incompatible interests and temperaments. Like his father, Wroth spent most of his time in local affairs—pursuing tenancies, consolidating his forest holdings, hunting and fishing. Both Sidney and Pembroke intervened on his behalf in a number of lawsuits at court, thus allowing Wroth to stay away from London and cultivate his rural friends and habits. Mary, however, continued to be a part of Queen Anne's entourage at court, taking part in masques and entertainments— activities I shall take up in detail in chapter seven. Her father acted as the queen's lord chamberlain, collecting and administering revenues and probably overseeing her household. Mary was also in constant contact with women friends. The Sidney letters make frequent reference to visits among Lady Wroth, the countess, and Lady Sidney, and the countess of Montgomery, Pembroke's sister-in-law. But there are none to any connections with Pembroke's wife or his mother.

While her husband stayed in Essex, Mary spent much of her time in London, continuing to stay, as she had while in her father's family, at Baynard's Castle. From the Sidney family correspondence, we can trace her frequently moving between Loughton or Durance, the Wroth's' residences in Essex, Baynard's Castle, and Penshurst. In 1609, Robert warns his wife that Mary and the Countess of Bedford were about to visit Penshurst: "What therefore your daughter will doe I know not, for shee is very eager to see you, before she goes her journey northwest: and the next week after this she must bee at home, because the King will bee in the forest." Mary is at Penshurst in August 1610; Robert expresses himself as anxious to see his daughter there a month or so later; Mary is back at Loughton early in October, and Robert visits her at Durance a week later and again the following month; Mary and the countess of Montgomery visit Baynard's Castle a few months later, and they are again together at Penshurst in August 1611. The men centrally involved in her life—her father and her cousin—frequently overlap in these visits; her husband is occasionally mentioned, mainly in connection with the unpaid dowry or occasional illness, but seems to be rarely away from one or other of his Essex homes.[34]

Although she married into the Wroth family, Mary continued to describe herself as a Sidney, much in the way her aunt had when she married Pembroke's father. Thomas Peacham's *The Compleat Gentleman* (1622) describes her coat of arms as that of the Sidneys. She inherited something of the family's reputation for patronage, and a number of poets addressed her, some by her married name but invariably making reference to her membership in the Sidney family. Her husband had other interests. As William Gamage, himself probably a distant relation of Lady Wroth's mother, noted: "Thy Durance keeps in durance none, I heare / 'Lesse be to pertake of thy bounteous cheere." Gamage footnotes "thy" with explanation that Wroth was "a famous housekeeper," an opinion echoed by Richard Nichols and, not least, Ben Jonson.[35]

At this point, indeed, enter the large figure of Jonson. *The Forrest*, in which "To Penshurst" and "To Sir Robert Wroth" occupy the first places after the mock-dedicatory "Why I Write Not of Love," has been read as a kind of manifesto of the Sidneian ideology of "housekeeping": Paul Cubeta argues that the spirit of Sidney "hovers over the *Forrest*," as both a commitment to the past ("To Penshurst") and a prophecy of the future ("To Elizabeth Countess of Rutland"). The collection also includes some poems associated with Pembroke and possibly Wroth ("That Women Are But Mens Shaddowes"), and one of Lady Wroth's brothers ("To Sir William Sydney, On His Birthday"). Of the fifteen poems in the collection, five, including four of the most significant, are associated with the Sidney family. Jonson's praise for the Sidneys—like that for Pembroke mentioned in chapter two—is that of a man enamored with a family associated with power, prestige, poetry, and (always a factor with Jonson) generous entertainment. Mary Wroth herself is mentioned in a number of his poems. In epigram 111, Jonson writes of her as "a Sydney, though un-named"; in epigram 105, he compliments her for her dazzling accomplishments: her bounty, fine dancing and hunting. She is, he asserts, the warrior-princess, "a *Nymph*, a *Muse*, a *Grace*": "so you are *Natures Index*, and restore / I' your selfe, all treasure lost of th'age before." In "A Sonnet, to the Noble Lady, the Lady Mary Wroth," he praises her love poems. Jonson, who on the whole scorned love poetry, "confesses" that after copying out her sonnets, he is "become / a better lover, and much better Poet." He goes on, not totally inaccurately, to characterize the conventional machinery of her poetry:

For in you were all *Cupids* Armorie,
His flames, his shafts, his quiver, and his bow,
His very eyes are yours to overthrow.
But then his Mothers sweets you so apply,

116

Her joys, her smiles, her loves, as readers take
For *Venus Ceston*, every line you make.[36]

The crucial poem is "To Sir Robert Wroth," which is usually read as a celebration of the reciprocity and generosity which are supposedly upheld in "To Penshurst." According to this reading, Jonson sees the Wroth estates as images of rural contentment and natural innocence. But if we set the poem in the context of Wroth's marriage, his wife's activities, and the ideals of manhood which the poem purports to uphold, a very different reading emerges. The poem opens, in fact, with an immediate backhanded compliment. Wroth inherited his father's distrust of the court and preference for hunting and country life, yet Jonson, the urbane haunter of court and taverns, exclaims: "How blest art thou, canst love the country, Wroth / Whether by choice, or fate, or both," and goes on to praise Wroth's lifestyle: while his estates are "neere the citie, and the court," he is fortunately untainted by this proximity, since unlike ambitious courtiers, glittering court ladies, or dissipated masquers, he does not resort to the pleasures of the city. In particular, Jonson eulogizes: "Nor, throng'st (when masquing is) to have a sight / Of the short braverie of the night." As a frugal housekeeper, Wroth is invited to contemplate disapprovingly "the jewells, stuffes, the paines, the wit / There wasted, some not paid for yet!"

When we consider not only to whom Jonson was writing but who was hovering in the background of the poem, we may be struck not only by the double-edged compliment, but by the risks he was taking. As he looked over his shoulder, he saw, first, Wroth's wife, one of those for whom "the short braverie of the night" was a central part of life. The other person he would have seen was Wroth's wife's cousin, whose intimacy with her was probably at the very least rumor, who was still owed for her dowry, and so had pointedly given the Wroths some "jewells" and "stuffes" that were "not paid for yet." Is Jonson indulging in sarcasm? As the poem goes on, and considering the multiple audiences, it is as if Jonson is trying to satisfy all of them. For Robert Wroth it was probably a compliment not only to have a poem addressed to him by a poet of Jonson's reputation (especially among his wife's relations), but also to be praised precisely for what he, not she, wanted to do— staying "at home," in "thy securer rest." But his wife and her cousin, for their part, might well have laughed up their sleeves when Wroth is described as dwelling "mongst loughing heards, and solide hoofes." Jonson is praising Wroth for exactly the characteristics his wife scorns. While she is masquing at court, he is at home with the cattle and the local squires. Jonson celebrates Wroth's rural life not as a moral exemplum but as that of an unsophisticated country gentleman. Unlike the Sidneys at

Penshurst, for whom country hospitality is part of a moral responsibility, for Wroth it is an opportunity for a "rout of rural folke" to "come thronging in." What Jonson quite explicitly calls "their rudenesse" is something that Wroth (as it were by nature) overlooks while his "noblest spouse" is sufficiently condescending to afford "them welcome grace." Jonson's conclusion praises Wroth by explicitly emasculating him:

> And such since thou canst make thine owne content,
>> Strive, *Wroth*, to live long innocent.
> Let others watch in guilty armes, and stand
>> The furie of a rash command,
> Goe enter breaches, meet the cannons rage,
>> That they may sleepe with scarres in age.

Behind this praise is a rejection of the masculine pursuits of politics, arms, law, business, "money, warre, or death." The poem concludes:

> Let thousands more goe flatter vice and sinne,
>> By being organes to great sunne,
> Get place, and honor, and be glad to keepe
>> The secrets, that shall breake their sleepe.[37]

The kind of man Jonson is praising Wroth for not emulating—indeed, for rejecting—is undoubtedly best exemplified in his immediate circle by Pembroke himself.

Even more ironic are the metaphors of gender that dislocate the poem's apparently harmonious vision. As in "To Penshurst," housekeeping is depicted as a return to the undifferentiated mother, a primitive unity where food, satisfaction, and acceptance are all instantly available. As Williams pointed out, in "To Penshurst" nobody actually works to produce the feasts; the fish offer themselves to be caught; all nature and its plenty are part of a universal flow.[38] It is a gently comic, pre-Oedipal fantasy of how nature and human beings were once united and provided for. In such a pattern the court represents an oedipal break; it is, by contrast to the idealized country, a raw, crude, masculine world. Staying at home, therefore, Wroth is demasculinized and sneered at. His wife is clearly most fulfilled when part of the court's perpetual movement, part of the masculine world dominated by the king and her cousin; he stays at home, since "when man's state is well, / Tis better, if he there can dwell." "Such," Jonson says to Wroth with, it seems, magnificent bravado, "be thou." He is playing Falstaff to Wroth's Shallow.

The poem is full of such comic mystifications. Wroth is praised for avoiding the litigious pursuit of land at court. And yet we know that is precisely what he was perpetually involved in, and that it was his wife who wrote, successfully, to the queen for interventions to be made on his behalf so he might rebuild Loughton. Someone—and it was usually his wife and her family, including her increasingly influential cousin—had to "sweat, and wrangle at the barre." Likewise, it is precisely because his wife, cousin-in-law, and father-in-law "goe flatter vice, and winne / by being organs to great sinne," that Wroth could enjoy the prestige of having the king come to hunt on his lands. Masculine power, most powerfully represented in the king, makes possible both the life of virtuous retirement and the world of the glittering court. The material details of labor, financial investment and exploitation—which in fact produce the harvest, enclose the forest, and pay the huntsmen—are, as in "To Penshurst," carefully ignored. As David Norbrook notes, someone like Wroth, living so close to Cecil's estates at Theobald's, a favorite retreat of the king's, "was bound to feel the need to keep up with the massive scale of conspicuous consumption indulged in by Cecil and the King." Cecil was referred to as "Robin the encloser of Hatfield wood," and Wroth himself was described by Chamberlain as "a great commander or rather by the Kings favor an intruder in Waltham forest."[39] J. C. A. Rathmell points out that "To Penshurst" can usefully be read as, in part, an expression of Jonson's anxiety that Robert Sidney might forget his moral duty and try to emulate the "costly piles." With "To Sir Robert Wroth," Jonson is also skating, with typical verve and bravado, on very thin ice indeed. As lord chamberlain, Pembroke had a major influence on the revels, in which Jonson and Inigo Jones received employment, annually gave Jonson £20 for books and—if Jonson's dedications to *Catiline* and the *Epigrams* are evidence—supported and admired him.[40]

Whether the wit of "To Sir Robert Wroth" afforded its primary addressee satisfaction, and his wife (and her cousin) some different kind of amusement, we cannot be sure. But we do know that the unease Mary's father expressed over his daughter's marriage may be reflected in the fact that the Wroths did not have a child until 1614. In his study of family life in early modern France, David Hunt notes that a woman of Wroth's class "exerted no effective control over her own reproductive functions. She conceived . . . according to a rhythm which in origin was biological and in practice closely related to the whim of her husband."[41] Childbearing was a primary part of her duty of forwarding the ambitions of her husband's family; yet Mary Wroth's only legitimate child was born ten years after her marriage and only a month before her husband, who presumably was the father, died. Her two illegitimate children were born in her period of widowhood—the first probably soon after she became a widow, the second within the next few years.

A month after the birth of her son James, Mary Wroth was widowed. Her husband's will was made the day before James was christened—with Pembroke as one of his sponsors, standing in for the king—and twelve days before Robert Wroth's death at Loughton on 14 March, 1614, probably of gangrene. He left behind him, as Chamberlain noted, "a young widow with £1,200 fortune, a son a month old, and his estate £23,000 in debt." Wroth did leave his wife a legacy of £1000, adding in his will that "I hartelie desire my sayed deere and loving wife that she will accept hereof as a testimony of my entire love and affection towards her, albeyet her sincere love, loyaltie, virtuous conversation, and behavioure towards me, have deserved a farre better recompense, yf the satisfying of my debts and supporting my house would have permitted the same." Robert Sidney once more had the opportunity to be grateful to his son-in-law that he did not have to pay the full amount of his daughter's dowry.[42]

In 1614 Mary Wroth was twenty-seven, a widow with a month old son and a heavily indebted estate which was to be managed by three members of her late husband's family, all named John Wroth—a cousin, brother and uncle to her husband. It does not sound a promising situation, and yet arguably the next decade was to prove the most eventful and satisfying period of her life. She was a widow, a lover, a mother, and a writer. All these roles were, in their different ways, means by which she carved out of a disadvantageous situation an unusually independent life.

First, despite her indebtedness, widowhood gave Mary Wroth a degree of involvement in public affairs and autonomy that she clearly had never achieved as a married woman. As Christianne Klapisch-Zuber puts it, if it was "marriage that brought a woman out of the paternal house and lineage, widowhood that often led to her return: women marrying into families were merely 'passing guests.' "[43] In common law a widow had a right of dower in one-third of her husband's lands, a right that was usually waived in return for a portion agreed in the marriage settlement. In Mary Wroth's case, the balance of the dowry remained unpaid and was forgiven in Wroth's will. But by virtue of her son's dying as an infant, she lost even a temporary hold over most of her married property. By permission of a special Act of Parliament many of Wroth's estates were sold at his death, while others were retained by his heirs. For her part, she kept Loughton and Luxborough and lived from the rents collected from the attached land. Pembroke was one of the guarantors of the deed drawn up in 1618 to regularize this arrangement. But since the estate was without a direct heir, and since she had lost most of the lands her husband had owned, she was in a real sense returning to the Sidney fold. In the next few years, she seems to have divided much of her time between Loughton, Baynard's Castle, and Penshurst—where her sister Phillip, recently married to Sir John Hobbard, gave birth to a son and where she herself may have given birth to her and Pembroke's two children. In the next few years various other references, some clear, some cryptic, surface. Many of them concern travel—as I noted in chapter one, a characteristic sign of an autonomy usually associated with men. Living in Essex, she was close enough to London and Kent to make frequent trips. There are records of visits to Penshurst, usually in the summer; visits to London to stay at Baynard's Castle; and visits by Robert to his daughter at Loughton. In the 1620s domestic expenses forced her to move house to Woodford, slightly nearer the Montgomery family, where Pembroke would have been a frequent visitor, and also close to a number of the more distant Herbert relations, including Edward Herbert, the poet George Herbert's brother whose son, William, named after his godfather the third earl, was born in 1626.[44]

Mary Wroth's connections with the court seem to have fallen off in her widowhood. By 1620 she was in her thirties, unconnected (at least officially) to any leading courtier, and past the days when as a girl or a newly married woman she could easily take part in court entertainments. But in 1619 she attended the queen's funeral, in which Pembroke was a pallbearer, and she became part of court gossip shortly after when she was linked with the earl of Oxford as a prospective marital prospect. Her real interests were elsewhere—again, in what would normally be men's activities. She was engaged in ongoing legal disputes over her land and to preserve her financial independence. At various times she leased or rented various of her lands. These rents proved inadequate, and throughout the 1620s she petitioned Secretary Conway, her father, and the king for help in avoiding her creditors. In 1623 she wrote to Conway for help, and a royal warrant of protection was issued, citing as justification her birth, quality, and intention to repay. But the next day Ellis Rothwell, a page of the Bedchamber, claimed arrears of rent for a London house, and Conway wrote to Lady Mary again, and then, three months later, to Robert Sidney, asking him to intercede with his daughter. Robert expressed great regret, and reassured the secretary of his daughter's good intentions. The king had recently (in 1622 and 1623) issued proclamations that the gentry should leave London and return to the country, "for the reviving and settling of hospitality and good government in this our kingdom," and Robert noted that despite his daughter's intention of obeying, Rothwell had tried to keep Lady Wroth to the lease. Her father added that in fact he knew little of her affairs, as she managed them herself. In 1624, before the last protection from debt had expired, she again wrote to Conway, noting that her "ill fortune" continued, but that she had paid off some of her debts either by "ready money" or by land, "by which means I have lessen'd my estate much." Records for 1625, 1627, and 1628 show similar petitions, and in 1635 we read that protection had been "divers times renewed," along with

Lady Wroth's continuing intention to give "content according to her desire" to all her creditors.[45]

From these records there emerges a picture of a determined, even stubborn, woman, intent on maintaining her independence, wrestling with legal and manorial negotiations, not afraid to use her court contacts and very much standing on her dignity. She may have been unhappy and struggling financially, but her courage is clear, as is the remarkable if unostentatious independence she was developing. Dominated by men— first by her father, then her husband and her lover—she was demonstrating more than the subservience and silence expected of a woman. In significant ways she carved out for herself spaces of autonomy. In particular, two areas I discussed at the start of the chapter are worth examining in detail—sexuality (including, as I suggested, motherhood) and writing. Her career as a writer will be the focus of chapters six, seven and eight; here I want to discuss the seemingly more "personal"— though no less culturally constructed—areas in which we can see her wrestling to establish some sense of herself.

Her relationship with Pembroke can be adequately, if not lavishly, documented. It is likely that many records, in both the Sidney and Herbert families, have been destroyed—in the former case, possibly deliberately; in the latter, in the Wilton House fire of 1647—but there are sufficient extant to indicate that the most significant relationship of her life was with her cousin. The evidence for the history of her involvement with Pembroke is a tantalizing mixture of public documentation and circumstantial surmise. The modern discovery of the affair is a fascinating one of an almost total cover-up by the Sidneys for nearly three hundred years. Nothing surfaced in biographical accounts of Lady Wroth, apart from puzzlement about the occasional "mistaken" (as it was termed) mention of a second son, until M. A. Beese discussed the Cardiff documents in her Oxford dissertation.[46]

A number of aspects of the relationship require comment. Adultery was officially regarded as a crime, however widespread it may have been. Blame fell almost entirely on the woman involved: Lady Anne Clifford noted in 1603 how "all the ladies about the court had gotten such ill names that it was grown a scandalous place"; Pembroke's affair with Mary Fitton was characteristically described as "a misfortune befallen Mistress Fitton." The patriarchal double standard meant that it was perfectly acceptable if male aristocrats were sexually promiscuous, but women faced greater approbrium. In his novel, *Couples* (1968), John Updike describes adultery of a "way of getting out in the world and giving yourself adventures."[47] I quote him not only to indicate a modern male nostalgia for sexual adventure and risk conceived in terms of a dim echo of the chivalric hero, but because for a woman in Mary Wroth's position, it was a real risk and adventure. What was at stake was not only her own sense of self but her very physical well-being and liberty. Characteristically, her partner in "adventure" had little to lose, where she could suffer possible pregnancy, as well as having her reputation, livelihood, and possibly (given the cautionary tale of Penelope Blount) her life at risk. As Shorter notes, in a society, "which maximizes male domination over females at every level," coercion was the rule, and coupled with an underlying suspicion, even fear of women's sexual appetites, it meant women who demanded sexual choice or independence often suffered dire social consequences. Younger women were inevitably the objects of powerful, older men, and it was probably a rare woman who could engineer some degree of social or economic control by means of her family's or husband's positions and who then could afford to indulge her own sexual choices. A widow was doubly vulnerable. There might well be resentment towards women who remarried, but it would have been no less suspicious to stay single. As Chaytor comments: "a too hasty remarriage could have been regarded as a dishonour to the dead husband but a lifetime of sexual freedom while enjoying his property might have been considered the greater insult."[48] Particularly interesting about Wroth's affair with her cousin, then, are three matters: first, the sexual independence it indicates; second, that their relationship was sufficiently stable or at least recurring to produce two children; and third, that her lover was her cousin. Each of these was such a breach with her assigned place in her society, such an "adventure" as to repay close examination.

First-cousin marriage was not forbidden: the marriage of "cousin germans" was "always *lawfull*, and sometimes . . . *Expedient*," as an expert later in the century expressed it.[49] But there does not seem to be a question of marriage in this case. Both married for family aggrandizement: Pembroke to acquire money and lands, marrying a woman of apparently little physical attractiveness or social grace—who eventually went, or more likely was conveniently declared, insane, largely for the financial benefit of her husband's family. Wroth, as we have seen, was married in a typical dynastic transaction: court connections traded for financial security. It is perhaps too tempting to construct a sentimental fantasy of the two cousins as tragic figures yearning to marry across forbidden bonds. But on a psychological level it seems clear how from her childhood on, Mary was incorporated into the family romances of the dominant men in her life. The object woman, to repeat Freud's phrase, is initially encoded as a woman within the family: with the young William Herbert, "immoderately given up to women," it was first his mother, and then his cousin, who was, in a sense, his sister, the nearest focus of his ambivalence about women and his own manhood.

But what of the family romance from the woman's point of view? How can we re-gender what has largely been described as if it were solely a man's, and not a woman's, prerogative to yearn to rediscover lost or impossible dreams in adult relationships? In chapter one I suggested that Wroth's—and, in patriarchal societies generally, the core of a woman's—family romance are dreams, first, of autonomy and agency, modeled on what is apparently enjoyed by the men with whom she falls in love or upon whom she is dependent; and, second, of mutuality and equality. What Kaplan terms "the incompatibilities of female desires and female ambitions with the social roles traditionally assigned to women" emerges in a combination of "submission and envy,"[50] and a search for an idealized relationship with a man who can share with her his apparently natural autonomy. The first of those men is the father. In *Fathers and Daughters*, Lynda Boose has drawn attention to the wealth of material on the father/daughter relationships in the early modern period. If the father gives his daughter to a husband he has chosen, then he maintains at least some symbolic control over her: the transaction "circumvents her ability . . . to choose another man, thus allowing him to retain vestiges of his primary claim" on her. Patriarchy, Boose notes, generally presents this control within an ideology of benevolence, but the daughter submits to it largely because she has no choice. When she finds she can, indeed, struggle against the father, she may find the alternatives are already too heavily inscribed by the father's image. She is haunted by contradictory desires: the security of the enveloping paternalistic family and the dangerous autonomy of sexual choice.[51]

What parts did Pembroke play in Mary Wroth's fantasies of autonomy? Was he a more glamorous father figure—younger, more autonomous, and more powerful than her biological father, with the double allure of someone both within and outside the family? By having two children fathered by her cousin, she was in a sense re-fathered herself, folded back into the family's dynastic desires, fulfilling them better than through her "real" marriage and at the same time remaining a Sidney. She could at once transcend her childhood incestuous idealization of the father while enacting a more than merely symbolic expression of it. What was usually available only in fantasy was thereby attainable to an alluring extent in actuality. But, as Kaplan and other feminist psychoanalysts make clear, the dream of another, more difficult, relationship haunts a woman's desires. It is that of bonding, not bonds; of mutuality, not the self-destructive hope that by abandoning herself to the will of another she will be given her "true" self. Why, asks Benjamin, has a woman's search for recognition so often culminated in "submission, instead of a relationship of mutuality?" Modifying what she sees as Mahler's "overvaluing of separation," Benjamin suggests that while relationships based upon domination have, sadly, been the norm in our history, there have been hints of the development of the "relational self" as an alternative fantasy narrative.[52] This dream of mutuality haunts *Urania*, and, at moments, *Pamphilia to Amphilanthus*. It constitutes the most radical aspect of Wroth's rewriting of the family romance.

Motherhood, too, I have suggested, may well have helped her reconfigure the family romance. We have no idea, it needs to be emphasized, whether her pregnancies were the eventual result of a long relationship with Pembroke (although it seems possible) or of stray encounters with a close and intimate relation to whom she felt obligated as well as attracted. Some of the mixture of celebratory fantasy and embitterment projected into clearly autobiographical aspects of *Urania* could reflect, as Roberts speculates, a longstanding commitment, even a secret betrothal, though they could equally reflect Susan Brownmiller's observation that rape underlies all traditional sexual relations and the reality that, in Shorter's words, "the women we encounter in the lists of unwed mothers are almost all women who were forced to go along" with the dominant male.[53] Sexual independence, including motherhood, took Mary Wroth back into the Sidney family, but it also may have afforded her a marked degree of autonomy and possibly deep-rooted and multiple psychological satisfactions.

There is no indication among the Wroth family records of her illegitimate children. They brought her back to the safety and, no doubt, in part, the reassuring undifferentiation of her "real" family of the Sidneys and Pembrokes—to the affection of her father, mother, and siblings, the relationship with her cousin, and the friendship of his sister-in-law. All, along with other family members, are represented, often in multiple characters and stories, in *Urania*. The experience of motherhood as a Sidney rather than a Wroth enabled her to recover a state of fusion with the nurturing matrix or mothering function of the family. In practical as opposed to psychological terms, the advantage she had, as the mother of illegitimate children, in being part of a powerful family was the possibility of secrecy or simply independence of the law. The first earl of Leicester, Robert Dudley, had an illegitimate son by Lady Sheffield; Penelope Rich had five illegitimate children by Sir Charles Blount; Sir Walter Ralegh left provision for his illegitimate son in his will. Like adultery, in the early seventeenth century illegitimacy was under increasing surveillance by church courts. A statute of 1576 empowered local justices to order parents of bastards to maintain them and to punish both mother and father. An act of 1610 required that mothers of illegitimate children be confined in houses of correction, at the expense of the father. But if the paternity was acknowledged, and the father was able to support the child, the matter probably would be ignored. In any case, such legislation would not easily affect a family like the Sidneys. As part of the residual indifference to aristocratic bastards, it was not uncommon for illegitimate children to be brought up with legitimate brothers and sisters. As Ivy Pinchbeck and Margaret Hewitt comment, "in the households of the great, throughout the sixteenth century and for many years after, acceptance of a man's illegitimate children persisted" among the aristocracy by contrast with a hardening of judicial attitudes towards middle- and lower-class illegitimacy. The "inescapable fact," they observe, is that "the state was only concerned with illegitimacy among the poor."[54] It seems that the two children were well protected by both the Sidneys and the Herberts—although most of the records we have allude to the children as Pembroke's. In addition to the family records, there is his cousin Edward's witty little congratulatory poem:

> "A Merry Rime Sent to Lady Mary Wroth upon the birth
> of my Lord of Pembroke's Child. Born in the Spring."
>
> Madam, though I'm one of those
> That every spring use to compose,
> That is, add feet unto round prose.
> Yet you a further art disclose,
> You can, as everybody knows,
> Add to those feet fine dainty toes,
> Satyrs add nails, but they are shrews,
> My muse therefore no further goes
> But for her feet craves shoes and hose,
> Let a fair season add a Rose
> While thus attir'd we'll oppose,
> The tragic buskins of our foes.[55]

Herbert must have sent the same verses, or conveyed the same sentiments, to Pembroke, since there is a letter, dated March 1620, in which Pembroke thanks him for his good wishes: "My Cos, I must give you many thanks for congratulating me with yo'r little cousin, who I thank God yet prospers like a blessing to me." In later years there are a few extant references to the children. William was aided by his uncle, the fourth earl of Pembroke, to a "brave living in Ireland," serving there as a soldier and, according to the Herbert records, dying unmarried. The family records note that Catherine married a "Mr Lovel neare Oxford," who may have been a tutor in the household of Mary Wroth's brother, Robert Sidney, second earl of Leicester, in the 1640s. If so, then as Sharon Valiant has speculated, her daughter may well have been the woman later known as Aphra Behn.[56]

The other major "womanspace" which Mary Wroth attempted to carve out for herself was her writing. Her poetry was her greatest continuing tie to her father, and one that further links her with other members of the Sidney family. It is obvious that she studied her uncle's and father's poetry well; it is less obvious that she was greatly affected by her aunt's pious poetry (on the other hand, as I shall note in chapter eight, there is a number of friendly representations of Pembroke's mother in *Urania*). In Wroth's writing, especially in the repetition compulsion patterns of passivity and masochism in both *Urania* and *Pamphilia to Amphilanthus*, there are signs of what might be described as neurotic displacement, vulnerability to depression, and helpless passivity before the father figure, Nonetheless, the very act of writing—the assertion of the significance of fantasy, the detailed planning, revision, circulation and publication (as well as the choice to refuse to circulate or publish)—seems to have opened up both material and psychological agency that confounds the masochistic stereotypes by which she was otherwise interpellated. In the Sidney family, poetry seems to have been held to be an appropriate activity for a woman. In chapter six, I will speculate on the connections with her cousin's poetry: do we have "a seeming historical necessity for the heterosexual woman who wants to create, to write—and be read— to couple herself, in fact or fantasy . . . with a man who also writes or wrote," what Hélène Cixous has termed the necessarily "hierarchized" writing couple? As with other areas of Wroth's life, her writing career was certainly heavily dependent upon authority figures, especially men— a phenomenon, Cixous argues, that is a "seeming historical necessity for the heterosexual woman who wants to create, to write—and be read— to couple herself, in fact or fantasy . . . with a man who also writes or wrote."[57] I do not simply mean that the many references to her love for her cousin constitute the meaning of the poems: they draw on and extend the Petrarchan tradition too suggestively to be read so reductively. But many seem to be projections of Wroth's wishfulfillment fantasies about her relationship with her cousin, especially in the early sonnets of the collection. The two lovers of both *Pamphilia to Amphilanthus* and *Urania* are first cousins whose love must—for no explicable reason—be kept secret. There are also recurring puns on the name "will," too many to be coincidental.[58]

But while there are unquestionably frequent references to Pembroke in *Pamphilia to Amphilanthus* and *Urania*, Wroth's struggles have a wider cultural significance. The poems present a fantasy of autonomy by a woman struggling in what they repeatedly term a "labyrinth." I suggested earlier that Wroth's writing is an act of self-assertion, but she is unavoidably caught up in discursive positions that she occupies only at the cost of self-violation. The recurring use of the word "molestation" is a sign of this tension. Behind the term are both physical realities and myths. Assault and domination may well have been part of Wroth's own experience of sex but, as well, she is evoking part of the cultural unconscious, the fears built into being a woman in a masculinist society. It may be, too, that a woman expressing any degree of sexual autonomy or demand falls victim to one of patriarchy's recurring myths about sexual molestation, which warns women that if they stray from their assigned place they may suffer (deservedly, they are threateningly warned) rape. Molestation is thus what Anna Clark terms an "extension of the social construction of male sexuality as active, dominant and aggressive."[59]

As I will suggest in chapter eight, the same groping towards some degree of self-assertion can be seen in *Urania*. There are indications that much, if not all, of the romance was written after Wroth was widowed and that at least part of it was written at Baynard's Castle. In 1640 the earl of Rutland wrote to Lady Wroth: "You once showed me a manuscript in your study at Barnard's Castle. Meeting here with your Urania I send the enclosed and beg you to interpret the names as I have begun them."[60] The biographical displacements I have already indicated make *Urania* a "family romance" in a number of senses. Pamphilia and Amphilanthus are first cousins who, as Pamphilia notes, have had "long conversation as from our youthes." He is "exquisite" in "all true vertues," including poetry; his only lack is his inconstancy, as Pamphilia—who is masochistically faithful and continually denyies her love for him, at least in public—frequently notes: "inconstancy was, and is the onely touch thou hast, yet can I say, but thou art constant to love." Indeed, "never," Pamphilia puts it to him with a little force, "art thou out of love." "Women," she warns him, "are ominous to thee, shunne them, and love her firmely who onely loveth thee" (*Urania*, pp. 78, 112, 115, 312–13).

In *Urania* we can find conscious autobiography, wishfulfillment fantasy, as well as the projection of deeper demands of the unconscious upon a fantasy landscape. The romance obsessively displaces personality, familial, gender, and broader social contradictions into a series of compulsively repeated narratives. It shows how women function as a terrain for male fantasies and also how a woman's fantasies, even though empowered by her place in the complexities of the patriarchal/incestuous family romance, are starting to search for voices of their own. I say "dramatize" advisedly, because not only do Mary Wroth's literary and personal lives stage a crucial phase of one of our history's great cultural dramas, but also because, along with her cousin, she took some part in the dramatic displays of the court—the pageants, masques, and tourneys by which the Jacobean court staged many of its shared fantasies of permanence and harmony. In chapter seven I will analyze Mary Wroth's play, *Love's Victory*, considering it in the context of the family's interests in drama, theater, and the pageants of display and spectatorship that dramatic performance enacted.

A number of biographical references in *Urania* drew Mary Wroth into public controversy when it was published. The first part was published, incompletely, in 1621—and when it became controversial, she claimed (probably truthfully) that it appeared without her consent. Chamberlain noted that a number of courtiers thought that the author "takes great libertie or rather license to traduce whom she please, and thinkes she daunces in a net," and commented upon "certain bitter verses" written by Lord Denny who accused the *Urania*'s author not only of "wrathfull spite" in writing "an Idell book," but of sexual looseness:

> Yet Common oysters such as thine gape wide
> And take in pearles or worse at every tide . . .

> Thus hast thou made thy self a lying wonder
> Fooles and their Bables seldome part asunder.

His poem concludes with a piece of tart advice: "leave idle bookes alone / For wise and worthyer women have writte none." It is headed: "To Pamphilia from the father-in-law of Seralius." In her reply, Wroth protested that Denny's interpretation of her "harmless booke" shows that "oysters have enflamd your blood," and that his "slaunderous flying flames . . . prove your self the drunken beast," concluding: "Take this then now lett railing rimes alone / for wise and worthier men have written none." She complained to Denny that the verses read as if they were by "some drunken poett" and affirming her "owne innocencie; which is as cleare and pure as new borne; what ever such like slanderous conceipts have layd upon mee," and concluding: "now I shall pittie your rash follie, and wish you amendment of understanding; and to take this as a mornings work." Denny replied the next day that he was not the author of the verses, but that *Urania* was, nevertheless, slanderous, a "booke . . . which all the world Condemns." He reminded Wroth of the comparison between her book and the writings of her pious aunt, Pembroke's mother, the recently deceased countess of Pembroke, hoping

> that you may repent you of so many ill spent yeares of so vaine a booke and that you may redeeme the tyme with writing as large a volume of heavenly layes and holy love as you have of lascivious tales and amorous toyes that at the last you may followe the rare, and pious example of your vertuous and learned Aunt, who translated so many godly books and especially the holly psalmes of David.

It was, Denny concluded, and without specifying whom he meant, owing to "the great honor I bear somme of your noble allies and my deerly

honored frends," that he forbore "to write what I might." Continuing
the controversy with some spirit, Wroth denied his threats, and (as far
as we know) the last word was Denny's when he affirmed that: "for
those noble Allies of yours I will ever honour and serve, when you
have make the worst of mee you can divise unto them." The name
of Pembroke is never mentioned among the "noble Allies" who might
have been protecting her. But the following March Wroth wrote a letter,
found among the Denbeigh papers, which, Briley speculates, may well
have been addressed not, as Roberts asserts, to William Fielding, first earl
of Denbeigh, but Wroth's cousin himself. In the letter Wroth beseeches
the recipient to recall past connections, saying that "your favour may
make all well with his Majesty." We recall Denny's sneer that she would
not have been so bold if it had not been for her friends, her "noble
allies." There is no evidence any official action was taken but Wroth's
fear of it may be seen in her writing to Buckingham, asserting that she
had never intended to publish the work and that copies had been sold
against her will.[61]

I have suggested that the years between her husband's death and the
birth of her second child, probably around 1621, may have constituted a
fulfilling time for Mary Wroth. After Denny's attack and her withdrawal
of *Urania*, we hear virtually nothing of her. Her literary voice may have
been silenced by the disapproval of the court just as she was marginalized
by her lifestyle and the choices made for her by her status as widow,
mistress, and mother. We have no record of her reaction to Pembroke's
death. Their relationship may have been long over, and we can only
speculate about whether she was in the congregation that heard his
funeral sermon and noted the exhortations to avoid the vanity of the
court, its "quick-sand of Mutabilitie, and inconstancie." She was to
live another twenty or more years, probably largely at Loughton. It
is recorded that she made occasional property deals. In 1643 a transfer
of Luxborough was made to her for the rest of her life, and in 1645
she was listed as an owner of land at East Wickenden.[62] Her death is
referred to in passing in a Chancery deposition of 1668, as probably
having occurred some fifteen years earlier.

What was Mary Wroth doing all those years? Was she with her
children? Did she write? Did she have casual or long-term relationships
of any kind? Had the passion for her cousin burnt itself out? Did
she choose, or was she forced to live quietly, with her memories, as
a forgotten, almost totally marginalized figure whose historical time
had not so much passed as not yet come? Within the Freudian incest
pattern, the mother/sister figure is called to demonstrate that she too
is consumed by suffering and self-denial because she is unable, finally,
to fall into the embrace of the son/brother. As a cousin, Mary Wroth

must have fulfilled many of the fantasies of her cousin/brother, but at the cost, except for perhaps six or seven years after being widowed, of her own voice and autonomy. Re-gendering the family romance meant for Mary Wroth the partial and contradictory exploration of patterns of experience at once dependent on and yet subtly different from those assigned to her, primarily by the men, the fathers, of her life. The male family romance pattern grows out of the simultaneous repudiation and anxious dependency on the mother. It tends to lead to difference as a denial of commonality, a sense of autonomy expressed in adventure, disconnection, and a fragile reliance on unity imposed by outside forces and allegiances—Mahler's category of the not-fully-born. Pembroke is by no means alone in the history of Western patriarchy in his reliance on domination and restless adventure as ways of defining himself. Nor is Wroth alone in at once envying the assertion of agency enjoyed by men and at the same time drawing subtle strength from the enfolding support of her sexuality, her connections with family and "womanspaces" of many kinds. We are seeing if not the beginnings, at least a self-conscious articulation of post-renaissance Western individualism—and, moreover, the crucial emergence of an element characteristically ignored in the standard accounts of its beginnings, the matter of gender domination.

Within the broader cultural patterns emerging from early modern England, the life and writings of Mary Wroth—and their complex interconnections with the Sidney men—articulate, however fitfully, what Williams terms "pre-emergent" signs of an articulated femininity that, in later centuries, has become less marginal, and by means of which we are now starting to rewrite the history of the ideologies and material practices of our culture. As we put the writings and lives of both Pembroke and Wroth into our history in the decade of the quincentennial celebrations of Columbus's voyage, we might usefully emphasize the irony of the New World's exploration as a work of masculinist domination, conquering, destroying, pillaging, populating. It precluded what might have been another opening up in the history of Western men and women, the expansion of the frontiers of bodily freedom and ego formation through the exploration of sexuality, which (perhaps because it was historically and ideologically centered in the female) proved so much more gradual and had to wait many centuries.[63] In the spasmodic and contradictory gendering of the family romance within the Sidney family we can sense its first stirrings.

4

Late Petrarchism:
The Inter(dis)courses of the
Sidney Family Romance

. . . as they may but see the lyning of our outermost garment, they straight
think that Apollo honours them . . . if we will not suffer them to smel on
our smockes, they will snatch at our petticotes . . . At the end of mens faire
promises is a *Laberinth* . . .

Jane Anger

By demonstrating the part played by perverse impulses in the psychoneuroses,
we have quite remarkably increased the number of people who might be
regarded as perverts. It is not only that neurotics in themselves constitute a very
numerous class, but it must also be considered that an unbroken chain bridges
the gap between the neuroses in all their manifestations and normality . . . the
extraordinary wide dissemination of the perversions forces us to suppose that
the disposition to perversions is itself of no great rarity but must form part of
what passes as the normal . . .

Sigmund Freud[1]

Petrarke hed and prince of Poets all"[2]: thus *Tottel's Miscellany* introduced what for English poets between Wyatt and Mary Wroth was not merely an an important literary space, but a set of codes with enormously broad cultural impact. The Sidney cousins' poems are made up of the traces and struggles of many texts, but the single name that stands above them all is that of Petrarch, who gave them (and us) one of the most seductive conceptual schemes by which to discuss sexual desire and its relationship with language. Francesco Petrarch (1304–74) remains one of Western Europe's seminal figures.[3] Although regarded in his lifetime primarily as a historian, humanist, and general man of letters, it is through his vernacular poetry—the *Trionfi*, and in particular his lyric poetry, the *Canzoniere*—that much of Petrarch's impact was transmitted to later centuries. His collection of lyric poems, written to a woman he hardly knew whom he calls Laura, was started in the 1340s and given a definite shape almost twenty years later, a decade after her death on 6 April 1348. Over Petrarch's lifetime, the *Canzoniere* had undergone modifications, finally consisting of 366 sonnets, divided in two parts: 1–263 before Laura's death, 264–366 after.

For three centuries much of what Foucault has termed writing "the truth of man's sex" was mediated through Petrarch—or, more accurately, through what became known as Petrarchism.[4] Generations of commentators and imitators elaborated a collective (mis)reading of his poetry of such power that it was impossible to locate oneself within the discourse of writing sexuality into poetry outside Petrarchism. Commentaries on the poems abounded throughout the fifteenth century; major imitations of them appeared in Italian at the same time, in Spanish in the late fifteenth century, and in French shortly after. By the time the English poets started to read him seriously in the second quarter of the sixteenth century, Petrarch had been mediated to them by nearly two hundred years of imitators, commentators, and adaptors. They were read (and rewritten variously) as a diary of sexual desire, a handbook of rhetorical ornamentation, a systematic exposition of love; as neoplatonist, Stoic, Ovidian, Christian, and Aristotelian. Petrarchan poetry could be solemn, witty, or blasphemous; slavishly imitated or scurrilously mocked. "Anti-petrarchist" sentiments are as much a part of the Petrarchan mode as the more obviously serious poems for which Petrarch is revered as philosopher, psychologist, and master rhetorician. Laura herself could be interpreted by neoplatonist commentators as an earthly lover drawing the soul towards Good, or towards God (as in Spenser's *Amoretti*); she could also be presented as an erotically enticing yet tantalizingly frustrating court lady to be wooed, complained at, or scorned.

I will look first at Petrarchism as a flexible rhetoric of erotic desire. It sees love as a frustrating though inspiring experience, characterized by a melancholy yet obsessive balance between desire and hopelessness, possibility and frustration. Its fundamental characteristic is conflict or paradox, usually expressed as a balance of powerful opposites, forces in or outside the lover which simultaneously move him on and hold him back. As Leonard Forster explains, "later generations were less interested in the balance than in the antitheses," and it is "this elaboration and exploitation which is the essence of Petrarchism." While Forster warns us against describing Petrarchist poets as being conscious of working within a system—it was "for them a natural mode of conventional utterance and conventional behaviour in certain circumstances"[5]—nonetheless, from our perspective, we can see Petrarchism as just that: an intriguing, systematic ordering of the discourse of erotic desire. Today, even if we recognize frustration and contradiction as recurring parts of our own experiences of love, we may see Petrarchism as archaic and artificial, and (as I shall suggest soon) there are aspects of it which have been individually destructive and socially exploitative over hundreds of years. But that it seemed "natural" over a period of perhaps three centuries shows how ideology, the social glue of a particular culture, works.

Now to particulars. Petrarchan poetry is written predominantly in the subject position of a suffering male lover contemplating a beloved's, usually a woman's, effects on him. From thousands of poems, a composite beloved can be readily constructed, her physical parts described or modestly alluded to. Such charms would often be set forth, either rapturously or satirically, noting, even listing, her ravishing physical characteristics, her golden hair, doe-like breasts, rosy cheeks, and other physical charms. The most crucial characteristic is the contrast between her fair outside and her icy or stony heart, which inevitably causes the lover suffering. But Petrarchism focuses on such physical characteristics less than their effect on the lover. Typically, it is expressed as what (I will soon suggest) we might fairly term masochism, the woman's supposedly causing her lover to feel cruelty, disease, distress, and pain. Her effects upon him are described as being like fire, ice, blindness, even mental instability, and yet he is inevitably drawn to her, puzzled over his self-torture. The peculiar impasse of Petrarchan love involves frustration balanced by hope, the love of God by the love of the world, obscurity by fame, passivity by restlessness, public by private, icy coldness by the fire of passion. Consummation—indeed, even presence—is rare in this poetry. The beloved is notable primarily for her absence; presence is not conducive to love or poetry. Indeed, there would be no need to write if presence were attained.

The second major characteristic of Petrarchism is, therefore, that it is more than simply a rhetoric for declaring passionate but frustrated love. While it may seem to focus on the depicting and idealizing of the beloved and to offer her patient, unrewarded service, it is rather a theater of the lover's own desires: rarely are the beloved's accorded autonomy; even more rarely is there a desire for mutuality or negotiation. She is the subject of his anguish, manipulation, and struggles of conscience. What does Petrarch's Laura reply to him? What does Philip Sidney's Stella reply to Astrophil's earnest self-regarding pleas for favor? We are told occasionally, but generally, the beloved's words are given to her by the poet. She is located within a discourse in which she is predominantly a focus of his gaze, obsessions and insecurities.

The Petrarchan poet, then, could focus on the beloved's external beauties, her surroundings, even on objects associated with her: a favorite pet, her handkerchief, or other accouterments; perhaps more spiritual qualities such as her chastity, unapproachability, wisdom, virtue. But the real focus is on her effects on the poet himself; she is the means by which his identity and autonomy can be established. Both her characteristics, and the events of their relationship put him in a state of deliciously anxious fluidity, stimulating a rhetoric for the construction of a remarkably fluid self in a world that is unpredictable, uncertain, always threatening. Petrarchan love is claustrophobic, self-conscious, and introverted. The "self"—the sense of being a "subject"— that emerges from such poetry is consequently an especially insecure one, and the poem is an attempt to achieve some momentary stability. The Petrarchan "I" is a device that looks as if it is stable, but in fact it puts into discourse a radically decentered self. Petrarchism thus provided a perfect language for the aspiring courtier in that it created a discourse in which his restless, anxious self could be temporarily stabilized. Greenblatt has written of the "self-fashioning" of the Renaissance courtier, but the phrase perhaps implies that the courtier is totally in control of his choice. As we follow through a collection of courtly lyrics, we discover that the self that writes is continually rewritten, and the more it writes, the more words interpose themselves as frustration, as negative mediations between the desperate subject and its object of desire, or between, in Eugene Vance's words, "the spoken signifier and its signified, dispossessing both into a centerless, unending productivity." Hence the longer the self of the Petrarchan sequence pursues its goals the less likely they will be materialized—"the less its signifiers point to some expressive or referential context: they point, instead, only to the discourse in which they begin and end."[6] The desired object constantly recedes: its primary function is merely to frustrate the final, unreachable, guarantee of the identity of the self which pursues it.

When we also consider the larger structure of Petrarchan sonnet sequences, the ways in which they might be organized by poet or editor, a similar unresolvability presents itself. The sonnet form obsessively accretes minute and often seemingly random details. We come to the unresolved end of one sonnet and then are pressured to go on. Many readers attempt to deal with this impasse by looking for narrative continuity to provide a comforting unity. Should a sonnet sequence be read as a narrative? Cumulatively rather than randomly? Typically, linkages may be suggested by the poet, or the lover, even (at times) the lady, but such hints of a plot are invited rather than imposed. Neely has argued that in a typical Petrarchan collection fragmentary composition, reflecting the randomness and unpredictability of the experiences of desire, might be followed by a careful rearrangement by author or editor to suggest the outlines of a general sequence. A common rearrangement would be to start with an introductory sonnet setting forth the initial attraction of lover to the beloved and often discussing the lover's need to express himself in poetry; this would typically be followed by poems showing the ebb and flow of the lover's suit; a set of concluding poems might detail his loss of her. But some collections (for instance, Drayton's *Idea*, which went through six editions) changed radically over their lifetime, with each new arrangement allowing for modifications of the sequence. Germaine Warkentin notes that the "collectivity" of Petrarchan sonnet sequences is built on the concept of *varatio* (variety), "a simple but flexible structural concept: that of a work exhibiting the variety of the moods of the lover, set forth in *rime sparse* or separate lyrics," a principle which, she adds, English poets tended to imitate more and more loosely.[7]

Petrarchism, then, afforded both its writers and readers a suggestive mixture of poetic workshop and psychological encounter session. It provided a space in which the poet could experiment, trying out figure and form; it offered a psycho-erotic model in which ideological and social tensions were acted out. The sonnet itself is such a space—a stanza, a small room, "much excellentcie ordred in a small room," as Pembroke's tutor Daniel put it.[8] It is often argued that, through the course of the sixteenth century, there is a distinctive English adaption of Petrarchism. It is seen, the argument goes, most especially in Wyatt's or Sidney's unusual emphasis on the moral dilemmas of erotic experience and in the relative neglect by English poets of the spiritual dimension of Petrarch's love for Laura. It was also adapted outside as well as inside poetry—to very precise political purposes, especially in England, where the fact of the Virgin Queen on the throne produced an extraordinary transference of the Petrarchan manner to politics. Elizabeth systematically encouraged her (male) courtiers to relate to her in the role of Petrarchan lovers, always in hope, caught between desire for advancement and fear of losing their places, singlemindedly devoted to the hopeless attainment of her favor, and grateful for any token. So Petrarchism was not simply a charming and sophisticated fashion for court entertainment or for fictionalizing love affairs. It became, especially in the last twenty years of the century, part of public policy. The Elizabethans perceived Petrarch's poems as a rhetorical master-text, adaptable to the increasingly self-conscious rhetorical world of the court, where display and self-aggrandizement were, paradoxically, associated with appropriate humility, and thus became the means of acquiring place and the possibility of power. Elizabeth turned her position as a woman to advantage by encouraging her courtiers to adopt the role of a Petrarchan lover.

Behind the poems of the two Sidney cousins lay not only this long and flexible poetic tradition, but a family of poets. Pembroke's mother never wrote in the Petrarchan mode, but some of her verse translations of both the psalms and, in particular, of Petrarch's *Trionfi della Morte*, show a sophisticated awareness of Petrarch's impact. The two most immediate members of the Sidney family who wrote major collections of Petrarchan love poems were Mary's father Robert and the cousins' dead uncle, Philip. Sir Philip Sidney was "our English Petrarke," claimed Sir John Harington, who "often conforteth him selfe in his sonnets of Stella, though dispairing to attain his desire." From about 1581 or 1582, when Sidney wrote *Astrophil and Stella*, and especially after 1591, when it was first published, readers sighed over its tragi-comic enactment of what Sidney calls "poor Petrarch's long deceased woes." *Astrophil and Stella* marks the triumphant maturity of Elizabethan poetry and the first full, belated but spectacular, adaptation of Petrarchism to English aristocratic culture.[9]

In Sidney's poetry Petrarchism is more than a style of verse or even a rhetoric of desire. For him, poetry and its social uses were inseparable. In *Astrophil and Stella* the court, the primary institution shaping the writing of poetry is evoked in the tournaments, the gossip of "curious wits" or the "courtly nymphs" who populate the poems, and the continual sense of them as a well-placed and sophisticated audience. But more than just the glittering surface of the court energizes the poems: despite his posthumous reputation as the perfect Renaissance courtier,

Sidney's career was one of political disappointment and humiliation; he seems to have been increasingly torn between public duty and private desire, much in the way the hero of his sonnet sequence is. What gives Sidney's life and poetry alike their particular caste is an inwardness, not necessarily or exclusively autobiographical, that in large part arises from the way his Protestantism interacts with the psychologizing rhetoric of the Petrarchan mode. In his political career, Sidney was a hotheaded Protestant aristocrat; in his poetry, in A. C. Hamilton's phrase, he was "a Protestant English Petrarch."[10] The inwardness of the poems—not necessarily, it should be noted, their supposed autobiographical dimension, but their concern with Astrophil's self-conciousness, even self-centredness, as lover, poet, courtier, and, through Astrophil, with the "self" we partly take on when we read—is a blend of Protestant and Petrarchan self-obsession, played out across the political tensions of being a courtier in the court of Queen Elizabeth.

Because it is clear that Mary Wroth in particular studied her uncle's poems very closely, it is important to survey them. *Astrophil and Stella* is a sequence of 108 sonnets and eleven songs that anatomizes the love of a young, restless, ambitious, and self-conscious courtier, Astrophil, for a court lady, Stella. The lover's aim is set out in the opening sonnet, where he claims "I sought fit words to paint the blackest face of woe / Studying inventions fine, her wits to entertaine." We are taken into the familiar world of Petrarchan convention and cliché: Astrophil is the doubting, apologetically aggressive lover, Stella the golden-haired, black-eyed, chaste, (usually) distant, and (finally) unobtainable beloved. The landscape is familiar—hope and absence, frustrated desire alleviated temporarily by writing, the beautiful woman with the icy heart who pitilessly resists siege and yet encourages her admirer, and the lover's final anguish at her "absent presence" (Sonnet 104). Yet however unsatisfied Astrophil's love, the sequence is characterized by a sophisticated playfulness. Sidney invites his readers to share his enjoyment at the varied follies and complexities of human love. We laugh with him; we laugh at or are sympathetic with (or perhaps disapproving of) poor Astrophil. But what of Stella? Does she share in the fun? Astrophil does not want us, although it is arguable that Sidney might, to call into question the power of his anguish or the centrality of his struggles of conscience. Stella is, like other Petrarchan mistresses, acknowledged only as she is manipulated by or impinges on Astrophil's consciousness. She is the product of her poet-lover's desires. Sidney's sonnets provide a theatre of desire in which the man has all the active roles and in which the woman is silent or merely iconic, most present when she refuses him or is absent. *Astrophil and Stella* is encoded within an overwhelmingly male-dominated discourse.

At this point I invite my reader to imagine these poems being read, perhaps in the late 1590s or early in the new century, by a young woman, perhaps at the time she, too, was starting to enter the court—specifically, the author's niece, Mary. How would she locate herself in relation to the poems? Where could she locate something akin to her own sense of agency? Even in fantasy? On which figures might her fantasies fix? On the poet? Or his partly fictional character, the lover? Or the beloved? Do the facts that she is a Sidney, perhaps already an aspiring writer herself, and a woman, make a difference to her reading? Even if Stella's replies are not in most of the poems (and where they are, as in Song 8, they are, we should note, reported to us through Astrophil's words), what might she say? Is her silence the repression of the character? Or is it, more directly, that of Sidney? Or of a whole cultural blindness that fixed women as objects of gaze and analysis within a discourse they did not invent and could not control? And how did a reader who was a woman locate her interests in that discourse?

An older criticism faced (or avoided) some of these issues by focusing on the biographical origins of the sequence and identifying the meaning of the sequence with the author's life. In part as an outcome of the Romantic valorization of poetry as the overflow of "sincerity" or "genuine" experience, earlier critics sentimentalized the obvious connections between Sidney's life and the fiction of Astrophil's love for Stella into a poetic *roman-à-clef*. But however naive a reading, it may also have been part of Sidney's niece's reading. Sidney certainly plays with some identification between himself and Astrophil and between Stella and Lady Penelope Rich (née Devereux) for whom Sidney was once suggested as a husband. Lady Rich lived until 1607 and was close to the Sidney family, as was Fulke Greville, who is also referred to in the collection. Reading the poems within the family may well have smoothed over some of the rhetorical subtleties with which Sidney complicates the relationship between his characters and the events of his life. Alan Sinfield points out that "the hints of Sidney in the poem" are made deliberately ambiguous by bringing the poet to the surface of the poems alongside and in a shifting relationship to the lover, so that any desire to see Astrophil unambiguously "as a fiction or as Sidney" or "a stable compound" of both "is frustrated."[11] And just as Sidney manages simultaneously to have much in common with Astrophil, be sympathetic with him, and yet to criticize or laugh at him, so the gap between Stella and the historical Lady Rich is even wider and always shifting—at best one can regard some of the references as sly or wistful fantasies. But read within the multiple Sidney cousins' family romances, such subtlety might go unnoticed. Part of the fascination Petrarch had for English poets, after all, was a puzzlement about how Petrarchan conventions might fit such "real" experiences.

One aspect of the collection, and the Petrarchan mode generally, to which Mary may well have responded with some intensity, then, was its offering a language by which to articulate "personal" dilemmas. It provided a mode of confession in which the confesser and confessor are, initially at least, the same person. Of course, once the poems are written and offered to readers other than the poet, another especially seductive aspect of Petrarchan rhetoric takes over. The Petrarchan lyric is typically inaugurating, requiring completion in its audience's experiences and responses. The continual isolation of the "I," focused in Astrophil's obsession with the self, directs us continually to our own self-consciousness. Even Sonnet 37, one of the two so-called "Rich" sonnets, where references to Lord and Lady Rich seem to be directly made, is especially effective because of the witty complexity of its appeal to multiple audiences. It starts as a therapeutic exercise and then, in the final line, turns outward to an audience which knows, or now knows, or at least may have become curious about, the identification of Stella with Lady Rich. Was Penelope Devereux Rich in the original audience? Would she have been embarrassed or amused? Either would be possible—just as other listeners' and readers' reactions, and therefore their readings of the poem, could have varied from indignation to titillation, puzzlement to disapproval. What might have been Sidney's niece's response? To what extent would it have been self-regarding? "This is about me, too." Or: "This is about 'us'." And what about other readers, in and outside the family, whom Mary might have known or with whom she might have discussed the poems? Harington's reading of the sequence as romantic gossip is one such; and the fact that the pirated 1591 edition of *Astrophil and Stella* omitted the "Rich" sonnets might give credence to a biographical reading. Another reading close to the family circle is Greville's, whose *Caelica* is in part an extended negative commentary on the celebration of erotic self-indulgence that constitutes one strand of Sidney's collection. In recent years, indeed, it has become fashionable to see Sidney's poems as condemning Astrophil, even to see him by the end of the sequence learning from his moral errors. It is a reading that wishes, perhaps, to see "Leave me ô love, which reachest but to dust," a sonnet which predated *Astrophil and Stella*, as a satisfactory conclusion to the collection, and the final *Astrophil and Stella* sonnets, 107 and 108, as a resolution. Yet counteracting such readings is the way Petrarchism is built precisely on the power of a lack of closure, on the perpetual deference of desire's consummation.

Did Mary Wroth and William Herbert, in fact, read their famous uncle's poems? It seems inconceivable that they did not. In the case of Pembroke, it was made clear, over and over, that he was the family's heir to the mantle of the famous dead hero, as a soldier, a patron of the arts, a statesman, and (it is therefore likely) as a poet. His mother was one of the editors of his uncle's writings, and many of his manuscripts had been entrusted to her care. But Mary Wroth was also seen as the inheritor of the family muse, not least because her own father was also a poet, working in the Petrarchan mode and clearly basing his own poems on his dead brother's. For the other important predecessor of the Sidney cousins is Mary's father, Robert. It is only in recent years that it has been widely known that Robert wrote poetry—P. J. Croft's rediscovery of the poems dates only from the 1970s—and even in his lifetime it seems to have been known pricipally to the family. During his life and after, Robert was overshadowed by the brilliance of his elder brother. In his early life Robert had none of Philip's prestige or flamboyance. He dutifully went on a tour of Europe, pursued by letters of advice from his brother as to his reading, chivalric bearing, friends, and finances. In 1585 he accompanied Philip, who had been appointed governor of Flushing, to the Low Countries, and was present at the Battle of Zutphen where Philip was mortally wounded. In short, Robert underwent the usual initiation of the Elizabethan courtier—with the additional burden of being the younger brother of the mercurial Protestant knight so admired by European statesmen, courtiers, and men of letters. In 1584 he married Barbara Gamage after some rather sordid negotiations, though, as I noted in chapter three, their letters later show them to have grown into a most loving couple: he constantly addresses her as "sweet heart" or "dear heart," and the letters are full of sadness over his absence from her and their growing family. In 1594 he wrote "there is no desyre in me so dear as the love I bear you and our children . . . you are married, my dear Barbara, to a husband that is now drawn so into the world and the actions of yt as there is no way to retire myself without trying fortune further."[12]

The intense strain of being absent from both his family and the court during the 1590s is evident throughout Robert's letters. Indeed, we might say with a little (obvious) exaggeration that Philip had the good fortune to die in 1586; Robert had to live on. In 1587 he was his brother's chief mourner and, like his sister Mary, may have turned to poetry as a similar, though less public, attempt to continue his brother's intentions for poetry. He may have decided that Mary, more permanently settled at Wilton in the 1580s with the increasing comings and goings of Greville, Spenser, Daniel, and other poets, was better placed to forward the Sidneian literary revolution, since it was to her that he sent the one extant copy of his manuscript, possibly in one of his much anticipated but infrequent visits to his family in England. It is clear from verbal echoes that Mary read her father's poems, so it may well have been that he had other copies made; or perhaps she would have visited Wilton or Baynard's Castle, where the countess's copy might have been kept. When the countess of Pembroke was revising Philip's psalms, she kept two working manuscripts, one at Wilton, one at Baynard's; she worked on them separately, sometimes transferring changes and experiments between the two copies.[13]

Like his brother's, Robert's poems take the form of a Petrarchan miscellany of sonnets and songs, although they show a greater variety of metrical and stanzaic patterns than the normal sonnet sequence of the 1580s and 1590s—this is a characteristic he shared with his sister, whose *Psalms* involve the most impressive formal experimentation in English verse before Hopkins. But if Robert shares something of his sister's technical daring, nevertheless the most important influence is that of his brother. The sequence is clearly modeled on *Astrophil and Stella*: it mingles sonnets with longer, more emotionally diffuse songs, and, like Philip's, Robert's sequence contains occasional transformations of biographical reference into deviously ambiguous fictions. The whole sequence is characterized by an opaque melancholy, a mood of disturbance and brooding which, while endemic to Petrarchan sonnets in general, nevertheless takes as its subject Robert's reading of his own political and personal career, not least as a member of the Sidney family. But while the collection is a typical Petrarchan miscellany, it is even less united than *Astrophil and Stella* by narrative or characters.

When we set Robert's poems alongside Philip's, as both the cousins would have had the opportunity to do, what do we discover? Robert does not possess Philip's dazzling control of changing dramatic mood within a poem: the emotions of his verse express themselves in broader sweeps, concentrating on generalized feelings about pain, disillusion, absence, and death. But his ear is highly sensitive, and his poems often reverberate with deep, sensuous moods. Poetry made up a small part of his life, though his commitment to its craft and insight was intense. Like his daughter's (as we shall see), the strengths of Robert Sidney's poems lie in the ways their broodings on the great commonplaces of Elizabethan life—time, absence, grief, deprivation—reveal much of the pressures upon poetry by virtue of its place in the ideology of the court whose influence continually haunted him. Most of Robert's poetry was probably written during his long, frustrating tour of duty in the Low Countries, perhaps started (like his sister's) in the late 1580s, but (at least in the only manuscript copy extant) copied probably some time between 1596 and 1598. Perhaps turning to poetry was a reaction not only to his exile from England, but to the melancholy duty of following in his brother's old post. It is possible that having used verse as an emotional relief, it lost its importance for him once he actually returned to England. Much of Robert's verse could therefore be read as a moving expression of a frustrated male politician's escape-world, yearning for the security of his wife and family back home at Penshurst.

But to offer a biographical explanation of these poems would be to oversimplify them, however much that aspect of the poems may have impressed his daughter, who would certainly catch the geographical and probably many of the personal references. Sidney's sentiments are highly typical of late Elizabethan courtiers and courtly poets. Like his brother's, Robert Sidney's poems are sites of struggle where the "self" of the poems is a cultural creation not to be simply identified with the historical figure who held the pen and wrote them. They were the means by which Sidney tried to write himself into the world just as, as I will show in chapter six, his daughter's were.

So there are clearly poems where details from Sidney's life are certainly used, where "the hardy captain, unused to retire," speaks directly of his turning from the Low Countries where he feels exiled, "to the West," where "love fast holds his heart" (Sonnet 7; Song 6). The sixth song of the collection is an especially revealing piece—as well as being perhaps his most impressive poem. Like Ralegh's haunting "As You Came from the Holy Land," it is based upon the traditional lost ballad of a pilgrim traveling to Walsingham. Robert Sidney's version is an evocative 136–1ine dialogue between a pilgrim and a lady who presumably represents Robert's wife, while "the knight that loves me best" and whose "griefs livery wears," and who "to the West . . . turns his eyes" is Robert's wistful projection of his own exiled self, held by duty to the Low Countries away from "the lady that doth rest near Medwayes sandy bed." Penshurst Place, the Sidney home, where Mary grew up, stands on the Medway River just outside Tonbridge and almost due west of Flushing (Robert actually revised this particular line to read "near ritch Tons sandy bed," which of course refers to Tonbridge).

The sixth song is the most clearly autobiographical poem in the sequence, projecting the partly calculated, partly wistful, view of a frustrated personal and political career. Its primary readers were, no doubt, Sidney's immediate family: his wife, sister, and (perhaps a little later) his growing daughter, who was probably about nine when the poem was composed. The bulk of the collection, in traditional Petrarchan fashion, is ostensibly concerned with love, and is similar to a host of sequences written in the 1590s, such as Daniel's *Delia* and Drayton's *Idea*. The diction is typical of the English *petrarchisti*. The lover's "soul" exists in "purest fyre" (Song 4); he accepts both the joys and griefs of love, in his "bonds of service without ende" (Sonnet 13). This is the altogether familiar Petrarchan world of plaint and paradox: on the one hand, the high idealism of the lover who affirms the beauty of "those fair eyes" which "shine in their clear former light" (Song 12); on the other hand, the "pains which I uncessantly sustain" (Sonnet 2). The beloved's beauties are "born of the heavens, my sowles delight" (Sonnet 3), while the lover's passions are "purest flames kindled by beauties rare" (Sonnet 4). As he contemplates in pleasurable agony how she takes "pleasure" in his "cruelty" (Sonnet 25), he asks her why she "nourishes" poisonous weeds of cold despair in love's garden instead of the plants and trees of love's true faith and zeal (Song 22).

This basic Petrarchan situation of frustration, contradiction, and paradox is decked out in familiar neoplatonic garb. The world is a dark cave where love's lights never shine except through the beloved's eyes, the "purest stars, whose never dying fires" (Sonnet 1) constantly burn a path between the heavens and the lover's soul. Sexual desire is rarely explicitly mentioned: the dominant mood is that of melancholy; it focuses to an unusual degree on the lover's helplessness and especially on torture, disease, and violence. The lover is a lashed slave, flung from rocks, a leper, racked by gangrene, and repeatedly in violent wars. As I will show in chapter six, similar though more explicitly self-directed violence also characterizes his daughter's poems.

Robert's poems are less versatile metrically and metaphorically than Philip's, and have little of Philip's sly humor. Typical is the brief, pessimistic Song 17, which on one level, at any rate, seems to reflect upon a deeply tragic event in the poet's experience. The first stanza sets the note of brooding melancholy:

> The sun is set, and masked night
> Veils heaven's fair eyes:
> Ah what trust is there to a light
> That so swift flies.

In the second stanza of this superb, cryptic little poem, the speaker (unusually, for Sidney and the tradition generally) is perhaps a woman; the poem expresses a helpless, brooding bitterness:

> A new world doth his flames enjoy,
> New hearts rejoice:
> In other eyes is now his joy
> In other choice.

Sidney's brooding over absence, delay, and loneliness have a conventional enough tenor: the lover suffers incessantly from "griefs sent from her whom in my soul I bless" (Song 23); continually he feels that "delays are death" (Song 18), as he waits "on unknown shore, with weather hard distressed" (Sonnet 22). He presents himself repeatedly as an exiled and neglected knight who has beseeched the pilgrim of the

144

Walsingham poem to give his abandoned lady his undying devotion. Such common Petrarchan motifs are often made peculiarly effective by the grave, deliberate, melancholic movement of the lines, which convey the passion, the hopelessness, and yet the continuing devotion of the lover. That tone of solemn devotion is also something that characterizes his daughter's poems.

Intellectually, Robert's verse is not as rich a revelation of the peculiar strains and repressions of the period as Philip's. An aspiring and anxious courtier, directing his poems at particular (rarely, of course, directly stated) political ends, his lyrics are intellectually commonplace. Nor, indeed, do the religious references suggest that he shared his brother's and sister's theological interests. Where religious references do occur in the poems, they are used to darken the established mood or to glance at a necessarily understated political aim rather than to transform a conventional motif into a profound religious speculation. Robert's poems acquire their urgency from their articulations of the political powerlessness not simply of their author but of a particular class of men.

From the elder Sidneys' involvement in Petrarchism it can be seen that the Petrarchan manner was clearly more than a literary fashion; it must have seized upon something very deep-rooted in the culture's "inner lives" to have had that longevity. A major critique of Petrarchism is long overdue. Since my focus in this and the following two chapters is on two poets at the end of a very long and complex history, I can only make suggestions along the lines that such a revisionary reading of the whole Petrarchist tradition might take. But it is an important project, and should involve paying attention to more than a recital of rhetorical devices or to ways in which the tradition allegorized religious or erotic commonplaces. Above all, we need to take note of the blatant yet (at least in standard scholarly accounts) unnoticed gender politics of this enormously influential discursive system.

As a starting point, here, with changes that I will discuss below, is a stimulating recent account of the "inner life" of Petrarchism, which extends some of the points with which I have started my discussion of it:

> Petrarchism is theater, the production of a scenario, for which characters—in the form of people, parts of people, and nonhuman (including inanimate) objects are cast. The performance is played before an audience, a crucial member of which is the Petrarchan lover himself viewing [himself] performing . . . Petrarchism is a detour that, at best, leads asymtotically to intimacy: it never arrives . . . Petrarchism is centered not upon the partner, but upon the lover . . . The pain and frustration of earlier times live on unresolved, carried within, always a potential threatening force motivating one to resolutions that never quite work, to an undoing never quite done.

This probably would be accepted as an accurate, if incomplete, account of the major dynamics of Petrarchism. The writer, however, would not easily be recognized as an expert in the field—although he was certainly a world authority in his own. In quoting his opinion, I have cheated, but only slightly: apart from a few brief elisions, by substituting the words "Petrarchism" or "Petrarchan lover" for the words the writer actually used. What I have given is a quotation from one of the late Robert Stoller's studies of erotic behavior. The words Stoller uses are "perversion" and "perverse person." He goes on to draw conclusions that would also be acceptable (were we not now alerted) as a description of other aspects of Petrarchism. The perverse situation (I restore Stoller's terms, though the reader is invited to substitute for it as we move along) is scripted to help the lover deal with the overwhelming power of the object of his desire. Since her full reality cannot be faced, she can be accommodated by the lover's mind only if she is accorded less than full personhood. He therefore depicts her as the "possessor of selected parts or qualities only. He anatomizes them. And if even that is too intimate," he turns from human to "inanimate objects, such as garments, granting them a certain amount of humanness." The careful scripting of these erotic scenarios is seen as an "aesthetic task," undertaken in the spirit of (dare one say it?) *sprezzatura*: the perverse scene is "most pleasing when it is seamless, when it does not give hints that it was constructed, when it looks as if it sprang full-blown from unconscious depths. If not created spontaneously . . . then it should look as if it was."[14]

My argument is not that "Petrarchism" ought to be added to the list of common paraphilia, along with coprophilia, kleptomania, or exhibitionism. Such a classification all too easily becomes reified into a moralistic dualism implied by such categories as "normal" and "pathological," which Freud certainly encouraged and which a century and a half after *Psychopathia Sexualis* still dominates popular discussion of sexuality. Like the far more perceptive Freud who elided the "perverse" and the "normal" in one of this chapter's epigraphs, I want to suggest rather that the longevity of Petrarchism was based on the remarkable extent to which it incorporated the major fantasies of patriarchal gender assignments and sexual pathologies. Here, for once, I am (partly) in agreement with Paglia, who sees Spenser's *Faerie Queene* as "an encyclopedic catalog" of the "perversions" of "Petrarchan stereotypes," akin to "Krafft-Ebing's *Psychopathia Sexualis*: not only rape and homosexuality but priapism, nymphomania, exhibitionism, incest, bestiality, necrophilia, fetishism, transvestism, and transsexualism."[15] Beyond the rhetorical conventions of Petrarchism the men and women who were interpellated into it played far more than a set of rhetorical scripts. They were acting out patterns of perversely repetitive strategies that were the outcome

146

of the dominant gender assignments of Western patriarchy. Historically, Petrarchism was predominantly a male discourse, and its central psycho-cultural trope is the quintessential male perversion, fetishism. It characteristically incorporates other typical male perversions, including aspects of both sadism and masochism, exhibitionism, voyeurism, and—at times, catering for more specialist tastes—transvestism, pedophilia, and necrophilia. When considering Mary Wroth as a reader of her father's and uncle's poems, and when (in chapter six) looking directly at her own poetry, I shall raise the question of what happens when a woman enters this predominantly male discursive playground. In either the reading or writing situation, are there signs of what Kaplan terms the "characteristic female perversions"? The central one, extreme submissiveness, is clearly relevant to Wroth, as is—at least in the sense of "stealing" the Petrarchan subject position—kleptomania: she read her father's and uncle's poems and her own show evident signs of learning from that reading experience; she read in (and in a sense was "written" by) the whole Petrarchan tradition. But since she also wanted to write, we might ask whether such "theft" and appropriation can be acts of agency. When is stealing justified? As to the other characteristic "perversions," whether there is space even in as hospitable a discourse as Petrarchism for self-mutilation (including self-cutting, surgical addiction, and trichotillomania), female impersonation, homovestism, anorexia, and the role of "the incest wife" remains to be seen.[16]

I joke, and yet I am deadly serious. We all, even today, carry with us the remnants of discursive systems we inherit from our cultural pasts and of which we often have little conscious knowledge or control. In our attempts to make sense of our desires, their unpredictabilities, joys, losses, repressions, and recurrences, necessarily we have recourse to these remnants. We are subordinated to them and steal from them. We construct stories, for ourselves and others, about those acts. It is (maybe) some comfort to know what Freud noted, that unlike other animals, human beings "are creatures whose sexual lives are governed almost entirely by fantasy," and that the fantasies we, all of us, construct or live out inevitably draw on the narratives through which our earliest, polymorphously perverse yearnings were realized or repressed. Nevertheless, as Freud also puts it in the remark with which I started this chapter, "the extraordinary wide dissemination of the perversions forces us to suppose that the disposition to perversions is itself of no great rarity but must form part of what passes as the normal."[17] Comfort? It depends on the degree of pain with which we live out our family romances. But perhaps to know more of at least some of the specific contradictions in which we are caught is to at least open the possibility of agency, if only to the extent of choosing the strategies by which we might try to achieve it. After all, it is real men and women, not merely fictional figures or "subject positions" or "structures of feeling," who have suffered from, as well as been transfigured by, their own and others' compulsions, needs, and lacks, and it behooves us to understand what languages our cultural pasts have given us, and denied us, to cope with our desires. Far more than a fashionable literary mode or set of moral commonplaces is at stake here.

My argument can, I believe, be widely illustrated by poets from Petrarch until well into the seventeenth century and beyond: as a number of commentators have noted, Petrarchism is alive and well even in aspects of contemporary popular culture, and in not a few of our scripts of desire. Erotic idealization, as has often been pointed out, is a form of "oppression through exaltation," in which the object of idealization (usually a woman) rarely exists in a relationship of mutuality or as the subject of her own desire. She is "overvalued," as Freud put it, in order that she can be, the lover hopes, exclusively the subject of his desires. Whenever she does act in relation to her own wishes—predominantly by rejecting him—she is castigated by him as cruel, a beauteous outside framing a heart of stone, or in psychoanalytic terms, the punishing mother figure from whom he is expelled and whom he continues to desire. It is as if she compensates for a deficiency, a lack, in the wholeness of the male lover, thereby putting into question that wholeness and its apparent power. Within these compulsively repeated patterns, the Petrarchan lyric traditionally presented itself as a man's appeal for mercy based on an acknowledgment of fear of discontinuity and helplessness before (or even in the absence of) the cruel, hard-hearted, alluringly yet frustratingly chaste mistress.[18] Her effects on him are like those the child feels in the birth, weaning, and separation/individuation process, or whenever he must leave the comfort of the mother and is thrown alone into the world, yet finding himself inevitably drawn, in reality or fantasy, back to her, puzzled yet reassured by the familiarity of his tortures. She is the all-powerful mother, simultaneously loved and hated, on whose nurturance he is totally dependent, and yet from whom he must break if he is to achieve his (and the gendered pronoun is deliberate) individuation. However much the beloved's absence may be bewailed, it is therefore, paradoxically, both welcome and necessary. The poem, as many commentators point out, cannot be written in the beloved's presence, and so absence becomes a precondition for writing of the miseries of her absence. That works as a clever and recurrent trope. But on the psychological level, it indicates something more deeply rooted in the gender construction of the male. The Petrarchan idealization of the beloved is characteristically accompanied by fear of her. When she does respond, the male lover typically finds some way not just to express gratitude and dependence, but to assert his further power. He cannot bear the full presence of the beloved because her claims on him are so overwhelming, and he knows that he must reject her if he is to assert his male autonomy.

If the beloved embodies both the alluring security and the threat of the mother, whom the male desires and rejects, and yet to whom he is inevitably drawn back, he needs to construct a satisfying narrative of this struggle—to justify it to both her and himself. The presence/absence paradox in Petrarchism is an adult narrativization of Freud's *fort/da* game, in which the child pushes the toy away in order to have the pleasure of having it come back (and also, as the game acquires more potent fantasies, to punish the object for its power over him): "the vicissitudes of the male in his sexualization lead him to fight from the beginning to escape the temptation of returning to his former fusion with the maternal image, holder of primitive power, the phallic mother, the great nurturing mother."[19] What is the story that such a lover constructs? Characteristically, he alleges that it is the beloved's cruelty, not his own desires, that is depriving him of fulfillment. His only means of avoiding the chaos of abandonment is to control her, or at least fold her into a narrative in which she is his. The classic Petrarchan trope is the lover's devotion to the beloved's picture; he constructs his narratives around the stimulation he gains from looking at it or from the mental image he holds as if it were also a picture of her. She thus becomes his creation, and her autonomy consists only in being "constant," holding still, in the picture frame as it were, so he might fix the particular image of her which he desires. The thought that she might have her own desires is rarely considered, although the effects of this obsessive male scopophilia—the pleasure gained by viewing objects of desire—upon the woman herself are angrily explored in some of Wroth's poems.

This brings me to another of the long-acknowledged characteristics of Petrarchism: the power it affords to sight, specifically the voyeuristic gaze. Within the Petrarchan system—and perhaps we can widen our own gaze and speak of patriarchy in general—the activity of seeing, as a substitute for (and sometimes a preliminary to) actual physical control is, in Freud's words "the most frequent pathway along which libidinal excitation is aroused." Predictably, Paglia sees voyeurism and scopophilia not merely as inherently male (an arguable position, perhaps), but celebrates it as the essence of the "aggressive eye" of high western art. The "sexual character of western seeing" is, she asserts, at the center of our Apollonian triumphs over (female) nature. This is certainly not, I think, an argument that a man could easily make today. Stoller argues, on the other hand, that scopophilia is predominantly a gender disorder (that is, a disorder in the development of masculinity and femininity) constructed out of a tradition of hostility, involving "*rage* at giving up one's earliest bliss and identification with the mother, *fear* of not succeeding in escaping out of her orbit, and a need for *revenge* for her putting us in this predicament." In Petrarchism the lover's admiring eye attempts to fix the mistress not just as a beautiful object that he wishes to possess, but often as a guarantee against the threat she represents. Psychoanalytic studies of scopophilia have seen the gaze embodying a "pre-oedipal fear . . . of merging and fixing with the mother," which may be protected against only by incessant watching. Stoller argues that "sexual excitement will occur at the moment when adult reality resembles the childhood trauma—the anxiety being re-experienced as excitement."[20] The viewed object is thereby detoxified, relieving the voyeur of his fear either directly or by being projected upon, and so shared with, another. The viewer enjoys closeness without the fear of engulfment. Scopophilic pleasure can be secretive or the man can make sure that the woman "exhibits": that is, she knows she is being seen and apparently involved in his fears, and her knowledge represents his superego giving permission for his own look/show impulses.

How do these characteristic male strategies for dealing with fears that may seem so basic to our culture's construction of gender be-come encoded in Petrarchan poems? The male gaze is predominantly directed, most obviously in the blazon, at a woman as the sum of separable parts. Nancy Vickers points out that the distinction between a woman's "beauty" and her "beauties" is a consistent feature of the whole Petrarchan tradition. The "whole body" of Petrarch's Laura, she argues, appears to him at times "less than some of its parts," and the technique of describing the mistress through the isolation of those parts "became universal . . . When late-Renaissance theorists, poets, and painters represented woman's body," Petrarch's verse justified their aesthetic choices, making her "available to be partitioned, with each of her features accorded object status separate from the totality." As the duchess of Newcastle wrote—a woman voicing the seemingly natural ideology of patriarchy—daughters "are but branches which by marriage are broken off from the root from whence they spring, and ingrafted into the stock of the other family, so that daughters are to be accounted but as movable goods or furnitures that wear out."[21] Thus a woman is rendered passive and (in the sense Shakespeare puns in sonnet 126) passively rendered. There were obvious analogies in material practices. As in the case of Mary Wroth herself, women, especially in the aristocracy, were required to consider themselves as family commodities, detachable parts of the family that could be traded, sold, given and received in return for security, comfort, and advancement. The blazon—the ubiquitous list-poem that blatantly articulates the objectifying focus, part by part, on the beloved's features—can thus be seen as a discursive homology to such practices as the marriage negotiations to which Pembroke submitted his prospective wife and to which Mary Wroth was subjected by her father, prospective husband, and (since he had substantial financial support involved in the marriage) Pembroke himself.

It is not that the representation of (or gazing at) human bodies or acts in art is inherently wrong. Nor, as Rosalind Coward points out, is it inherently objectionable to gain pleasure from the representation of parts of the body. "In viewing pictures which we might find pleasurable," she argues, "it is often a detail on which we might focus: a certain expression in the eyes, the nape of the neck, the way a hand rests on a part of the body." It is rather that the predominant codes of patriarchal representation—and, clearly, not just in Petrarchan poetry— are overwhelmingly invasive, even violent, requiring the submission of the female body to passivity and fragmentation as a means of controlling the viewer's own fears. When T. S. Eliot's Prufrock voices his anxiety that the "women" will "formulate" him with their looks, as they would an insect, he is clearly voicing a man's apprehension of finding himself subject to the way women have felt positioned by the male gaze for centuries. "Every perversion," writes Kaplan, "is an effort to give some representation to, while controlling, the full strength of potentially mur- derous impulses, generated by fears of both being controlled and losing access to the person who will serve to control that fear."[22]

Petrarchism is intimately, and inextricably, bound up with the pre- mier male perversion that seeks to come to terms with the fear of the beloved's overwhelming power, fetishism. Clinical studies suggest that the fetishist is usually not trying to victimize or control the beloved, since fetishism is, like Petrarchism itself, directed at the effects of the beloved upon the lover, not the reverse. His goal is rather to find just the right intensity of the beloved's power that he can, for the moment, deal with. If her effects on him become too overwhelming, how much, he asks, can he bear without banishing her? The fetish is the attempted answer to that question. "A sexual fetish," notes Kaplan, "is significantly more reliable than a living person . . . when the full sexual identity of the woman is alive, threatening, dangerous, unpredictable, the desire she arouses must be invested in the fetish . . . fetish objects are relatively safe, easily available, undemanding of reciprocity." Likewise, the fetishistic narrative is designed to divert attention away from the "whole story by focusing attention on the detail." Unlike a real woman, who may (presumably!) have desires of her own, and therefore in patriarchal society, be even more threatening to the supposedly autonomous male, the fetish can be commanded, assigned multiple or contradictory parts, and (except in the masochistic scenario, a special case to which I come soon) will not make demands of its own. Fetishes are created as nodes of meaning within the narrativizations of the earliest, most primitive of family romances, the desires to emulate, replace or seduce the parents. They acquire their magical power as part of the primitive fantasy structure of the child contemplating how large, powerful, and irresistible his or her parents seem. In adult life, fetishism "entails a displacement of sexual desire away from the whole identity" of the beloved to some accessory, they (or chain of substitutes for them) may be reactivated and often enormously elaborated in adulthood, their origins long lost under the accretions of later narratives. Kaplan comments: "the extravagant sexual theories of little boys may be outgrown and forgotten but they are never entirely given up. They are repressed and temporarily banished from consciousness but persist as unconscious fantasies that are ready to return whenever there is a serious threat, imagined or actual, to a man's hard-earned masculinity."[23]

Fetishism, though rarely discussed as such, has in effect long been noticed as a major ingredient of Petrarchism. Fetishes, of course, may be anything that the erotic imagination imbues with metonymic power—shoes, clothing, pets, portraits, locks of hair, odors, sounds. The clinical literature is full of stories of the bizarre, banal, outrageous, and ordinary in this most widespread of male paraphilia, as, indeed, is the Petrarchan tradition. It is as if the lover can deal with a woman best—or, as he would put it, when he most admires her—only when he can estheticize her, when her beauty and desirability are a compliment to him, and the power of her physical presence no longer a threat. He uses, to employ a photographic metaphor, a freeze-frame, capturing her for all time, not as true to life, but true to what he can bear to in relation to the ways the ways he has learnt from his culture to depict women and their effects on him. His move, from the real to the fetish, is precisely the reverse of Orlando's determination in *As You Like It* to move from the world of fantasy to the world of the real: "I can live no longer by thinking" (5. 2. 50).

Another standard trope of Petrarchism is that of rejection: the lover's mistress is absent, unkind, loves another, has a cold heart that denies her fair outside; he himself has no peace and yet is continually at war; he burns and freezes. There is, in short, a strong strain of masochism involved in the Petrarchist pose. In this case, the scripts are subtly different from those I have so far discussed which assert male dominance and independence and yet necessitate finding a way back to the love object that. Masochism, according to Freud and much popular parlance, is bound up with sadism, and there are no doubt cases where the same person is caught up in both. But the partner of a masochist does not have to be a sadist. The peculiar script of masochism is that it requires

152

only a cooperator, who need not even be aware that he or she has been co-opted into the masochistic narrative. The essence of masochism is the pleasure taken in delayed gratification, in the pain of denial and waiting: the masochist "waits for pleasure as something that is bound to be late, and expects pain as the condition that will finally ensure (both physically and morally) the advent of pleasure." Masochism involves assigning to the other the absolute power of forbidding pleasure—in the case of male masochism, giving the all-powerful mother the power of the Law to rule absolutely, at least within the script he laid down, his life and death. Such a description hardly needs examples from the Petrarchist canon. It is most widespread in the "serious," less so among the "witty" Petrarchists; it is especially found in those for whom love is a substitute for or pathway to God, and where self-denial and delayed gratification are means to what in *Astrophil and Stella*, 63 Sidney terms "heavenly bliss." It is ubiquitous in Petrarch, in Sidney, in Shakespeare. It is found less in Donne, and by the time Petrarchism has reached the Cavalier poets, it has virtually been eliminated and replaced by the masculine bravado of scorn. Pembroke's poems contain little of it, except as part of a posture to be repudiated by a more direct misogyny. Masochism, however, and of a far more deterministic kind, is a predominant strain of Wroth's poems.

This leads to the crucial question at the center of this chapter. What place does a woman occupy in Petrarchism, which is so obviously a predominantly male discourse? To answer that, one might focus on the degree of autonomy a male poet allows the woman in his verse. She (and the personal pronoun is barely appropriate since "she" is so completely "his" creation) is entirely a product of the discourse that she supposedly shares. She is asserted to control her lover's destiny, and yet she is allowed to operate only within a structure of control and domination. She is the object by means of which he can indulge his anguish, his pleas, his manipulations. Either way, despite his assertions of despair and dependence, in no sense is she ever an agent: she has no choice but to be sexualized, and she is not accorded reciprocal power. If she "move," she is fickle, whereas if he does so, it is part of the necessity of being male, as Donne argues at the end of "A Valediction: Forbidding Mourning."

In this chapter I have suggested that, as a reader of Petrarchism and of its impact not merely in the history of poetic styles, but very specifically within the Sidney family, the two Sidney cousins might well have shared certain assumptions and loyalties generated by the family, but were probably very divided by characteristically gendered reading strategies. The history of reading is not merely a history of ideas about reading, constructing ideal models of reading as predictable from the "intentions" of texts; it is a history of real, material readers, men and women, and of the complex social formations that produced them as readers. Just as texts are written within particular social formations, so they are read within what Bennett terms "reading formations," a selection or repertoire of assumptions, attitudes, material practices about how and to what ends to read, who should read, and for what purposes, as coded by institutional, class or gender, or other social factors.[24] Reading is always culture specific, and what appear to be the natural practices by which reading occurs are in fact culturally produced, and so always a site of cultural struggle. The reading of her father's and uncle's poems by Mary Wroth is a dramatic demonstration of these assertions.

We can get a sense of the nature of her reading of their poems and the tradition behind them by asking what kind of reading self their poetry asked for and, in a very real sense, tried to create. Or (another way of putting the same question) what role is the reader asked to occupy in reading the kind of poetry that both Wroth and Pembroke were writing? An immediate difference can be noted between the two cousins' social situatedness in relation to Petrarchan poetry. Most of the poets writing at the time were male courtiers or public servants, and they directed their poetry towards a readership of similar men. The interpellated reader of most kinds of Elizabethan writing is primarily male, a privileged member of a community linked together by the acceptance of a certain view of civil order, supposedly based on a system of universal moral virtues and metaphysical principles. Part of a poet's training was to be aware that the power of poetry resided in the forcefulness of the image that was presented to what Cicero termed the mind's eye of the reader. Sidney emphasizes how poetry aims to produce visible images to move a reader. Peacham and others set out a hierarchy of appropriate rhetorical figures, emphasizing how the reader must seem to see a "lively Image" rather than "a reporte expressed with the tongue." The true poet, writes Sidney, "holdeth children from play, and old men from the chimney corner"; poetry is a more effective teacher than history or philosophy because its power is rooted in its ability to "move." "Delight" captivates a reader; "moving" produces an effect on the will, since, Sidney argues—switching back to an Aristotelian dictum—"it is not gnosis but praxis" which "must be the fruit" of teaching: "truly I have known men that even with reading Amadis de Gaule . . . have found their hearts moved to the exercise of courtesy, liberality, and especially courage."[25] On the surface, such statements still preserve the determinative nature of the writer's intention—that the effective poet communicates a "message" to a responsive reader who will thereby be moved to virtuous action; this puts the reading of poetry in line with the reading (or hearing) of the homilies. But Sidney confesses that poetry's ability to move its readers is not automatic; men may not be moved at all, or may not translate vision into praxis. The channel of communication between text and reader, that is to say, doesn't necessarily go in one direction. Reading is inaugurating, it may open different meanings: they may be called wrong but, nonetheless, they are loosed into the world.

Such an incipient interactive or even inaugural model of reading also finds justification in Elizabethan rhetorical theory. Elizabethan educators praised language that was copious, plural, overflowing; that readers can create multiple meanings from language is one of its most admirable features: words generate other words and so produce other matter. That realization is characteristically noted in a mixture of celebration and anxiety. Some complained that the Latin and Greek languages were too "copious and plentiful" or criticized their "inkhorn terms," others that the inrush of new experiences in the age meant, in Ralph Lever's plaintive but revealing phrase, that there were "more things, then there are words to expresse things by," or in Mulcaster's more optimistic judgment, that "new occasions" bring "furth new words." The implication is that language's multiplicity might get out of hand, and there is a widespread desire that it should be disciplined and controlled, and thus cleansed, as Nashe put it, "from barbarisme." But to make language "gorgeous and delectable" was one thing; to make it a hodgepodge was plainly unacceptable, especially in a society where political and cultural control was paramount. Social order might well be threatened by a language run riot. It is not merely a literary argument when Puttenham insists that the language of poetry should be that of the court and its environs.[26]

The Petrarchan lyric tradition enacts the contradictions of these reading positions. Petrarchan rhetoric worked by a remarkably keen sense of its readers' participation in the concretization of poems. In English poetry, from Wyatt on, there is a tendency to become more aware of varied audiences, to adopt rhetorical strategies which would involve different kinds of readers and readings by means of dramatic personae, both heightening the effect of seemingly "individual" voices in the poems and asking for response or for the participation of different audiences, often by direct address. In particular, what develops is an increasing sensitivity to and uneasiness about the nature of the reading "self," especially in the way the poem's "I" invites a reader or hearer to become part of the poem's experience. Part of the "delight" of poetry, to use Philip Sidney's term, is the way that when I read I become part of the "suture" effect, as I oscillate between the reading position the poem asks me to take up as I read and the "self" I (or at least think I) am. It is as if the "I" of the poem were both present and absent in my reading, alongside me, looking over my shoulder rather than simply identified with me, there and yet unable to be seen in the mirror I hold up to myself. The "mirror" is the poem: the particular frisson we get from reading the poem is this fictional we—the overlapping "I"s of the poem's readings—who makes the poem's meanings. The "I" of the poet is just one of the "I"s contained by the poem. To adapt some phrases of Barthes, the poem is not lines of words realizing a single message; they are "multi-dimensional spaces in which "a variety of writings," including those of the poem's readers, "blend and clash."[27] And the "I" of a Petrarchan sonnet is never stable. It is a shattered, decentred voice that searches in vain for stability, unable to capture the plenitude of significance it attributes to the object of its desire. It is likely, I suggest, that something of the hostility to this disturbing multiplicity of the reading experience underlies many of the objections to fictional discourse, not just love poetry, in the period, including Spenser's and Fulke Greville's. Reading a love poem, especially one that is (to use Sidney's terms) moving and persuasive, looses, even creates, many unpredictable feelings and desires. The experience can have a disturbing effect on the reader whose own repertoire of desire is called into play.

The relevance of this excursus into the early modern reading formation to the Sidney cousins' reading of the Petrarchan tradition and their own family poets is that we can see the potential for the emergence of self-consciously gendered reading positions. In the case of Mary Wroth, what variations and distortions occur when a woman reads Petrarchan poems with her own writing in mind? What happens when a woman reader becomes aware that she is interpellated to occupy the places of both the ostensible object of the poet's devotion, the focus of the "I"'s gaze, and the subject position of the poem itself? What opportunities did that contradictory or "split" position give a woman reader at this time? Did it enable her to discover a voice that she herself owned, if not "individually," at least as a woman voicing the shared subjectivity of other women? As chapter six will show, the view of reading that emerges through Wroth's poetry is certainly not triumphantly clear on these issues: it is necessarily timid and contradictory. But reading her poems as themselves "readings" of the Petrarchan tradition and her family's contribution to it shows that her stance as a reader of the position she is asked to occupy, as a woman, ranges from passive uneasiness to outright anger. She could simply read in the interpellated male default position and not notice. Or she could notice, in which case she becomes a split subject. Or she may resist, even if with great difficulty. In Wroth's poems there is evidence of all three reading strategies. In particular, there is a masochism born of frustrated wishes to emulate the apparent freedom of male readers from such contradictory roles, and a desire for an autonomy that the roles in which she finds herself caught continually deny her. As we know from her life, sexual assault and domination may well have been part of Wroth's own material experience but, as well, she is evoking, as part of a cultural unconscious, a resentment at being assaulted by her positioning as a woman reader of a masculinist discourse. In Wroth's writings, we are looking at the slow and con-tradictory emergence, however fitfully, of alternative gendered subject positions in the reading situation. If there is, in the early modern period, as many have argued, the emergence of a new sense of subjectivity, a claim for a unique and essential interiority, Wroth's poems also record the stirrings, against enormous odds, to establish an equivalent female subject position.

Such, then, is something of the gender politics of the reading and subsequent writing experiences that underly the Sidney cousins' poems. It amounts to a sweeping indictment of Petrarchism as a constricting, de-structive distortion of the possibilities of human desires and possibilities. Petrarchism reinforces gender hierarchies and dichotomies; it registers pain rather than fulfillment as central to desire; it allows for autonomy to be ascribed predominantly to the lover who speaks at the same time that it enacts the opposite; it valorizes unfulfilment and avoids the possibilty of mutuality as the basis for fulfilling relationships. It enacts some of the most destructive, "perverse," scenarios of interrelationships in our culture. Is it fair to bring such a "contemporary"—some would say somewhat moralistic—perspective to bear on such a venerable poetic tradition? For some, raising issues of gender politics might be felt to be bad manners, naive and socially inappropriate—not merely in Pem-broke's circle, to whom such issues would have seemed absurd. Even if Mary Wroth gives voice in some of her poems to sentiments that do approach such criticism, they were not publicly circulated, and were by a woman in any case. But today, it may seem heavy-handed to condemn a whole tradition of poetry, even the gender politics of a whole culture, for what has been an overwhelmingly "natural" practice. Such issues, I suggest, have been too long overlooked in the construction of our social and literary histories. One can still acknowledge the residual pleasure afforded by particular cultural practices like Petrarchan poems while at the same time one trying to situate them within our cultural history—and then, also, examine the cultural conflict set up by these two, ideologically at odds, forms of "enjoyment." At times, no doubt, one of those women similarly positioned among such contradictions was Pembroke's cousin, who, in the family tradition, had written her own collection of songs and sonnets. It is to the poems written in this family tradition by the two Sidney cousins that I now turn.

5

"Sophisticate Affection":
The Poetry of the earl of Pembroke

The only way that Mr. R could get a satisfactory orgasm was to cut off a lock of his wife's hair during foreplay or ocasionally after he had already penetrated her. He also indulged in daily masturbation while fantasizing that he was cutting a woman's hair . . . As he walked through the city, he would peer into every barbershop he passed with the hope that he might see a woman having her hair cut.

Louise Kaplan

The boy does not merely disidentify with the mother, he repudiates her and all feminine attributes. The incipient split between mother as source of goodness and father as principle of individuation is hardened into a polarity in which her goodness is redefined as a seductive threat to autonomy.

Jessica Benjamin[1]

o read Pembroke's poems is a frustrating experience in many senses, the first of which is simply the normal (or perverse) scholarly kind. We have what purports to be an authoritative edition, published thirty years after the poet's death, entitled *Poems, Written by the Right Honorable William Earl of Pembroke, Lord Steward of his Majesties Houshold, Whereof Many of Which Are Answered by Way of Repartee, by Sir Benjamin Ruddier Knight. With Several Distinct Poems, Written by them Occasionally, and Apart.* There are two separate prefaces, implying that the volume brings together as many of Pembroke's poems as a well-connected and assiduous editor could find, along with some contributions by another poet, Benjamin Ruddier, or Rudyerd, a long-time friend and political dependent. As it turns out, fewer than half of the eighty-two poems in the volume are probably Pembroke's, and only four Rudyerd's.[2] On close reading, the two prefaces are self-serving and contradictory. It is true that the volume does bring together what are most of Pembroke's surviving or identifiable poems: outside the volume (which I will refer to henceforth as *1660*) there is an additional handful of other poems in various manuscripts or printed miscellanies of the period (c.1610–70) which can be definitely attributed to him or of which, without definitive evidence, he is one of the likely authors. In addition, the poems themselves are further frustrating in that even over-reading them with a prurient amount of curiosity, they provide us with few autobiographical references. They make no explicit reference to Pembroke's relationship with his cousin, although there are lines that may refer to her. This, as I shall show in the next chapter, puts them in direct contrast with her poems, which are full of both explicit and implied references to him and their relationship.

Nonetheless, Pembroke's poems do provide an intriguing opportunity for studying the production and reception of poetry in the Jacobean court and the ways by which the writing (and reading) of Petrarchan love poetry was primarily encoded as a gendered activity, one especially appropriate for a male of Pembroke's class and ambitions. For this powerful political figure, poetry was a demonstration of his confidence

233

POEMS,

Written by the

RIGHT HONORABLE

WILLIAM

EARL OF

PEMBROKE,

Lord Steward of his Majesties Houshold.

WHEREOF

Many of which are answered by way of Repartee,

BY

Sr BENJAMIN RUDDIER,

KNIGHT.

With several Distinct

POEMS,

Written by them Occasionally, and Apart.

LONDON,

Printed by *Matthew Inman*, and are to be sold by
James Magnes, in *Russel-street*, near the *Piazza*,
in *Covent-Garden*, 1 6 6 0.

Title page from Poems . . . *by the earl of Pembroke,*
published 1660. Reproduced by permission of the Folger
Shakespeare Library, Washington, D.C.

in his privileges and accomplishments as a male courtier; studying his poems reveals, too, something of the mechanisms by which he was interpellated into a system of class and gendered assumptions within which he was extremely comfortable, and which undoubtedly seemed "natural" rather than gender-specific, and in which his cousin was far less happy. "You know," Ben Jonson told him, addressing his patron's authority by mentioning two major symbols of male and class superiority, how "to use" both "yo'r sword and yo'r pen."[3] Such ease was, however, not simply derived from his "personality" or even his talent, but primarily from the ideology of gender and class assignments which appeared naturally and comfortably to be "his."

The confidence and dominance afforded by Pembroke's gender and class status are also obvious from the largely unjustified praise he received for his poetry. One of the most admired characteristics of Pembroke's uncle, Philip Sidney, had been that he was not only a patron of poetry but a poet himself, and in dedicating A Poetical Rhapsody to Pembroke in 1602/3, Francis Davison announced that Sidney's nephew also deserved a "Lawrelle Crowne." This was undoubtedly a tactful way to address the young heir of both the poetic mantle of the Sidneys and the Pembroke title, although Jonson, who regularly received £20 a year for books from him, preferred to concentrate on Pembroke's learning and judicious taste, adding as well fulsome tributes to his lordship's high moral character, rather than dwelling on his poetry. But William Browne, one of Pembroke's occasional employees as well as a prolific poet himself, claimed that "in all our Land / None can more rightly claim a Poet's pen," and Anthony à Wood likewise praised "those amorous and not inelegant Aires and Poems of his composition."[4] There are many similar tributes. Hence an initial question to ask about Pembroke's poetry is whether there is any justification for such praise. In fact, it is easy to construct a case for Pembroke as a moderately interesting minor poet, sufficiently eclectic in his tastes to be seen as transitional between so-called Elizabethan, Metaphysical, and Cavalier styles, and even in some ways anticipating the development of neo-classicism. The degree of derivativeness in his verse certainly could be used to demonstrate the influence of such poets as Campion, Jonson, Donne, or Carew, all of whom Pembroke knew and over whose careers, as lord chancellor, he exercised varying degrees of power and patronage. His poems have, however, received scant modern attention from either editors or commentators, who (by and large) are not beholden to his patronage.

Some preliminary discussion of the canon is necessary. First of all, there is the puzzle presented by 1660. There is no entry in the Stationer's Register for the book, but the titlepage states that it was prepared for the press by John Donne the Younger, and printed by Matthew Inman for James Magnus.[5] Inman was a printer whose shop was located at Addlehill, Thames Street, from 1660 and 1663 or 1664; Magnus was a bookseller on Russell Street from 1660 to 1679; he specialized mainly in plays and prose fiction. In addition to certain major editorial problems, which I will discuss below, the book was carelessly printed, with some lines omitted and some poems run together. It is likely that few copies were printed: Beese noted that a standard run for such a book was probably only about three hundred. For over one hundred and fifty years, evidence for its history is scanty. A number of copies surfaced in nineteenth-century book sales at Quarles, Sotheby's, and elsewhere. Of those that are extant, very few are perfect: some lack the title page or have pages missing or canceled.[6]

In 1817, *1660* was reissued by Bensley and Son, together with a summary of Pembroke's life by Sir Egerton Brydges. Some poems were shortened; a number of lines were asterisked out, with moralistic comments to justify the censorship; and the punctuation was heavily modernized. "I have striven," remarks Brydges, "probably in vain," to "water" the "withered . . . turf" of Pembroke's poems in an attempt to "reanimate the form, as well as to restore the laurel crown of him, who was the son of *Sidney's Sister*, and whom Ben Jonson and all the poets of his day have celebrated."[7] In 1841, in his edition of Sir Benjamin Rudyerd's *Memoirs*, J. A. Manning printed those poems in *1660* attributed to Rudyerd, along with those of Pembroke's that were supposedly written in association with him. Then, for a further century, little attention was given to Pembroke's verse. In 1934 and 1961, respectively, Beese and Robert Krueger presented, in the form of Oxford B.Litt. theses, what purported to be modern critical editions of *1660*. Neither was subsequently published. Where noted, I have drawn upon their researches and speculations, although both are, in different ways, unsatisfactory and incomplete. In 1959 Gaby Onderwyzer published in the Augustan Reprint series a cramped facsimile edition of what she believed to be Pembroke's contributions to *1660*. As scholars from Grierson to Buxton have commented, an adequate modern edition of Pembroke's poems remains an urgent task. The investigations I have made are sufficient only for my purpose in writing this book—although I will present evidence on Pembroke's poems that would be useful for the preparation of a modern edition of his poems.[8]

Now for the intriguing and frustrating story of how *1660* was assembled. It is not only—for those who acknowledge the (no doubt) perverse pleasure in such scholarly matters—an intriguing puzzle, but (more germane to my study) it lets us into something of the part poetry played in the intellectual and emotional life of its author. The editor of *1660* was John Donne, sometime clergyman, editor, extremely minor poet, and son of the famous poet and divine. From 1640 he lived in Covent Garden, and in the last years of his life he prepared a number of his father's works for publication, including *A Collection of Letters made by Sir Tobie Matthew* (1660) and *XXVI Sermons* (1661). As an editor, the younger Donne was, R. C. Bald noted, the "frequent exasperation of modern scholars: he proofread poorly, allowing misprints, did not check sources," and made "weak or spurious attributions." Beese comments further that Donne's editing is "seen at its worst in the *Pembroke-Rudyerd Poems*." One poem is printed twice, separate poems are printed as one, and there are many scribal errors, showing that "Donne did not make the slightest attempt to edit the text. [and] it is to be feared that he scarcely read the poems through."[9]

The poems were dedicated by Donne to the countess of Devonshire, one of the friends with whom Pembroke had dined the night before his death in 1630. By 1660 this lady was in her seventies. The daughter of one of James's early favorites, Edward, Lord Bruce, she was the widow of William Cornwallis, second earl of Devonshire, who had died in 1628, and during the 1630s she had been widely known as a generous patron, to Waller and Hobbes among others. Like Mary Wroth, she was involved in many property lawsuits after she was widowed, but, unlike Wroth, an early biographer noted, "after some years care and management she had the pleasure of seeing all her Lord's debts discharged, and his estate clear from encumbrances." Donne flatters her by saying that the preservation and publication of Pembroke's poems is "no small addition to all your great titles and other excellencies," and he reminds her that though astrologers "could foretell the time that he should leave us"—a reference to the well-publicized prophecy of Pembroke's death around his fiftieth birthday—the publication of his poems "could set no date to the fame that he should leave behind him." The poems, expostulates Donne, now have been "awakened by your ladyship's command, and under your patronage" have been ordered to "come abroad." While it is likely that some of the poems Donne printed were indeed procured from the countess of Devonshire, following the dedication to her he added a further note entitled "To the Reader," which states that the poems were furnished by the musicians Henry Lawes and Nicholas Lanier. In this second and contradictory account of the poems' origins, he also implies that many of them were of dubious attribution, and states that he would continue to look for "many more ready to supply their room, which were not come unto my hands when I published these." The note was probably inserted while the manuscript was at the printer's and does not mention the countess of Devonshire at all.

I count probably twenty-five poems in *1660* that are almost certainly or most probably by Pembroke. They consist of his contributions to a poetic debate between love and reason written with Rudyerd, along with a miscellaneous collection of songs and lyrics, mainly found in the first third of the volume. There are a further twelve poems, principally in the last third of the collection, that are attributed to Pembroke with no (or else dubious) authority, although there is no external evidence for alternative authorship. A further twenty-one are attributed to Pembroke and are certainly not by him: their actual authors include Carew, Ralegh, Brooke, North, Drayton, Wotton, Strode, and others. There are four poems definitely by Rudyerd, plus another eleven attributed by Donne to Rudyerd but not, in fact or all probability, by him. There are six unattributed poems that are by neither Pembroke nor Rudyerd. The initial eight or ten poems in *1660*—the debate with Rudyerd and some lyrics, perhaps provided by the Countess of Devonshire, possibly by Lawes and Lanier—are fairly easy to identify as Pembroke's. Thereafter, apart from some interspersed poems by North, Wotton, Dyer, and Drayton, up to about page 54 of *1660*, Donne had gathered together those poems that he believed (usually correctly) to be Pembroke's. He was, however, seemingly already starting to add others' poems to fill out the collection. From about page 54 to the end, *1660* is simply a miscellaneous collection of lyrics which Donne assigns to "P" or "R" without any firm authority, though with an occasional fortuitous guess. He was probably drawing on both published and unpublished verse miscellanies, perhaps even a number of loose sheets. He may be sincere when he says in "To the Reader" that he hopes to find further poems by Pembroke, but, as it stands, the collection is a monument to careless attribution and incompetent editing. Outside *1660*, I have located another eight poems definitely or probably by Pembroke, and four additionally possible, which brings us to a total of between forty and forty-five extant poems definitely or probably by him.[10] Without a cache of other poems being discovered (and it is not at all impossible that the 1647/8 Wilton fire destroyed some[11]), we will never be able to make a claim for Pembroke as more than an occasional poet. As for their quality, the poems we do have may demonstrate, as Brydges in his quaint way put it in 1817, "the moral and intellectual endowments ascribed to him by the luminous pen" of the earl of Clarendon, but when considered as (that admittedly question-begging term) "literature," they certainly cannot be seen as much more than the "slight amusements of literary leisure."[12]

However few, Pembroke's poems can nonetheless be used to add some intriguing pieces to the account of the Sidney family romance. When and how regularly was Pembroke active as a poet? Was he, like Sir Walter Ralegh, an "occasional" poet, writing irregularly but stirred to write by particular public or personal events, scribbling witty repartees in verse and slipping them, as a headnote to one of Ralegh's poems puts it (whether literally true or not) into ladies' pockets?[13] Did he write his poems during a relatively brief period, when he was trying to display himself as a bright young courtier? Or was he more or less active as a poet throughout his life? Why was it important for him to write poetry at all? What can they tell us of his relationship with his cousin? Or, indeed, of any of his relationships within the family? Can we perceive any connections with the writings of Pembroke's more prolific uncles Philip and Robert, his mother, as well as his cousin? Why did he write the kind of verse he did? Can we point to characteristic male fantasies that consistently emerge from them? Do they contribute anything more to the contradictions of gender roles that we have seen in Pembroke's career?

First, when did Pembroke write his poems? The only poem by Pembroke in print before 1660 is "Disdain me Still," which was published in two miscellanies, A Book of Ayres (1611) and A Pilgrimes Solace (1612). Another, printed without attribution in 1660, "When Phoebus first did Daphne Love," was published in Dowland's Third Book of Songs (1603), but it is probably by Charles Rives (flourished 1595). The Pembroke/Rudyerd debate poems probably date from after 1602, when the two men most likely knew each other at the Inns of Court. They had been up at Oxford at the same time ten years before, but Rudyerd was eight years older than Pembroke, and so it is more likely that they met at Gray's Inn, when Pembroke was admitted as a member and Rudyerd was also in attendance. When we turn to the manuscripts in which Pembroke's poems are found, MS 2067 in the National Library of Scotland (which contains William Drummond's transcription of a poem by Pembroke not found in 1660), is datable not later than 1609. A poem on the death of the earl of Salisbury, also not published in 1660, was probably written shortly after that event in 1612. Other manuscripts confirm dates that are in some cases certainly, in others probably, in the first decade of the century. In short, it is likely that most of the poems of Pembroke's we have were written in the years he was first at court, and almost certainly his poetic career, if we can distinguish it by such a title, was over by the end of the first decade of James's reign, much in the same way as his participation in masques and tourneys seems to have ended by the time he was elevated to the position of lord chamberlain in 1616. Since Wroth was being noticed as a poet by 1613, some of the two cousins' poetical activities may have overlapped.[14]

Puttenham's observation in the 1580s regarding a "crew of courtly makers Noble men and Gentlemen of her Majesties owne servants, who have written"—if not all "excellentlie," as he claimed, at least reasonably competently, and some extremely well—applies well into the seventeenth century.[15] The number of commonplace books in which Pembroke's poems are found (at least fifty from the period c.1610–70) gives us a glimpse of the primary means by which his poetry circulated. Compiled by students, courtiers, or merchants, the commonplace books (along with printed miscellanies, which often used commonplace book material) are fascinating revelations of the taste of both courtly and middle-class audiences. Utilitarian doggerel is mixed with delicate lyrics, moral tags with erotic plaints. Pembroke's poems are found along with the work of other fashionable or socially well-placed poets, including Donne, Ralegh, Carew, Randolph, and other minor versifiers, like Sylvester or Strode. Some were clearly moderately popular: some of his poems are found in at least twenty manuscript sources. There are many minor variants, no doubt largely caused by careless copying, though some may be the product of deliberate adaption. Stanzas may be added or references changed: the poems Pembroke and other amateur "courtly makers" were writing were, in a sense, never complete, but, as Richard Newton puts it, "always the possession of [their] last possessor." Heard as recitation or song even before they were circulated in handwritten or printed form, such poems are part of a conversation, infinitely adaptable, moving from one interlocutor to another. Perhaps, one might observe, no poem is ever complete: it is always in process, different each time it is read, reading being a kind of rewriting, and all texts being, in one sense, to adapt Barthes's celebrated term, "writerly." But there is a particular histori- cally located form of writerliness at stake here. It is as if they do not "belong" to particular authors but rather to their hearers and readers. They are what Arthur Marotti calls "coterie social transactions," written for or within a group of friends, perhaps on particular, though relatively common, social or erotic occasions. Poetry was part of the cultural dress code of the complete courtier, not a means of self-advancement: poetry held no career expectations for Pembroke. Many of his poems read as if they are written, as it were, by the coterie rather than by any individual member of it. The authorship of poems written in such circumstances is frequently, therefore, difficult to establish. The poems seem to speak with the voice of a collectivity rather than an individual; often the poets appear to be *scriptors* or spokesmen for the dominant views of a whole class, or at least the coterie within and for which they wrote—and which, in a real sense, produced him. The quintessential court amateur poet, like Pembroke, went with whatever fashion he found congenial; he was, in C. S. Lewis's words about Ralegh, "blown this way and that (and sometimes lifted into real poetry)." The poem found in Drummond of Hawthornden's papers, along with an answering poem by Drummond, may have been written when the two men met in 1603 when Pembroke went north as part of the entourage to greet King James, or when Drummond visited London in 1606 and saw the performance of

Ford's *Honour Triumphant*, in which Pembroke took part. As Marotti points out, one of Pembroke's poems, "When mine eyes first admiring of your beauty," is found in one of the commonplace books in the Rosenbach collection, conflated with a version of Shakespeare's sonnet 106, probably because the copyist, or someone else read them as being concerned with the same topics.[16]

A useful comparison is again with Donne (in this case, the elder Donne, not his son, the incompetent editor). As an ambitious outsider—in his case, in terms of class and religion if not gender—Donne attempted to turn his social insecurity to advantage, with poetry as one of the means by which he tried to attract not just notice but acceptance and, not incidentally, financial security. Pembroke had no need to struggle against the hegemony of either class or gender power. The prime purpose of his poetry was simply to display himself as a confident participant within the dominant social class. He is content to let the dominant aesthetic ideology of the male-dominated court and its acceptance of the decorativeness of lyric poetry speak through his verse without the anguish of having to call into question the system that brought them into being. He finds a pattern of discourse already existing and a role waiting for him to fill. Familiarity, not innovation, is what is valued in coterie verse, since it reinforces its readers' sense of belonging to the same group as the author. The values and commitments that emerge from such a poem are those of a group and a tradition rather than that of a novel or idiosyncratic voice. Each lyric is, to use Jameson's term, "a *parole*, or individual utterance, of the vaster system, or *langue*" of a dominant class and gender discourse. Indeed, the formal unity and, in performance, the harmoniously unified voice of the lyric are mechanisms designed to smooth over any particularizing and ideologically disruptive possibilities.[17] One poem of Pembroke's, for instance, is an elegant and relaxed variation on a theme familiar to readers of Marlowe, Ralegh, and Donne. He inserts himself into the cultural assumptions behind such poetry in order to demonstrate his skill and familiarity with its social role:

> Dear leave thy home and come with me,
> That scorn the world for love of thee:
> Here we will live within this Park,
> A Court of joy and pleasures Ark.
>
> Here we will hunt, here we will range,
> Constant in Love, our sports wee'l change:
> Of hearts if any change we make,
> I will have thine, thou mine shalt take.

Here we will walk upon the Lawns,
And see the tripping of the Fawns;
And all the Deer shall wait on thee,
Thou shalt command both them and me.

The Leaves a whispering noise shall make,
Their Musick-notes the birds shall take,
And while thou art in quiet sleep,
And the green wood shall silence keep.

And while my herds about thee feed,
Love's lessons in thy face I'le read,
And feed upon thy lovely look,
For beauty hath no fairer book.

It's not the weather, nor the air,
It is thyself that is so fair;
Nor doth it rain when heaven lowers,
But when you frown, then fall the showers.

One Sun alone moves in the skye,
Two Suns thou hast, one in each eye;
Onely by day that sun gives light,
Where thine doth rise, there is no night.

Fair starry twins, scorn not to shine
Upon my Lambs, upon my Kine;
My grass doth grow, my Corn and wheat,
My fruit, my vines thrive by their heat.

Thou shalt have wool, thou shalt have silk,
Thou shalt have honey, wine and milk;
Thou shalt have all, for all is due,
Where thoughts are free, and love is true.

(*1660*, pp. 38–39)

This particular poem would have been widely recognizable as a variant on a common theme, represented by well-known poems like Marlowe's "Come live with me and be my love," Ralegh's "The Nymph's Reply to the Shepherd," and Donne's "The Baite." The discourse that has produced this poem is coded by matters of class (aristocratic, privileged, leisurely) and gender (male, dominant, self-indulgent) more than by any purely "aesthetic" considerations, let alone any biographical revelations. Its focus is not so much the poet's inner life as the desires and values of its audience, specifically those of a coterie of men united by class outlook, and indulging their enjoyment of poetry as a relaxing social ritual. They are content to have poetry, like all art, be what one Jacobean courtier and minor poet, Donne's friend, Sir Henry Wotton, unabashedly called "an instrument of state."[18] In such a poetic, form and idea are conceived of as a faithful reflection of the social harmony of which they are part and which they are designed to celebrate. To introduce, as I shall now, questions of class or gender politics would simply have been in rather bad taste. My argument, predictably, is that this poetic mode and the social values it assumes are gendered discourses. Submerged beneath the assumption of universalism in this poetry are not value neutral but very specifically coded by class and gender assumptions.

The younger Donne's second introductory note to the reader in *1660* informs us that "in the collecting of these Poems (which were chiefly preserved by the greatest masters of music, all the sonnets being set by them) I was fain first to send Mr. Henry Lawes, who furnishing me with some, directed me for the rest to send into Germany to Mr. Lanear . . ." Regardless of the accuracy of Donne's claim, many of Pembroke's poems were, in fact, set to music, and their affinities with music reinforce their ideological context. They are designed to represent not so much a precise—let alone an individually particularized—emotion so much as an invitation to share or recollect a collective, socially approved, emotion. In responding to the poems, there is no need to know, they imply, more than the surface. Again, to foreground any ambiguity, tension, or urgent personal voice would be socially inappropriate, as would any dark brooding or even perhaps any emotion recollected in tranquility. Pleasing language and melody—what Stevens calls "idealized talk" and Lewis "a little music after supper"—combine to give the sense of grace and relaxation of an elegant soirée attended by a group, if not of friends, at least of members of the same privileged class.[19]

We can, in fact, provide even more specific connections between Pembroke's lyrics and court music. Like most nobles of his class, Pembroke employed musicians at both Baynard's Castle and Wilton House. As Graham Parry notes, "soloists or small consorts of lutes and viols played to the great men of the court to indulge their humours or assuage their melancholy."[20] Pembroke's musicians included Thomas Tompkins, one of the most eminent composers of the period, and John Dowland, another celebrated composer, was employed by both the Sidneys and Pembrokes. Two other prominent musicians associated with Pembroke were those mentioned in Donne's preface to *1660*, Nicholas Lanier and Henry Lawes. Lanier is particularly known for his contributions to the development of the declamatory air, in which the speech rhythms of the verbal text largely determine the rhythmical shape of the music. Between about 1615 and the mid–1620s, he set a number of songs in the court masques, but there is no indication that he set any of Pembroke's. Lawes was far more closely associated with Pembroke: he and his brother William, also a musician, grew up near Wilton, where their father was a minor official at the cathedral. By about 1615, Lawes was at court, where Pembroke, who as lord chamberlain had at his disposal posts in both the Chapel Royal and the King's Music, appointed him to a position in the royal household. In 1630/1, a few months before Pembroke died, Lawes became a member of the King's Private Music. He set many lyrics by current poets, and further extended the tradition of the declamatory air by adapting the techniques of Italian recitative. The Lawes Manuscripts contain settings of almost four hundred songs, and it may well be that Lawes provided Donne with some of the poems that were printed in the second half of *1660*. In his *Ayres and Dialogues* (1653), Lawes claimed that "as for those copies of verses in this Book, I have rendered their Names who made them, from whose hand I received them."[21] "Canst thou love me and yet doubt" is one:

I.

Canst thou love me, and yet doubt
So much falshood in my heart,
That a way I should find out
    To impart
Fragments of a broken love to you,
More then all, being less then due;
O no! Love must clear distrust,
Or be eaten with that rust:
    Short love liking may find jarres,
    The love that's lasting knows no warres.

II.

This belief begets delight,
And so satisfies desire,
And in them it shines a light
    No more fire;
All the burning Qualities appeas'd
Each in others joyning pleas'd;
Not a whisper, not a thought,
But 'twixt both in common's brought;
    Even to seem two they are loth,
    Love being but one soul in both.

(*1660*, p. 23)

Lawes's setting of this short, delicate lyric is in 4/4 time; it starts with an appropriately querulous first accent and then falls into a pattern of recitative in a style rather more like that of Campion than Dowland. The final lines are particularly beautifully modulated, lingering and melancholy. Another of Lawes's settings of Pembroke's lyrics, "Oh let me groan one word into thine ear," is also particularly haunting:

> Oh let me groan one word into thine ear,
> And with that groan break all my vital strings;
> Thou that wouldst never, now vouchsafe to hear
> How *Leda*'s bird on sweet *Meander* sings:
> So dying tapers lend their fiery flashes,
> And deadest Cinders have some burning ashes.
>
> Those were the looks that once maintain'd my strength,
> Those were the words that all my parts did cherish;
> And what (Unkindest) wilt thou gain at length,
> If by the same, I miserably perish:
> This, that a frown did in a minute starve,
>   That which a smile did many years preserve.
>
> (1660, p. 52)

This small lyric shows both Pembroke's lyrical skill and Lawes' settings at their best. The poem suggests a civilized, courtly occasion, asking for verse and a musical setting that move elegantly, simply, and without disrupting the atmosphere, which is designed to soothe and relax. With another lyric, "Dear leave thy home and come with me, / That scorn the world for love of thee," two musical settings exist, one by Henry Lawes, the other by William, his brother. William turned the lyric into a four-part song, tender and serious; Henry's setting is a single-voiced air, light, gay, and appropriately cynical.[22] Other poems set by Henry Lawes and found in *1660* include "Since every man I come upon," attributed to Rudyerd, but probably by John Grange; "Not that I wish my Mistress more or less," and "Be not proud, cause fair and trim," both also probably by Grange; and Neville's "Till now I never did behave." Outside the poems from the Lawes collections, there is at least one further musical setting of a poem probably by Pembroke, "Chloris sighed and sang and wept" is found in at least twenty other printed and manuscript sources, many of which attribute it to him. One manuscript has a musical setting by "Mr. Bales," who may be Richard (or Alphonso) Bales.

Setting Pembroke's lyrics within the history of song gives an important indication of their occasional quality. We can get some further perspective on them when we place them within the history of verse styles.

Drawing on Russian formalist studies of lyric, Schleiner distinguishes between three modes of poetry in the early seventeenth century, what she terms "song," "declamation," and "conversational speech."[23] "Song" is characterized by metrical smoothness, "declamation" by moderately smooth meter, and "conversation" by a greater degree of metrical roughness. Most of Pembroke's poems fall in the middle category. There are occasional abrupt openings, though none have the violence of Donne's "For God sake hold your tongue, and let me love," or Suckling's later "Out upon it, I have loved thee / One whole day." Pembroke will sometimes write in long, though still relatively smooth, syntactic units: his lines are rarely interrupted by parenthetical insertions to convey the sense of direct speech. But there is some indication of his use of the declarative or recitative style: instead of trying, as the typical Elizabethan song does, to create a "synchronous complex of attitudes," his poems usually build up a series of smoothly connected, relatively simple emotions. The result is, in the best of the poems, pleasing, restrained, providing little surprise but often a quiet and charming pleasure. Thus some of his poems are written in fairly regular short-lined meters—ballad measures, trimeters, or tetrameters:

> Say pretty wanton, tell me why
> Thou canst not love so well as I
> Sit thee down, and thou shalt see,
> That I delight in none but thee.
>
> Say pretty wanton, be not coy,
> For thou alone art all my joy;
> If a smile thou wilt not lend,
> Yet let thy gentle ears attend.
>
> If thou stop those gentle ears,
> Then look upon these brinish tears;
> Which do force me still to cry,
> Pitty me now, or else I dye.
> (1660, p. 73)

This three-stanza poem, not found anywhere other than in 1660 (where it is mistakenly run together with "Fairest fair, my Love, my Jewel") and unaccountably ignored by Krueger, is a simple, melodic song in tetrameters, with end-stopped lines; when enjambment occurs it does so without breaking phrases, never between subject and verb, though occasionally between verb and complement. This particular lacks the "strong lines" typical of a Donne poem and is closer in mode to some of Jonson's. But frequently in Pembroke's verse there will be parallelism,

172

subordination, and the use of conjuncts and disjuncts to convey the speaking or "recitative" voice, as in the opening of his poem that Mary Wroth inserted as written by Amphilanthus in *Urania*:

Had I love butt att that rate
Which hath binn ordain'd by fate
To all your kinde;
I had full requited binn
Nor your slighting mee had seene,
Nor once repinde
Neglect to find.
                    (Wroth, *Poems*, p. 217)

What Schleiner terms the "musical" qualities of Pembroke's lyrics is usually subordinate to the "declamatory" voice. There are occasional poems that do feature patterns of repeated sounds and rhythms, as in the typical late Elizabethan song that starts: " Fairest fair, my Love, my Jewel, / Wilt thou never cease to grieve me?" (*1660*, p. 74). But more typically, the poems' effects are achieved through clear rhymes, repeated grammatical structures, and without using sustained patterns of sound. The declamatory style could accommodate occasional speech inflections, thereby making the emotional effect more complex. It also serves to emphasize ideological contradictions that are only just held in check by the lyric grace. Whereas in the Elizabethan song the regularity produces an effect of generalized feeling, with the declamatory lyric, there is less time to build up effects, and the changes in pace and diction underline the meaning and the impression of a speaking voice:

Muse get thee to a Cell; and wont to sing,
Now mourn, nay now thy hands, thy heart now wring;
And if perhaps thine eyes did ever weep,
Now bleed, and in eternal sorrow sleep;
O, she that was, and onely was, is gone,
And I that was but one, am left alone.
                              (*1660*, p. 28)

Here the effect nicely mixes a smooth melodic form, mild enjambment, parallelism and subordination, and a careful blend of tones with mild exclamations and questions. There is also a similar blend of figures of sound (including alliteration) with figures of sense, so the cohesion of the poem is achieved through both phonological and lexical patterning. The diction is not the characteristic hard consonants and consonantal clusters of many of Donne's *Songs and Sonets*, but neither is it the languid consonantal movements of many of Campion's or some of Sidney's songs. It has some degree of formality, rarely becoming informal or

173

colloquial—although where there is a a distinct audience presupposed, as in the answer poems with Rudyerd, a more informal diction and syntax will enter, as in these opening lines: "It is enough, a Master you grant *Love* / At one weapon, 'twas all I sought to prove" (*1660*, p.11). Rarely, however, will the diction become idiosyncratic or elliptically compressed; most of Pembroke's metaphors are conventional, with occasional careful and controlled elaboration or illustrative anecdote.

What are the broader cultural effects of such a stylistic register? Verse forms and diction are the bearers of ideology no less than metaphor and allusion. In reading Pembroke's verse we can see an eclecticism that matches the social role of his poetry. He is perhaps responding to the relatively new fashion of "strong lines" much in Jonson's way, by what MacDonald Emslie terms "Tottelizing Donne,"[24] using the effects of informality and idiomatic surprise on occasions, but generally favoring the melodic comfort of the song. The desired effect is to efface controversy, to adopt and reify the default position stylistically as well as ideologically. Equally conventional is the atmosphere of Platonized Petrarchism that dominates the poetry. The poems concentrate on generalized observations of loss, absence, and idealistic devotion. We encounter the familiar Petrarchan metaphors which by the time that Pembroke is writing have degenerated into cliché: idealism and deprivation; beauty and rejection; personifications of love as a warrior, a cheat, a transformer of men into beasts:

> Thou mak'st food loathsome, sleep to be unrest;
> Lost labour easeful, scornful looks a feast.
> And when thou wilt thy joies as far excell
> All else, as when thou punishest thy Hell:
> O Make that Rebel feel thy matchless power,
> Thou that mad'st *Jove* a Bull, a Swan, a Shower;
> Give him a love as tyrannous as fair,
> That his desire go yoaked with despair.
> Live in her eies, but in her frozen heart
> Let no thaw come, that may have sence of smart.
> Let her constant silence never break,
> Till he do with repulse to hear her speak.
> And last, such sence of error let him have,
> As he may never dare for mercy crave.
> Then none wil more capitulate with thee,
> But of their hearts will yield the *Empire* free.
>   (*1660*, pp. 6–7)

The surprising opaqueness of the verbal registers of Petrarch's *Canzoniere* had for two hundred years given poets an unusually adaptable

174

instrument: not only an intriguing, systematic ordering of the discourse of erotic desire but a sourcebook for rhetorical display and self-indulgence. By the time Pembroke is writing, the paradoxes have become too easy, articulated without anguish, the enjambment reducing the tension of the lines, as does the witty turn at the end. The lover is "restless," a prisoner, blinded; the mistress is a jewel, a picture, unkind. The tone is not particularly serious: Pembroke was writing his poems at the end of a very long and hospitable tradition, and what has been called "witty" or parodic Petrarchism had been long established, not least (in England) by Pembroke's uncle Philip.

I move next to the dangerous yet inviting question: to what extent can we see these poems as autobiographical? As I noted in previous chapters, both contemporary and later readers have often constructed narratives from the foregrounded "I" of *Astrophil and Stella* in order to read the poems as biographical revelations. The Petrarchan lyric's typical rhetoric of confessional sincerity looks as if it is not merely a shared psychosexual code, but an overheard confession, with the poetic act—frequently asserted in the poems to be conceived in pain, loss, or embarrassment—supposedly derived from direct personal experience. A few poems of Pembroke's do clearly make references to his life. A poem not printed in *1660*, but found in both the Cecil Papers and a manuscript in the Chatham Library, Manchester, "You that reade [in] passing by," was written in memory of Robert Cecil, Earl of Salisbury, who died in 1612:[25]

You that reade [in] passing by
Robert Earle of Salisburye
Know yt in so short a story
You can never find more glory.
All ye secrets on him laide,
He the staffe of treasure swaide,
Gave his Master all the gaines
Of the wardes; reserv'd the paines,
Govern'd all with so cleane handes
As most malist silent standes,
All that snarle shall be soone
Found Doggs barking at ye moone.
This Tombe hath his boones possest
Heaven and friendes preserve the rest.

Here the referent is obvious and the occasion for the poem identifiable, even if the relationship between the persona of the poem and the author may be problematic. Another poem where Pembroke's public life intruded, at least in the public nature of the poem's occasion, is in the series of answer poems written with Rudyerd that are arranged together near the beginning of *1660* as well as in a number of manuscripts. In the records of Gray's Inn, Rudyerd is named as having written for the law students' annual entertainment, and the poems by him and Pembroke in *1660* may have been composed for a similar event. Written in heroic couplets, with wit that would have been appropriate for a mock-legal debate, they take sides over the question whether reason or love is to be preferred in a lover. Pembroke takes the part of love, arguing for its superiority over reason on conventional grounds, at times acknowledging "I do not sever Love from Reason's law, / But say that they in one sweet yoak do draw" (*1660*, p. 11). Throughout these poems, there is a fine and witty control of the verse lines, which generally show an excellent sense of audience. Even if it is conventional enough, one of the poems concludes with a finely provocative prophecy:

> But to conclude debate, whilst you are free,
> You may make *Love* even what you list to be,
> As those that will describe an unknown Land,
> Place Cities, Rivers, Hills, where none do stand;
> Even so you deal with Love, and streight will know
> How far he shoots, that never felt his bow;
> One day you may, and then confess with me,
> You love his Fetters more then to be free.
>
> (*1660*, pp. 20–21)

There is a fine sense of repartee in these poems, but typically, they speak to an occasion, and to the poetical and social tradition in which they are produced, rather than to Pembroke's own experiences.

The most intriguing autobiographical question with Pembroke's po-etry—one where one wishes to slip into the easy simplicities of Croft's biographical reading of Robert Sidney's verse as being directly about his supposed extramarital affairs, a reading which, in fairness, might well be based on fact, and possibly shared by some of the readers in the family circle[26]—is what they might tell us of his relations with Mary Wroth. The answer is, frustratingly, very little, though the very absence of explicit references—given the insistence, as I shall suggest in the next chapter, with which Wroth sprinkled her poems with references to him— may be significant. Pembroke's verses are those of a man indulging in cool "sophisticate affection" (*1660*, p. 48), as one of his poems puts it. The court lyric offered a kind of playspace in which a poet could experiment, less to make direct confession of erotic experience than to define his level of accomplishments in relation to a a long tradition of such poems and the social expectations that shaped them. Details from his life might then be permitted to appear if socially appropriate. As in so much of his life, Pembroke found an easy role to play, and he proceeded to play it as well as he needed. There are undoubtedly poems that could be read in connection with his relationship with his cousin, but the posible references are so general that they could be applicable to any mistress, or none, as in this heavily erotic complaint of a secret lover:

We have been private, and thou knowst of mine,
(Which is even all) as much as I of thine:
Dost thou remember? Let me call t' account
Thy pleasant Garden, and that leavy Mount
Whose top is with an open Arbour crown'd.

(*1660*, p. 57)

One poem is addressed to a tall mistress (we might recall Whyte's reference to the young Mary Sidney as uncommonly tall), and another mentions a common interest in poetry. But such references are no more specific than that. Nor do we have an indication that any of Pembroke's poems were written for Mary Fitton, although there is a remarkable passage in a letter from Sir William Knollys, Mary Fitton's erstwhile protector, about his own "affection" for his charge, who was clearly horrified by Knollys's attentions. Knollys is, he confesses to Mary's sister, Anne:

... cloyed with to much & yeat readye to starve ffor hunger, My eyes see what I can not attayne to, my eares heare what I doe scant beleve, & my thoughtes are caryed with contrarye conceipts, My hopes are myxt with dispayre & my desyres starved with expectation, but wear my enjoying assured, I could willinglye endure purgatorye ffor a season to purchase my heaven at the last . . . I could complayne off fortune which ledd me blyndlye into this baren desert where I am readye to starve for want off my desyred ffoode & off myselff that would suffer my reason to be betrayed by my will in ffollowyng so blynd a guide.[27]

The letter is a fascinating indication of the commonplace nature of Petrarchism in the discourse of desire at the time.

One indication of a poem that may have been written for Mary Wroth is "Had I loved butt att that rate." Wroth included it in the continuation of *Urania*, where it is attributed to Amphilanthus, the main male character, who is based upon Pembroke. It is also found in four other manuscript sources, three of which attribute it to "E. P.," and one in which it is signed "pembrooke":

Had I loved butt att that rate
Which hath binn ordain'd by fate
    To all your kinde;
    I had full requited binn

Nor your slighting mee had seene,
　　Nor once repinde
　　Neglect to finde,

For I ame soe wholy thine
As in least sort to bee mine
　　My hart denies;
I doe think noe thought butt thee,
Nor desire more light to see
　　Then what doth rise
　　From thy faire eyes,

Deer I blame nott thy neglect
In excess of my respect
　　The fault doth rest;
Thou dost pretty love impart,
As can lodge in woemans hart
　　Non showld bee prest
　　Beeyound ther best,

But when I did give thee more,
Then againe thou cowldst restore,
　　And woeman bee,
I made thee against thy will
To remaine ungratefull still
　　By binding thee
　　Soe much to mee.
　　　　(Wroth, *Poems*, pp. 217–18)

The poem is conventional enough, though Wroth gives it an intriguing context when she says that Amphilanthus composed the poem to express his love for his (then) admirer and would-be betrothed Antissia, but then readdressed it to a "higher" lover, his cousin Pamphilia, who sings it.[28]

Do these poems bring us any closer to Pembroke? If these are supposedly "autobiographical" poems, the "I"s are hardly "individual." Even in the Salisbury poem the speaking position is complex—obviously that of a fellow politician, one public man bidding farewell to another, but also that of a younger, aggressive, albeit less secure, politician, eyeing his own rivals as much as his dead mentor or friend. It is a public tribute, concerned as much with "image" as it is "sincere." We get no unambiguous sense of what an older criticism might have called the man "behind" the poem—what is recorded is the public role, the constructed self of the public tribute. As readers, we are instructed, even threatened, to agree with the position Pembroke—as opposed to, say, Northumberland and his supporters—takes on Salisbury's career, much as Ralegh rejects, indeed curses, any possible dissenting readers at the end of "Praisd Be Dianas Fair and Harmless Light": "A knowledge pure it is hir worth to know, / With Circe's let them dwell that think not so."[29]

Far more important than possible autobiographical references are the issues I raised in the previous chapter about the Petrarchan mode of poetry. I want especially to ask what Pembroke's poems tell us of the ideological, particularly the gendered, assumptions from which they grow. It should be clear that, however opaque a discourse they inhabit, these poems are indeed profoundly revealing of their writer's gender and class assignments. As I will suggest in the next chapter, the contrast with his cousin's angry reworkings of essentially the same hospitable poetic tradition could not be more stark. Wroth was seeking in large part to define her writing of poetry as an act of agency, struggling to establish the sense of autonomy that the Sidney men enjoyed by, as it were, nature. Her sense of authorship involves large and—given the hostile response by certain well-placed, male courtiers—even dangerous claims to independence. Pembroke's poetry simply assumes a coterie audience, and presumes that its readers and listeners will not ask certain questions; certain responses are simply inappropriate, out of court, so to speak. The restrained lyric voice, the preponderance of monosyllables and the non-demanding syntax do not simply "express" or "reveal" a simple, sincere sensibility; rather, they create a sophisticated sense of occasion that the reader is asked politely to accept or which, it is assumed, the appropriate reader already possesses. It is poetry designed to express class solidarity by excluding any reference to class, verse that asserts an authoritarian gender politics by taking masculinist power for granted. It embodies the coherence of a group where hierarchies are established but fragile, and therefore not to be discussed, and where poetry knows its place—decorative, subordinate, and in that it is controlled and authorized by men, overwhelmingly feminine. Nonetheless, despite themselves—especially when they are looked at by later readers who are not part of that initial audience—these poems can enact what Lawrence Venuti terms "ideological subversions potentially destructive of [the] privileged social group"[30] that they are designed to celebrate. While the social order to which the poems owe their allegiance presents itself as timeless, they are unable to suppress the passing of time in the chaotic world outside the drawing room or chamber in which they were read or sung. Gender, agency, and class are, as I shall suggest in chapter six, explicit issues of great moment in Wroth's poems; without some consideration of them we would not be able satisfactorily to solve crucial problems of text, transmission, even authorship. With

Pembroke, the issues seem less central, which makes it all the more important to raise them.

Most of Pembroke's poems are love poems. They focus on male desire that is ostensibly heterosexual, even though it is intimately bound up with homoerotic bonding between the courtiers who make up the dominant members of his audience. Its overall ethos of male domination and female submission is often disguised in a rhetoric of the lover's insecurity and abasement. Desire presents itself to the lover as a paradoxical experience in which the presence of the beloved may be rare—and often is as threatening when it does occur. To deal with the threat of both the absence and presence of his mistress, the lover tries to depict her as a collection of separable bodily parts, characteristics, memories and mementos, and focuses obsessively on their separate or cumulative effects on him.

However minor a figure, at the end of a very long and complex tradition, Pembroke may be, his poems are therefore predominantly in line with mainstream Petrarchism. They focus not on a woman's physical characteristics but their effects upon the male lover. Even if a tone of sophisticated complacency undercuts any seriousness, these effects are, again typically, predominantly paradoxical and negative: deprivation, frustration, and pain are the recurring effects the mistress has upon the lover. Love is never a mutual experience: autonomy and agency are always privileges of one partner or the other. Helplessness, possession, or loss of control, and retaliation are the main modes of interaction. Paradox dominates: he joys in his misery; he feels her presence when she is absent. He juxtaposes the "Law" of his love with his "Priviledge"; he idealizes his mistress in her absence. She is overvalued so she can be, the lover hopes, exclusively the subject of his desires:

> I seek your love, and if you that deny,
> All joyes that you and all the world can give
> My love-sick soul would little satisfie
> Which wants your Grace, not food to make it live.
>
> (1660, p. 33)

Whenever she does act in relation to her own wishes—predominantly by rejecting him—she is castigated by the lover as cruel, the cause of his "violent distress" (1660, p. 3). Such terms evoke caricatures of women, juvenile figures of fear, but they are ubiquitous in Petrarchism. They provide an easy solution to what might be more complex and difficult to deal with within the male fantasy structure. Moreover, such a scenario means that by controlling whatever it is—or so he fantasizes—that a woman threatens him with, he does not have to deal with "the woman's part" in himself. That, as I suggested in the previous chapter, is one of the most disturbing aspects of the Petrarchan script. "All too often," as Kaplan puts it, a man's "independence and assertiveness are founded on an infantile ideal of what a real man should be. He has very little opportunity to integrate the feminine and masculine aspects of his identity." Men, she goes on, "are not born sadists. However, when their humiliating and frightening feminine strivings rise too close to the surface, some men are driven to rape, mutilation ansd mutilation homicide"—or, in terms of Petrarchism, to metaphors of violence and what Wroth terms "molestation."[31] Instead of acknowledging a woman as an equal "other," Petrarchism helps produce a male subject who gives himself up to juvenile speculations and dualistic generalizations about the power of women. When she does respond to him, the male lover typically finds some way not just to express gratitude and dependence, but to assert his further power: "I left you," one of Pembroke's poems is headed, "and now the gain of you is to me a double Gain" (1660, p. 25). He must reject her if he is to assert his male autonomy. A manuscript poem, either by Pembroke or John Hoskins, is a typical variation on this trope:

Absence heare my protestation
  Against thy strengthe
  Distance and lengthe,
Doe what thou canst for alteration:
  For harts of truest mettall
  Absence doth joyne, and time doth fettle.

Who loves a Mistris of right quality,
  His mind hath founde
  Affections grounde
Beyond time, place, and all mortality:
  To harts that cannot vary
  Absence is present, time doth tary:

My Sences want their outward motion
  Which now within
  Reason doth win,
Redoubled by her secret notion:
  Like rich men that take pleasure
  In hidinge more then handling treasure.

By absence this good means I gaine
  That I can catch her
  Where none can watch her

In some close corner of my braine:
   There I embrace and there kiss her,
   And so enjoye her, and so miss her.
                  (Bodleian Eng. poet. f.9, fol 43)

Behind the recurrent presence/absence paradox, and the insistence on the controlling male gaze, lies an underlying male fear of the effect the woman has upon the lover. In some poems this fear is dealt with by idealization, but another way of dealing with that fear is by ridiculing the woman. As an example from Pembroke's poems, we can glance at "One with admiration told me," a lively, cynical ballad found only in two other manuscript sources, including the Lawes MS, as well as in *1660*. It takes a mock-Platonic perspective on a tall mistress:

One with admiration told me,
He did wonder much & marvel,
(As by chance he did behold ye)
How I could become so servile
To thy beauty, which he swears
Every Ale house Lettice wears.

Then he frames a second notion
From thy revoluting eyes,
Saying, such a wanton motion
From their lustre did arise,
That of force thou couldst not be
From the shame of women free.

Then he blames the work of Nature,
'Cause she fram'd thy body tall,
Alledging that so high a stature
Was most subject to a fall:
Still detracting from thy worth,
That which most doth set thee forth.

So the *Buzzard Phoebus* flies,
When the *Eagle's* piercing eye
See those noble mysteries
Which adorn the azur'd skye;
Bravest objects so we find
Strike the weaker judgements blind.

For I know thy native beauty,
Teaching Art her imitation;

182

Ows no mortal Power a duty,
But as free from alteration
(If not whiter) as the skin
Of the spotless *Ermylin.*

And those Love-alluring Darts
Shot from thy tralucent eye,
To the knowing man imparts
Such an awful Majesty,
That each man may read the mirror
Of thy mind, and he his error.

If thy curious body's frame,
To thy making add no splendor,
Why adore we *Cynthia's* Name,
And our Poets most commend her
When amongst her Nymphs she crushes,
Cedar-like 'mongst lower bushes.

But my *Julia* I am sure,
Be thou low or high of stature,
Thou from blemish art, and as pure
As the yester-night-born creature;
And though blind men talk of light,
None can judge that wants his sight.
                    (*1660*, pp. 50–52)

Putting aside the vague possibility that the tall "Julia" refers to Mary
Wroth, the compliments to the woman in this poem are presented in a
typically amused and cynical tone, which assumes as the poem's primary
audience to be not the mistress herself but other men—friends and
acquaintances perhaps of the poet, who can all be expected to respond
to women, tall or otherwise, in similar vein. This generic woman is
reduced to an object of lazy, patronizing desire, her particular physical
characteristics merely add to her temporary interest as a plaything. The
speaker looks for approval not to her (her availability is taken for
granted and "she," after all, is a fictional construct of male fantasies that
can fit any woman) but to his male associates. By a skillful manipulation
of tone and lightly worn mythological references—a seemingly careless
display of masculinist coterie wit—and by concluding with an appropriately firm cliché, which supposedly summarizes what the audience
is assumed to think, any interrogation of gender or class assumptions
and biases is meant to be rendered irrelevant. But beneath the surface
jocularity and the easy cynicism of male bonding, there are serious and

disturbing issues of gender politics. Why this fixation on avoiding direct and intimate contact? Why the unwillingness to accept the equality of another's desires? In agonal relationships, in order to keep the forces of frustrated infantile rage from being turned back on the self, women are made to serve the role of scapegoat for men's insecurity, awareness and fear of separation, individuation, and contingency.

Are there any ways by which these fantasies of erotic domination and submission might be replaced by (or, more optimistically be seen as displaced yearnings for) wholeness and mutuality beyond the antagonism of bipolar gender assignments. Not, it seems, in male Petrarchism. The predominant way by which the Petrarchan lover tries to deal with the threat represented by women is, as I explained in the previous chapter, through the dominant male strategy of fetishism. Fetishism entails "a displacement of sexual desire" away from the identity of a woman to some accessory or garment, some object ancillary to her being. By virtue of its partial nature, its power, unlike that of the beloved herself, can be controlled and manipulated. Though rarely discussed as such in standard accounts of Petrarch, the fetish has, in effect, long been noticed as a major ingredient of Petrarchism, which is replete with celebrations of the beloved's dress, her hair, her pets, her house, or her habits. The classic fetishistic move assumes that it is easier to deal with and "miss" the over-whelming power of the beloved when one is alone, when the lover has the beloved in fantasy rather than in the flesh: "sometimes all a man needs is his fetish, for embedded in the fetish is the drama, the characters, the stage set, and an entire history of the lost desires and confused imaginings of childhood."[32] A poem of Pembroke's from 1660, "When mine eyes, first admiring your rare beauty," is a particularly intriguing example:

> When mine eyes, first admiring your rare beauty,
> Secretly stole the Picture of your face;
> They, fearing they might erre, with humble duty,
> Through unknown pathes, convey'd it to that place,
> Where Reason and true Judgment hand in hand
> Sate, and each workmanship of sences stand.
>
> Reason could find no Reason but to love it,
> So rich of beauty was it, full of Grace:
> True Judgment scan'd each part, and did approve it
> To be the model of some heavenly face;
> And both agreed to place it in my heart,
> Whence they decreed it never should depart.
>
> Then, since I was not born to be so blest,
> Your real self fair Mistress to obtain,

Yet must your image dwell within in my brest,
And in that secret Closet still remain:
Where all alone retir'd, I'le sit and view
Your Picture, Mistress, since I may not you.

(1660, pp. 54–55)

On one level (the level of coterie entertainment which the poem privileges and which it wants its readers to accept without questioning), it is a nicely crafted compliment, working logically, using firm touches of allegorical narrative, and conveying an potentially disarming mixture of self-pity and possessiveness in the final stanza. In terms of the sexual politics of late Petrarchism, however, it is far more revealing. Sight, and by extension rational visualization, is what is used to conjure up the power of the woman, even when she is absent. The lover freezes the beloved into an image, a statue, a picture, at a moment of his choice: "it protects him from becoming conscious of some wishes and fantasies that would otherwise frighten and humiliate him." To survive, he must divide and fetishize her. As Kaplan comments, in every perverse scenario, "something or someone is treated as a fetish object, which is why fetishism is considered the prototype of all sexual perversions."[33]

Written on the decaying edge of the tradition, Pembroke's poems contain little of classic Petrarchism's male masochism, except as part of a posture to be repudiated by a vigorous assertion of male domination acompanied by some (often very direct) misogyny. But there are some masochistic notes. The lover asks to be rejected in order to generate a compensatory overvaluation of his beloved: "Disdaine me still, that I may ever love" (Kaplan comments relevantly that "the strange idea that sexual masochism is a male perversion becomes more likely when we realize that a crucial aspect of the perverse strategy is to give expression to a man's feminine wishes and longings while still keeping him in a position of masculine power." The observations of the modern feminist therapist here leap across the centuries.) He beseeches her: "Let not my sighs, nor tears, thy virtue move," since (in a revealing reminder of the mothering metaphor), love's "Nurse is Scorn" (1660, p. 5). ("In that way," notes Kaplan, "he can identify with the position of the masochist and fulfill his unconscious and shameful feminine longings without anyone's being the wiser.")[34] Women know, another poem asserts, the keen edge of male masochism: "And women know when they retire, / It makes true Love love dearer" (1660, p. 72). Masochism, however, and of a far more deterministic kind, is a predominant strain of Wroth's poems, as the next chapter will demonstrate. More typical in her cousin's poems is the assertion that while a woman is blameworthy if she is inconstant—"The Evening kind, / The morning of another mind"

(*1660*, p. 2)—a man can always justify his leaving. "Disdain me still,"
which was, as I noted earlier, printed by Dowland in 1611, is particularly
relevant here:

I.

Disdain me still, that I may ever love,
For who his love enjoyes, can love no more
The War once past, with Peace men Cowards prove,
  And ships return'd, do rot upon the shore.
Then though thou frown, I'le say thou art most fair,
And still I'le love, though still I must despair.

II.

As heat's to life, so is desire to love,
  For these once quench'd, both life & love are don;
Let not my sighs, nor tears, thy Virtue move,
  Like basest Mettle, do not melt too soon:
Laugh at my woes, although I ever mourn;
Love surfeits with reward, his Nurse is scorn.

(1660, pp. 5, 45)

It is a simple, witty lyric, posturing with mildly paradoxical bitterness,
its cynicism tempered into a courtly melancholy by Dowland's musical
setting. The argument, such as it is—the lover pleads that his mistress *not*
love him, so that he may continue desiring her—is a typically watered-
down Petrarchan paradox. Like all of Pembroke's lyrics, its desired effect
is to amuse, to pass the time pleasingly and make no further demand
on its readers than, perhaps, memory (and desire for a repetition) of the
pleasure to which it refers. We are in the world so richly evoked in the
opening scene of *Twelfth Night*. In its gender politics, "Disdain me still"
also invokes the decadent aestheticism of that play. It is unselfconsciously
masculinist. The analogies—with war, commerce and metallurgy—are
the commonplaces of an unselfconsciously male courtiers' world, its
view of women rudimentarily dismissive except as a stimulus to further
male desire. Indeed, the only acknowledgement of a female role in the
production of desire—and no less masculinist for that—comes in the
final line, where love is characterized as a petulant spoiled male child
and his "Nurse," his sustainer and protector, is "scorn." Women are a
necessary stimulant, at best a pleasant diversion, necessary caretakers for
brats, but otherwise threatening in their relations with men. Reflecting
this male fear, women must be kept on display, their each movement and
habit sexualized not merely for the benefit but the protection of the male
onlooker. Laces, fabric, hair, eyes are all constructed to be evaluated by
the controlling spectator. That the impression of women on the speaker

186

is so overwhelming is less attributable, therefore, to anything inherent to particular women than to the discourse that is producing Woman, either as rapturous fantasy or as victimizing, disillusioning hag. Either way, in no sense is a woman ever seen to be an agent. In terms of the period's gender politics, such libertinism afforded the thrill (albeit cheap) of indulging in male sexual promiscuity while upholding the dominant ideology of transcendent purity and idealism.

In such poems, the surface idealization of women has broken down and been replaced with an explicit carnality: it appears to have crossed a frontier from the Petrarchan mode, and yet it retains its dependence on it. The Petrarchist fetishization of the female body continues, as does the focus on the lover's feelings and self-exploration. As Malcolm Evans comments, "the Petrarchan influence is never fully expunged in the bulk of English love poetry in the first half of the seventeenth century . . . As an international lovers' discourse . . . the Petrarchan text, to apply Derrida's phrase, has no outside."[35] Overall, Pembroke's poems are overall characterized by a tone of lazy, "sophisticate" emotion: the physicality of love is rarely denied. Nature, one poem smirks, placed alluring odors in sexual organs to entice, giving "from the curious shop of her rich treasure / To fair parts comeliness, to baser parts pleasure" (1660, p. 94). Joking about a woman's sexual attractions is, of course, a way of distancing her threat. Commenting on some of her cases, Kaplan notes that "merely the thought of a woman's inner sexual and procreative organs—her vagina and her uterus—can be a reminder of [men's] frightening wishes to be eternally united with Mother in some smooth, womblike utopia where the rough and troubling realities of everyday existence can no longer disturb the peace." The much commented upon physical directness of Cavalier and Restoration poetry—especially that of Rochester some half century or so later—may be seen in these terms. The male who uses such distancing strategies, notes Kaplan, is afraid "that some awful fate would befall his penis if he should insert that most prized organ into the cavernous emptiness of a vagina. Yet so desperate is he to prove his masculinity that he must have erections and he must enter the vagina as many times as possible." Here we are moving beyond Petrarchism, and into the dark fear of the enigmatic and threatening female genitals that, later in the century, haunts Rochester's poetry, which he can control only by violation, compulsion, and finally annihilation. That reaction even brings us into the aura of the Marquis de Sade. "The more we become adept at reading perverse scripts," writes Kaplan after surveying the characteristic male scenarios, "the more we come to realize that every perversion is an effort to give some expression to, while yet controlling, the full strength of potentially murderous impulses" arising from the gender system of our culture.[36]

Am I taking such a flippant piece of misogyny too seriously? One may, indeed, confess it is a well-sustained and organized mildly amusing piece, typical of its occasion as a piece of light court entertainment, characteristic of the late phase of decadent Petrarchism where the tradition has been invaded by so many others that it almost belies the label. But there is more that needs to be said, since there are broader issues of cultural politics at stake. As I noted at the end of the previous chapter, to concentrate on the sexual politics of such a slight lyric, or on any of Pembroke's, would seem to be over reading with a vengeance, were it not that his poems grow out of both a distinctive cultural milieu and a deeply-rooted and long lasting system by which love and desire have been formulated. This whole poetic tradition, I suggest, betrays a vast and powerful set of cultural assumptions. In some of her poems, Mary Wroth gives voice to sentiments that approach such criticism, but the poems were not publicly circulated, and they were by a woman in any case. We do not restore a woman's possibility of, or rights to, agency by aestheticizing, in whatever supposedly loving detail, her body, let alone mementos of her presence or absence. To be thus positioned not merely by the slightly boorish wit of a minor poet, but by a whole tradition that encouraged such attitudes to be seen as "natural," is a cultural phenomenon of some importance. In Pembroke's lifetime, at times, no doubt, one of those women so positioned among these contradictions was Pembroke's cousin who, in the family tradition, had her own collection of songs and sonnets, and it is to them I will now turn.

6

"Watch, gaze, and marke":
The Poetry of Mary Wroth

The women I have seen in clinical practice who present such images of spatial
containment and inner space also have masochistic fantasies in which surrender
is called forth by the other's power to penetrate, to know, and to control their
desire. Yet in these fantasies we gradually discern a strand of seeking recognition
for a force that originates within, a force imbued with the authenticity of inner
desire . . . what is experientially female is the association of desire with a space,
a place within the self, from which this force can emerge.

Jessica Benjamin

Can this be me? The disposition of idealised bodies, anatomically like our
own, in postures of dominance and subjugation, is not intended to do anything
for us.

Marion Glastonbury[1]

Despite their apparent obviousness, the words we use to describe gender assignments are sites of continual struggle. "Man" and "woman" are sliding, not stable, signifiers. Nor are the material practices that embody our lived sexual roles adequately descibed by the tragic limitations of such binarism. New forms of gender assignment emerge; new patterns of what we persist in calling "masculinity" and "femininity" are engendered. Representations never fully correspond to lived experiences, yet experiences are given form only by means of their representations. No literary text attempting to articulate gendered experiences is, therefore, ever "merely" literary; inevitably part of the history of ideologies, it opens political, religious, racial, class, and gender related questions—and perhaps the more intensely so when it is situated on the margins of the dominant literary forms of its society, where it is a reminder that any moment in history is constituted by a multiplicity of material practices and that what appears to be dominant depends, in part, for its power on what has been, at least for the moment, marginalized.

Mary Wroth's poems constitute a major document in tracing the ways both assigned and lived gender roles were under pressure in the early seventeenth century. The first collection of Petrarchan love poetry in English by a woman, *Pamphilia to Amphilanthus* was published in 1621, appended to Wroth's prose romance, *The Countesse of Mountgomeries Urania*. The date is important: even in the time it was written, it was a culturally marginal work. 1621 is some thirty years after the main vogue of sonneteering in England (and twelve years after even Shakespeare's belated and probably pirated collection appeared). In the previous decade Wroth had been mentioned by family members, a few friends, and dependents in a predictably adulatory manner as an inheritor of the Sidney poetic genius, but the actual publication of *Pamphilia to Amphilanthus* received virtually no notice. Nevertheless, along with the poems she inserted into *Urania* itself, *Pamphilia to Amphilanthus* is a major document at the end of the dominant tradition of Renaissance love poetry and a focal point in the long struggle to challenge the assumptions and practices of that tradition. It is a prime source for our attempting to read, today, what it was to be gendered as a woman in early modern England, and to try to write within and against the structures of desire determined by that gender assignment.

Vilified when they appeared in print, Wroth's writings were virtually unknown, except as curiosities, until the mid–1970s. After over three centuries of neglect, they are currently receiving an increasing amount of attention: since 1977 there have been three editions of her writings (with a further one, the complete *Urania*, awaited), a monograph, a collection of critical essays, and a number of articles and chapters of books on her.[2] Much of the (very sparse) earlier attention she received was because she was a member of the Sidney family, but today it is largely because of the seriousness and power of her writing. Wroth is certainly the most important woman writer in English before Aphra Behn: we are not dealing as we are with Pembroke, with an undeniably minor writer for whom poetry was just a spasmodic pastime. Simply in terms of the amount of poetry she wrote, Wroth deserves careful attention. There are over two hundred of her poems extant: 103 in the 1621 version of *Pamphilia to Amphilanthus*; another nineteen in *Urania* itself (some of which had been in an earlier manuscript version of *Pamphilia to Amphilanthus*, now in the Folger, which also contains an additional six poems that were excluded from the 1621 edition); another fifty-six in the published *Urania* and a further eighteen in the unpublished second part that were excluded from both versions of *Pamphilia to Amphilanthus*; and, finally, nine separate lyrics in her verse play, *Love's Victory*. It is possible that there are still more unidentified in manuscripts. So far as dating is concerned, from some internal references at least a few were probably written in the first decade of James I's reign—the period for which we have the most detailed documentary evidence for the liaison between Wroth and Pembroke—and some may have been circulating by 1613, when Jonson refers to Wroth's poems making him both a better lover and a better poet.[3] There is no way of saying definitely which poems Jonson saw; if the poems he praises were indeed part of what became *Pamphilia to Amphilanthus*, they were no doubt revised in subsequent years, even as late as 1618–21, when Wroth was probably composing *Urania* and deciding which poems should be inserted into the romance. The years 1614–21, after her husband's death—when she was sexually and socially independent, when she bore her two illegitimate children, and when she wrote *Urania*—was most likely a period of great insecurity but, quite possibly, unexpected satisfaction to her. Even if it originated earlier, *Pamphilia to Amphilanthus* was almost certainly revised in these years, and records more directly than her other writings her struggles against the constraints of

Deare cherish this, and wth itt my soules will
nor for itt i am away doe itt abuse,
alas itt left poore mee your brest to chuse
as the blest shrine wher itt would harbour still;
Then favor shew, and nott vnkindly kill
the hart wch fled to you butt doe excuse
that wch for better, did the wurse refuse,
and pleasd I'le bee, though hartles my lyfe spill,
Butt if you will bee kind and iust indeed,
send mee your hart wth in mines place shall feed
on faithfull loue to your deuotion bound:
Ther shall itt see the sacrifises made
of pure, and spottles loue wch shall nott vade
while soule, and body are together found; /

Cruell =

Page from the holograph manuscript of Lady Mary Wroth,
Pamphilia to Amphilanthus. *Reproduced by permission of
the Folger Shakespeare Library, Washington, D.C.*

being a woman. Much of the power of her poetry lies in the record of those struggles.

In writing in the Petrarchan mode, Mary Wroth was following paths that were (to put it mildly) heavily trodden. Not only are her poems among the last recognizably Petrarchan poetry in English, but they are doubly "belated," to use Harold Bloom's term, in relation to her own family.[4] The commitment to the poetic vocation and to the details of craft that all three of the first generation Sidney poets—Philip, Mary, and Robert—showed is evident in her poems, but no doubt being a Sidney was itself a provocation to write, even for a woman. That she took her writing seriously can be documented from the extensive changes she made over perhaps a decade to the poems. The holograph copy in the Folger contains corrections which were later included in the revised text appended to *Urania*, and many of the poems were moved back and forth between the main body of the prose romance and the appended sequence. The Folger manuscript is perhaps rather like the manuscript of Greville's *Caelica*, essentially a private, cumulative collection designed primarily or even exclusively for the author herself.[5]

Even though they are far less frustrating than Pembroke's, Wroth's poems still present any modern editor with a dilemma in reconstructing their history. If the 1621 printing is used as the copytext, then the editor needs to either ignore or find a way of sorting through printer's accidentals, and then must somehow fit in or append those poems found only in the Folger copy. If the Folger manuscript is used as copytext, then an undatable ordering, even though with authorial accidentals, becomes the basis for the edition, and the reordering, additions and omissions of 1621 are obscured. In my edition of *Pamphilia to Amphilanthus* (1977), I chose the former course; in her edition of the complete poems (1983), Roberts followed the Folger text, but used the ordering of 1621. Neither is entirely satisfactory, and that in large part is because of the nature of the collection. As with most Petrarchan sequences, even as it was being written it was being reread and rewritten by its author. Adapting Deleuze and Guattari's terms, Roger Kuin has suggested that we should view the Petrarchan text as a desiring machine, combining the "power of the continuum" with "rupture in direction" in its "capacity for an unlimited number of connections."[6] *Pamphilia to Amphilanthus* might be best seen as a continuous text, unravelling as it is put together, never resting in a final form, in which a variety of discoveries, demands, and changing occasions clash and contradict.

As with Pembroke's poems, we are clearly in the familiar world of belated Petrarchism—plaint and paradox, sophisticated but general emotions, rhetorical smoothness and lyric grace frequently counterpointed by the disruptiveness of question or cry, and beneath all the Petrarchan stock-in-trade of juxtaposed despair and joy. If Pembroke's poems are often more "Cavalier" than "Petrarchan," Wroth's poems often read as if they would be at home in the collections of poems that had been fashionable twenty and more years before. But the cousins share the central Petrarchan inheritance: as with his, it is easy to construct from her poems a miscellany of such Petrarchan clichés, almost three hundred years old by the time she is writing. Love is "truth, and doth delight," and yet makes the lover "true slave to Fortune's spite"; it is at once the "hottest beames of zeale" and shows a "coldenesse" which "can but my despaires descry." The lover's spirit is "cloyd with griefe and paine," captive and yet free; the joys of love are rapturous and yet "heape disdaine" on the lover; the spring which the lovers see around them reflects back on the "sad sowrs / Which from mine eyes doe flow" inside the lover's minds, which exist in the delicious agony of frustration and indecision: "Restlesse I live, consulting what to doe, / And more I study, more I still undoe" (*Poems*, p. 151). Such conventional paradoxes and complaints are frequently dressed in stylized neoplatonic garb, thus bringing Wroth closer to some of the poetic fashions of the Jacobean and Caroline court lyric. At times, in some of her less felicitous moments, her verse can sound like the drabbest of poets thirty years earlier, at others like a Jacobean court wit. Overall, her preferred style is closer to the direct voice of a Jonson than the elaborate wit of a Donne. Jonson may well have admired those many poems with direct and uncluttered metaphors:

> Sleepe fy possess mee nott, nor doe nott fright
>   Mee with thy heavy, and thy deathlike might
>   For counterfetting vilder then deaths sight,
>   And such deluding more my thought doe spite.
> (Poems, p. 95)

Around 1610, perhaps about the same time as she was starting to write what became *Pamphilia to Amphilanthus*, Lord Dudley North dedicated a treatise on poetry to her, which contains a strong attack on what was to become known as "Metaphysical" poetry and a defence of the plain Jonsonian style. Predictably setting his argument in terms of the prestige of the Sidney family, he claims that "the admirable inventions and matter of your unimitable Uncles extant works flourish in applause of all"; further, he praises such features as "the well wrought and exquisite harmony of their Cadence," their "round, cogent cleare and gracefull delivery," and asserts (again in accord with Jonson) that "the best eloquence is to make our selves clearly understood." It may well be that Wroth herself was starting to write with such notions in mind about the time that North was writing. Her poetry can therefore be placed in a transitional position between Elizabethan "drab" verse and the Jonsonian style which grew from it. Wroth's poems rarely catch the lyric qualities of Elizabethan song: in the terms I used to speak of Pembroke's poems, even the "songs" in *Pamphilia to Amphilanthus* are brooding and melancholy, "declamatory" rather than songlike. But the most significant aspect of her writing arises from the contradictions between the predominantly masculinist rhetoric of the Petrarchan sonnet and her sense of her own gendered position as a woman, lover, reader, and writer. What was it for a woman to write a blazon? To gaze at a woman's beauties, her "ruby lips, pearl teeth, damask cheeks, face, neck, chin, formed of purest snow" (*Newberry 1*, fol. 24) may seem a "natural" default position for a male writer. But what happens when the passive object of such "devotion" wants to write in the same mode? To what extent is she aware of being a multiply split subject? The conventional answer is that she should not notice: that the form itself dictates the response. But that is to assume that the "neutral" reading position is not gendered, while in fact it institutionalizes a wholesale gagging of women readers and writers. In 1630 the courtesy book writer Robert Cleaver voiced the whole culture's proscription of women's language when he recommended that "as the echo answereth but one word for many, which are spoken to her, so a woman's answer should be in a word." A very condition of Wroth's permission to write poetry meant that she had to locate herself within a tradition that largely denied her, as a woman, a place from which to speak.[7]

Pamphilia to Amphilanthus is more various than most collections of Petrarchan sonnets,[8] and not surprisingly, critics intent on finding a "unity" to the whole—quite apart from the textual problem discussed above—have perceived quite different structural organizations. Jeff Masten argues that we should see *Pamphilia to Amphilanthus* not as a single collection, but as several sequences of poems copied into a single manuscript. This, he argues, accounts for the unusual numbering, which starts at #1 at several places and has blank pages between groups of poems. McLaren sees the 1621 order as divided into two, the title sequence and an unfinished "Crowne of Sonnets"; May Pauliessen sees four sequences: the opening one courtly, witty, and frequently flirtatious; the second, more erotic, "occult, more debauched"; third, the "Crowne"; and then a concluding group focusing on spiritual love. Roberts agrees on a four-fold structure, but sees the focus differently: an opening section of fifty-five sonnets and songs focusing on Pamphilia's struggle for love; a second on the darker side of love; the crowne of sonnets in which different versions of love are debated; and a final section in which unpredictability, pain, and loss are all acknowledged as an inevitable part of love.[9] Roberts's reading is a pleasurable and comfortable (in Barthes's sense) narrativization, but, as we read any sustained collection of Petrarchan lyrics, inevitably we discover that what holds it together is less (or not only) the "story" but the arbitrariness of desire, the surges of discontinuity and surprise. It is as if the self that writes is continually being rewritten by the experiences it seeks to enclose and comprehend.

As I noted in the two previous chapters, the Petrarchan poem centers on its fragile and self-obsessed "I." It is a device, at once rhetorical and psychological, that functions to provide an impression of stability and continuity to the experience the poem tries to encode, but so often what the poem records (and evokes) is a disturbing instability. Part of the power of Petrarchism had traditionally been that it encouraged its readers (including the poet) to acknowledge that the self that writes feels not harmony but continual dissatisfaction. Except under the most stringent ideological constraints the Petrarchan "I" is always under attack, always liable to be surprised by change, dislocated by the pull of impossible futures and indelible pasts. In Wroth's case this painful discovery is all the more threatening because of the way the poems highlight the dilemmas of her gender assignment.[10]

Petrarchism involves the encoding of a set of recurrent, perhaps even inherent, male strategies for dealing with desire. I say "perhaps even inherent": a more optimistic reading suggests that they are typical of a society that rigidly hierarchizes gender differences along the lines of domination and submission. In this chapter I want to ask what variations and distortions occur when a woman, traditionally occupying the place of the ostensible object of the poet's devotion, the focus of the "I"'s gaze, takes up the subject position itself? Necessarily caught up in the enormously powerful discourses of an authoritarian patriarchy that went far beyond poetry, what opportunities did a woman poet at this time have to discover a voice that she herself owned, if not "individually," at least as a woman voicing the shared subjectivity of other women? In a poetic tradition where male formulations of desire were so dominant, could she settle for (or even envisage) anything more than fragmentation? Would it be the "same" fragmentation as that articulated on behalf of the male subject position? While these questions are fundamental to our understanding of Wroth, and all will recur in my discussion, rather than treating her as a "woman poet"—as if that were a self-explanatory category determined by a fixed gender role—I want to raise questions about how her options and possibilities as a writer were affected by her gender assignment. In chapter three I suggested that in her life and especially in her relations with her father, husband, and cousin, she was struggling to re-gender the fantasies and narratives of the Sidney family romance. Here I want to show how that process works out in a particular discursive form, the Petrarchan sonnet collection, which had traditionally been as rigidly coded "male" as the society that had engendered it.

There is no doubt that Wroth's poems, far more than those of her cousin, ring with a distinctive voice, one that speaks powerfully to her age and beyond. It is a rhetorically confrontational voice, something which derives only in part from the insistent sense of audience in the Petrarchan tradition. It typically makes demands on its audience for attention that seems, on occasion, defensive to the point of petulance:

> Bee you all pleas'd? your pleasures grieve nott mee:
>   Doe you delight? I envy nott your joy:
>   Have you content? contentment with you bee:
>   Hope you for bliss? hope still, and still injoye:
> (Poems, p. 91)

Frequently, it is a voice that seemingly resents speaking at all, at least so as to be overheard. Yet while reluctantly acknowledging the presence of listeners, the poems nonetheless convey a sense of active dialogue and dissension: conversations rather than monologues emerge through the poems. This is a paradoxical effect arising from the encoded situation of a woman writer: desiring to write, she finds herself unauthorized to do so by the very form she chooses in which to write. She resents being overheard trespassing on ground already occupied, but it is ground that she must nonetheless step firmly upon. Wroth is uncommonly effective at setting up multiple voices within the poem that belong to the speaker herself, brooding alone, giving herself advice:

> Yett is ther hope: Then Love butt play thy part
> Remember well thy self, and think on mee;
> Shine in those eyes which conquer'd have my hart;
> And see if mine bee slack to answere thee.
> (Poems, p. 86)

As in her uncle Philip's *Astrophil and Stella* or many of her father's lyrics (even some of her aunt's sometimes intensely dramatic psalm metaphrases), Wroth's poems stage the process of internalization by which both women and men alike were positioned by contradictory erotic and social demands. And sometimes, like those of her male relations, Wroth's poems show her heroine trying to withdraw from public responsibilities, even from public view, in order to deal with the internal dialogue of her desires. As in her father's and her uncle's poems, public or ideological contradictions are internalized as private debates. But in *Pamphilia to Amphilanthus*, most of these psychological divisions arise specifically from a woman's gender assignment:

Why should wee nott loves purblind charmes resist?
Must wee bee servile, doing what hee list?
Noe, seeke some hoste to harbour thee: I fly

Thy babish trickes, and freedome doe profess;
Butt O my hurt, makes my lost hart confess
I love, and must: So farwell liberty.

(*Poems*, p. 95)

To what extent are these poems autobiographical? Can we trace any consistent (or significantly inconsistent) relations between the "I" of the poems and their author? Or are we dealing, as we were with Pembroke, with the apparent anonymity of coterie verse? Unlike her cousin's poems, Wroth's include a tissue of narratives taken from her own life, the most obvious of which refers to her relationship with her cousin. Kristeva speaks of poetry enabling us to "play around that exquisite border where the 'true' trips over into the 'make-believe'," and, especially in the early sonnets of *Pamphilia to Amphilanthus*, there are a number of references to the relationship between the two cousins that seem to hover titillatingly between personal revelation and fantasy, perhaps in the way that Philip's "Rich" sonnets do.[11] Pamphilia claims that "many Poets write as well by imitation, as by sence of passion" (*Urania*, p. 77). The names attached to the sequence's hero and heroine— the names also of the main characters of *Urania*—mean, respectively, "all-loving" and "lover of two." That they are in part a projection of Wroth's wishfulfillment fantasies about her relationship with Pembroke, what she conceived as her own fidelity and his lack of commitment, seems undeniable. The two lovers in both the poems and romance are first cousins, whose love, we are told, though for no explicable reason, must be kept secret. It is clear, moreover, that while he gains from such secrecy, she suffers privately from lack of public recognition of her love. In *Urania* this insistent secrecy lasts even after the two have concluded a public vow of commitment: as I shall show in chapter eight, it is as if they both are and are not committed to each other, just as their love both is and is not secret. In the poems, although likewise no reason is provided, secrecy is also a given: "thy chiefe paine is that I must itt hide / From all save only one who showld itt see" (*Poems*, p. 107). Like the romance, too, the poems give clear signals about the "real" identity of the protagonists. There are recurring puns on the name "will," conventional enough in themselves, but too many to be coincidental. Such references include, from the sixth poem: "Long have I suffer'd, and esteem'd itt deere / Since such thy will; yett grew my paine more neere" (*Poems*, p. 88); or, two poems later:

But now, itt seemes, thou would'st I should thee love;
    I doe confess, t'was thy will made mee chuse;
    And thy faire showes made mee a lover prove
    When I my freedome did, for paine refuse.

                                     (*Poems*, p. 90)

In a song late in the collection, Wroth puns on both her cousin's name and her own, asserting that "your chiefe honors bee in this / By worth what wunn is, nott to leave," and admonishing him that "if worthles to bee priz'd / Why att first will you itt move, / And if worthy, why dispis'd?" (*Poems*, pp. 137–38). Merging the figure of Cupid with the male lover, she acknowledges that instead of falling in love with the "wanton boy" who shot her, she has found herself in love with "Will," who is the object of her poetry, and who is therefore even more dangerous than Cupid himself: "When love came blindfold, and did chaleng mee / Indeed I lov'd butt wanton boy not hee."[12] In a poem in the the Folger MS, the poem's speaker identifies "Will" with her own will, and begs him not to seek freedom from the bonds of love. As Pauliessen suggests, the enigma or riddle of the poem is that, despite the poem's admonition to do so, "Wee will not seeke to free will." In another sonnet where she puns on her cousin's name in the opening line, "Deare cherish this, and with itt my soules will," the second part of the poem reads like "a coy letter of a proposal of love" to Will, suggesting that his heart will not be abused in the exchange: "Butt if you will bee kind, and just indeed,/ Send mee your hart which in minds place shall feed." One poem in particular makes the biographical reference extremely clear:

How like a fire doth love increase in mee,
    The longer that itt lasts, the stronger still,
    The greater, purer, brighter, and doth fill
    Noe eye with wunder more, then hopes still bee

Bred in my brest, when fires of love are free
    To use that part to theyr best pleasing will,
    And now impossible itt is to kill
    The heat soe great wher Love his strength doth see.

My eyes can scarce sustain the flames my hart
    Doth trust in them my passions to impart,
    And languishingly strive to show my love;

My breath nott able is to breathe least part
    Of that increasing fuell of my smart;
    Yet love I will till I butt ashes prove.

                              (*Poems*, pp. 114–15)

As Roberts notes, this is "one of the very few places in which the identification of Amphilanthus is made explicit."[13] The poem marks the end of the first section of sonnets and is signed "Pamphilia."

There are enough such references that if these poems were circulated among Wroth's family and close friends, the autobiographical level would surely have been recognized. J. B. Broadbent speaks of the "air of public intimacy" of such verse, with its tone of a friendly correspondence that we are invited to overhear. Unfortunately, none of Wroth's poems seem to be "answer" poems like those Pembroke wrote with Rudyerd, so the connections between the two cousins' poems are generic rather than specific. What they share is the ubiquitous Petrarchan paraphernalia: metaphors of lovers stealing glances, the contradictions of love, its magnetizing disdain and compulsive misery. Stretching matters somewhat, we could put Pembroke's "If her disdaine" alongside some of Wroth's sonnets and see it replying to a number of hers. But if we are, as Pauliessen argues, in the middle of a coterie, it is a coterie of all Petrarchist poets, a ubiquitous rather than a private lexicon, with only occasional specific references to note.[14]

So far as a narrative is concerned, only the opening sequence of forty-eight sonnets and six songs seems to have any plausible internal coherence, and that at such a general level that no precise sequence of biographical references could be constructed. It seems likely, indeed, that this group of poems was organized into a sequence. It starts out with two sonnets dealing with the opening of a love affair. The speaker feels, not entirely happily, that she has been picked out by love (1); this victimization has occurred in an encounter within the court (2); she thus finds herself in the conventional Petrarchan state of oscillation between misery and hope (3-5). This opening group of six sonnets culminates in an assertion in which she indicates that the source of her joyful grief lies in the desires of another: "Long I have suffer'd, and esteem'd itt deare / Since such thy will"(6). (I will not, at this point, pause over the gender politics of that subservience to another's desire, but will return to it and like sentiments later.) A song is placed after each group of six sonnets, except the last: in song 1, Pamphilia bewails the contrast between the spring outside and her internal winter, and vows that if she is not happy, she will at least make poetry from her miseries. The second group (sonnets 7-12, song 2) resumes the bewailing of her fate: the pun on "will" is again in evidence. She writes poetry to contain her misery (8), and asserts that she is married not to her beloved but to sorrow (9). Her lover arrives, a weary traveler (10), causing her increasing torments, especially as she lies awake at night (11, 12). The second song, concluding the second group of sonnets, depicts her weeping, alone, at night. The third group (sonnets 13-18, song 3) again starts with a sonnet begging that she, "one, who att your will, yeelds to the grave," will be spared destruction (13), even though she cannot resist him (14). This is followed by four sonnets (15–18) and a song on sleeplessness.

The next group (sonnets 19–24, song 4) continues the concern with sleeplessness and brooding alone. Pamphilia considers her plight while her beloved is outside hunting (23), and warns herself against jealousy (24). The following group (sonnets 25–30, song 5) focuses on her absence from the beloved. A light, courtly song (song 4) announces the theme, and then the following sonnet (25) pleads with him to return from his journey. The next sonnet once again points to the identity of the beloved, begging him for an exchange of hearts (26), especially as he produces only hopelessness and grief in his absence (27–30). The fifth song is, appropriately, a complaint against time. The sixth group (sonnets 31–36, song 6) opens with Pamphilia lying down, asking Fortune for comfort: she regrets that love has to be snatched from time (31), thus producing increasing frustration. She describes herself as a hive of love (32), is aware of and even glorifies in being watched in public (33, 34), even though she feels her love is hopeless (35) and must be hidden from all except one (36). The song that concludes the sequence concerns eyes, the means by which she is watched. The seventh group (sonnets 37–42, song 7) opens with poems on night (37) and banishment (38), followed by an expression of the inadequacy of her poetry, even when it is admired (39). The group concludes with two sonnets on emphasizing that true love is an inner state (40, 41) and one affirming that her great love is also her great woe (42), while the concluding song of the group also dwells on sorrow. The final group (sonnets 43–47) starts by imagining her lover as a light shining everywhere except where she is: "But now alas, your sight is heare forbid, / And darkness must these poore lost rooms posesse." Again, her state is contrasted with the burgeoning spring (44), as she bewails her lover's absence (45). Once again punning on "will" (46), she acknowledges she has engaged in a forbidden love and that, therefore, her devotion is hopeless (47). Then, in the final sonnet, signed "Pamphilia" in the Folger manuscript, she simply acknowledges that however unfulfillable it may be, she cannot help the increase of her love, and once again, in this culminating sonnet of the sequence, explicitly acknowledges the commitment to "Will": "Yett love I will till I but ashes prove."

In this way, one can, then, construct a coherent reading of the main sequence of *Pamphilia to Amphilanthus*. But what does such a reading give us beyond some extremely general narrative coherence and some scattered if undeniable biographical references? When we have "identified" the beloved as a fantasy projection of Pembroke, what have we gained? More important than tracking down biographical references, I suggest, are the ways in which Wroth's poems are written by broader discursive structures, and therefore, as I did with Pembroke's, I turn to the poems as articulations of cultural, not merely individual, narratives.

Far more self-consciously and with more evident effort than a male poet working within the Petrarchan tradition, Wroth has to struggle to define her own voice in her poems against overwhelming gender stereotypes. How does a woman poet write within such an overwhelmingly male discourse? What emerges through her poetry is a variety of moods, only some of which she shares with male poets in the tradition. They range from passive uneasiness to outright anger at the treatment that she, as a woman, receives. Some of these feelings are common to male protagonists of Petrarchan poems, but others seem to grow more directly from becoming conscious of what it is to be assigned the "woman's part" in a relationship. And some are directed towards the very structures that have brought her poetry and, more broadly, her very sense of being a woman, into existence. Like a kleptomaniac, she must steal what has hitherto been the prerogative of the male. Drawing on both case studies and theoretical work by Otto Fenichel and Gregorio Kohon, Kaplan explains how in a society where power rests largely in the hands of a few superior males, the kleptomaniac may feel both revenge and erotic excitement. Cautioning that how "the theft relates to her childhood deprivations and humiliations can be understood only by a reading of her unique unconscious script," Kaplan nonetheless notes that there are some prototypical kleptomania scripts. In the clinical literature, some relate specifically to modern commodity fetishism, with consumption as an outlet for anxiety and emptiness; others more readily grow from pre-capitalist society where the power possessed by men and desired by women also included language, movement, autonomy of many kinds. Kaplan sees Joan of Arc as a historical prototype: as Denny's reaction to the publication of *Urania* shows, men can be content when a woman's ambitions are held within approved limits, but should she "openly declare her ambitions in territories that have been defined as masculine," then she may have to "awaken the infantile fantasy that [her] intelligence is a stolen trophy," and often she must "run for cover" in her "masquerades of womanliness." Historically, Kaplan notes, when women have expressed themselves in politics or writing, males have commonly reacted by constructing the image of the virago, "convinced that the castrated ones are out to castrate the phallic ones." Denny's virulent reaction to Mary Wroth's leaving the approved confinement of pious translator and "stealing" the roles of erotic poet and romance writer is the classic reaction, even to the point of his anger being articulated as sexual abuse. Her reaction to withdraw the work and retire from public exposure is likewise the classic reaction of the abused victim of the patriachal system.[15]

We do, however, have the spoils of her thefts. In *Pamphilia to Amphilanthus*, Wroth explores a series of situations in which her protagonist searches for the causes of her restlessness. In some poems she focuses on the very institution that from early in her life had complemented her family as the institutional reinforcer of her gender assignment, the court. Often her suspicion of the court is conventional, emerging in the commonplace *otium* of the pastoral:

> Love as well can make abiding
> In a faythfull shepheards brest
> As in Princese whose thoughts sliding
> Like swift rivers never rest.
> (*Poems*, p. 117)

Less conventional, however, is the insistence that becomes repeated, even obsessional, as the collection moves along: that the court should be left "to faulscest lovers" (*Poems*, p. 93). Such rejection characteristically suggests that the true lover may find his or her happiness in the country, since there too infidelity and, especially in her case, imprisonment and frustration are found. Love is fundamentally deceptive, whether in the court or the fields. A woman is happy only when alone, in some rare private space—which may be only inside her head—where she can be silent with her memories. Even there, in the supposedly comforting stability of her mind, however, she discovers she cannot escape. The intense melancholy of the sequence is more focused than the usual betrayal of the Petrarchan plaint. It is rooted in a woman's alienation from the court and from the continual pressure to occupy the disempowering roles which the court and the wider patriarchal society it represents have constructed for her. Her innermost thoughts, "stolen" from the public world in which she must perform demeaning roles, are hers when she is alone. The poems thus present a fascinating gendered variation of a common Petrarchan paradox: she is trapped yet free. *Pamphilia to Amphilanthus*, then, enacts a distinctively gendered fantasy of autonomy. Pamphilia's speaking, even to herself, is like Wroth's writing itself, an act of self-assertion. But it is never an easy achievement: the more agency is affirmed, the more she finds that, because she is a woman, she must struggle in what the poems repeatedly term a "labyrinth." Both Wroth and Pamphilia are unavoidably caught up in discursive positions that they occupy only at the cost of self-violation. In psychoanalytic terms, a turn to writing—like any act of agency—is to turn from the mother to the father, to choose assertion, activity, possession of the phallus over passivity, castration, and

204

masochism. Nowhere would such moves be a greater breach with the gender assignment of a woman than in a noble family in early modern England. Yet once presented to her—in the form of sexual possibilities or the encouragement to write—the choice is one that must be taken. This is a recurring pattern in Wroth's work: in *Urania* women seem inevitably to be punished for making sexual choices, yet they insist on making them since, however dimly, it is through such choices that they are offered the possibility of emulating or stealing for themselves the autonomy apparently enjoyed by men.

In the previous chapter I argued that Pembroke's poetry, in common with the Petrarchan tradition, articulates a range of characteristically male perversions. Wroth's poems, I suggest, illustrate the classic klepto-maniac tendencies of the woman living in a repressive society and want-ing to affirm herself. But, like Pembroke's, her poems display a broad range of what Kaplan terms characteristic "female" perversions. Most especially, they betray a masochism born of frustrated wishes to emulate the apparent freedom of men and a desire for a mutual relationship that the masochistic, self-destructive desires in which she finds herself caught continually deny her. The "molestation" on which I commented in chapter three is a recurring metaphor for her situation. Kaplan writes of how we use our fantasy lives to work over the "ordinary, expected traumas of childhood," but if these traumas are reinforced by society as the child grows up, then the mind may be crippled not only from them but by the very survival mechanisms she has "to enlist to continue to think and feel." Behind the term "molestation," then, may be historically specific physical realities and powerful myths. Molestation is thus closely related to what Clark terms an "extension of the social construction of male sexuality as active, dominant and aggressive."[16] Once a woman starts to resent being regarded as the property of a man, she might well regard the traditional proprietal sexual actions of a patriarchal husband as invasive and "molesting" in a direct physical sense. Part of a sense of agency is the right to say no; to have that no taken as rebellion, or as in fact saying yes, is part of "molestation." Wroth is evoking part of the cultural unconscious, the fears built into being a woman in a society in which gender relations are structured by an ideology of bipolar authoritarianism.

Within *Pamphilia to Amphilanthus*'s rewriting of the Petrarchan scheme, these contradictions of a woman's gender assignments often emerge as a discontented passivity and are given a distinctively masochis-tic edge. The conventional emphasis in Petrarchism on love as an inva-sion of a (supposedly) more powerful beloved encourages a stance of helpless passivity by the lover. The conventional masculine response is to look for relief or rescue not directly to the beloved but to a fetishized token for her absent presence, even to a higher love, perhaps to God for whom she is, at least in his rhetoric, a privileged though imperfect substitute. Wroth associates the lover's anguish not just with conventional postures of pain or martyrdom—Cupid "still adding fire / to burning hearts," or the feeling that one is kept in a cage, or the recurring metaphor of a labyrinth in which the lover suffers (*Poems*, pp. 85, 121, 127)—but, more characteristically, with the emotional and physical retreat, even regression, into the roles that have been assigned to her as a woman.

But such a move may be tactical, not merely reactive: in which case it might be seen as an attempted act of agency. As Benjamin comments, "the masochist's wish to be reached, penetrated, found, released—a wish that can be expressed in the metaphor of violence as well as in metaphors of redemption—is the other side of the sadist's wish to discover the other." The masochist's desire to experience her "authentic, inner reality in the company of another parallels the sadist's wish to get outside the self into a shared reality."[17] Pamphilia describes herself as desiring isolation and silence—desiring, that is, precisely what the dominant ideology prescribes for women: to have her organs of self-assertion, her mouth (for speech), her genitals (for sexual self-assertion), and the door or gate of her room, house, or garden closed or locked.[18] She knows that by voicing her miseries, pursuing love, or going abroad, she could overcome her victimization, but instead she accepts her assignment of silence, isolation, and frigidity. Her posture is frequently described as sleeping, or near sleep, or lying down in a small space, and addressing the shadows around her as comforting, even if confusing. In one poem she broods:

How oft in you I have laine heere opprest,
  And have my miseries in woefull cries
  Deliver'd forth, mounting up to the skies
  Yett helples back returnd to wound my brest.
                    (*Poems*, p.104)

In the next sonnet, she states that "lay'd downe to ease my paine," she still is trapped and can rise only by the aid of "Fortune," who is interestingly described as a fellow woman lover, who "in her bless'd arms did mee inchaine." As she rises, she acknowledges that even with another woman, she is responding rather than initiating: "I, her obay'd, and rising felt that love / Indeed was best, when I did least itt move" (*Poems*, p. 105). Discussing what he believed to be the inherently masochistic situation of being a woman, Freud claimed that it consisted of neurotic passivity, whether shown in ordinary timidity or the "extreme instance" of sexual satisfaction being "conditional upon suffering physical or mental pain at the hands of the sexual object." Either way, he saw it as an individual aberration, and one inherent in being a woman. But the construction of female (or for that matter, male) masochism in our cultural history is far more complex than Freud's account. The unconscious is not a given, biological "place"; it is rather a metaphor for those assumptions and practices whereby the contradictions of a society's ideology are repressed, transferred, and reproduced. The passivity that Pamphilia sometimes displays—and I choose that exhibitionist term deliberately—is more a cultural construct than the "individual" neurosis of which Freud speaks. "Female masochism" is not, as Freud thought, biological: even though biological factors enter into its being women's most characteristic perversion; it is predominantly the result of women's socialization and gender assignments in patriarchal society.[19]

In the Petrarchan scheme the lover typically asserts that he becomes the victim of the power of the beloved. From such a systematization of the dynamics of desire, it seems that only two possible gender positions are possible, "one of rapacious domination, the other of docile submission."[20] Yet though the (male) lover may assert that he is trapped or paralyzed by the power of the (female) beloved, he is inevitably the active participant: he pursues, is called to public duties as courtier or soldier; he speaks out, hunts, fights, complains. A man has the independence to move, to be restless, unfaithful, or simply assume the freedom to move through the world; a woman remains at home, constant, reassuring, mothering. Wroth's emphasis on Pamphilia's constancy never removes her from this male fantasy in which a man assumes he may move, travel, or choose, and a woman stays at home. The woman's role is to be the focus for his self-division and his physical and emotional restlessness. Moreover, her absence or coldness, while a matter for complaint, and the cause of his insecurity, is often the necessary stimulus for his being able to feel that self-division and to write about it. If she were present, which he desires, he would not write, which he also desires. She is therefore required to be absent so he can desire her presence, a paradox that Greville grimly deconstructs in *Caelica* 45, when he insists that absence, far from being the ideal state of love, the "glorious bright" of absence is in fact, pain:

But thoughts be not so brave,
With absent joy;
For you with that you have
Yourself destroy:
The absence which you glory
Is that which makes you sorry
And burn in vain:

For thought is not the weapon,
Wherewith thought's ease men cheapen,
Absence is pain.[21]

Greville's is a rare, unqualified demystification of the Petrarchan pose by a male poet. Wroth's critique is more detailed and more interesting because it is written by and on behalf of a woman.

The role of Petrarchan mistress in which Pamphilia finds herself is primarily, then, a passive one. Her desire is defined and licensed by her lover's "will." She is positioned by forces, reified as "love," that are, she assumes, outside her control, and the range of feelings she is permitted consists almost entirely of the largely negative ones of entrapment, loss, and bondage. Unlike her male lover, she has no recourse to other activities by which to develop a sense of autonomy. She accepts that she must wait upon his initiative: the female "complement to the male refusal to recognize the other is woman's own acceptance of her lack of subjectivity, her willingness to offer recognition without expecting it in return."[22] She makes herself available to her lover when he chooses to visit her. Her satisfactions are those of the master/slave relationship, finding satisfaction in submission, humbling herself not out of fear but because she has been socialized, in the family and beyond, to find self-recognition in service. Moreover, she feels, in part, that she is a willing accomplice in her own victimization, as if the "molestation" she experiences is not merely a consequence of her being a woman but in some sense her own fault. A woman is more helpless than a man before love's deceptiveness because she does not have the male assumption of agency in love—represented by his ability to move, change, accept or even revel in unpredictability. She cannot claim any autonomy, it seems, without submitting to further pain and disillusion. In waiting and being hurt by him, she feels that she is at least being reached: her pain gives her authentication. As Masud Khan noted in his study of perversion, it is important to find a witness for one's psychic pain, the audience allowing for the achievement, however temporary, of a deeper sense of achievement. "Molestation" may thus be the alternative to psychic breakdown.[23]

The dominant code by which women have historically been made available for male pleasure rather than their own (or even for mutual) pleasure, is based on this reification of what had tradionally been praised as a woman's constancy. Donne's poem of that name dramatizes, albeit amusingly, the male nervousness before the threat embodied (literally) in women that they will be untrue, unavailable, beyond possession. The reassuring mother must always be, if not present, at least available when need calls. Elaine Beilin has argued that "constancy," which is particularly intensely apostrophized in the final sonnet of *Pamphilia to Amphilanthus*, has a "fundamental importance" in Wroth's scheme, and that "separated from Amphilanthus . . . Pamphilia is wholly dedicated to the love of virtue."[24] But repeatedly in Wroth's poems, constancy seems to be a role forced upon a woman in a dangerous environment, a defensive posture at best, an assigned and unavoidable role within an aggressively patriarchal situation at worst—and far more typically. In her constancy, Pamphilia has internalized the residual female role of possessing a "faith untouch'd, pure thoughts . . . wher constancy bears sway" (*Poems*, p. 134). In one of the later sonnets she acknowledges that "No time, noe roome, no thought, or writing" can give her "loving hart" quiet, and yet she is powerless to give up her love:

> Yett would I nott (deere love) thou shouldst depart
>   Butt lett my passions as they first began
>   Rule, wounde, and please, itt is thy choysest art
>   To give disquiett which seemes ease to man.

The erotic Cupid can give only "disquiett"; by contrast, the divine offers "glory," presented as a relief from the perpetual disease of erotic desire:

> When all alone, I think upon thy paine
>   How thou doest traveile owr best selves to gaine;
>   Then howerly thy lessons I doe learne,
>
> Think on thy glory which shall still assend
>   Untill the world come to a finall end,
>   And then shall wee thy lasting powre deserne.
>   (*Poems*, p. 141)

Constancy, then, is hardly the virtue it seems. Indeed, *Pamphilia to Amphilanthus* is a remarkable demystification of the ideal of constancy as, in effect, a device of patriarchy to keep women under control and available whenever the needs of their struggles for individuation become unbearable: women need to be in a state of unchanging constancy so as to relieve men of some anxieties. Amphilanthus' own sister Urania points out to Pamphilia that "tis pittie . . . that ever that fruitlesse thing Constancy was taught you as a vertue" (*Urania*, p. 400). Men are not required to be constant. Why then should women? This is a theme on which *Urania* dwells incessantly, as I shall show in chapter eight. Whereas a courtier, like Amphilanthus, has a sense of assigned agency, the autonomy of continual adventure and innumerable mistresses, Pamphilia must wait, resigned and insecure, threatened by her love and by her own faithfulness:

Love grown proud with victory,
  Seekes by sleights to conquer me,
  Painted showes he thinkes can bind
  His commands in womens mind,
Love but glories in fond loving,
I most joy in not removing.
                     (*Urania* p. 549)

The "painted showes" of the court—including the masques and celebrations that had won Wroth herself some momentary "glories"—are
here taken as a metonymy for the seductive attractions by which the
court lady is assigned her passive, decorative role. Love, like the court
itself, is characterized by superficiality and insecurity. And the speaker?
Do we read the last line as "most" or "must"? If as "most," then the
passive, masochistic, self-punishing role has been accepted; if "must,"
then the reluctance to accept such a role is inevitable but still resented.
Either way, constancy, with its idealized tone of willing devotion and
dedication, is proved to be deceiving, a construct designed by men to
keep women in subjection.

Perhaps the idealization of constancy throughout the sequence can
be read as a clear, if singularly depressing, indication of how a dominant
masculinist ideology has been internalized by a woman. Seen in that
light, it acts to conceal the contradictions of Pamphilia's assigned roles.
The ninth sonnet records a protracted degree of bitterness at such an
assignment, as it caustically describes the lover married only to sorrow
in a socially constructed world where faithfulness, although imposed
as a duty and a sign of belonging to a male lover, seems nonetheless
an imposition:

Bee you all pleas'd? your pleasures grieve nott mee:
  Do you delight? I envy nott your joy:
  Have you content? contentment with you bee:
  Hope you for bliss? hope still, and still injoye:

Lett sad misfortune, haples me destroy,
  Leave crosses to rule mee, and still rule free,
  While all delights theyr contrairies imploy
  To keepe good backe, and I butt torments see.

Joyes are beereav'd, harmes doe only tarry,
  Dispaire takes place, disdaine hath gott the hand:
  Yett firme love holds my sences in such band
  As since dispis'ed, I with sorrow marry;

Then if with griefe I now must coupled bee
Sorrow I'le wed: Dispaire thus governs mee.

(Poems, p. 91)

The poem is racked by a deep helplessness. Demands are made upon the speaker that are seemingly irresistible; petulant defiance seems the most positive alternative to helpless acquiescence. Although one of the more extreme of the sonnets, it is typical in that love is presented not only as deceptive and disruptive, as it is so often to a male Petrarchan lover, but as enforcing helplessness and passivity. A woman is a "stage of woe" (Poems, p. 111) on which others' desires rather than her own are acted out. Her constancy, the virtue with which she is most praised (and thereby by what she is imprisoned), may be opening her to further victimization. Writing on "mourning and melancholia," Freud speaks of the melancholic's sense of loss involving "painful dejection, cessation of the interest in the outside world, loss of the capacity to love, inhibition of all activity and a lowering of the self-regarding feelings to a degree that finds utterance in self-reproaches and self-revilings."[25] Many sonnets show Pamphilia withdrawn to her bed, both night and day, brooding over her misery and her lover's absence. But where Freud insisted that narcissistic melancholia was an "individual" neurosis, Wroth's poems show how thoroughly it is socially constructed. It is as if the need for secrecy, the sense of non-fulfillment and above all the awareness that the beloved is an active agent elsewhere—hunting, traveling, moving through more complex social worlds—provides a contrast that is at once humiliating and yet inescapable. Pamphilia's withdrawal is an attempt to restore some sense of an acceptable self-representation. She needs the sense of her own loss and pain to buttress any feelings she retains of having a coherent sense of self.

Discussing Pembroke's poetry in the previous chapter, I noted that one of the recurring metaphors of male Petrarchism is the controlling power of the male gaze. It is built upon an assumption so deeply rooted in our history's dominant ideologies of perception and knowledge production that it has overwhelmingly seemed unassailably true. Men gaze at women; women are gazed at and, as Kaplan puts it, "the man's excited responses to her body reassure the woman that she actually exists."[26] What response could a female protagonist have to such a situation? Was it possible to construct an alternative to the dominance of the gaze? Part of Pamphilia's enforced (or chosen) passivity—her acknowledgement that love "indeed was best, when I did least it move"—is the awareness that she is being both watched by others for signs of her love and thereby in a sense given an identity by their gazes.

Within recent feminist theory, the psychosocial dynamics of the gaze have been much debated. A standard viewpoint, represented by the work of Tania Modleski and Laura Mulvey, has focused on the male gaze as the normal subject position for the viewer of classic cinema, and the need to develop an alternative point of view, especially for women viewers. More recently, Gaylyn Studlar has argued that, on the contrary, many films interpellate a male viewing position not simply based on the desire to over-see and dominate, but rather on a masochistic fear/desire of being dominated and absorbed themselves by women. Both analyses, of course, may be pointing to the variety of ways by which the dominance of the male subject position has been reinforced. Either way it is clearly rooted in the way our history has constructed our dominant gender assignments. But perhaps it is possible to discuss the confounding of such situations by the woman's own active participation in the gaze. As Constance Penley puts it, if the gaze in traditional art is "an inscription of the look on the body of the mother, we must now begin to consider the possibilities of the mother returning the look."[27] What happens, in short, if "she" looks back at "him"? Or even actively watches herself being watched and instead of feeling positioned as an object, and assumes "gazing back" is a viable subject position? If vision connotes aggression and control, can a woman—even while she knows she is the object of the gaze—appropriate its power? Wroth's poems explore a number of these possible subject positions. At times Pamphilia is "molested" by her role as an object of the desiring gaze; at others she tries to escape the gaze of lover and other people's, in loneliness, isolation, or sleep. Such reactions are attempts to avoid the repetitive constructing of sexual relations by patterns of male desire and domination and female submission. In such relationships the values of the patriarchal male predominate: they emerge as the urge to overwhelm, penetrate, defeat, and triumph over.

As I suggested in the previous chapters, an analysis of the gender politics of Petrarchism suggests that this, one of the dominant discourses of desire in the western world, has been overwhelmingly destructive for at the very least half of those human subjects caught up in it: the traditional Petrarchan situation against which *Pamphilia to Amphilanthus* is written is part of a historical pattern of "normal" sexuality as defined by Western society, in which, as Stoller puts it, "an essential purpose is for one to be superior to, harmful to, triumphant over another."[28] The seeming neutrality of "one" in Stoller's remark covers the preponderant historical identification of assumed control with the male. Beneath the language of sexual dependence, idealized admiration, even (occasionally) sexual reciprocity to which the Petrarchan lover lays claim, there is a predominantly one-sided emphasis on domination and submission. One of the poems in Wroth's opening sequence in *Pamphilia to Amphilanthus* is a remarkable critique of this whole tradition. It attempts to subvert the dominant male subject position by appropriating not only the gaze, but its pleasure:

> Take heed mine eyes, how you your lookes do cast
>   Least they beetray my harts most secrett thought;
>   Bee true unto your selves for nothings bought
>   More deere then doubt which brings a lovers fast.
>
> Catch you all waching eyes, ere they bee past,
>   Or take yours fixt wher your best love hath sought
>   The pride of your desires; lett them bee taught
>   Theyr faults for shame, they could noe truer last;
>
> Then looke, and looke with joye for conquest wunn
>   Of those that search'd your hurt in double kinde;
>   Soe you kept safe, lett them themselves looke blinde
>   Watch, gaze, and marke till they to madnes runn,
>
> While you, mine eyes injoye full sight of love
>   Contented that such happinesses move.
>
> (*Poems*, p. 106)

The poem opens with a warning against indiscretion, but the tone is unusually paranoid, as if guarding not just against betrayal of a secret with which the woman has been entrusted, but of the multiple "selves" in which she lives. The tactics of the poem, indeed, become not the passive slipping into the role of a secret lover or of the modest object of another's forbidden desire, but the more aggressive one of "catching" or trapping and defeating "all waching eyes." It is a matter of self-identity, not merely of love—primarily a matter of acknowledging how the self is constructed. Given that identity consists in being assigned a multiplicity of roles, that very multiplicity and its contradictory assigned positions will, she determines, become her basis for action. Her fantasy of female agency becomes based on her returning the gaze, on reminding herself to "looke with joye for conquest wunn," and acknowledging that it is her own active desire—accepting her construction by the contradictory gazes and returning them—that affords her power. Stoller remarks—as so often, irritatingly essentializing but nonetheless pointing to a seemingly fixed aspect of Western patriarchy—on the little boy's assumed "right to sexual looking and a little girl's training that she is not to permit that looking." Placed within the history of gender assignment, Wroth's Pamphilia marks an attempt, however spasmodic and isolated, to break with such a pattern. She is not merely fixed by the gaze, but turns it to an active and defiant exhibitionism. She has started to reappropriate herself as a subject, distancing herself from the narcissism of self-involvement and starting to see herself as a man might see her. But because she appropriates both the traditional gender roles and so sees with both the eyes of a woman and the gaze of a man, by involvement and reflection, she acquires a secret authority unknown to the men who gaze on her and think they control her. It is the clearest expression of the fantasy of emulation, what Kaplan terms "a retribution scenario, a vengeance on those who have been assigned to abandonment and mutilation."[29] Or, more optimistically put, she has asserted her right to gaze back, just as her poems assert the right to talk back.

This poem also reflects upon another part of the Petrarchist situation, the interpellation of the reader (him)self as a voyeur. The gaze of the (male) reader is a part of the male display built into Petrarchism: Sidney's poems, for instance, typically look out to their audiences, often with a wink or an invitation to laugh, inviting his reader's amusement as well as disapproval of or sympathy with his dilemmas. *Astrophil and Stella* is typical of the mode: it is what Barthes terms a playful text,[30] one that depends strongly on an audience, inviting our participation, asking us to watch, identify, judge, laugh, and learn. But it assumes a "universal" gaze that in fact is that of the dominant male, and the sympathy it asks for is for the suffering lover, wanting separation from and yet desiring the presence of, the woman. What we are asked to watch and assume to be "natural" is the textual/sexual spectacle of another human displaying him- or herself according to gender-specific stereotypes—or refusing to, which in its effect on the viewer amounts to the same thing. Women display for men; men display for themselves, and then are authorized to display, in writing, their accounts of the experience. What happens when such a situation is complicated by having a woman protagonist/poet? By a woman who displays herself, not merely sexually but textually as well, in her act of writing? The reader's trajectory of desire makes his (or her) complicity more complex. Where the male reader/spectator can see his own gendered roles in harmony with those valorized by the poems, the gaze can appear neutral. When the gaze is complicated by gender, either by a woman reader or, in the way that operates in Wroth's poems, by a woman writer, then the male power over objects in the Petrarchan scheme is called into question.

At this point, my excurse in chapter four into reading theory and a discussion of the place of gender in reading acquires some immediacy. Wroth's poems, parading the gender of both their author and protagonist, catch us in a reading situation where the shifts in subject position call into question any "natural" order of gender. We are not simply observing the woman's acceptance of the conventional role of cruel beauty and perpetual tease, produced to both generate a man's desire and overcome his fears of that desire. However fitfully it is occurring, we can observe the slow and contradictory emergence of alternative subject positions for women and, implicitly, for men. As Belsey, Francis Barker, and others have argued, before the development of the humanist subject in the seventeenth century, women were afforded places within the period's dominant ideology only by being incorporated into structures and discourses which assigned them subsidiary roles, as objects of others' desires, not as subjects of their own. There is, in the early modern period—in *Hamlet*, most forcefully—the emergence of a new sense of subjectivity, a claim for a unique and "essential interiority, which, even if it is never fully articulated and is therefore historically "premature," nonetheless anticipates the emergent claims of a bourgeois subjectivity that will emerge in the next century or more. Wroth's poems record the stirrings—against enormous odds, it needs to be stressed—to establish an equivalent female subject position. Her poems' struggle to find an authentic voice for a woman are related to the frustrations of gender assignment. The dominant gendered subject positions of early modern England did not permit such autonomy to a woman writer or protagonist—any more than they did, as Dollimore has argued, to gays. But we can note, across the range of constructed gender roles, points of strain and contradiction where alternatives are struggling to emerge.[31]

As I noted in chapter four, the dominant gender politics of Petrarchism are constructed so that the male lover-poet can fulfill his desires even if his beloved is absent. If she is present, he is fulfilled as a lover; if absent, as a poet. He therefore plays, according to his own rules, an elaborate version of the *fort-da* game Freud so famously described, moving her at his will back and forth, from presence to absence.[32] Within the Petrarchan framework, however much a man may protest, he has the autonomy to love or leave, to write or be silent. But a woman? If she is not accorded her own desire, what role can she claim? What starts to emerge in *Pamphilia to Amphilanthus*, taking on even greater significance in the stories in *Urania*, is a counter-discourse of indignation and envy of men's autonomy and movement, what are termed their "adventures." Pamphilia also yearns for her own "adventures." Even if they are denied her, over and over she struggles to find them and, through them, a sense of an individuated self that seemingly is "natural" to a man. So if the residual oppression of "constancy" is, in the end, part of the patriarchal entrapment of women, producing at worst a subordinated passivity and at best anger and envy, against it must be set surges of defiance and claims of autonomy. The two areas that stand out within the poetry are those which, as I have suggested, we can observe struggling within Wroth's life as a whole—her writing and her sexuality.

Writing is an act shared by Pamphilia with her creator. So far as Wroth's writing is concerned, we should not underemphasize its importance as an act of self-affirmation, even a defiance of patriarchy, despite the encouragement afforded by being a member of the Sidney family. Mary E. Hazard has noted that, typically, a Petrarchan poet fashions for (him)self a fictive role (which may at times be close to that claimed by the poet outside the poems).[33] The one constructed in *Pamphilia to Amphilanthus* for both writer and character is more varied than most. It certainly includes, as we have noted, passivity, "constancy." But it also includes a measure of defiance and self-assertion that echoes something of the desires of the author herself. Even though her family probably encouraged her to see herself as a writer, Wroth took that permission far more daringly than, say, her aunt, the countess of Pembroke, had. To write a prose romance, a pastoral play, and, perhaps above all, a collection of Petrarchan love poems, was to go well beyond what the family might have seen fit—and it is significant that it was in part because she exceeded what were felt to be the decorous precedents of translation and devotional works set by her pious aunt that Wroth was bitterly attacked by Denny upon the publication of *Urania*. Even, as Masten suggests, the seemingly mundane acts of arrangement, revision, and circulation of her poems—or, he insists, not to be underestimated as an act of choice, the refusal to circulate them—were acts of defiance. Within the poems, too, writing is depicted as a way of giving a woman not merely reactive roles to male desires but multiple and changing voices of her own. Like the male Petrarchan lover, Pamphilia determines to "seeke for some small ease by lines," only to realize that "greife is nott cur'd by art." Poetry "tires" her mind, yet the "debate" it produces in her makes her realize that it is her thinking, brooding mind that is carving out an area of autonomy—even through her pain—which affords her not only comfort but power (*Poems*, pp. 90, 91, 92). While others, men in particular, may be subject to the whims of the king, or to some "pleasing past time" required by their roles at court, she has, she claims, a small but autonomous space to explore:

> When every one to pleasing pastime hies
> Some hunt, some hauke, some play, while some delight
> In sweet discourse, and musique showes joys might
> Yett I my thoughts doe farr above thes prise.
>
> (*Poems*, pp. 99–100)

Masten's argument that the poems "encode" a desire for "withdrawal from circulation" has some force here. Refusing to voice one's love and doing so in anguished public language is, of course, a conventional trick of the Petrachan poet—"they love indeed, who quake to say they love" as her uncle Philip's volubly silent Astrophil put it in *Astrophil and Stella*, 54. But *Pamphilia to Amphilanthus* is not trying to carve out a space for a dominant male subject who can be assured of his audience even (and perhaps especially) when they are eloquently told not to listen to his inner and supposedly private revelations. The space Wroth is trying to establish is for a female subject, one who necessarily has to absorb and neutralize metaphors that have been encultured by dominant male practice: "When others hunt, my thought I have in chase." Masten points up the paradox that Wroth "is writing in Petrarchan discourse to write against it," but there are broader cultural issues at stake: in so doing she is contradicting on more than the level of conceit the encoded subject position of the male speaker of Petrarchan poetry. She claims withdrawal as a tactic of self-affirmation for a woman's subjectivity.[34]

If writing is an act—or at least an enacted fantasy—of agency, what of desire itself? If, as Marx put it, praxis—meaning sensuous human activity, the practices of the body—is the basis of real power, what space is *Pamphilia to Amphilanthus* trying to carve out not only for its protagonist but also for its author, and for the language and praxis of women's desire? As I have suggested, much of Pamphilia's desire emerges as pain, deprivation, molestation, by which sexuality is experienced as harm, shame, self-obliteration. Wroth overwhelmingly offers us a distinctively privileged perspective on the negative eros produced by male domination and female masochism. This perspective allows us to see the relative paucity of love "objects" to which a woman had access in the early modern period. Freud noted frequently that repressed objects of desire are represented by a series of unsatisfying substitutes: Pamphilia's growing self-awareness, her "waking" as a lover, brings her the realization of the distinctive kind of cruelty Cupid affords women.[35] He is responsible for love's "wounding . . . delights," the producer of displays, for male delectation, of "endless torments" upon "this stage of woe," ending in self-immolation, even death. Repeatedly the lover is "in chaines" or trapped in a "labyrinth" (*Poems*, pp. 86, 92, 111, 123). The recurring labyrinth metaphor is the nightmare underside of a woman's private space. The extremely popular mazes in Elizabethan and Jacobean gardens reflect an obsessive concern with what Wotton termed a "very wilde Regularitie," a special place designed to transgress the restrictions of the house and its regime of harmony and control. But such a view is from the perspective of the proprietor of the house or the architect. For someone lost in the labyrinth, the point of view may be very different. The private chamber is an area of orderliness and control, however compromised by its surroundings; the labyrinth consists of potentially infinite attempts to find an escape: it constructs a series of "tense" blind spaces that produce incessant, frustrated, "restless" movements to escape. Petrarch had used the labyrinth as an image of the cognitive and emotional confusion in love, and there were a number of commonplace analogies between the labyrinth and the sonnet itself.[36]

The "crowne of Sonetts dedicated to Love," which are grouped together towards the end of *Pamphilia to Amphilanthus*, explore some of these difficulties from the viewpoint of the woman lover trapped within, certainly not a designer of, labyrinths. The "crowne" consists of fourteen sonnets, the last lines of each constituting the first line of the next. Roberts speaks of the "universalized concept of love" in the Crowne and Beilin of its "catalogues of love's divinity," but the Crowne sonnets are more distinctive for their demarcation of contradictions than in its acceptance of some kind of transcendent resignation.[37] The labyrinth is, despite its emphasis on puzzlement and entrapment, a metaphor of action: one enters a labyrinth and tries to find one's way out, or to its heart, or both. Pamphilia, surrounded by alternatives, nonetheless insists that contradiction and difficulty offer her more fulfilling choices:

> In this strang labourinth how shall I turne?
> Wayes are on all sids while the way I misse:
> If to the right hand, ther, in love I burne;
> Lett mee goe forward, therin danger is.
>
> *(Poems, p.127)*

Her determination is to "take the thread of love," to be constant to her growing sense of self, to "feele the weight of true desire," and to produce a mutual, united love. Such agency within contradiction allows each lover to open him(or her)self to previously unsensed possibilities: "Itt doth inrich the witts, and make you see / That in your self, which you knew nott before" (*Poems*, pp. 128, 130). Yet even in such a fantasy of love, stasis—what she terms "constancy"—is never the end. The final poem points to the self-exploration that love has opened up, not to achieve a final goal so much as to begin a never-ending search: "Soe though in Love I fervently doe burne,/In this strange labourinth how shall I turne?" (*Poems*, p. 134).

So far I have read Wroth's poems in terms of their struggle, fitful but not entirely accidental, to assert some sustained, even momentary, agency for women. They articulate one of the dominant fantasies of the woman's family romance, to achieve the same sense of agency that has been promised, as he emerges from childhood, to the boy: becoming a man, he will, like his father, assume independence, autonomy, power over others, especially over women. There are, however, signs in *Pamphilia to Amphilanthus* of another counter-discourse taking shape. There is, for instance, the acknowledgement that the victimization of women is not Pamphilia's alone: other women share her helplessness or anger. The poems frequently address other women, sometimes an un-named friend and sometimes, as Naomi Miller points out, those women who have been described in the lines of men's poems. In the sonnet just quoted, for instance, Fortune is described as Pamphilia's supporter. Fortune is, conventionally, female and a consoler of the suffering male; but because the poem is spoken and written by a woman, Fortune takes on a less conventional role. She becomes a fellow female sufferer, helping Pamphilia face the anguish of being a mistress whose desires are controlled by her lover. The community of "oprest" women lovers in the poems includes Night, Reclining, and other personifications of the assigned female passive role, providing, as Miller puts it, a "litany of parallels" with Pamphilia's grief, which in some of the poems often deepens into anger at being pressured by overwhelming social forces into accepting the roles society thrusts upon them because they are women. As Lamb notes in her splendid analysis of anger in *Urania*, "the Renaissance offered women few healthy models for encouraging the expression of justified rage or for acknowledging the heroism of their ordinary lives."[38] It offered even fewer models for an alternative fantasy of genuinely mutual constancy.

The experience of most women in the early modern period—that they were not possessors of their own bodies, that they did not have a sense of choice and deliberation in their gender assignments—causes, as Erikson noted in his classic studies of life stages, "the most pervasive anger."[39] How can a fantasy of mutual constancy be generated from such a situation? We are used today to women's relations to their own bodies being, no less than for men, a source of power, vulnerability, betrayal, a space of agency as much as of restriction. Such a spectrum of relations with a sense of self was only barely becoming possible in the early modern period. Wroth's poems are a kind of dream space, in which only dimly graspable subject positions are being tentatively and partly unconsciously explored, interacting with more powerful discourses of restriction. *Pamphilia to Amphilanthus* is a dream of a still to be found autonomy that will lead not to dominance but to mutuality.

7

"Like one in a gay masque": The Sidney Cousins in the Theaters of Court and Country

You live in the face of a glorious Court, where your eyes are daily fill'd, as with Magnificence, so with Vanity, yet you shall doe well, otherwise, to cast them aside from such gorgeous Spectacles [and] empty and indefinite agitations.

Thomas Chaffinge[r], 1630

Here's trifling foolish banquets, torchlight, lutes,
fantastics, antics, counterfeits, prick-songs . . .
The Earl of Pembroke quaffs the fumes and chats
throughout the play—he's all embroidery,
pompoms and glitter, gold-clocked hose . . . I see
comedy and tragedy together . . .
Who's best on stage? These daughters leave
their fathers, all for love . . .

Pamela White Hadas[1]

The conflicts and contradictions of a society can be found in the texts of "popular" culture no less than in the valorized "canonical" or (to adopt Puttenham's sixteenth-century term) "worthy" kinds of writing. Of course, what counts as "canonical" or "worthy" may shift radically over time, and the literary kinds in the early modern period that have been accorded greatest prestige in our time were little regarded, even scorned, by the intellectual and educational authorities in their own. Right at the bottom of Puttenham's strictly hierarchical listing of the poetical kinds are those poems that we may take most seriously. After the most laudable aim of praising God, the principal function of poetry is to praise "the worthy gests of noble Princes," to be "the memorial and registry or all great fortunes."[2] Thus epic is preferred above pastoral, satiric, or (finally) lyric, and it is of course the latter, at least among poetry, that modern taste has preferred.

Of the writings that come to us from the late sixteenth and early seventeenth centuries, unquestionably the most admired, and even widely read (or viewed) today, are the scripts written for the public theater. In their own time, the plays of the public theaters were scorned by Puttenham and Sidney, and even at times by those who wrote them, most notably, of course, by Jonson. Yet the constitutional, economic and broader ideological crises of the early modern period were surfacing in Jacobean popular theater in ways that other literary forms rarely registered, and the plays were helping to put into circulation radical and disturbing ideas and practices that more dominant cultural forms, including the epic poem, were attempting to marginalize. The public theaters, as part of the age's entertainment industry, were therefore— no less than the family, school or church—one of the many cultural or, in Althusser's term, ideological "apparatuses" by means of which men and women were interpellated into not just the dominant beliefs, but (a point often forgotten in Althusserian criticism) the tensions and contradictions—and therefore possible points of growth—of their society. The public theater of the period was open to a wider range of social pressures than the insulated, though far more prestigious, cultural forms

221

dominated by the court, such as the court masque. Where the masque was part of the court's mystification of power and allegiance, the public theater was a "site of experimental institution-making," existing as it were on a cultural fault line between the city and the court, the city and the country, and even between men and women.[3] Where the court masque excluded oppositional forces, the drama of the public theater, not necessarily consciously or at times willingly, gave voice to them. In the public playhouses, the ideological tensions that were to shape the early modern world were starting, however dimly, to be apprehended by men and women, both individually and as members of particular classes and of gendered and racial groups.

The theater was, however, not only a place, a building, an institution. It was also an extraordinarily powerful metaphor that served to organize the thinking and feeling of men and women. Players "act"; the playwright or theater company "dramatizes"; a company "stages" a play; above all, men and women are, as the great Renaissance cliché had it, actors on the great stage of the world, the everyday theater of fools and fooling, comedies and tragedies. As modern scholars reconstruct the world of playhouses, acting companies, and script making in this period, we discover that more than actors, lists of properties, and box office receipts are at stake: not only did the poor players strut upon the stage, but the great social conflicts of the time were acted out there. Likewise, as we reconstruct the world of politics and court machinations, we find not only the clash of ideas and political or economic interests. There are also clashes of style, rhetoric, accent, roles, and presentations of self: a remarkably self-conscious sense of theatricality and role-playing characterizes this supposedly more serious world. Humanist educational ideals and practices alike stressed the need for the aspiring courtier to present himself self-consciously as an actor on the great stage of the world. The gendered "himself" here is deliberate: the dominant ideology of women's self-presentation insisted on a rhetoric of modesty, withdrawal, and subservience rather than assertion and ostentation, a difference in gender assignment in the wider social world paralleled by the forbiddance, at least on the public stage, of women actors.

These initial remarks are, of course, commonplaces in the current view of the place of acting and theater in early modern England. "Dramatic," "playing," and other metaphors were concretized not only in the public, court, and private theaters, but on the stage of politics and in the public presentation of self; the lexicon of the theater provides powerful "key words" for our understanding of the cultural contradictions of the early modern period. The Sidneys' contributions to the drama and the development of the theater are almost as rich and contradictory as the theatrical metaphor itself. The two Sidney cousins inherited not only varied but highly contradictory interests in the theater and the drama. Both took part in many of the theatrical activities in the court. Pembroke was also a patron of the public theater, and, as lord chamberlain, had direct control over the country's theaters. Wroth wrote one of the earliest extant plays by a woman, and in her writings, *Urania* in particular, she broods over the age's fascination with the theatrical metaphor from a perspective that is often startlingly aware of gender differences. In this chapter, therefore, I will contrast the interests and activities of the cousins, and then consider the theater and the dramatic as powerful metaphorical structures in their lives and writings. What emerges is something broader than a study of their interests in the court masques or in the public theater that was shared across two generations of the Sidney family: what we discover are the complex ways in which theatricality and (in many senses) the dramatic and theatrical were part of the Sidney family romance.

In the *Defence*, the cousins' uncle, Sir Philip Sidney, had voiced the astringent prejudices of élitist humanism against public theater. As many apologists for Sidney have pointed out, he died before Shakespeare and Marlowe even started to write plays for the stage, and of the plays that he could have known, the "notable morallity" and "stately speeches" of *Gorboduc*, which he praised, were undoubtedly better than anything written before the 1580s. Nonetheless, some key principles enunciated in the *Defence* are rigidly antagonistic to the performative spectacles of the public theater. Sidney criticized *Gorboduc* for being "faulty both in time and place"; but he was far more scathing about "all the rest," in which:

> you shall have Asia of the one side, and Afric of the other, and so many under-kingdoms, that the player, when he cometh in, must ever begin by telling where he is, or else the tale will not be conceived. Now ye shall have three ladies walk to gather flowers, and then we must believe the stage to be a garden. By and by we hear news of shipwreck in the same place, and then we are to blame if we accept it not for a rock. Upon the back of that comes out a hideous monster with fire, and then the miserable beholders are bound to take it for a cave . . .

—and so he continues, poking fun at precisely the mixing of kinds that was to produce not only *As You Like It* and *The Winter's Tale*, but also his niece's *Love's Victory*. But even worse, at least in the minds of some Protestant moralists, with whom Sidney had not a few political sympathies, not only would such incompatible literary kinds be inappropriately mixed in these "gross absurdities," but another kind of disordered mixing would be encouraged: audiences could be assembled together whose members were both drawn from different classes and whose gender identities—especially remembering the cross-dressing involved in having boy actors play women characters on the stage—might all too easily be challenged or blurred. The public theater was therefore a socially indecorous institution in terms of its representations (the plays), its representers (the actors), and those indulging in the representations (the audiences).

Then, another of Sidney's concerns was one shared by extreme and many moderate Protestants in his time (and, it might be added, not a few of today's Puritans of both left and right): how can we ensure that representation has the effects we desire? How can we trust art and "literature" to further our particular agendas? With scripts designed for public performance and therefore open to multiple readings or misreadings, writing takes on a dangerous, or at least an inconvenient aspect: it becomes unpredictable in its effects, open-ended, inaugurating rather than closing down the generation of meanings. Such matters were becoming of increasing concern to the poets and theorists of the late sixteenth century: Sidney's *Defence* is at times uneasily caught between the demands of what he terms the "infected will" and the "erected wit," and for *homo seriosus* (among the Sidney circle, Fulke Greville and, indeed, Pembroke's mother herself) come to mind, writing could all too easily become not merely imitative or deceptive, but morally and theologically reprehensible.[4] All the more unfortunate when it becomes even less socially responsible by taking the form of a script for a troupe of actors to titillate and confuse a socially and gender mixed audience. How is meaning to be controlled in such circumstances?

Pembroke's mother took it as part of her devotion to her brother to encourage plays that would promote his literary and moral principles. The closest models available were the closet dramas on historical themes being written in the French academies, in particular those of Robert Garnier, whose *Antonie* the countess had translated by 1590, four years after Philip's death. Two years later she took the unusual step for a woman of having the translation published, with two further editions following in 1595 and three more by 1607. The combination of high learning, pious moralization, and classical form in Garnier's plays was precisely designed to advance the Sidneian ideals in the face, as Joan Rees puts it, of those "new dramatists who had sprung up since Sidney's death" and who "threatened to sweep away the cherished ideals before them on a great wave of popular and 'barbaric' drama."[5]

Yet at the same time as the Countess was encouraging, actively or by example, writers like Fulke Greville, (*Mustapha*, 1599; *Alaham*, 1601), Samuel Daniel (*Cleopatra*, 1594; *Philotas*, 1595), and William Alexander (*Darius*, 1603; *Croesus*, 1604; *Julius Caesar*, 1609) to write plays similar to her own translation of Garnier, her husband, the second earl, was providing support for a very different kind of drama. A number of the early public theater companies—the Queen's Men (1590, 1596), Strange's (1593), Worcester's (1595, 1596), and Essex's (1596)—are recorded as having played at Ludlow on their provincial tours, while, as Hannay notes, the number of performances by touring companies in Shrewsbury, where the second earl routinely presided over the Council of the Marches, greatly increased during his tenure as lord president of Wales.[6] In London, he lent his protection to a number of the public theater companies, not the least of which, the company actually known as Pembroke's Men, probably played a brief part in the development of Shakespeare's early career. As modern scholars piece together the ambiguous records of these early companies, we can rather dimly see Pembroke's Men as an ill-defined group that briefly took some stable shape in the shifting fortunes of the London theater companies in the 1590s, playing at the Swan, seemingly sharing its members and perhaps its identity with the Admiral's Men. Chambers traces Pembroke's interest in and protection of the company as far back as 1592: it may have played at court in 1592–93, though a letter from Henslowe to Richard Alleyn suggests it had little success otherwise. Temporary members seemed to have included Shakespeare, Burbage, and the Dutton brothers. By 1597 the company included Jonson among its members, but *The Isle of Dogs* scandal, in which Jonson and others were imprisoned, effectively disbanded the company, though there are occasional provincial and London references to it—or at least to its name—thereafter. Chambers further suggests that the company's repertoire included Marlowe's *Edward II* (1592), Shakespeare's *Titus Andronicus* (1594?), and a number of history plays, some of which may have been by, or at least worked on by, Shakespeare.[7]

It is not surprising that with the varied interests of his parents, William Herbert grew up with an interest in drama, both the increasingly popular, commercial, and socially unruly theater of the London companies, and the more exclusive private theatricals of great houses and royal court. One of the first state visits King James made after his accession in 1603 was in December of that year to Wilton House, where Pembroke, just over the disgrace of the Mary Fitton affair and no doubt reveling in his newly inherited title, summoned the King's Men to play. Despite Chambers' assertion that a letter once existed from Pembroke's mother remarking that "the man Shakespeare" was "with us" and that *As You Like It* was played, there are no records extant of what plays were in fact presented at Wilton, but it is, nonetheless, an indication of the close connections between Pembroke and the public theater.[8]

Throughout his career as a courtier, Pembroke in fact continued a very active interest in drama, and in 1616, after some conventionally sordid horsetrading, he became lord chamberlain, where his duties included the overseeing of the licensing of all plays, although in practice virtually all the day-to-day work was handled by his subordinate, who oversaw the Office of the Revels. When Pembroke first became lord chamberlain, the master of the Revels was Sir John Astley; there was a series of attempts to have the office revert to a Pembroke appointee, a move opposed by Buckingham, who at that point was moving rapidly to a position of political domination. Jonson, as a protegé of Pembroke, was suggested for the position, but eventually one of Pembroke's distant cousins, Henry Herbert, the brother of Lord Herbert of Cherbury, bought the reversion of the position from Astley, who was eased out of the-day-to-day operations of the position while still retaining the title.[9] In 1623 Herbert visited Wilton and was knighted as a reward for his willingness to cooperate with Pembroke's moves to consolidate his power against Buckingham. Yet Pembroke's interest in the drama does not seem to have been simply that of a distant bureaucrat or manipulative politician: when Richard Burbage died in 1619, Pembroke wrote to Lord Duncaster of his having avoided a "supper given by the Duke of Lennox in honor of the French ambassador," which, he said, "being tenderharted could not endure to se so soon after the loss of my old acquaintance Burbadg."[10] His connection with Burbage, long a principal actor in Shakespeare's company, may be an indication of why, in 1623, the Shakespeare First Folio was dedicated to the two "incomparable brethren," Pembroke and his brother, the earl of Montgomery, the husband of Mary Wroth's closest friend, Susan, countess of Montgomery. In short, we get a picture of a nobleman who conceived, with some enthusiasm, that the public responsibilities of his rank and family included the conscientious support and responsible oversight of (as well, almost certainly, attendance at) the public theater as well as (at least during his youth) participating in court entertainments. In his case the concern with theater seems to have exceeded even the admittedly substantial interests of his family: one of the consistent strands in Pembroke's character seems to have been a preference to let his responsibilities follow his personal pleasures, and in theater no less than in what Clarendon, made perhaps of sterner stuff, less indulgent to socially marginal frivolities like the public playhouses, termed his "immoderate" liking for women.

Pembroke was also an active participant in court dramatic performances—masques, tilts, and probably private theatricals—and it is in these colorful examples of the self-indulgence of the Stuart court that he is perhaps most characteristically displayed. Recent scholarship has revealed how the dramatic activities of the court were never mere entertainment, but politically crucial articulations of political policy and of the location and distribution of power. "These Things are but Toyes," said Bacon, but "Princes will have such Things. . . ." Therefore the masques were, in the words of Henry Wotton, a shrewd cynic as well as a diplomat, "art become a work of state."[11] The court entertainments of the Christmas season, for instance, were not simply (and perhaps rarely) convivial occasions for merriment but rather ritualized occasions for announcements of policy, displays of allegiance, and sumptuous displays of propaganda. Althusser's celebrated formulation of how ideological state apparatuses work to interpellate members of a society by incorporating and "hailing" them has its perfect manifestation in the functioning of Stuart court entertainments: staging of demonstrable truths in the very presence and effectively scripted actions of the court from the king down the social hierarchy to the least and most insecure gentlemen and ladies.[12]

Early in the reign of James, the court masques were largely organized within the queen's household, with Queen Anne herself taking an active role. She had a love of spectacle, costume, dancing, and also a desire to reproduce in England the opulence and indulgence of continental courts. The Sidneys and Pembrokes were major players in her endeavors. As early as May 1603, Mary's father was created Baron Sidney of Penshurst, and given the place of the queen's lord chamberlain and surveyor, the second highest official in her household, second only to Cecil, who was appointed lord high steward. Sidney's title was not entirely ceremonial. In addition to the collection of the queen's revenues and overseeing the courts of survey—which meant, to Rowland Whyte's intense relief, that Sidney became increasingly involved with the manipulations of the Jacobean court, absence from which, Whyte felt, had hindered Sidney's career—Sidney was required to make continual public appearances at masques, tourneys, ceremonies, and funerals. According to the family accounts, a great deal of his own resources were put into providing appropriately elaborate costumes and entertainments. While it had been to the more austere court of the last years of Elizabeth that Robert Sidney first sent his "Mall," with the new reign his oldest daughter occupied a more colorful place as one of the ladies of the queen's household. Typically, Whyte—who also benefited considerably from his employer's elevation—best articulates the role appropriate to a daughter of the queen's new chamberlain when he comments that she had "dawnced before the Queen two galliards with one Mr Palmer, the ablest dawncer of this tyme; both were much comended by her Majestie; then she dawnced with hym a corante."[13] Those are precisely the terms on which a daughter of a family like the Sidneys would be most advantageously displayed at court. She was to be decorative, an embodiment of the graces and accomplishments provided by her education, qualities that would make her, however briefly, a fitting companion to royalty. Then, as quickly as possible, she would be noticed as a good match, and a marriage completed that would be benficial to the family—or, at least, not disadvantageous. It was always to some extent a burden for one in Robert Sidney's position to have daughters.

After her marriage, and no doubt because of her father's status, the new Lady Wroth was given a role in the first masque written for Queen Anne, Jonson's and Jones's *Masque of Blacknesse* (1605). She played the nymph Baryte, processing with Lady Walsingham, who played Periphere, carrying "an urn, shered with wine," to signify the earth's fruitfulness. Other women taking part included her cousin Anne Herbert, Pembroke's future sister-in-law Susan Herbert, and Lady Penelope Rich. Each lady appeared as one of the twelve daughters of Niger, dressed in blue and gold, with peacock feathers in their hair. All carried fans inscribed with names and *imprese*. Mary Wroth's father attended the performance, which was on Twelfth Night, 1605, at Whitehall, dressed in a suit costing the large sum of £80, made "of Ashe coulor satten cutt with a peach coulor taffetie and laid with silver lace." Audience and masquers alike celebrated the occasion with conspicuous ostentation, although Dudley Carleton disapproved of the masque, saying that while "their Apparrell was rich," it was "too light and Curtizanlike for such great ones." Three years later Wroth's participation in the sequel to *Blacknesse*, *The Masque of Beauty*, was commented upon by the Italian poet, Antimo Galli, in a narrative poem dedicated to Pembroke that devoted a stanza each to his wife and his cousin.[14] Although records are scanty, Mary Wroth may also have performed in—and almost certainly must have watched—*Hymenaei* (1606), *The Masque of Queenes* (1609), and *Oberon* (1611). *Urania* makes reference to *Lord Hay's Masque* (1607) by Campion and possibly *Tethys Festival* (1610) by Daniel. Wroth and Pembroke also took part in a now-lost pastoral called *The May Lord*, written by Jonson and presented probably sometime before 1612. She was a keen observer of the theatrical effects achieved in the masques: McLaren has shown just how closely the descriptions of the masques in *Urania* draw upon specific details of Jones's designs, especially for the effects of spectacular surprise.[15]

Pembroke was also an active participant in court entertainments, "drawn," as Dick Taylor puts it, to the masque by his "own temperament, interests, and early environment and by his desire for court advancement."[16] He was in the inaugural masques for King James, including Daniel's *The Vision of Twelve Goddesses* and the anonymous *Maske brought in by a Magician of China*, in which he took the role of first masquer, opening the action by presenting the king with an *impresa* "in a shield with a sonet to express his device" and a jewel worth £40, for which in fact James had already paid. The following year Pembroke was also first masquer in the masque for his brother's wedding, upon which

I commented in chapter two, an occasion distinguished, according to Carleton, by "no small losse that night of chains and jewells, and many great ladies were in shorter than their skirts."[17] The other masque of 1604, *Blackeness*, created by Jonson and Jones, featured Mary Wroth and (although there is no record) probably Pembroke as masquers. The 1605–6 masques, which included Jonson's *Hymenae*, show no record of Pembroke's participation—probably, Taylor suggests, because it was designed for the marriage of Essex and Frances Howard, and Pembroke's rivalry with the Howards was already developing. In the 1606 season a pageant written by John Ford, *Honour Triumphant*, was performed. Four knights errant, played by the duke of Lennox, the earl of Arundel, Pembroke, and his brother, now earl of Montgomery, defended four idealistic propositions. They were, respectively, that "knights in ladies service have no free-will," "Beauty is the maintaineer of valour," "Fair Lady was never false" (which was Pembroke's), and "Perfect lovers are only wise." A month later their challenges were formally answered by four more cynical knights with four counter-propositions, the counter to Pembroke's being: "Fairest Ladies are falsest, having fairest occasion." One notices how the idealized misogyny of courtly Petrarchism so "naturally" permeates the rhetoric of court politics. Pembroke may also have been in *The Masque of Beautie* (1608), and was in the *Haddington Masque* (1609) and the *Squire's Masque* by Campion (1613). The tilts held on the anniversary of James accession, 24 March, were annual events in which Pembroke was a regular performer as late as 1616, when he became lord chamberlain. In 1610 Pembroke was especially honored as Prince Henry's server, and brought out two peach-colored, velvet-draped horses resplendent in white pearls. Wotton recorded his impression of the 1613 tilt that it was the two Herbert brothers who shone out above all others: "The two best, to my fancy," he wrote,

> were . . . the two Earls brothers: the first a small exceeding white pearl, and the words, *solo candore valer*. The other a sun casting a glance on the side of a pillar, and the beams reflecting, with this motto, *Splendid refulget*. In which devices there seemed an agreement; the elder brother, to allude to his own nature, and the younger to his fortune.[18]

In 1613 Jonson wrote *A Challenge at Tilt* as one of the entertainments for the wedding of Robert Carr and Frances Howard, after the divorce of the bride from the earl of Essex on the grounds of his impotence. The bride's "virginity" had been attested to by a somewhat suspect procedure, and a year or so after the marriage the implication of both bride and groom in the murder of Sir Thomas Overbury constituted one of the age's major scandals. But at the wedding Jonson's masque was presented—along with other masques, including

Campion's *The Somerset Masque*, Middleton's *Masque of Cupid*, the anonymous *Masque of Flowers*, and Jonson's *Irish Masque at Court*—as the sign of reconciliation between the court's main factions. Built around a debate between two cupids, acted by pages of the bride and groom, the debate over who constitutes the "true" Cupid was adjudicated by Hymen, who decided that they were equals, both being the offspring of Venus and Mars. The piece concludes: "And may this royall court neuer know more difference in humours; or these well-grac'd nuptials more discord in afflictions, then what they presently feele, and may ever avoid." The hope expressed here was represented by the Howard family and supporters appearing among the combatants in the colors of the groom, with the two Pembroke brothers, who were known to be opposed to both the Howards and the marriage, appearing in the colors of the bride. The masque thus became a means of making a political statement, and representing, in Jonson's words, "a strife, wheren you bothe winne . . . a concord worthy all married mindes emulation, when the louver transformes himselfe into the person of his belov'd."[19]

After 1616 Pembroke seems to have no longer taken an active part in court entertainments. He was, after all, approaching forty, and it was probably beneath his new dignity as lord chamberlain, not to mention a challenge to his physical capacity, to appear in tilts and even the less physically demanding masques. Once he became lord chamberlain, however, he was responsible for overseeing all the court's entertainment as well as having final control of licensing the public theater. As I noted in chapter two, he seems to have used his office, consistently though usually not ostentatiously, to promote his political agenda in his role as the "backstage leader of Parliamentary Puritanism." In 1623, it is likely, at the very least, that he judiciously failed to intervene to prevent the acting of *A Game at Chesse*, in order to allow its anti-Spanish and anti-Buckingham sentiments to influence public opinion at the height of the crisis over a proposed Spanish marriage for Prince Charles, and then organized a light punishment for the erring participants: Henry Herbert was called to account for licensing the play, but the matter seems to have never been proceeded with, and the actors received only a letter of warning from Pembroke himself.[20]

We need at this point to stand back from this fairly straightforward chronicle of patronage, playing, and participation in court entertainments and consider some of the broader cultural implications. Together and separately, the two Sidney cousins took their roles in a variety of narratives scripted by their family, class, and gender assignments. Among them were the roles they played out within the courtly and popular theaters. Both performed in the court's most prestigious art forms, the masques, tilts, and similar entertainments, each being willingly interpellated into the royal court's ritualized image of its own order and power. The most obvious difference between the two cousins concerns their theatrical interests outside the court. Pembroke was a patron, probably an enthusiast, of the public theater. His London residence was (almost literally) a stone's throw from the Blackfriars Theater. His closer associations with the public theater are not unrelated to his class and gender assignments. Wroth's life as a woman in the court, however, meant that she acquired a very different perspective on the theatrical dimensions of her life. As a lady-in-waiting and occasional dancer, she played an appropriately decorative and silent part in the margins of the spectacle of the court; if she had been trained to have an agenda of her own, it was simply to be seen, as a graceful, minor contributor to the dazzling visual display that mirrored for its participants the gloriousness that was a central part of the court's self-image. Like one of her characters in *Urania*, she "both saw those sports the Court affects, and are necessary follies for that place, as Masques and Dauncings, and was an Actor my selfe amongst them" (*Urania*, p. 457). Pembroke was likewise a minor participant in the orchestrations of court display, but, as a man, "naturally" he took on more active roles as a dancer, tilter, and challenger, and in his highly visible public roles as patron and political authority.

One of the roles that Pembroke did not play was that of playwright: of the two cousins, it was Wroth who actually wrote a play, even though it was never published and may not have been acted, even privately. So far as we know, too, she had no direct contact with the public theater, although Miller has argued that, especially in *Urania*, there are many signs of Wroth's interest in a concept of the dramatic and the theatrical very different from those derived from the masque and the specular theater of the court: many revelations occur in dramatic dialogues that echo the conversations between heroines and confidantes, like Beatrice and Hero, in Shakespeare's comedies. But what McLaren terms "the mechanics of seeming" in *Urania* suggests that Wroth was aware that court theatricals displayed what must have been, especially for a woman, an all too familiar metaphor for the gender politics of the court. Several key episodes occur in "theaters," which are depicted not merely as sites of dramatic entertainment but of enchantment and self-discovery, as if one of the functions of artifice and role playing were to reveal the origins and destiny of the actors, not merely the roles they play.[21] When Pamphilia asserts that "an Actor knowes when to speake, when to sigh, when to end: a true feeler is wrapped in distempers, and only can know how to heare" (*Urania*, p. 314), she may be displaying a disdain for feigned emotion, but the sorrowful queen and every other character in the romance are constantly on display, arranging scenes to display themselves as surely as the Jacobean courtiers in their elaborately staged performances, on stage and off. Pamphilia arrives at the House of Love in calculatedly spectacular fashion, in a "Chariot of Watchet, embroydred with Crimson silke, and purle of silver." Bacon pointed out that the "glories" of tournaments are "chiefly in the Chariots, wherein the Challengers make their entry."[22] When King Antissus of Romania arrives with his knights to take part in the Accession Day tournament—thus echoing the same event in the court of James—they are referred to, not without some extended irony, as actors (*Urania*, pp. 123, 99, 341, 386). In *Urania* there are a number of scenes in which the male propensity to self-display and self-advertising are satirized. The sly humor, directed even at the matchless Amphilanthus, is both consistent and serious: the pressures and contradictions of the court, whereby men had to constantly struggle for recognition, produced what Greenblatt terms a "virtually fetishistic emphasis on manner," and meant that performative and adaptive role playing became a supposedly "natural" part of the male courtier's identity.[23] Wroth's romance gives us a demystification along gendered lines: it enacts a woman subject's acknowledgement of the power of and yet alienation from the "naturalness" of male display.

Theatrical metaphors, then, carried a particularly intense ideological weight in the lives and writings of the Sidney cousins, not least in relation to the politics of gender. The very act of being a woman author itself involves playing parts that are, as it were, not found in the accepted scripts for women. Yet to take on the role of a writer, as Heather Weidemann points out (and Wroth's treatment by Lord Denny attests), does not in itself produce a "happy proliferation of subversion."[24] If taking on an unfamiliar role, disguising, and trying to play new parts all suggest liberation from assigned gender identities—as they do, at least for a time, in Shakespeare's comedies, most obviously in *As You Like It*—they may equally signify the oppression of never having any owned subject position, which is what Pamphilia complains about when she exclaims "O afflictions, how many severall ways have you . . . how many maskes, how many false faces can you procure, to delude inocent faith" (*Newberry 1*, fol. 21). The fragility of the theatrical metaphor is never far from the surface in such remarks. The commonplace Renaissance metaphors of the world as the theater of God's glory or the court as a theater of magnificence assert a correspondence between specular surface and underlying reality, where what is acted is part of the natural and providential. But the world of theatricality in *Urania* is fundamentally insecure and untrustworthy. The acceptance of the self as theatricalized never allows a man or, especially, a woman an escape from assigned roles and actions. If a woman wants to attain to even a fantasy of autonomy, she must act within the confines of the roles assigned to

her. In one of the many patently autobiographical episodes in *Urania*,
Wroth tells the story of Lindamira, in which a court lady has her queen's
favors withdrawn. Lindamira's career at court is ruined: " . . . all her
favour was withdrawn as suddenly and directly, as if never had . . . the
night pass'd, they are in their old clothes againe, and no appearance of
what was." Instead of abandoning the court, she finds that she can only
function by "remaining like one in a gay Masque" (*Urania*, p. 424). She
has, it seems, no real self, no owned desires, no stable point from which
she can assert her desires apart from those assigned to her as a woman
in the court.

The story of Lindamira is one indication of how Wroth's awareness
of the theater was not confined to being gazed at in the masques. Yet it
must have been especially from studying the masques that Wroth realized
how she and other women were trapped and, indeed, molested, in a
theatrical space of far more moment than that provided by the masque.
Before 1632 and the innovations introduced by Queen Henrietta Maria
to court entertainment that were so disapproved of not only by the
Puritans, but by courtiers like Dudley Carleton, women took part only as
silent dancers.[25] Even that had been, in the first decade of James's reign,
regarded somewhat uneasily. In *The Masque of Queenes* (1609), Jonson
had introduced court ladies, but men or boy actors still played the female
roles in the anti-masque. Bel-Anna, Queen of the Ocean, personifying the
queen herself, is described as simply reflecting her husband's masculine
virtue, "humbling, all her worth / To him that gave it." She is, we are
told, " a spectacle so full of love and grace / Unto your court." The
masques may have shown Wroth how patriarchy's traditional commod-
ification of women's sexuality was blatantly demonstrated in the silent
women on display in the processions and dances of masques and court
entertainments. They are scripts for entertainment, but also scripts of
gender assignment in the wider world. The ideology of sexual hierarchy
and gender assignment in the masques is consistent and blatant: in
Campion's *The Lord's Masque*, male masquers are "men fitt for wars,"
the female masquers are statues that are eventually transformed into
"women fitt for love." If the active male body is at the heart of the
male fantasy of autonomy, the umoving female body is meant to be
a body on display, and, by implication, available to be touched at
will by the males.[26]

In previous chapters I commented on the paucity of modern analyses of the gender politics of Petrarchism; for all the modern interest
in Jacobean masques, it is curious that there has been little analysis
of their gender politics. It may be that the masque is so obviously
archaic and of largely antiquarian interest that it seems hardly worth
subjecting to rigorous cultural analysis. But the masque was the most

prestigious "literary" form of the age, one in which a vast proportion of the court and therefore the country's wealth was invested, and no less than, say, Disneyland or Madonna today, deserves analysis, at the very least, to reveal the ways by which it formed and articulated its society's dominant ideologies—not least those of gender. Wroth is all the more interesting, therefore, in that she provides the rare occurrence of a critique of the masque and its gender assumptions from a woman's viewpoint—and by someone who took part in masques. Her treatment of the ways women and women actors are produced by their dramatic contexts is valuable precisely because it is articulated by a product of the system she is attempting to demystify. What Weidemann terms the instability that "necessarily attends the construction of the female subject" in the period is all the more powerful because of its being spoken by someone who was in the subject-ed position within the system she is critiquing, further who had been marginalized, and, at the time she is writing, was like Lindamira, expelled from it. Is *Urania*, as Lamb suggests, in part motivated by Wroth's anger towards the court that cast her adrift?[27]

Over and over, Wroth's female characters describe the pressures they feel beset by in terms of theater, performance and display. The forsaken Lindamira feels she can regain the queen's favor only by "remaining like one in a gay masque," even while "she was only afflicted" (*Urania*, p. 424), and she ponders her tactics of self-presentation, deciding that her best image is to "effect silence," returning to the state of Jonson's and Campion's female statues. Theatricality, like gender assignment itself, is beset by ambivalence. Taking part in a masque, like entering the court itself, offers the illusion of power, even or perhaps especially to the otherwise powerless female subject. But, in fact, it creates her as the product of both a collective gaze and the gazes of individual men. What reactions might a woman have in this situation? In chapter six I discussed a poem in which Pamphilia was able to, as it were, turn the gaze back on the gazers. But that is a rare note. Usually the situation is one in which the woman is perplexed, even victimized:

Like to the Indians, scorched with the sunne,
The sunn which they doe as theyr God adore
So ame I us'd by love, for ever more
I worship him, less favors have I wunn,

Better are they who thus to blacknes runn
And soe can only whitenes want deplore
Then I who pale, and white ame with griefs store,
Nor can have hope, butt to see hopes undunn;

234

Beesids theyr sacrifies receavd's in sight
Of theyr chose sainte: Mine hid as worthles rite;
Grant mee to see wer I my offrings give,

Then lett me weare the marke of Cupids might
In hart as they in skin of Phoebus light
Nott ceasing offrings to love while I Live.

(Poems, p. 99)

Whether, as Roberts suggests, line five refers to Wroth's memory of
having taken part in *Blackenesse*, what Weidemann terms "theatrical
consciousness"[28] is certainly at the forefront of the poem. Pamphilia
describes herself as a masquer, "receavd" in sight of the court; without the identity afforded by the court and its ritual theatricals she is
"worthless." Yet to be chosen to play a role in the specular theater of
the court is to be disclosed as the court's creation, and so individually
exploitable and expendable. At best it may serve to reveal the constructed
nature of being a woman—but that may be an unbearable burden for
her, since there appears to be so little possibility of changing her state.
To discover that one is constructed in ways one did not suspect is a
recurring and disillusioning discovery in *Urania*: the work actually opens
with a "masked" woman, a shepherdess who has just learnt to her
bewilderment that she is, in fact, high born, and who thus is unable to
say who she "really" is. This opening episode is an ironic reversal of the
classic family romance: instead of the pleasurable fantasy of having noble
parents, Urania is distressed to find that she is not, as she had supposed, a
humble shepherdess. Thereafter, as the work unfolds, the divided desires
of the book's title character become characteristic of all the women. In
the main group of plots, centered on Pamphilia, despite her insistence on
truth and transparent virtue, she continually finds herself regretting that
she must play roles in accord with others' desires: "Pamphilia made some
signe of Joye, but a Signe indeed it was for how could joye come where
such desperate sorrow did abound, yet the Seeming gave great content
to all the beholders (*Newberry* 1, fol. 21). She continually blames herself
for appearing to dissemble: "when did I ever play so foolish a part? justly
may I bee condemned for this error, and blamed for so much lightnes"
(*Urania*, p. 321).

Yet how can a woman in the court avoid playing parts? Obviously
enough, Pamphilia's roles include those of a queen, a friend, a daughter,
but also, more deviously, those of a lover, a deceiver of rivals in love,
and especially that of a contented friend to her cousin, while at the
same time vowing love to him and bewailing his continual infidelities.
In the masque presented by the seer Lady Mellisea, as in the Jacobean

court, the masquers sing and perform, then pull off their vizards, and dance with the ladies. Wroth presents an image of nostalgic happiness, an idealized picture of "Emporesses, all the kings, and princes. . . ." Then it is as if such an ideal image is always in danger of disappearing: "Butt heere we have longe stayd, therfore we must a while leave this Court in all hapines, and content" (*Newberry* 1, fol. 15). That seems to have been, for Wroth, the overwhelming force of the theatrical activities and the theatrical self-presentation of the court: to draw attention to its own ephemeral nature, while never providing the means to construct an alternative. Late in the 1621 edition of *Urania*, the princess Lisia tells of how a lady is suspected of scandal at court, leaves, and then tries to recreate the ideal image of joy and gaiety:

> at last [she] sought company, some she got together, but of what sort? those that were of the age before, who having young minds rumbled up their old carcases, and rubd over their wrinckling faces like old wainscot new varnished: and little sweeter was some of their beauties . . . an noise they also made of mirth, banqueting and inviting company, but all would not serve, the glaringst signe, or greatest bush, drawes not in the best company: no more did they make the Court much the fairer. Dance they did, and all ridiculous things that ancient, but young made women could invent to do . . . Lord how I admird the alteration, and the place, being changd from what it was, as much as from a Court to a Playhouse.
>
> (*Urania*, p. 486)

It is an astonishing demystification of the court, its theatricalities and self-dramatizations projected upon the women interpellated into its self-admiring system. How intriguing, too, that it is the playhouse that is used to represent at once the downfall and disgrace of exile from the court, and yet, by extension, an alternative to it.

Perhaps the most striking example of the theatrical metaphor in *Urania* is the complex episode in the second part which is centered on a masque presented in Pamphilia's honor by her eventual husband, Rodomandro, King of Tartaria. The masque celebrates the triumph of Honor over Cupid; it thus stages the Tartarian king's high-minded virtue by comparison with his rival Amphilanthus, who is identified with Cupid. Rodomandro plays his role so well, conveying his deep and virtuous love for Pamphilia so effectively—if not to the love-torn queen, then certainly to the assembled company—that Amphilanthus reacts with violent jealousy, and confronts Pamphilia with his love. He promises absolute fidelity to her, and together they take public vows of intent— "performed," we are told in an ambiguous ceremony to which I shall return in detail in the next chapter, "butt nott as an absolute marriage though as perfect as that" (*Newberry 1*, fol 14). But their vows are never fully consummated, a lesson underlined by the masque. Cupid is subjected to Honor, just as in her life as a queen Pamphilia must submit to Honor rather than Passion, and in Wroth's love for her cousin had to be subordinate to the demands of the family and her role in its aggrandizement.

Reading Wroth's life in relation to *Urania*'s concerns with the theatrical, an intriguing contrast between the two cousins emerges. In his career, as in his poems and letters, Pembroke presents himself as a male wanting to be in control of the events in which he was caught, a man who risked little, keeping his private affairs strictly subordinate to his public roles, never (at least after the Mary Fitton affair) allowing passion to triumph over honor. By contrast, his cousin, as a woman, was far more subject to others' desires, except (and perhaps only briefly) in her writing and her sexuality. As Pamphilia's struggles show, a woman may create a fantasy of control; but generally, to take a part in the specular theater of a male-dominated world is, for a woman, to lack any material agency. Hence it is all the more intriguing that, of the two Sidney cousins, Pembroke remains the relatively aloof patron of the drama, the presider over court entertainments; Wroth—positioned as a woman as part of the spectacle of the court and its theater—wrote a play. Her venture into playwriting, however, is indicative of the limited possibilities afforded to women: where Aphra Behn fifty years later could write plays for the public stage, Wroth's was designed at most for private presentation. Until 1989, when it was first published, it existed only in two manuscripts, one imperfect, and it was probably rarely read for over 450 years.

Love's Victory is a pastoral drama in five acts. It portrays the highly idealized romantic interactions of four couples, whose wooings and boo-hooings are overseen by Cupid and his mother Venus. It was most likely written about the same time as the continuation of *Urania*, in the early 1620s. Both Roberts and Barbara Lewalski speculate that it might have been written for private performance, perhaps for Sir Edward Dering (1598–1644). He was a collector of plays and known to present private performances, possibly including women actors. He was also a near neighbor of Wroth's family home in Kent. Dering may have owned the original, unfinished manuscript of the play, now in the Huntington. But there is no evidence for its having been acted at his instigation or at any other time.[29] Lewalski has traced the generic conventions within which it operates: those of the pastoral tragicomedy, which puts into dramatic form the typical atmosphere and themes of the pastoral eclogue. Tasso's *Aminta* (1580) and Guarini's *Il Pastor Fido* (1590) are the best known examples of the form. Sidney had disparaged such works as "mongrell Tragedicomedie," but by the early seventeenth century tragicomedy had become a respectable and—if we extend its scope to include related and equally mixed works like Shakespeare's *The Winter's Tale*—popular dramatic kind. In 1610 Fletcher offered a definition, claiming that "it wants deaths, which is inough to make it no tragedie, yet brings some neare it, which is inough to make it no comidie." Lewalski suggests that Wroth probably had only a general awareness of the controversies over the nature and legitimacy of tragicomedy, but in writing *Love's Victory*, she certainly "looked to the canon of the new kind—Tasso, Guarini, Daniel, Fletcher—to provide . . . the horizon of generic expectations," which included lyrical songs and choruses, stock characters and a miraculous ending. There are four pairs of lovers. Recent readers of the play have suggested there are various family references in their names and relationships. The most prominent male lover, Philissus (Philip Sidney?), is in love with Musella (Muse+Stella?), but fears, wrongly as it turns out, that she loves his friend Lissius (Matthew Lister, Pembroke's mother's physician who was, it was gossipped, seen as a possible husband for the dowager countess?) who in turn comes to love Philissus's sister Simeana (Mary Sidney, Pembroke's mother herself?). To complicate the action, Silvesta loves Philissus, but renounces her love for him in favor of Musella, and also rejects the love of the unsophisticated Forester, at least until the play's end. The flirtatious Dalina and the boorish Rustick (yet another satiric portrait of Wroth's late husband?) are also united at the end. Other minor characters interact with these four main couples: Arcas, who tries to slander Philissus and Musella, and so is the play's obligatory villain; the outsider Climeana, who courts Lissius far too blatantly; Fillis and Lacon, who are respectively, the rejected suitors of Philissus and Musella.[30]

The most important characters in the play's scheme, however, are the two gods, Venus and Cupid, who preside and quarrel over the activities of the mortals. When Lissius scorns the power of love, Venus is insulted and orders that Cupid's hitherto merely mischievous intentions towards the mortals should become more intensified. She announces at the end of Act One that she "would have all to waile, and all to weepe" (l. 387), and then at the end of Act Three that she is still dissatisfied that some of her victims are "to slightly wounded" (3. 336). Musella reveals to Philissus that her father's will has commanded her to wed Rustick and that she therefore must give him up. Finally, however, Venus intervenes in the lovers' favor, claiming that the miraculous survival and uniting of Philissus and Musella is her own work and giving judgment against the villain Arcas. At the end, like the monarch mingling with the dancers in a masque, the mythological figures appear to and join with the mortals. The play's end can thus be read either as a sentimental celebration of true love winning out or as McLaren argues, something more elevated, a demonstration of the power of Venus and Cupid to humble everyone in the play, even those who seem most immune to love. All the lovers, Cupid assures Venus,

> . . . shall both cry, and sigh, and wayle, and weep,
> And for owr mercy shall most humbly creepe.
> Love hath most glory when as greatest sprites
> Hee downward throwse unto his owne delights.
>   (2. 405–08)

Love's Victory has an attractive languidness that, if we look at the history of dramatic forms in the period, not only has affinities with the masque, but anticipates the pastoral plays encouraged by Queen Henrietta Maria in the late 1620s and 1630s. There is no evidence that Wroth returned to court to take part in those pastorals: she would have been, after all, a woman in her forties, with a scandalous past, a reputation for frankness or even slander, in debt and without landed or financial power, a poor relation of a family whose influence on the national scene was waning. But it is intriguing to see how her work anticipates many of the fashions that were the taste of the court in the next decade or more.

The conventional machinery of the plays written for Henrietta Maria are all patently evident in *Love's Victory*: the paraphernalia of Cupid's arrows, love's secrecy, hope, jealousy, impossible chastity, and fortuitous interventions of the deities are all commonplace ingredients of the court entertainments of the 1630s—just as they had been of romance stories, poems and dramas over the previous half century and throughout the long and devious tradition of romance narrative back to the Greek romances. The play's clichés are the familiar ones of the tired Petrarchism typical of much of the court poetry of the time, including Pembroke's: love is "a paine which yett doth pleasure bring," (2. 94), at once a mystery, a gift from heaven, and a perpetual betrayal. These undemanding paradoxes are dressed up in the equally conventional landscape of the court masque: " . . . a Landt-shape of Forrest, Hils, Vallies, Cottages, A Castle, A River, Pastures, Heards, Flocks, all full of Countrey simplicity," as Jonson describes it in *The Sad Shepherd*.[31] On a much grander scale, what Jonson depicts is also the landscape of *Urania*. In fact, in the continuation of the romance, there is an episode that uses the same material: a group of shepherds and shepherdesses, led by a brother and sister, undergo similar experiences. Names also recur: Arcas, Rustick, Magdalina. In the *Urania* version, a group of young princes and princesses, some of the "lost children" around whom some episodes of the continuation of the romance are built, have been kidnaped by the Sophy of Persia, and they gather together to recount their experiences.

The episode serves as a metaphor of escape from the violence in the world outside the pastoral, an attitude that is taken to an extreme by Folietto (a shepherd rather like Rustick), who asserts that even the sufferings of love are largely fictional. In Wroth's dramatized version of the situation (we have no way of saying which was a reworking of which), the political context is omitted. Nonetheless, even in the more seemingly escapist world of dramatic pastoral, the complex world of politics does manage to creep in. On the most elementary level, Wroth brings references from her own far from serene life into the pastoral. The most obvious are the probable references to her (presumably, when the play was written, late) husband in the character of Rustick, who is unsophisticated and vulgar, and unaware of the love between Musella and Philissus; and finally both revealing his ignobility and obligingly allowing a wish fulfillment ending to occur by abandoning his claims to Musella and disavowing all the promises she has self-sacrificingly made to fulfill her father's will that she should marry him. His gesture is perhaps a wistful fantasy on Wroth's part as she looks back on the relations between herself and her father, her cousin, and her husband. The scripts of the family romance play out over and over.

What is most attractive about *Love's Victory* is its humor. Jonson had insisted that comedy was a necessary part of court entertainments, even when they were designed as serious celebrations. *Love's Victory* is permeated not only by humor, but by a crisp irony, which is consistently directed even towards the presiding deities. Their threats are more fustian than serious, and most of the action is lighthearted. Rustick is the continual butt of lighthearted joking: he expresses his love for Musella in terms similar to Sidney's Mopsa in *Arcadia*: she is "whiter then lambs wull," her eyes "play / like Goats with hay," and her cheeks are red as "Okar spred / On a fatted sheep's back" (ll. 337, 341–42, 348–49). In addition to the overt comedy of the play, its treatment of love is also intriguing. Beneath the clichés of "Love's sweet pleasing paine" (3. 372) are some interesting contradictions. As McLaren suggests, much of the action centers on characters' difficulty in communicating, trying to convey their affections and choices to the partner of their desires. Further, she suggests, it is the women who are faced with special difficulties, since they are interpellated into erotically passive roles. The malice of Venus's commands—"they shall have torment when they think to smile" (1.402)—translates into an anxiety born of their roles as women. It is they who are most disadvantaged in communicating and choosing. The extent of the masochism and paralysis in *Pamphilia to Amphilanthus* and *Urania* is never approached, but it is important to note that the one woman character who claims some degree of sexual autonomy, Dalina, is clearly disapproved of. She blatantly asserts:

This is the reason men ar growne soe coy,
When they parceave wee make theyr smiles owr joy.
Lett them alone, and they will seeke, and sue,
Butt yeeld to them and they'll with scorne pursue.
Hold a while of, they'll kneele, and follow you,
And vowe, and sweare, yett all theyr othes untrue.
Lett them once see you coming then they fly,
Butt strangly looke, and they'll for pitty cry.
(3. 249–56)

As the play unfolds, such sentiments are clearly set up in order to be silenced. Yet at the same time, *Love's Victory* implies that there are some limited areas of female agency. The dominant ideology of pastoral romance is that life represents a harmonious movement, through misprision and misfortune, to a happy marriage in which individual desires are reconciled with social stability. It is the ideology of a benevolent patriarchy typical of Shakespeare's *As You Like It* or *A Midsummer Night's Dream*. There are forces opposed to or skeptical about such a pattern, but they generally exist to be firmly rejected. In *As You Like It* it is Jaques who opposes such harmony; in *Love's Victory*, significantly, it is a woman, Silvesta, who vows to remain dissociated from men and marriage:

Butt farewell folly, I with Dian stand
Against love's changinge and blinde foulerie,
To hold with hapy and blest chastitie.
For love is idle, hapines ther's none
When freedom's lost and chastity is gon . . .

Now love's as farr from mee as never knowne,
Then bacely tyde, now freely ame mine owne.
(1. 126–30, 157–58)

Where the play's heroine, Musella, is overjoyed to be finally married to her beloved and gives appropriately dutiful thanks to the presiding deities, Silvesta claims that independence is preferable, and her rejection of the ideology of benevolent patriarchal marriage is certainly rendered as a far more attractive alternative than Jaques' rejection of the happinesses of the "country copulatives" at the end of *As You Like It*. Silvesta believes it is possible to "make a cleane shift to live without a man" (5. 187). The emphasis on "freedom" and being "mine own" is not rendered ironically: it is clearly an affirmation that defies, without obviously negative consequences, Venus's warning that unless mortals follow her dictates, they "will butt frame / Words against your selves."

241

Women, according to Venus, should accept their parts in the play of love: "Love the king is of the mind / Please him, and hee wilbe kind." (2. 324–25, 330–31). Being "mine own" may not be a sustainable fantasy, but it does mark a woman's assertion of her right to the kind of individuation that seems natural to men. It is, however, worth pointing out the intriguing contradiction here. Being "mine owne" would not meet with the approval of the age's moral orthodoxy for men or women, as the figures of Richard III, Iago, or Edmund remind us. Yet such characters, as Shakespearean commentators have long pointed out, are putting into play an emergent sense of the individualized subject, the Cartesian "I," that in less than a century will seem as "natural" as it seemed "unnatural" around 1600. All the more significant, therefore, that, as I have suggested, being "mine owne" is at the core of Wroth's gendering of the family romance: for a woman, being like a man involves a degree of autonomy rarely presumed by a woman, and it is significant that it is one of the recurring fantasies of *Love's Victory*.

As in Wroth's other writings, *Love's Victory* also places a strong emphasis on female friendship, as a "womanspace" not to be ruled by men. The sharing of stories and gossip—something to be benevolently exchanged among both men and woman, though initiated and presided over by the women—is an attractive aspect of the play that connects it with both *Urania* and *Pamphilia to Amphilanthus*. It is, however, worth noting Arbella Stuart's tart remark about the ladies in Queen Anne of Denmark's court (who would have most likely included Mary Wroth herself) and their indulgence in the kind of entertainment favored by Wroth's characters:

> . . . certain childeplayse remembred by the fayre ladies. Viz. I pray my Lo. give me a course in your park. Rise pig and go. One peny follow me. &c. and when I cam to Court they weare as highly in request as ever crackling of nuts was. So I was by the m.rs of the Revelles not onely compelled to play at. I knew not what for till that day I never heard of a play called Fier. but even persuaded by the princely example I saw to play the childe againe.[32]

Trivial though they may have been (though presumably no more than the gossip and boys' games of male courtiers), such activities, especially when exclusively the province of women, may be seen as part of an attempt by the politically powerless to carve out a distinctive space of pleasure and discovery for themselves. In Act Four of *Love's Victory*, the lovers play at riddles, and Rustick is laughed at for his ignorance—perhaps another jest at Wroth's husband, who, as we can see from Jonson's poem to Sir Robert Wroth, preferred the company of rural friends and animals and may well have been impatient at such courtly pastimes. As Lewalski notes, the satiric portrait of Rustick not only permits Wroth some amusing asides at her late husband's expense, but also allows her to align herself with the emerging ideology of the Stuart court's valorization of the urban pastoral, as opposed to the rustic values of the country, and to stress the dominance of the women, secure in their own discursive space. In the third act, the game is played only by the women, who share their stories of past loves. Dalina tells stories of what the moral orthodoxy of the time would term her fickleness—though another way of describing her activities might be in terms of sexual autonomy and experimentation, activities presumably acceptable for men, but forbidden to women. As in *Urania*, Wroth stresses that voicing such desires may lead only to pain, and thus a woman is well advised to accept her place within a benevolent marriage. Dalina's desire for the security marriage offers, therefore, comes through in her amused but still serious vow to accept the next proposal she receives. Simeana then tells of her constancy and of her secret hopes regarding an unnamed lover. Fillis tells of her unrequited love for Philissus. Climena tells of following a lover who later rejected her and of her present love for Lissius. While there are warnings that each may not necessarily be telling the whole truth, the scenes are a touching and (especially when Simeana and Climena quarrel) amusing revelation of the mixture of subjection, fantasy, and realism of women's roles in trying to find some alternative spaces within a gendered script they did not write.

For we can also see emerging from the scene what Lewalski terms "an implicit feminist politics"[33] that is unusual in the genre in which Wroth is writing. Not only is Venus rather than Cupid the dominant presiding deity, but more importantly, among the mortals the women's actions are more dominant and forceful. I have argued that the dominant fantasy of the woman's family romance is in effect to occupy the brother's place, to have the possibility of inheriting the father's autonomy and movement. But there is another, perhaps more mature, fantasy in the family romance for women and men alike, one that is often enacted in *Urania* but only hinted at in *Love's Victory*, as it was in *Pamphilia to Amphilanthus*. It is the fantasy of a mutual love regardless of gender, an erotopia of mutuality. It is a fantasy of community, not of competitive individualism. Significantly, therefore, where the values of community and human relations are central, it is significant, as Miller puts it, that they are mainly asserted by the women. Musella is a faithful confidant to men and women alike, especially in helping to reunite Lissius and Simeana. Dalina advises Simeana to act cautiously at first, and then, when they hear Lissius's confession of his love, to respond encouragingly. Musella in particular articulates for herself and her companions a clear range of choices and options: while misjudging Philissus's love for her, she does eventually respond to him, and takes Simeana's advice to think through her situation. Musella discovers herself in conflict with her mother's desire that she obey her father's will, and she contemplates:

> . . . my state
> Agreed on by my father's will which bears
> Sway in her brest, and duty in mee. Fate
> Must have her courses, while that wreched I
> Wish butt soe good a fate as now to dy.
>
> (5. 12-15)

Ethical questions arise here that were common to women of Wroth's class and which she herself had been deeply affected by, above all: is Musella bound to marry Rustick because of her father's will? Unlike many women in the Jacobean court, including perhaps Wroth herself, Musella seizes the initiative. It is she who decides that she and Lissius should visit the temple of Venus, where they will either find some mysterious end to their dilemma or die together. In a pastoral romance, as in a daydream, the miraculous wishfulfilment comes true.

Thus at the play's end we can see an interesting contradiction. We could say that the triumph of the lovers is as much a victory for perseverance as for love. The pastoral genre, of course, prepares us for a marvelous ending—the revival of the statue of the dead Hermione in *The Winter's Tale*, the return of Cymbeline's children, the reuniting of Pericles, Thaisa, and Marina—but as with Shakespeare's romances, the miracles at the end of *Love's Victory* are as much decided by human, and specifically female, agency as by supernatural intervention. Philissus and Musella go to the temple; they are about to stab themselves in a last act of mutual devotion when Silvesta offers them a more convenient method, a poison that (seemingly) kills them. Then she and Simeana inform the others what has happened. Rustick disclaims all rights to Musella, at which point the apparently dead lovers revive. This happy ending against all possible odds, including death, must have embodied a common fantasy for Wroth and her circle: that in the opposition between duty and love, reason and passion, if love could be pursued absolutely, it would be rewarded by the gods. Venus claims that Silvesta has been an "instrument ordain'd," and "when Venus wills, men can nott but obay" (5. 490, 536). These sentiments reassert the pastoral convention that all events are benevolently controlled by a mysterious providence; they also reassert the equal beneficence of providential patriarchy—yet that conclusion has been made possible by the devotion and cunning of the lovers themselves, especially the women. And at the level of fantasy enactment, something even more intriguing is emerging: the autonomy of men, envied by women, is maybe not finally satisfying, even to men.

Enacted even briefly, contained in *Love's Victory* is, once again, a fantasy of mutuality. Hinted at in *Pamphilia to Amphilanthus*, the same utopianism haunts the longest and most intriguing textualization of the family romance of the Sidney cousins, *The Countess of Mountgomery's Urania*, and to that I will now turn.

8

"SOME THING MORE EXACTLY RELATED THEN A FIXION": THE COUNTESSE OF MOUNTGOMERIES URANIA

Psychoanalysis [is] the telling and retelling of stories, stories of a particular life, until analyst and analysand finally come to a consensus on a better story or on their best possible story. This would be the one that more widely encompasses the previously repressed and disavowed, one that makes better sense of the puzzling motley of symptoms, behaviors, and dysfunctions with which the analysand had initially presented herself for treatment.

Robert Wallerstein

The longing for the missing phallus, the envy that has been attributed to women, is really the longing for just such a homoerotic bond as boys may achieve, just such an identificatory love. This is why there are so many stories of women's love being directed toward a hero such as she herself would be—the wish for disciplehood, serving an idol, submission to an ideal.

Jessica Benjamin[1]

246

Mary Wroth's *Urania* is a long prose romance, in some ways very like her uncle's *The Countess of Pembrokes Arcadia*, in some ways very unlike. It was published in part in 1621 as *The Countess of Mountgomeries Urania*, named for its author's friend and Pembroke's sister-in-law, Susan Herbert, the wife of Philip, earl of Montgomery. The 1621 *Urania* consists of 558 pages, and it ends with an incomplete sentence: " . . . And." It is followed by the sonnet sequence discussed in an earlier chapter, *Pamphilia to Amphilanthus*, named after the main characters of the romance, the first cousins, Pamphilia, Queen of Pamphilia, and Amphilanthus, Emperor of the Romans. A holograph manuscript of a second part, clearly a continuation of the 1621 volume, though not recommencing exactly where the published version leaves off—McLaren speculates that there is a bifolium missing—and with some of its stories occasionally inconsistent, is in the Newberry Library. It is currently being edited by Josephine Roberts as part of the first complete edition of the work, due to appear in 1994.[2]

The publication of the first part in 1621 seems to have been rushed, probably from a mixture of motives on the part of both author and printer. Wroth, it has been occasionally suggested, might have wanted to publish the work to help allay her debts. This is highly unlikely: the phenomenon of best-selling romances lay far in the future. In fact, it is likely that she had no idea that the publishers, John Grismand and John Marrot, had even obtained a copy. They registered *Urania* on 13 July 1621; when it appeared—no later than 14 December, when a copy is recorded as having been sold in Scotland—it was incomplete, with the last line finishing in mid-sentence. The printer was Augustine Matthews, who had a record of illicit publications. He printed it without any preliminary material except for an elaborate title page designed by Simon Van der Passe—the designer of surviving engravings of both Pembroke and his mother—which reproduces a scene early in the work. Analyzing the production rate of contemporary printing houses, McLaren has shown that it was likely printed hurriedly, and in only small numbers, before its author discovered the existence of the pirated edition. When Wroth

Title page from The Countesse of Mountgomeries Urania, *published 1621. Reproduced by permission of the Folger Shakespeare Library, Washington, D.C.*

found the work was to appear, McLaren suggests, she probably accepted it as a *fait accompli*; but when she found it was being interpreted, by Lord Denny at least, as referring satirically to embarrassing events at court in which members of his family had been implicated, she tried to withdraw it from circulation. The flurry of correspondence and poems between Wroth and Denny, discussed in chapter three, then followed, and the book may have been withdrawn. Just over twenty copies are known to survive today.[3]

Approaching a work as complicated as *Urania*, an overview may be helpful, even if it is bound to sound either short and banal or long and wordy. *Urania* concerns the adventures—amatory, dynastic and chivalric—of a number of closely woven, imaginary royal and noble families, who indulge in seemingly infinitely convoluted interactions that range across an imaginary Europe, mainly in Greece and nearby countries. It has a cast of thousands, almost innumerable plots and subsidiary stories, stock figures, shifting settings, sudden transitions, debates, allegorical scenes, and interspersed poetry. It is held together by three structural devices.

The first is a series of set pieces—each somewhat like the Garden of Adonis or the house of Busyrane in the *Faerie Queene*, or the climactic scenes in Jonson's and Jones's masques—which involve elaborately described enchantments and provide major revelations for the characters involved in them. The second is the recurring focus on the family relationships of Queen Pamphilia, especially her connections with her first cousin, the Emperor Amphilanthus, the romance's repeatedly praised perfect knight (and perpetually fickle lover). Their meetings, sunderings, conversations, and adventures are interspersed with a bewildering assortment of stories, mainly relating to other members of their families—Pamphilia's brothers Passelius, Rosindy, and Philarchos, and her sister Philistella; Amphilanthus's brother Leonius and his sister Urania, who is also Pamphilia's closest friend. While it is overly simple to see Pamphilia entirely as a projection of the author and Amphilanthus as a projection of Pembroke, there are too many parallels between Wroth's situation and Pamphilia's to ignore, and the major characteristics of Amphilanthus are certainly not unrelated to those of Pembroke. The titular heroine, Urania, who appears in the work's opening pages, quickly takes on a subsidiary role. She largely becomes a friend and confidante to Pamphilia and Amphilanthus. Can we detect in her a fictional projection of the countess of Montgomery? Evidence from the Sidney correspondence certainly suggests she and Wroth were very close, and it might have been possible that she was a confidante of Wroth and Pembroke. Within the romance, Urania certainly plays a sisterly role to both main characters, scolding Pamphilia for her unjustified and masochistic constancy, upbraiding Amphilanthus both for his fickleness and his doubts about Pamphilia's love. She advises, teases, and reprimands her brother and cousin, and, like many of the work's minor characters, undergoes a number of her own adventures: she discovers, like Pamphilia, many of the disillusions of love before she marries Steriamus, King of Albania.

The third unifying structural device is that the stories in *Urania* are at once all different and yet the same. They are like the narratives of the unconscious or compulsive daydreams; or like the limited number of obsessively repeated stories we all have, which originate in our earliest desires and relationships as a variety of tales of adventures, miraculous achievements and tragic losses, and which we project over and over into our adult experiences. In the case of *Urania*, the stories return, again and again, to the events of Wroth's upbringing, marriage, family relations, and her obsession with her cousin's love, his fickleness, and in particular his autonomy and power as a man.[4]

Generically, *Urania* is a mixture of dynastic and chivalric romance, *roman à clef*, and, as Ann Shaver suggests, something bordering intriguingly on what would later become the psychological novel.[5] Such a combination was extremely popular at the time. All across Europe, between about 1570 and 1670, a striking flowering of prose romance occurred; in England from about 1570 on, a great variety of short and long romantic prose fiction was written or translated, adapted, or imitated from Italian, Spanish, French, and earlier English sources. Verse romances, both English and Continental, were reworked into prose versions; and many of the writers of the Elizabethan younger generation, mainly of a different class from Wroth and her uncle—Gascoigne, Greene, Lodge, Nash, Deloney, Forde—produced a variety of native examples. Towering above them all was Wroth's uncle Philip's *Arcadia*, which was the most admired piece of prose fiction in English before Samuel Richardson's *Pamela* (1740). For almost two centuries it was imitated, completed, translated, summarized; it was used as a mine of plots and situations for writers of prose fiction; stories from it were excerpted and dramatized; it was regarded as a storehouse of lost moral wisdom. The most popular tale within the complex fabric of Sidney's work, the noble and tragic love between Argalus and Parthenia, was probably at least as familiar to English readers during the seventeenth century as the story of Romeo and Juliet, and it inspired poems, plays, and a variety of chapbook condensations or summaries over the next century.

Why was romance so pervasive, not only in verse and prose narratives, but in drama, and even in unlikely places like works of popular theology like Thomas Beard's *The Theatre of God's Judgements*? Frye has described the fundamental narrative structure of romance as a recurring quest for transcendence—either a search for a return to some lost, authentic mode of being or, in a more utopian mode, the articulation of some possible, unalienated future.[6] The classic romance pattern is an often extremely complicated quest, usually that of a young man in search of an ideal, frequently represented by a bride, a lost kingdom, or some personal or communal goal of purity or transformation. His "adventures"—a term that in *Urania* accumulates multiple and contradictory meanings—are characteristically varied and unpredictable, but they are united by both his goal of fulfilling the quest and the reader's drawing moral lessons from his struggles to achieve it. The settings are exotic and romantic: enchanted islands, unpredictable seas, fierce monsters, and distressed ladies; coincidences, revelations and miracles continually occur. The heroes and heroines are idealized; the villains and challenges exaggerated; terrible dangers threaten; barriers and temptations must continually be overcome; fortunate or magical rescues abound. The desired effect upon the readers is summed up in *Urania* by Follietto: "ledd by charmes, hawnted, and abus'd . . . made to think any thing, and all was noe thing, soe as you had seen the manne, you scarce cowld have beeleev'd a longe time after that any thing was true you sawe" (*Newberry 1*, fol. 4).

Frye also writes of the "pervasive social snobbery" that pervades romance.[7] Even in modern variants of the genre, the adventures of romance are articulated in terms of an ideology of class hierarchy: its heroes and heroines are invariably projections of a society's highest residual status, whether in terms of class, as in Wroth's time, or money and leisure, as in the popular romances of our own. Even in romances in which the heroes and heroines are unapologetically from the lower orders, the values they aspire to are those of their society's elite, whether conceived of in terms of class, riches, status, or (in the case of current pulp romances) access to material goods, high fashion, and exotic vacation spots. Romances idealize not only a society's dominant objects of fantasy, but (despite their idealistic tone) they are related closely to the material realities of the time. Indeed, romances are like the imaginary worlds of children: naive, but not innocent, structured by a repertoire of blatant class allegiances, gender stereotypes, and racial prejudices, which have been absorbed from the family and then projected repetitively into story after story. It is "impossible," we are told, "for Knights and Ladies to travell without adventures" (*Urania*, p. 342). As in the narratives of the family romances Freud originally depicted, the imaginary families of *Urania* are more noble, more powerful than Wroth's own.

In addition to the analogies we can draw with the huge number of similar works at the time, as Mendelson interestingly comments, to find analogues with a work like *Urania* in its own time we need look no further than the daydreams and family romances of the adolescent subculture of the upper classes during the period. The characters parade forth typically idealized figures and actions that must have exemplified the daydreams and fantasies at the time, especially, in a society that systematically infantalized its women, those coded as female. The heroes and heroines have "great beauty, high birth, rich possessions, absolute command, and what is most, matchelesse love, and loyaltie." Their actions are all enveloped in glowing idealism: "One day as the King and Queene were walking in the Garden, attended on by all the Princes, Ladies, and Knights of the Court . . ." is a typical opening sentence for the work's many episodes (*Urania*, pp. 163, 56). But however like daydreams they may be, many of the stories of *Urania* are also uncannily close to some of the real events of the 1620s. Just as Elizabeth had encouraged her courtiers to think of their relations with her in terms of Petrarchan idealization, so the politics of the last years of James's reign and that of Charles were frequently cast in terms of chivalric romance. When Charles and Buckingham made their secret but abortive voyage to Spain to arrange a marriage for the prince, James addressed them as "sweete boyes, and dear knights, worthie to be putte in a new romance." The blurring of "romance" and "reality" in such examples suggests that while romance tries to draw its readers into what Sidney termed a "golden world," that world is never as innocent as it pretends.[8] Even in *Arcadia*, in so many ways the age's most significant prose work, there are signs of the incipient breakdown, even at its apparent height, of the cultural hegemony it celebrated. It is arguable that *Arcadia*, like the *Faerie Queene*, is an unfinishable work, its elaborate display and complexity an epitome of its author's uneasiness before the questions his work was starting to raise but which could never be settled within an increasingly archaic literary form. *Urania* likewise occupies a pivotal position in this complex, untidy development. It has an additional element not present in *Arcadia* and rare in any other romance in English until the middle of the eighteenth century, the emergence of gender as a major issue.

In fact, despite its chivalric caste, *Urania* has an insistent domestic atmosphere. It is the work of a woman writer, who, in turn was the product of complicated family values and demands, produced within an ideology of obligation and assignment against which she struggled. All the accretive senses in which I have used the term "family romance" in connection with the Sidneys culminate in *Urania*. It was written, as *Arcadia* was, within and initially for a family circle: it was dedicated to Pembroke's sister-in-law, the countess of Montgomery; it was probably written in part at the earl of Pembroke's London house, and probably circulated among immediate members of the family and courtly friends. Throughout the work the family, as a crucible of both repression and of dreams of transcending gender limitations, is a recurring topic. It is full of family and coterie jokes and references, many of which are no doubt lost on us, some of which are still explicable. Most blatantly, in the words by which we are told the story of Lindamira, it is "some thing more exactly related then a fixion" (*Urania*, p. 429), the seemingly compulsively repeated story of its author's involvement with her cousin. It projects her wishes and fantasies about their relationship and makes continual references to their connections within the multiple networks of the Sidney-Herbert family. Then, specifically considering Freud's definition of family romances, *Urania* projects a fantasy world created by a woman who clearly chafed against the limitations of her role as daughter, wife, mistress, and mother. It is full of dreams of autonomy and independence, dreams of glory and power that far transcend what material life could provide, except fitfully. It is also haunted by wistful, and sometimes angry, dreams of mutuality between men and women. *Urania* is a work that is produced by, romanticizes, struggles against, and spasmodically overcomes (in ways in which the author herself was probably in part aware) the powerful ideologies of family and gender that had determined how she conceived of herself as a woman. It is a major cultural document for laying bare the mechanisms by which the men and (more particularly) the women of the early modern period were assigned their gender roles. As Rosemary Jackson notes, fantasy does not transcend our world: "it has to do with inverting features of this world, re-combining" familiar material that may have to be concealed or repressed if the world which refuses to otherwise allow for the expression of the fantasy is to be negotiated successfully.[9]

At the most basic level, we can find family romance motifs throughout the work. It opens with an ironic reversal of one of Freud's classic symptoms—with Urania wishing that she might be ignorant of the fact that she is a princess and not, as she had hitherto assumed, a simple shepherdess:

> Alas *Urania*, said she, (the true servant to misfortune); of any misrie that can befall woman, is not this the most and greatest which thou art fallen into? Can there be any neare the unhappinesse of being ignorant, and that in the highest kind, not being certaine of mine owne estate or birth? Why was I not stil continued in the beliefe I was, as I appeare, a Shepherdes, and Daughter to a Shepherd? My ambition then went no higher then this estate, now flies it to a knowledge; then was I contented, now perplexed.

> (*Urania*, p. 3)

Later in the work, Amphilanthus himself exclaims: "Why didst thou not make me a Forrester, or a Shepheard, or any thing, so I might enjoy my love?" (*Urania*, p. 299). These are cries like those of the neurotics described in Freud's essay, who project their frustrated desires back upon the family in which the desires were generated. Many of *Urania*'s stories are, in fact, rather thinly disguised rewritings of episodes in Wroth's life, some of which are fairly easy to identify. The most obvious is the story Pamphilia tells of Lindamira—presumably, an anagram of Ladi Mari. She is the eldest daughter of "a brave young Lord . . . second sonne to a famous Nobleman" who had married romantically. Lindamira herself was "a Lady of great spirit, excellent qualities, and beautifull enough to make many in love with her"; but she loved another. When the queen, who had hitherto favored Lindamira, suspected the affair, "all her favour was withdrawn as suddenly and directly, as if never had: *Lindamira* remaining like one in a gay Masque, the night pass'd, they are in their old clothes againe, and no appearance of what was" (*Urania*, pp. 423–24)—perhaps a revealing comment upon Wroth's disappearance from court life and a possible indication of royal displeasure at the cousins' affair. Other family references abound. Quilligan points to "the strange plethora of brothers" and how the women "suffer not only their wayward lovers but their brothers' wayward actions." In a family like that of the Sidneys, the oldest son would have provided the closest example of the privileges and independence that she, as a mere daughter, would have been denied. Further, as I noted in chapter two, the discrimination involved in her being a daughter was compounded by her being the oldest child, with her younger brother William having the privileges of the family heir. From the start, her gender meant that she was accorded fewer privileges and promised less independence. Parents, one character in *Urania* notes, may have "a cruel & tirannical power over their children," and, as Carolyn Swift has pointed out, marital misery enforced upon daughters by ambitious fathers is a recurring motif in the work.[10] Even though virtuous daughters are trained to "esteem obedience beyond all passions," they may need to be forced to obey their fathers if the order of kin and dynasty are to be served. And, once married, and assumed into another family, how do married women cope? Many tolerate their husbands by "hunting and other delights abroad, to take away trouble . . . at home" (*Urania*, pp. 35, 5, 434).

Also easily recognizable is the story of Amphilanthus rescuing Bellamira from the perils of widowhood by returning her to her father, who had originally forced her to marry Treborius, whose name suggests "forest dweller"; he is one, we are told, who frequently entertains the king, who "going to see his Countrey in Progresse, my husbands house was found fit in his way, so as he lay there, and was by him freely, and bravely entertained, he being as bountifull in his house, as any man." If that reference reminds us of Jonson's praise of Mary Wroth's husband in "To Sir Robert Wroth," we should not forget Jonson's snigger at Wroth's preference for the company of the local squires and huntsmen when we read that Bellamira confesses that she would "dissemble" whenever her husband "praised rude sports, or told the plaine Jests of his Hunts-men." Before her marriage, Bellamira had been taken to court by her father, and it was there that "before I knew what love was, I was his prisoner." There she had fallen in love with a man other than her husband, who loved a princess, though "no more then" men "generally do." "Never," we are told, was a man "lord of so many womens soules, as this my lorde had rule of, who without flatterie, did deserve it, never being unthankfull for their loves," a trait which, like Pamphilia and the author of *Urania* herself, Bellamira excuses (*Urania*, pp. 424, 334, 326–27). Then she tells how, soon after, her husband dies and, not long after, her only son. The final pages of the continuation give another, barely disguised (though rather contradictory) account of the events of Wroth's marriage, where we are told of the death of Pamphilia's son and husband and her return home to her father, accompanied, on somewhat ambiguous terms, by Amphilanthus.

Other recognizably autobiographical stories in the work include the obvious wish fulfillment fantasy of the acceptance of the cousins' liaison by Pembroke's mother, who, in the figure of the Queen of Naples, a poetess and patron of poets, approves of the cousins' love: "the Queen blessed them both, as truly hers, and as hers they lived a while with her in truest delights, and comfort, wher they can bee better left, wher more cherished, then wher the hart, of the bravest of her sex, makes her self a subject to please them" (*Newberry 2*, fol. 1). There is also mention of a prophecy—presumably Wroth knew the story of the prophecy about Pembroke—"by an old man . . . whose skill was very great in the Art of Divination" that a certain man "should never live to fiftie yeares of age" (*Urania*, p. 155). Amphilanthus is also described as a poet. Quilligan points out, however, that while Wroth further underlines the identification of Pembroke and Amphilanthus by ascribing a poem of Pembroke's to the emperor, she does so only in the unpublished second part of the work. So, she comments, though Amphilanthus is said to be "famous for his poetry," throughout the entire text, no poem of his actually appears, "almost as if Wroth could neither risk identifying him in public nor deny the identification by supplying him with a poem of her own."[11] In the continuation, two of the more important new characters are illegitimate children—Andromarko, the son of Polarchos, and Faire Design, whose father is not named, but who is designated to be the heir of Amphilanthus. It would have been difficult for Wroth to have written in these characters without thinking of her and Pembroke's children.

Such references point to the way in which Wroth, as well as writing out the same story over and over, is also fragmenting aspects of her life into her characters and events. She projects her own frustrations and dreams into the figure of Pamphilia, who, we are told, "had so great a spiritt, as might be called Masculine" (*Newberry 1*, fol. 57). Lamb suggests that the story of the queen is Wroth's "revenge upon the society that had cast its author out of its circle for transgressions that seem almost mundane among the array of possible topical accounts of adultery, incest, and murder in her work." *Urania* is thus the enactment of a fantasy of resentment and desire for something more fulfilling than her society has assigned her as a woman.

Significantly, the one aspect of family life that emerges positively is mothering. Much of the action of the second part is taken up with the search for lost children, the sons and daughters of many of the kings and queens in the first part. There are, in fact, two long episodes dealing with the lost children in part two, though as McLaren suggests, had she ever revised the second part of the work, Wroth might well have conflated them.[12] According to one version, two children are held on the island of Cressante. They are the son and nephew of the duke of Athens, who had been sent to live with their grandmother and great-aunt, the dowager queen of Naples, when they were captured by giants, offspring of a family that, in the first part, had tried to kidnap Pamphilia. The children are imprisoned in a castle with many "devilish inventions" to prevent their escape, including a door in a pillar that set one way is impermeable to "hunderds of armed men," but set another "itt looseneth itt, soe as if a childe com on itt, it falls open the unhapy falls in, the trap flyes up, and locks againe as fast as ever" (*Newberry 2*, fol. 35). Mirrosindo, Rosindy's third son, tells Pamphilia that all the abductions of the royal children, and others who are vaguely alluded to, are part of a grand, seemingly cosmic enchantment which the work never develops. As McLaren notes, Wroth's "inability to retain control of her material is unfortunate because she obviously intended to convey something very important" in these complicated episodes.[13] The children are finally released with the help of Amphilanthus. By the time the story is picked up again, we are told that they are imprisoned on a different island, near Tengo, and are guarded by a "Monstrouse Giant" along with "a hundred Giants more and Giantesses" (*Newberry 1*, fol. 34). Amphilanthus arrives, sees "a valt, and a most lamentable cry of Children," and ten children are rescued—even though they are seemingly a different group from the ones imprisoned on Cressante.

At one point Pamphilia expresses her desire to have children, and she and her husband, Rodomandro, King of Tartaria, like Wroth and her husband, do have one son. But Pamphilia's wish is to have children with her cousin Amphilanthus, even though we are told when he rescues the lost children that he is extremely formal rather than friendly: he "saluted them, and blessed them, but had small discourse for them, seldome having had conversation with Children" (*Newberry 1*, fol. 34). Why is this seemingly gratuitous detail added? Why, indeed, do many of the details of Amphilanthus and Pamphilia's relationship seem inconsistent? It is as if Wroth wants to insert details that make sense autobiographically, but without regard for their fictional relevance or consistency. Pamphilia and Amphilanthus, we are repeatedly reminded, are first cousins: she is the daughter of the king of Morea, whose brother the king of Naples is the father of Amphilanthus. "Cousinage" in a number of senses is scattered throughout the work. Amphilanthus is her "bravest Cosin"; the "false delight" that Pamphilia's rival Artissia feels when she sees Amphilanthus holding Pamphilia's hand is a "cosening thing"; and Artessia, justly suspicious of Pamphilia, reminds her that Amphilanthus is not only "matchles" but her "Cousin." When Artissia accuses her of loving him "more, then respectively," Pamphilia acknowledges that they had "long conversation as from our youthes" as the basis of their affections; but, she adds, "besides, our bloud claiming an extraordinary respect." Later in the work she again protests, this time while confessing her love to his sister Urania, that she "loved him for himselfe, and would have loved him had hee not loved mee, and will love though he despise me" (*Urania*, pp. 266, 52, 78, 400). In the phrase "will love" do we hear echoes of the concluding sonnet to the main sequence of *Pamphilia to Amphilanthus*? Such references add up to an an amusing and yet— except as autobiographical revelation—somewhat gratuitous emphasis on the family relationship between the two lovers.

The cousins' love, we are repeatedly but inexplicably told, must be kept secret. Secrecy in love was a courtly romance convention, but usually because the lovers involved were already married to other people, or because there was some irremediable barrier between them. But there are no such barriers here. We are simply told repeatedly that Pamphilia vowed "not to carry the tokens of her losse openly on her browes, but rather weare them privately in her heart." So, "in all her extremest sufferings," she keeps her love secret. She goes to a favorite spot in the forest:

> Sweete wood said she beare record with me, never knew I but this love. Love, answered the wood being graced with an Echo. Soft said she, shall I turne blabb? no Echo, excuse me, my love and choyce more precious, and more deere, then thy proud youth must not be named by any but my selfe, none being able to name him else, (as none so just, nor yet hath any eare except his owne) heard me confesse who governs me. . . .

As none but we doe truly love, so none but our owne hearts shall know we love.

(Urania, pp. 76, 264)

Decorously borrowing the predominant male perversion of fetishism, Pamphilia kisses the picture she wears of her cousin in secret; in public, she asks casually, almost indifferently, about him: "as one might judge, shee asked for the rest for his sake, because she would name him, or named him last, as more to sticke in memory." But there is no doubt about her love for him: over and over we are told of her single-minded devotion to her cousin. Late in the first part we are given a premonition of a happy ending, when "all the lovers should be made happy with their long desired loves in marriage," but (needless to say, without motivation) "only *Pamphilia* was unpromised, for she was her own, but as she had unfortunatley given her selfe" to her love for her cousin. Like Pamphilia, and with even less motivation, since he is by nature a philanderer, Amphilanthus tells nobody his love for his cousin, "holding that too deare, even for his friend to heare" (*Urania*, pp. 315, 341–42, 263, 302).

The plot proceeds on this level of gratuitous masochism. Pamphilia's "fortune is," we are told, "to lose all" (*Newberry 2*, fol. 22). Late in the work she marries Rodomandro, King of Tartaria—almost invariably referred to dismissively as "the Tartarian"—when she learns that Amphilanthus has married the Princess of Slavonia, although we learn later that he has been tricked into the marriage by being persuaded by his tutor (possibly a projection of Hugh Sanford, who was active in Pembroke's marriage negotiations) that Pamphilia had already married. But the lovers remain an ambiguously devoted couple. Near the end the two are brought together when Amphilanthus discovers the deceptions to which they have both been subject and when Pamphilia's son and husband are—we are told perfunctorily, as if the author is killing them off for motives of her own—dead. Then, of course, it is (the melodramatic capitals unquestionably justified) Too Late. But when Pamphilia's father, we are told, "arrived in Tartaria hee found a great change, the king dead, his dearest Pamphilia a widow, yett the mother of a brave boy, who soone after his arrival to that Court also died, wch moved the Queene to leave that Country, and go unto Pamphilia, and ther with her father live as contentedly as sad people could doe" (*Newberry 2*, fol. 58). Escorted by her cousin, she returns to the protection of her father.

Amusingly, it is as if Wroth wants her heroine to both have a secret love and have it known as well—a not uncommon contradiction in intense adulterous or forbidden liaisons in many societies. In the first

258

book, Amphilanthus goes with Urania and Pamphilia to the woods and there, "the only man for truth of perfection that the world held," laying his head in his sister's lap and holding Pamphilia's hand, and he begins "to discourse, which they so well liked, as they past a great part of the day there together." When Pamphilia believes (as she often does, with justification) that Amphilanthus has been unfaithful to her, she gives way to "nightly complaints, to teares, sobbes and groanes." She tells Meriana a poem she has written on her "unquiet grief," she bewails the lack of news from Amphilanthus while Meriana (who seems at this point to both know and not know the identity of Pamphilia's beloved) tells her "stories she had knowne of" Amphilanthus. She is comforted by father, mother, friends, sisters, and in particular by Urania (who also seems to both know and not know the name of Pamphilia's secret lover). Urania gives her advice to be firm and resolute, even if, she pointedly says, she knew it "were mine owne brother had caused this mischiefe" (*Urania*, pp. 161, 392, 399). In short, there seems to be no reason (in the work) for the secrecy. It leads Pamphilia into some amusingly complex moral dilemmas to keep her love "secret." Her rival for Amphilanthus's love is Antissia, one of the most interesting of the minor characters, who is jealous, headstrong, passionate, and a poet like Pamphilia herself. She eventually marries Dolorindus, King of Negroponte after trying, out of revenge, to have him kill Amphilanthus. Antissia is, not without reason, suspicious and jealous of Pamphilia's affection for Amphilanthus, and Pamphilia—without any authorial disapproval—decides to lie about the relationship. She denies that her poetry has reference to him or that she loves him "more, then respectively," despite Antissia's noticing "his often frequenting *Pamphilia*'s Chamber," his "private discourse with her," his "seeking opportunitie to be in her presence," his "stolne lookes," his "fearefull but amarous touching her hand," or his "kissing his owne hand, rather comming from hers, then going to hers." Antissia's jealousy is patently justified, something that Pamphilia denies:

> Alas . . . can so base an humour as suspition creepe into so brave a heart as *Antissia's*? and to gaine such power there, as to make her mistrust her friend? Truly I am sorry for it; and would advise you for honours sake, quickly to banish that Devill from you, which otherwise will daily increase new mischiefes.

The next day the two cousins compound the deception by offering their mutual affection to Antissia:

> the King holding the Queene by the hand, met her at the gate. *Antissia* was so much joy'd, as she was but that cosening thing it selfe, ravished with false delight; she triumphed in the blaze, while the true fire burnt more solidly, and in another place. She was conducted to the Palace,

Pamphilia with her left arme embracing her, holding *Amphilanthus* with the right hand.

(*Urania*, pp. 78, 93, 266)

The encounters between the two cousins are often described in amusingly ambivalent ways. Early in the work, the prophetess Mellisea tells Amphilanthus that in love he will "bee most happy, for all shall love you that you wish," stressing not only his attractiveness, but his power to "command" love. "Yet," Melissea goes on, "you must bee crost in this you now affect," his love for Pamphilia, even "though contrarie to her heart." Amphilanthus vows that his apparent invulnerability in love is no compensation for losing Pamphilia: "take all loves from me," he exclaims, "so I may have hers." But Melissea's reply is that although "she loves you"—so setting up a situation in which both lovers apparently have the same goal—she adds that "it will proove your fault if you lose her . . . which I thinke, you will and must," thus exonerating Pamphilia (*Urania*, p.115).

The logic of these stories is the logic of dream or fantasy, justifiable only in terms of an unacknowledged (or unacknowledgeable) reality that lies outside the narrative. They are stories that are at once private and intimate and at the same time banal and collective. We would all, however ashamedly, recognize our fantasies and daydreams as the products, at least in part, of the commonplace stories and motifs of our own culture—rags to riches, love at first sight, overnight stardom, sexual irresistibility, heroic achievement. However such narratives grow from and return us to our own unconscious desires and insecurities— our desires for and fears of differentiation, our accumulated pleas for security, acceptance, or oneness throughout our lives—they are never only "ours": they are rooted in the complex demands of race, class, and gender that have already interpreted and given language to our earliest struggles—perhaps even our earliest flutterings in the womb, already placed within language by patterns of culturally produced discourses that will name and layer our unconscious. We struggle to discover and name what is ours from our beginnings; we discover it is never fully ours alone. We tell our fantasies in the narrative modes of our child- hood because they once gave us satisfaction. The "adventures" into which all the knights and ladies who people *Urania* find themselves thrown are projections into the chivalric-romantic terms of the time, of both individual and collective daydreams. Like a modern adolescent imagining him- or herself as a movie star even while glimpsing Holly- wood's corruption and superficiality, Pamphilia's adventures, and those of the interconnected families of the book, are narratives of passions, challenges, and achievements on a grandiose scale, while she herself is presented as a victim, unhappy, unrewarded, "molested," "all in the hell of deceit," and frequently blaming herself for wrongs done to her. When Urania advises her that she should reject any man who abuses her— "though," she says pointedly, "I knew it were mine owne brother"— Pamphilia dwells on her own unworthiness: "kil me at once for all; torture me not with sorrowes, I will truly and religiously confesse, I am not worthy of you," she exclaims to Amphilanthus. When she hears news of his coronation, she tells him in her mind that "this was once . . . belonging to me, but I was not worthy . . . sure else he had not alter'd." "I am yours," she confesses, "and may you not dispose of yours, as best doth like your selfe?" (*Urania*, pp. 494, 399, 395, 396). She consistently exemplifies Kaplan's description of the master/slave relationship in women's masochism, in which there are "only two possible positions, one of rapacious domination and the other of docile submission."[14] Only rarely, as I will show, do alternative fantasies, those of autonomy and (even more rarely) of equality and mutual constancy, emerge as viable.

I turn now to a detailed discussion of the work's main characters— or, more precisely, to the fantsy narratives they enact. The romance, as Nancy Miller has argued, has traditionally been built on two contradictory stories. One is that of the aggressive, questing male hero: its logic is to fulfill triumphantly the hero's assigned quest and thereby produce a happy ending; it is thus a reflection of the masculine fantasy of autonomy and conquest.[15] The other story is the heroine's. In most romances, it appears only piecemeal, because it is the woman who is meant to be the embodiment of, or the means to, the hero's goal, and therefore the more prominent her story becomes, the more subversive it is. It is part of the fundamental importance of *Urania* that this second, traditionally repressed or marginalized story emerges as the dominant strand of the work.

The first of these narratives centers on the figure of Amphilanthus, Emperor of the Romans. He is clearly a fantasy figure into which Wroth projects her idealization of, and at times her disillusions with, her relationship with the values embodied by her cousin. Amphilanthus looks like a typical male fantasy figure, the kind of heroes boys of the time would have dreamed of when they struggled against their real fathers. Frye argues that the male figures of romance, men of action and autonomy, represent the unfettered projection of the libido or desiring self for fulfillment unhampered by reality.[16] Amphilanthus is an obvious reworking of this traditional type. "Master of the greatest part of the Western World, and . . . Monarch of [Pamphilia's] heart," he is continually praised as "the most renowned on earth." When another hero is introduced, the narrator immediately reminds us of Amphilanthus's superiority: we are informed, for instance, that there is "not a braver man, a worthyer man, nor a fairer man att Arms" alongside Olymandor, "except Amphilanthus" (*Newberry 1*, fols. 9, 21). He dominates the traditional male domains of martial and sexual conquest. Yet because he is a character in a romance written by a woman, we need to focus particularly carefully on the relationship between author and character.

We discover, for instance, that characteristic male freedoms—military prowess, perpetual movement from one battle or quest to another, from one woman to the next—involve an autonomy that a woman envies but seemingly cannot herself achieve without risk, guilt, or self-punishment. Most especially, while Amphilanthus is brave, daring, and unconquerable, he is also, we are repeatedly told, continually unfaithful: "unconstancy was, and is the onely touch" (*Urania*, p. 312) by which, as it were essentially, we are to know him. He embodies, therefore, another male fantasy, that of being at once promiscuous and at the same time dedicated to one woman, who of course represents the stable mother figure to whom he can always return. He is presented as the more likable (at least we are meant to take it this way) precisely because he is imperfect, at once "the greatest, and yett as in lovers vassalage the lowest of creatures." He is "the whole worlds glory" (*Newberry 2*, fols. 26, 31), at the same time as he is "the falsest, ficklest, waveringst, and unworthiest," claiming, moreover—a characteristic of helpless victimization which is meant to link him to Pamphilia—that "I cannot rule my selfe" (*Urania*, p. 325). Accused that he is held to prefer "a ladys chamber above any other place," he responds openly, "and so I doe still" (*Newberry 1*, fol. 10). He vows eternal love to Pamphilia but eventually marries another, even while he is still not only fatefully attracted to his cousin—protesting: "Madame . . . if all vailes were taken away, and truth only knowne then should my blest blessings shine"—but is in fact contracted to her! Ever the sincere philanderer, "immoderately . . . given up to women," he is (also like Pembroke) a poet, writing to or about his avowedly one true love, Pamphilia, but happy to let former mistresses take copies of his poems. In short, Amphilanthus is an intriguing variation not just on a common romance pattern—in Freud's terms, the unfettered male id—but, more accurately, a combination of the dominant male fantasies of Western patriarchy, at once bound to and exploitative of women, defining his sense of self not only by the violent overcoming of his rivals, but by his conquest and control of women.

These are all fantasies that are overwhelmingly male within our cultural history. Why, we need to ask, is such an ideal being articulated, so seemingly uncritically, by a woman? The second of the work's two major narratives tells, over and over, something of an answer to that question. While Pamphilia may be, in large part, a fantasy projection of the author herself, she embodies far broader cultural fantasies than just her author's. She is enacting the subordination of women's desires to those of men in the early modern period and, to a large extent, well beyond. On the biographical level, *Urania* is Wroth's enactment of a day dream—"her owne solitary waulke, wher she tooke full libertie"— in which, despite having to use the romantic chivalric terms given by her class and gender assignments, she tries to imagine what her life as the "truest wife" of her cousin might be "really" like (*Newberry 2*, fols. 23, 26). But what defines the limits and possibilities of that "really"? The terms in which Wroth depicts her heroine, and her reactions to her cousin, also reveal, and probably in ways of which she was at least partly aware , the restraints under which she and other women at the time and well beyond were assigned their gender roles.

Pamphilia's name suggests a combination of Sidney's two heroines, Pamela and Philoclea, and her role in *Urania* is, in part, that of the quintessential romance heroine, embodying the contradictory characteristics that patriarchal men require their women to have. At once chaste and alluring, sorrowing and provocatively "apparreld in a Gowne of light Tawny or Murrey, embrodered with the richest, and perfectest Pearle for roundnesse and Whitenes, the work contrived into knots and garlands," she embodies allurement and unapproachability: "her necke was modestly bare, yet made all discerne, it was not to be beheld with eyes of freedome" (*Urania*, p. 141). She is also, as a queen, a woman of enormous power, a fantasy figure for women of an independence and power that would rival men's. Yet while Wroth stresses Pamphilia's majesty and status, she also emphasizes the extreme constraints and frustrations under which Pamphilia lives. Where other women seem to have more freedom of choice in their loves, or at least are occasionally lucky enough to have their lovers become their husbands, Pamphilia seems designed to live out an extreme masochistic situation in which her independence is continually called into question by her helplessness, even by a measure of guilt. Kaplan describes recent clinical studies of modern working (or even simply assertive) women who feel they deserve to be punished for aspiring to take on the autonomy or power of men; such a woman may fear that she will be "castrated and abandoned unless she paid for this terrible crime by becoming the suffering mistress of a womanizer who made her into something compliant." Kaplan comments, in a remark that finds uncanny precursors in both Pamphilia's and Wroth's situations, on how paradoxical it should be that a desire for submission and punishment is generated by what starts as a desire for recognition and mutuality. As Benjamin observes, such "masochism can be seen . . . not only as a strategy for escaping aloneness, but also as a search for aloneness *with* the other: by letting the other remain in control, the masochist hopes to find a 'safe' open space in which to abandon the protective false self and allow the nascent, hidden self to emerge."[17] Pamphilia's royalty is clearly a part of fantasy to be more powerful, like a man; but her masochism is a projection of a recognition that, at least for most women, the goal is unrealizable. Throughout, she feels "tyrannically tortured by love" (*Urania*, p. 51), and the only relationships in which she finds herself are conceived of in terms of domination and rejection, or (as in the case of her marriage) duty.

The torments and twists of Pamphilia's love for Amphilanthus are exhibited in a number of ritual set pieces throughout the work. The most important is the enchantment of the Crown of Stones near the end of the fourth book of the first part. Amphilanthus and Pamphilia have been hunting, and Amphilanthus goes missing. Pamphilia finds only a bone, some blood, and his abandoned armor, shield, and sword. Nearby, beneath a "Crowne of mighty stones," is a slain boar and a dead man. After hanging her cousin's armor on the rock, Pamphilia opens a stone door which appears magically in smoke, and she sees a vision of her rivals Musalina and Lucenia with Amphilanthus:

> . . . *Musalina* sitting in a Chaire of Gold, a Crowne on her head, and *Lucenia* holding a sword, which *Musalina* tooke in her hand, and before them *Amphilanthus* was standing, with his heart ript open, and *Pamphilia* written on it, *Musalina* ready with the point of the sword to conclude all, by razing that name out, and so his heart as the wound to perish.

Pamphilia attempts to rescue her cousin but, like Spenser's Scudamore outside the House of Busyrane, she is repulsed, and, waking from a faint, she finds all vanished except an engraved stone:

> Faithfull lovers keepe from hence
>   None but false ones here can enter:
> This conclusion hath from whence
>   Falshood flowes, and such may venter.

Some time later we read an account of the second part of the episode from another viewpoint, when we learn that Amphilanthus has encountered the same enchantment. According to his version, at the Crown of Stones he kills the boar, battles an army, and kills its leader, whose death cry sounds to him like Pamphilia—"and presently in stead of that young man, hee saw to his thinking *Pamphilia* slain, and by his hand." Then, like her, he enters the stone. He sees a vision of his cousin, "dead, lying within an arch, her breast open and in it his name"; like her, too, he is repulsed when he tries to rescue her, and finds "these words only written in the place of the entrance": "This no wonder's of much waight, / 'Tis the hell of deepe deceit." But unlike the constant Pamphilia, he is "called to for helpe by Musalina, her hee saw, she must be followed, Pamphilia is forgotten, and now may lie and burne in the cave, Lucenia must be rescued also." His compulsive infidelity, his being "immoderately given up to women" is what marks the difference between them, and yet (we are immediately told) it was not his fault, "Musalina having by divelish Art beene the cause of all this" (*Urania*, pp. 494–95, 554).

In the second part similar contradictions occur. The cousins spend "a while . . . in truest delight, and comfort," Amphilanthus escorting Pamphilia to her chamber "according to his custome"—we should recall his preferring "a ladys chamber above any other place" (*Newberry 1*, fols. 1, 13, 10)—and each vows to be faithful. When Rodomandro, King of Tartaria, comes to woo Pamphilia, Amphilanthus is intensely jealous, "wherfor faining some occasions of business hee rose and retired." Seeing him disturbed though (apparently) oblivious to the cause, Pamphilia retires to her chamber, wondering how best "to pasiphy Amphilanthus' burning thoughts," and "on her bed she found him layd, or rather throwne carelessly." Going to him, she asks: "what is the cause that you thus sigh, alas what can procure sadnes in you"? His response is: "fast clasping her in his armes, performing then ever hee had before or shee had permitted, boldly seising her and telling her that though he was aprised of her love yett his was so infinite." She points out that while it seems that he may look at any woman, she is apparently forbidden even to be pleasant to another man. They then proceed to the culminating (and most contradictory) episode in the whole romance, a public vow of intent of their love. Witnessed by Urania, Selarina, Antissus, Allanius, and others, they pledge eternal union to each other. Wroth's authorial comment is that "such a contract can nott bee broken by any lawe whatsoever" which, Roberts points out, makes it a *de praesenti* agreement and therefore, acording to seventeenth-century law, legally binding. We are told, rather ambiguously, that the ceremony "was performed butt nott as an absolute mariage though as perfect as that."[18] Is it some kind of spiritual marriage? Or simply Wroth's wishfulfillment fantasy about the more "perfect" relationship she had with Pembroke? Later in the story the two cousins marry other people. At her wedding "sad Pamphilia" is dressed in black, wears her hair down rather than up, as a bride would, and, we are told (as if the narrator is afraid we will not notice!), "her heart was long beefor married to a more beloved creature" (*Newberry 2*, fols. 14, 22, 23).

Such contradictions, inconsistencies, and overemphases can be explained by the conventions of romance characterization, or simply as

sloppy writing, but there is a fundamental consistency in the contradictions that can be resolved only at the level of authorial wish fulfillment fantasy: however unfaithful Amphilanthus may be, he is still,
we are repeatedly told, infinitely worthy of Pamphilia's love. Over and
over we are assured that "the iniury hee did" her is done "ignorantly"
(*Newberry 1*, fol. 8). Even when he is in attendance at her wedding,
he is described by the narrator as being "fitter to have bin the right
bride groome," and her kingdom, her "earthe and grounds," as "far
fitter for" Amphilanthus's "government" (*Newberry 2*, fols. 12, 24).
This view of Amphilanthus is shared by the narrator and Pamphilia
herself, who at one point states that his faults are due to the "noble free
fashion hee had, which gave ignorant or bold people to speake of him"
(*Urania*, p. 372). Where other knights are accused of boastfulness or
unnecessary self-display, Amphilanthus "was never Ambitious of such
curtisies" (*Newberry 1*, fol. 17).

The "adventures" of the characters in *Urania* are, predictably, stories of chivalry and courtship, the raw material of the games and fantasies of Wroth's class and gender. We are given a seemingly never-ending
procession of tales of beautiful young people playing at war and love,
repetitive fantasies of glory, prowess, sacrifice, and destruction of evil for
the cause of good. As I noted in chapter two, the Jacobean aristocracy
still took at least the trappings of chivalry with great solemnity: it
provided commonplace metaphors much as professional sports do for
most twentieth-century Americans. *Urania* is crammed with discussions
of tournaments, colors worn and changed, thundering horses, mutilated
bodies, broken lances, hacked armor, and the heroic ideals and exploits
of the cousin's friends and families. If the male characters are not march-
ing off to war—frequently in disguise so their heroic violence will be
performed with appropriate *sprezzatura*, nobly but modestly—they are
staging mock battles in their tilts and tourneys to defend their ladies'
beauty or virtue or their own honor.

Frye noted that the battles and tourneys that permeate romance
are ritualized actions "expressing the ascendancy of a horse-riding aristocracy," and that they "express that aristocracy's dreams of its own
social function, and the idealized acts of protection and responsibility
that it invokes to justify that function."[19] They are not only fantasies
of class, however; they are also fantasies of gender. The stereotypes
of romance have traditionally been male: in Renaissance romance the
quests, adventures, battles, and heroic loves displayed the prototypical
wishfulfillments of the "soldier-males" of the feudal and post-feudal aristocracy. The passionate celebration of ritual violence is seen in tourneys,
jousts, and wars—rituals of maturity, spiritual as well as physical rites of
passage. As Shakespeare's *Troilus and Cressida* dramatizes so effectively,

the early seventeenth century may have seen the growing dominance of newer technologies of war and different strategies of mass destruction from those of chivalry, but the traditional view of the aristocratic male warrior as an innocent, idealistic (and humanistically educated) youth lived on as a powerful individual and collective fantasy. It is therefore important to note that *Urania*, a romance written by a woman, should be dominated by such stereotypes. Parry notes, without perhaps being quite aware of the term he chooses, what he calls the "masculine vigour" of *Urania*, observing that "the author takes particular pleasure in the rituals of chivalric encounter, in set combats, and in its tournaments with their display of devices and *imprese*." Wroth's acceptance, at least on the surface, of the chivalric code clearly represents the seemingly immutable, "natural" force of a masculinist ethos by which the men of her class were brought up and into which the women, too, were interpellated. "Noe my lord," says the queen to her cousin, "you are borne to rule, and god forbid I should assume any such power over you" (*Newberry 2*, fol. 21). Recall that is for his apparent inadequacy in "guiltie armes" and "warre" that Wroth's husband was gently laughed at in Jonson's "To Sir Robert Wroth"; and, further, that it was her cousin who, like every aspiring courtier, tried to shine, under her anxious father's eye, in, as Robert Barret had put it, "warre and armes."[20]

Yet chivalric romance did not merely provide material for the fantasies of its members; as in the case of Philip Sidney, chivalric ideals frequently brought real, not just imagined, deaths. Destruction and domination are not merely fantasies. As I argued in chapter two, the ideology of subjugation and violence has extraordinarily and destructively intimate connections with the Western male psyche. Male violence may, as Theweleit argues, be seen in part as an attempt to cover over the tragically self-destructive complex of gender stereotypes of the "not-fully-born." For a man, the armored, near-anonymous body of a combatant provided a challenge to imagine his own masculinity. The act of penetration of the enemy by sword or lance is an obviously sexualized image: in the moment of impact, the victor bears down on his weapon, which causes a spurt of blood upon entry, as if the whole body has been turned into an armored phallus. Indeed, the warrior's sword, spear, or dagger transcends the sexual, since it can do something that flesh and blood cannot: penetrate, spurt, be withdrawn, and remain as erect as before (and if it breaks, be replaced by an erect alternative). The loser is he who first loses all his capacity for erection. As Theweleit notes of his warriors, "they meet to kill; and the only one to 'flow' " (like a woman, one needs to add) is the man who dies. The holes and gashes in his body are a signal of the enemy's reduction to the status of a woman and the winner's transcendence of self.[21]

267

The battles, jousts, and tourneys in *Urania* are therefore not simply to be seen within "literary" conventions. They are emblems of the desires and anxieties that lie at the core of a culture's myths of violence and domination. The armed knights who thunder towards each other on horseback, or who hack at each other with swords, are metaphors for both a fantasy of invulnerability and a longing for fusion with a trans-individual force that they have been trained to repress in themselves and of which they are afraid. The possible eruption of "the woman's part" in them seems often to trigger a panicked recourse to violence. "You are not a man for men at armes to discourse with," says Steriamus to the martially ineffective Leonius. (*Newberry 1*, fol. 31). When Amphilanthus becomes infatuated with Lady Lucenia (while he is supposed to be in love with Antissia, and "secretly" is really in love with Pamphilia), his immediate reaction, as if to deal with the unbearable confusion of emotion, is to suggest a joust, in which the various male rivals will fight "in defence of their Mistresses beauty" (*Urania*, pp. 136–37).

This pattern of recourse to domination and violence when faced with external threat and internal insecurity has been so deeply ingrained in our cultural history that it seems almost to be natural and outside gender. It shows its residual power by the fact that it is here articulated so strongly by—and within the romance, on behalf of—a woman. In *Troilus and Cressida* it is Cassandra who prophesies doom to the warring battalions of male warriors, and Shakespeare's history plays invariably embody a protest by a woman against the fantasy of male self-assertion through carnage and destruction—Hotspur's Kate, or Lady Macduff, for instance. But as the case of Ophelia shows, women were all too easily interpellated into male fantasies of power: they were, after all, "naturally" the rewards, the prizes, for which the knights battled, objects on which the males of the chivalric caste could project their ego aggrandizement, their denial of the possibility of failure, their fear of annihilation repressed in the orgy of destruction and possession. Violence and war are primary male metaphors for conquest and control. Women are the calm oases or fertile fountains from which the men drink after the dangerous terrain of their adventures has been passed through; the woman's passive, alluring yet forbidden body waits as a reward after the man has slain the resisting, and therefore mutilated, bodies of dragons, monsters, or human enemies. Thus Pamphilia's husband, the Tartarian, is praised for being "in the field . . . a fierce Marss, yett in a Chamber, he may among ladys bee as other men arr" (*Newberry 2*, fol. 21). In such a relationship, the woman is called upon to be the unmoving figure whose fidelity is rewarded only by the seemingly arbitrary return of her lover, always more fulfilling in anticipation or retrospect than in actuality, corresponding, one might speculate, to the sexual experiences of most women at the time. As Kaplan comments, "One way of keeping a tyrant in power is to imagine that he might chooose another slave." The fantasy of "the other slave" animates much of Pamphilia's thinking about her cousin, as does what Kaplan terms "the most common manifestation in women," the illusion "of being fixed and transformed by the magic phallus." Pamphilia is possessed by the idea that her cousin alone is invested with phallic power for her. It is he alone who can compensate for her humiliations: "when that certain kind of person—the ultimate phallic being—is found, that is, created and intensified by the woman, the erotomanic pursuit of this fictive phallic power assumes a force and intensity that eventually subsume and consume all a woman's strivings and ambitions."[22] Here, at the beginning of the modern era, a culturally produced fantasy structure that has animated and distorted women's (and men's) lives throughout our history is being given frighteningly forceful articulation.

Such observations call into question Beilin's argument that with *Urania*, romance becomes "a potentially 'feminine' genre" because it includes the "first extended fictional portrait in English of a woman by a woman." We need to probe far more deeply into the psycho-cultural complexities of that potential transformation than to note simply that women characters predominate, or that the "spirituality" or "virtue" of women is affirmed.[23] Such a reading simply repeats the traditional patriarchal division of the world into male activities (which matter) and female ones (which don't) a division implied in the conventional transition: "But now it is time to leave these affaires to *Mars*, and let his Mistris have her part awhile. . . ."(*Urania*, p. 264). Such a division both devalues potential alternatives to masculine hegemony and leaves unexamined the masculinist values of chivalry, domination, and violence themselves.

What, if anything, counterbalances the dominance of the masculinist chivalric world that must have been epitomized for Mary Wroth by her cousin? The obvious answer, as Beilin's reading implies, is love, the traditional antithesis to war. It might be thought that if war and conquest represent the "masculine" in heroic romance, love represents the "feminine," with the desiring machine of erotic love that permeates the "feminine" aspect of the romance as the apparent antithesis of the destructive machinery of militarism. But overwhelmingly, throughout *Urania* love is co-opted by the dominant masculine ethos. As Theweleit demonstrates, part of the warrior's simultaneous desire for and fear of fusion is directed towards the female—both within himself and in society at large: he keeps women in subjection so that he need not acknowledge the woman in himself. But women, real women, also exist outside the male fantasy of domination and fear, and so they must be somehow controlled in their "real," not just in their fantasized, bodies. To control them, they can only be supportive to male activities: insofar as women are permitted any degree of agency, it is to support and succor men. In *Urania*, as in the *Faerie Queene* and *Arcadia*, the repeated confrontations of rival emperors, princes, and knights represent part of the education of both men and women to accept violence and domination as the principal means of dealing with gender difference.

The stories in *Urania*, whether of love or war, then, are governed by the same masculinist values. In a revealing remark, we are told that Pamphilia "raild at the uncareful people who permitted her to have her fond desires without limiting her power," as if it were only the limitation, imposed by male dominance, that could make her happy. The firmer the limitation, the less discontent there would be for a woman, even for a queen in a world of make-believe. Women, "bred in Loves Schoole," we are told, "knew" their "paine," and Pamphilia, ever in the role of masochistic victim, had "misfortunes" that "farr surpas'd any hapiness she had ever seene." That pain and those misfortunes are so deeply inculcated into women's lives that there seem to be no means of protest except those sanctioned by the system against which she would protest. She therefore chooses to accept her role within "the cruel tortures, the everlasting gnawing sorrow of love or not of love, butt of love disdained" (*Urania*, pp. 165, 312; *Newberry 2*, fol. 26; *Newberry 1*, fol. 32). In doing so, she gives voice to what Benjamin sees as a predominant mark of the Western ideology of individuality that has affected all men and women: Independence from the mother as object rather than "recognition of her as subject" lies at the root of Western individualism, she argues. And because the ideology of individuality has been so bound up with the default position of masculinity, "the image of the other that predominates in Western thought is not that of a vitally real presence but a cognitively perceived object," overwhelmingly seen from the masculine subject position. A man may define himself by his willingness to recognize or withhold recognition from the other; a woman, on the other hand, is characteristically positioned to accept her own lack of subjectivity and to "offer recognition without expecting it in return." Her anxieties about lack of autonomy are handled by more and more complete submission. Thus, argues Benjamin, "submission for women allows a reenactment of their early identificatory relationship to the mother; it is a replication of the maternal attitude itself."[24]

In such a world, sexual agency is predominantly a characteristic of men. It can be expressed in explicitly erotic terms: "for what man lives, that glories not in multitudes of womens loves?" comments the narrator on Amphilanthus's "glorying" in having both Pamphilia and Antissia love him, in which situation (as usual) "all was as hee wished." But possessing erotic choice points to something deeper, something that goes beyond the mere possibility of sleeping (or speaking) around. Male-ness is distinguished by the permission of the culture to move and change in far broader ways. Men are assigned the freedom to not have others know their whereabouts or activities. We are continually meet-ing characters who ask what other men are doing, where their ad-ventures have taken them, when they disappeared, or what glorious deeds they have performed. Parselius, for instance, meets Leandus and Amphilanthus' squire:

> He demanded what he knew of his Master. Truly (replide he) nothing but the joy I conceive to heare by this gentle Knight that he is living: I parted from him in a greate storme, having been in *Germany* sent thither with an army from the *Pope* to assist the Emperour against the Duke of *Saxony*, who was slaine by his hand, and for this act was by the Emperour and the other princes made King of the Romans, having protected the Empire against such an enemy, since till now never having heard newes of him: but he ment to seeke still for you, and therefore left Germany, and in the Mediterran sea, my selfe, ship, and all my Lords treasure was taken by this Pirat . . .
>
> (*Urania*, pp. 270, 37)

This is a world of danger and unpredictability. It is a world that, within the reigning gender ideology, only men are capable of managing, since its key values are the male qualities of aggression and violence. Battle, the narrator tells us, is "the cruellest, and yet delightfullest Com-bate," the delight arising not least because of the lure of power over others it affords. "Brave knights" act, move, change; "delicate ladies," if they are true to their natures, stay at home, or—even when, like Pamphilia, they are queens—move only under the protection of "brave knights." A woman is "meant" to admire in a man "dainty fashion, rich cloathes . . . a noble mind, a free disposition, a brave, and manly countenance, excellent discourse, wit beyond compare," and to accept that he has, by his nature, a confident autonomy to which she cannot, without peril, aspire (*Urania*, pp. 63, 106). A woman's "natural" sphere of action is a walled garden in which she may walk, guarded by men. In Wroth's lifetime—if not the time she was writing—the exception was Queen Elizabeth, and Pamphilia's reluctance to marry has been seen as a reminder of Elizabeth. But Pamphilia clearly would marry Amphilanthus, were he not mysteriously unavailable—and as Roberts notes, there is a sense in which she does so, in: "such a contract can nott bee broken by any lawe whatsoever" (*Newberry 1*, fol. 14).[25] In any case (as Elizabeth I knew) even if she is independently minded, like Pamphilia, who is also a queen, a woman still requires male protection, even if it is sometimes discreetly disguised. Leandrus, for some time her suitor, converses with her:

> Is it possible (most excelling Queene) that such a spirit, and so great a Princesse, should be thus alone, and adventure without guard? My spirit my Lord (said she) as well guards me alone, as in company; and for my person, my greatnesse, and these walls are sufficient warrants and guardians for my safety. Yet your safety might bee more (said hee) if joyned with one, who might defend you upon all occasions, both with his love and strength, while these dull walls can onely incompasse you: but if traitors assaile you, their helpe will bee but to stand still . . .
>
> (*Urania*, pp. 178–79)

Only occasionally do women venture alone outside such confines. Antissia goes to the seaside to learn the adventures of some travelers; there are a few women warriors, fishers, and hunters. But whenever we hear a detailed story of such apparent autonomy, we find either it is done in accord with the wishes of their families' interests, especially their marital concerns, or else because the women are associated with some powerful male character. The queen of Naples, presented as the wisest and most independent of the women characters, is praised primarily because she is the mother of Amphilanthus. Women who, like Pamphilia herself, hold some title or even rule countries, give up their control and authority to the men they marry, and, as Shaver points out, these are frequently landless younger sons. In many cases, however, women's attempts to achieve any autonomy lead to unhappiness or even what is presented as perversion and self-destruction. Shaver has argued, indeed, that the work is full of unruly women, "unchaste, outspoken, disobedient, full of the confidence conferred by self-esteem," and almost invariably suffering or actually punished for their boldness. Limena describes how she is tortured "with daily whippings, and such other tortures, as pinching with irons" for her adulterous love. Ramilletta is "terribly tortured, and yet kept long in paine for her more lasting punishment, and lastly burn'd." Orelina is locked in a ship with a ravenous dog in the hope that it would "devouer [her], being one of the fiercest in all the Countrey" (*Urania*, pp. 72, 108, 459).[26]

The most protracted of these violent cautionary tales is that of Nereana. We learn about Nereana's life for the most part from Amphilanthus, who describes her to Urania and Pamphilia as "most ignorantly proud." Her main crime—not unlike so many of Shakespeare's heroines—is to challenge the prerogative of the male and pursue the man she loves. Thus she is not only that threatening creature, "so amarous a lady," but also inappropriately "Knight-like," the term by which Pamphilia reprimands her when they meet. She acts out the fantasy that all the women wish to live out, and her reward is to be accused of de-feminizing herself. Nereana is mistaken by the madman Allanus for his love the cruel Liana, and she is half-undressed, half-decorated, as the goddess of the woods before whom "he kneeled downe, and admired." As Shaver comments, "it is a brilliant parody of five centuries of woman-worship and fetish-creation, a marvelous cartoon of courtly love's inevitable results." Eventually she escapes and is finally discovered in a distraught condition by Prince Perissus, who sees her "true" nobility beneath her dishevelment and, reimposing the prerogative of the chivalric male rescuing the distressed damsel, takes "her to the Towne . . . in his owne Charriot [and] cloathed her according to her dignity." We are told that she has learnt "to overrule her old passions" (*Urania*, pp. 162, 163, 166, 288–89, 421). Thus her willfulness is tamed and she is accorded her appropriate place by the man, but only at the cost of her loss of dignity and autonomy, and after being "molested" because of the very sexual aggressiveness that is supposedly so admirable in a man. As Swift points out, "the knights who aid some desperate ladies abuse others, and it is often questionable whether the women are rescued or simply degraded once again."[27]

The story of Nereana points to the contradictions built into a woman's struggle to emulate the autonomy men take for granted. Inevitably there seems to be a conflict between any strivings for autonomy and her assigned roles in the hierarchies of gender. With the men, however, there are no such conflicts. They leave the women behind to wait for them and go off on continual "adventures." When Dalinea beseeches her lover Parselius to take her with him, "My deere, said he, pardon at this time my leaving you, for should I carry you where troubles are? no Sweet, remayne you here . . . deere love bee patient, and stay here." Unencumbered, the men range across a fantasy Europe where ceaseless adventures await them; they are continually seeking battles to fight, princesses to rescue, enchantments to encounter. The work's heroes are like Steriamus, always "forc'd by an adventure, calling [him] away," and "loving nothing more then change." Having a "travelling life" is what being a man means. Leandrus, we are told, "long . . . rid not without an adventure, those places affording many, and pleasant ones." When Parselius is journeying through Morea, he is thinking of Urania until he sees Dalinea:

> . . . who he so much admir'd, as admiration wrought so farre, as to permit him to thinke that she equal'd *Urania*, this was a sudden stepp from so entyre a Love . . . But into this hee is now falne . . . Uncertaine Tyrant Love, that never brings thy Favourits to the topp of affection, but turnes againe to a new choice. Who would have thought . . . ?
>
> (*Urania*, pp. 125, 57, 59, 471, 83, 102)

He stays with Dalinea, discoursing (private conversation are always the sign of lovers' enjoying themselves) despite his breach of faith with his former love. But, as Dolorindus remarks, "Courtiers you know will love choyce of Mistresses." "This Prince," we are told of the prince of Janbolly, "was one that least troubled himselfe with constancy, all women were pleasing to him . . . and varietie he had sufficient . . . yet here hee stayed a prety while, because it was thought hard to win her, or impossible to gaine her love." There are always other fair ladies available for the "changing sexe" (*Urania*, pp. 156, 463, 158). When defined by men's desires and needs, love seems inevitably to involve changeableness: "noe sooner mett, and as if in Metamorphoses, butt we must bee parted" (*Newberry 2*, fol. 13). Amphilanthus is the primary offender against the virtue of constancy, finding continual fascination in a variety of ladies even while he holds (we are repeatedly told) absolutely true to Pamphilia. But as McLaren notes, "Wroth does not show, or even suggest, that this 'blemish' affects Amphilanthus's standing as a Knight or even his virtue as a King."[28] When Amphilanthus is seduced by the Queen of Candia—whom Pamphilia tartly refers to as "that delightfull Queene the Cummone commaundress of mens harts"—or marries the Princess of Slavonia, he still remains her "right bride groome" (*Newberry 1*, fols. 21, 12). Even for Antissia, whom he has systematically deceived, and who tells him angrily that inconstancy is his distinctive mark, he remains matchless.

Yet, we need to ask, is there any evidence for women's own fantasies emerging through the work? Were women able to "own" fantasies at all in this time? In an age where the metaphors of sexual fulfillment were so overwhelmingly militarized, what effects can we perceive in the psychosocial profiles of both men and women? Can we read Wroth's apparent celebration of the masculinist myths of love, possession, and domination as an act of wish fulfillment, appropriating the stories of the "other" since there seem to be no alternatives? Or is there, at the edges of the seemingly replete ideology, cracks and fissures through which we can sense the "flow," to use Theweleit's metaphor, of a feminine discourse?[29] *Urania*, like *Pamphilia to Amphilanthus*, dramatizes the difficulties and the contradictions involved in constructing viable subject positions for women outside the dominant masculinist ethos.

Our search for such symptomatic difficulties and contradictions can start with the ways in which commonplace romance motifs are rewritten from the perspective of the women characters. Where chivalric romance is concerned almost exclusively with romantic courtship, *Urania* is predominantly concerned with the details and stresses of married life. Adultery, the staple of romantic love, is not only seen as a grand passion for men: the consequences, both positive and negative, for women become a major preoccupation of the stories Wroth tells. Women's sexual restrictions within arranged marriages are a recurring concern, and adultery is condoned, even at times celebrated, where it may lead to a more fulfilling relationship for women. Repeatedly, husbands are described as "a terrible and wretched barre in the way" of desire. Many of the liaisons in *Urania* are like that described by Dolorindus, in which "my loves husband grew to doubt his wife, which well he might . . . I had but one love, yet of force shew'd two; faith and sincere affection to my choyce dissembled: and a faign'd respect to her had chosen me" (*Urania*, pp. 148, 155–56). In the continuation, the adulterous Celia is praised for "soe prettily, and craftilie" carrying off her liaison with her lover. She is able to be with him and "injoyed a greater porssion of hapines then they had expected, and therefore the better to be borne." Yet, we are told, "this notable incroacher" upon the duties of marriage "is such a longing creature, and soe devouring as it is never satisfied" (*Newberry 1*, fol. 8). Overreaching themselves, they are discovered, yet their affair is not condemned.

When we look at the different gender roles in these affairs, with the exception of Nereana—whose violent fate is a terrible and protracted warning against a woman pursuing her own desires in love—it is always the men who are active, aggressive, making choices, and achieving (or failing to achieve) their amatory goals. By contrast, Pamphilia is characterized by her constancy. Despite being reminded that "this virtue hath limits," Pamphilia remains true to her cousin "at all times." "O stay," she cries in despair to him, as she sees him in a vision departing with yet another woman, "and live with me, follow not her, that loves thee not like me, forsake me not againe" (*Urania*, p. 400; *Newberry 1*, fol. 8; *Urania*, p. 492). In the enchantment of the Tower of Desire in Book One, the allegorical figure of Constancy is described as "metamorphosing her self into" Pamphilia's breast, whereas for Amphilanthus "inconstancy . . . presse[s]" him "on to more delight" (*Urania*, pp. 141, 111).

This opposition between men's inconstancy and women's constancy looks as if it constitutes the moral crux of the work. At one point, Amphilanthus cries out against his own inconstancy: "O for ever hated change, for ever detested change, for all earthly ills, the wurst . . . soe is my fault above that, ungrateful I ame, and to her, to whom my fault is unpardonable" (*Newberry 1*, fol. 34). Yet one of the most fascinating aspects of *Urania* is the way the traditional stereotypes of both constancy and inconstancy, and their associations with gender assignments, are subject to a thorough demystification. In the work's most radical statement, it is Amphilanthus's sister Urania who points out to Pamphilia, "tis pittie . . . that ever that fruitlesse thing Constancy was taught you as a virtue" (*Urania*, p. 400). For a major character like Urania to talk of constancy in that way is to call into question in an extreme way not just the particulars but the epistemological basis of traditional gender assignments. It is as if Spenser were to hand the universe over to the sway of Mutability without his final assertion in the two unfinished cantos of the *Faerie Queene* of God's providential control of the universe. To speak of constancy as something "taught" to women calls into question the "naturall"ness of the courtly idealization of women, undermines a man's talk of being enslaved by the various perfections of a woman, and challenges the seemingly natural assignments of gender. Women are "bred in Loves Schoole" to relate tales of love and to be emblazoned by their lovers, but not to initiate, let alone make multiple choices of, them. Men affirm that they cannot choose but follow after ladies, but the political reality is that women are commodities, pursued for their exchange value.

Nor is Urania's admonition of Pamphilia for her pointless constancy an isolated remark in the work. In Amphilanthus's hearing, Musalina advises:

> Lady, trust not too much; for believe it, the kindest, lovingst, passion-atest, worthiest, loveliest, valiantest, sweetest, and best man, will, and must change, not that he, it may bee, doth it purposely, but tis their naturall infirmitie, and cannot be helped. It was laid to our charge in times passed to bee false, and changing, but they who excell us in all perfections, would not for their honours sake, let us surpasse them in any one thing, though that, and now are much more perfect, and excellent in that then wee, so there is nothing left us, that they excell us not in, although in our greatest fault.

> (*Urania*, p. 375)

Yet it is remarkable that such comments, though they articulate a deep cynicism, are not expressed in moralistic terms. In Wroth's world, the autonomy represented by men's "adventures" is envied or becomes an occasion for anger; but it is not condemned. It represents not a moral weakness so much as a mobility and power "taught" to men and desired by women.

None of these contradictions, however, emerge sufficiently consistently in the work to constitute a rejection of the system that produced them. Benjamin asks why, over and over in our history, men's and women's strivings for mutual recognition have culminated in "submission, instead of a relationship of mutuality." All too often, she muses, a relationship built upon domination and submission, seems to offer the only way of breaking the "encasement of the isolated self."[30] Pamphilia's repeated response to advice like Urania's or comments like Musalina's is to subordinate herself to Amphilanthus, praising his perfection even while knowing of his unworthiness. Veralinda pointedly asks Pamphilia whether she "knewe any man, especially any brave men continue constant." As usual, Amphilanthus's inconstancy is immediately excused by her—"I would not my self have my Lord constant"—though she voices her wish with some tartness—"for feare of a miracle" and because, the narrator notes, Pamphilia has "seen Amphilanthus in severall slips already." When Veralinda asserts that "his hart and body is false and unkind," Pamphilia terms it "vain counsell"; to her exhortation to "lett him goe," Pamphilia admits, "I can nott butt grieve, when I think such excellency, can fall into so strange forgettfulness" (*Newberry 1*, fol. 40).

In Pamphilia's consistent masochism—and especially by contrast with those women figures in the romance who do claim some degree of agency—Wroth is articulating the difficulties of constructing a subject-position for a woman in the early modern period. In such a society, "to be a woman is to be unable to say 'I want that'," asserts Benjamin.[31] Though the cracks in the epistemology of gender hierarchy are starting to become evident, even on the level of fantasy the structures and assumptions on which a woman's life was constructed emerge as unavoidable. At times all she can hope for is to withdraw into her private musings on her losses. When she returns to her own country, we are told, "she joyed in nothing, nor communed with any but her owne sad selfe, which she cal'd her losse, and passions for it . . . yet she lost not her selfe . . . like that Lady she was, wherein she shewed her heart was not to be stirr'd, though her private fortunes shooke round about her" (*Urania*, p. 411). Losing "not herself" is the minimal goal that both Pamphilia and her creator Wroth try to achieve; both use writing to carve out a private space in which some sense of an integrated identity can be maintained, where a woman "soveraignises" over herself.

In chapter three I suggested that through Wroth's life and writings we can indeed see the fitful but significant development of a number of "womanspaces." One is the sense of community and mutuality, independent of supposedly inherent masculine concerns, afforded by family life or friendship. It is unlikely that a man writing at the time would have paid detailed attention to such matters as the emotional interdependence of women cousins, or the closeness of (and rivalries between) brothers and sisters. While the relationships between Euarchus and his son and nephew, and between the sisters Pamela and Philoclea are prominent in Sidney's *Arcadia*, they are generally set in terms of political or moral issues. Even the *Arcadia*'s examination of Basilius's family, which involves generational tensions, sibling relationships, and adultery, is described largely in terms of authority, governance, and obedience. In *Urania*, especially in the second part, there seems to be something more: an obsession with a sense of community afforded by domestic life—with marriage, parenting, family affections, and familial anxieties and loss.

John Frosch describes family romances as fantasies or narratives born of "the absence of the love object or the failure of reality to meet" our basic needs for autonomy and relationship.[32] The fantasies generated are designed to compensate for the lack of correlation between desire and the world, to repeat Deleuze and Guattari's formulation, they take the form of utopian completions of narratives that are apparently frustrated by reality, and for which fantasies provide more satisfying and immediate endings. This element of utopian fantasy in Urania—giving voice to a dream of autonomy not possible for the author in her real life—is embodied in romance's seemingly endless habit of interrupting and recommencing stories and also in the valorization of story-making itself. The enjoyment of "contented discourse" (*Newberry 1*, fol. 5)—which includes fiction-making, the withdrawal of a character to write or sing her inner thoughts, the sharing of gossip, tale or anecdote among a group of family or friends (usually family members), and (not least) the writing of poetry—has a major symbolic function in this world, not least for its author. Story represents a private space, an area of (even) temporary satisfaction, in which a narrative can be constructed that will at least allow an imaginary resolution of conflict and frustration. To tell a story is to seduce, oneself at least, with the illusion of desire satisfied: "Discourse procur'd conversation, sweet conversation, liking of it selfe; that liking, desire to continue it; that desire, loving it, and that man that affoorded it" (*Urania*, p. 103). In one scene we see Pamphilia, Amphilanthus, and a group of friends reminiscing about the "flowering time of their first lovings, everyone, nott nice, but truly telling their infinitely suffering passions" (*Newberry 1*, fol. 57). Many of the stories that make up *Urania* are told in retrospect, publicly, within a group of friends or a family group. Pamphilia and Urania spend much time "lying together, and with sad but loving discourse passing those dark hours" (*Urania*, p. 123). But, quite frequently, Pamphilia's stories are told when she withdraws to private retreats, where she can enjoy thoughts "too pretious for any eares butt hers." A favorite activity of hers is to go beyond the confines of house or palace, on "her owne solitary waulke, wher she tooke full libertie." She takes one such walk on her marriage night, "to give her passions some disburdening" (*Newberry 2*, fols. 47, 23).

Today, at least in the Western middle class, we take it for granted that we need private spaces where the rules, possibilities, barriers, and outcomes of our society and (not least) our families can be avoided with minimum interference from other people. To gauge the significance of Pamphilia's claims for privacy, we need to consider not only the places today where we construct our own private fantasies—alone, often in our rooms, or in bed—but also the material living arrangements that might have made such a retreat more difficult in the early seventeenth century, when a major transition between feudal and early modern notions of family privacy is being reflected in domestic architecture. In noble families like the Herberts and Sidneys, where the obligations of kinship remained strong, what today are assumed to be private or at least intimate experiences—birth, death, sex—were assumed to be parts of a public, dynastic domain: James I sporting in (or at least on) Pembroke's brother's marriage bed is a not altogether distant reminder of the concerns of a monarch for the appropriate marital arrangements of his subjects. The great houses of the Tudor and Jacobean aristocracy consisted of many undifferentiated living spaces, as if the family at large had the acts of its individual members under surveillance. The patriarchal and authoritarian nature of traditional society made private acts that were disapproved of by the family—romantic liaisons included—difficult to carry out. The seventeenth century sees the growth of more private living spaces—both beds and bedrooms become more privatized areas. In such ways, material transitions at least in part produce, not merely reflect, psychological and cultural ones. In the early modern period the desire for what Marvell, a generation later, with wonderful cosmic irony, termed a "fine and private space" in "To His Coy Mistress," constitutes a utopian desire of enormous moment, especially since it is voiced by a woman. Hence it is significant that throughout *Urania*, we are shown Pamphilia, and sometimes other ladies, taking refuge in such private spaces. In the opening adventure Philargus tells Urania how his mistress "retired into a Cabinet she had, where she used to passe away some part of her unpleasant life" (*Urania*, p. 10). Pamphilia frequently takes refuge in the woods where she can write or be alone with her thoughts:

> One day as the King and Queene were walking in the Garden, attended on by all the Princes, Ladies, and Knights of the Court, every one discoursing as best pleased them, *Pamphilia* walked alone, none daring to present himselfe to her.
>
> (*Urania*, p. 56)

Such a desire for privacy articulates a deep psychological and social yearning. It is the fantasy of one continually under surveillance, for whom privacy was a rare and valuable achievement. It bespeaks a need for control of one's own "stories," and an acknowledgement that a woman's stories need not be told on her behalf by her family and her society. It is a desire to complete stories of her own.

Heavily marked by gender and class, the spasmodic, emergent stories of *Urania* are overwhelmingly about autonomy, the continuing battles that a woman wages, throughout adulthood, to achieve the individuation

promised in infancy, accorded to men, yet denied to her. In the case
of men, they are stories of adventure, movement, and change as the
articulations of their natural rights; for women, they are stories of the
enormous allure and danger of emulating men. They are also, on rare
occasions, about mutuality, though heavily tinged with the difficulty of
its realization, at least between men and women. Many of them are
concerned with the articulation of desire, especially with writing:

> These passions oft did vexe her, and perplexe her soule, one day es-
> pecially when all alone in the Woods shee did thus complaine. Never
> at quiet tormenting passion, what more canst thou desire? What covet
> that thou hast not gaind? in absence thou dost molest me.

(Urania, pp. 203–04)

Such complaints, both about love and the necessity and difficulty of
putting love into words, are recorded in the poems scattered throughout
the work, as well as in *Pamphilia to Amphilanthus* itself. In developing
and revising both her romance and the accompanying collection of
sonnets, Wroth moved many of the poems back and forth between the
romance and the separate collection. Both works (and in some sense
they are best considered as a single work) record a dilemma about giving
public voice to private anguish. Poetry may even bring one to the edge
of madness, especially in the case of a woman poet. Indeed, we are
told of one who could "express . . . pretious thoughts, in a rare, and
covert way," but fell victim to a "frenzy" (*Newberry 1*, fol. 13). Pamphilia's poems are presented as attempts at both self-preservation and
self-assertion, and yet they always have a self-torturing edge. She vows
"not to carry the tokens of her losse openly on her browes, but rather
weare them privately in her heart," and determines to not "blabbe" her
love. Her poems, are often written in the "delicate thick wood" (*Urania*,
pp. 76, 264) to which she continually retires: she carves verses on trees or
writes them on sheets of paper, destroying some, showing some to a few
close friends, including Amphilanthus, but denying that he is referred to
and even at times that she herself is the author. Silence and reticence are
expected of women. She was a woman: therefore, she was to be silent
and to display herself gracefully. But in the secret life afforded by her
writing, she was striving, however fitfully, for her own language. As is
the case so often in *Urania*, the personal pronouns at this point become
blurred. To what extent are Pamphilia's struggles those of her creator? In
Pamphilia's poetry it seems that Wroth is writing out her own struggles
to find a poetic (and perhaps beyond that, a personal) language that
could be hers.

As we read *Urania* today, we can see two dimensions of the struggle
in which Wroth was caught which were largely outside her knowledge at

280

the time. The first is the enormous changes that even in her time, though not necessarily in her circle or her class, were emerging in women's lives. Even as she was writing, the terms of struggles that would be fought out in later years were being set up. The second is the historical outcomes of those struggles. Wroth lived and wrote within an ideology of gender assignments and within the fantasies they produced that together were profoundly destructive of many aspects of human maturity, for both men and women. Perhaps, to use Theweleit's analogy, early modern English society consisted largely of the not-fully-born: men for whom violence and domination were the natural means available by which they might rediscover a lost, undifferentiated world, and women in whose struggles can be seen futile yet unending struggles against that supposedly natural world. Pamphilia is warned that she "must nott expect the returne of the golden age, but remaine in this, a wurse then Iron" (*Newberry 1*, fol. 34). Greenblatt notes that "one of the highest achievements of power is to impose fictions upon the world and one of its supreme pleasures is to enforce the acceptance of fictions that are known to be fictions."[33] In *Urania* Wroth certainly achieved the first; the second was available only perhaps to the monarch and, to some limited extent, to a Buckingham— or even a Pembroke. The assumption that to impose one's own fictions on the world is itself desirable has been, historically, a male delusion. In Wroth's lifetime, at least, there seem to have been few possibilities of an alternative, more nurturing, communal desire. "All adventures," Pamphilia is warned by Urania, "were not framed for you to finish . . . The great Inchantment" under which we all suffer and struggle, "will not bee concluded this many yeares" (*Urania*, p. 321; *Newberry 2*, fol. 62).

9

RESTORING WHAT WE HAVE MISSED

I have restored what is missing, taking the best models known to me from other analyses; but like the conscientious archeologist I have not omitted to mention in each case where the authentic parts end and where my constructions begin.

Sigmund Freud

We need not look only, in a transforming history, for direct or public historical event and response. When there is real dislocation it does not have to appear in a strike or in machine-breaking. It can appear as radically and as authentically in what is apparently, what is actually, personal or family experience.

Raymond Williams[1]

All men and women (terms that over the course of this study have, at least for its author, become blurred and problematic) live out multiple histories, multiple stories of desire, achievement, loss, possibility, and impossibility. We do so within many and contradictory narratives we have inherited from pasts which we did not ourselves create, and yet which give us, often without our being aware that we are being incorporated within them, the only narratives we know. As we mature, we start to create what we fancy to be "our" stories; one of the great, encouraging illusions of the liberal post-Renaissance West has been that they are, indeed, "our" stories, just as one of the most powerful and confusing disillusions of the twentieth century—articulated by Darwin, Marx, Freud, Foucault, and many others—has been that they are not "ours" at all, that we are never fully aware of the range of stories from which we might choose, and that we are, in many ways far beyond our understanding, let alone control, always already chosen by "our" stories. A century after the "invention" of psychoanalysis, we are still living in the uneasy and often schizoid condition of both willing ourselves to construct "individual" dreams of autonomy, independence, agency, and also still discovering, some of us daily, how many of those stories lie in wait for us, always already told for us, sometimes without our knowing.

The primary subjects of this book were no less caught up in their own and their histories' stories and dreams. Yet they are also parts of ours. They lived on the shifting and ill-defined boundaries of two worlds: one that seems in so many of its material and emotional details unquestionably alien to most of us, and another that is frighteningly familiar. Their separate and intermingled lives therefore raise not merely "historical" questions, but questions about the contemporary presence of history, and perhaps questions about what is permanent, or at least recurring, and why, in our individual and shared histories. It is, incidentally, one mark of difference between our world and theirs (perhaps, for some of us, between our world and our parents' worlds!) that the questions and narratives of "permanence" or "universals" or "essentials" in human life used to pertain predominantly to beneficent, providential stories of the ends and purpose of the universe; now they are predominantly questions and narratives of our conditioning, our social construction, even our biological and psychological makeup. Paradoxically (some would say tragically), because we live by what Kristeva calls a "shattered imaginary,"[2] a plurality of contradictory narratives, we are often able to combine and recombine fragments of our different histories and make some attempts at stories that we feel to be "ours."

In our time and place, among the most powerfully counter-dominant narratives that have called into question the received stories of what it is, and has been, to be a human subject have been those of gender. In the last thirty years feminist thought and practice have assaulted the bastions not only of traditional scholarship but patterns of living far beyond the academy. They have brought women's concerns and women's histories into contemporary life; they have challenged us all, men and women alike, to rethink and re-act the relationships between our assumptions about gender and the rest of our lives. They have shown that the ideological tensions over gender are as much problems of politics as they are of sexuality. They have shown the need for a thorough rewriting of the received histories of our culture, to bring out both the narratives that were recorded but marginalized and forgotten, and those that were never recorded, never told, but were lived, without adequate means of symbolization or understanding. To recover and write out these persecuted histories is one of the great obligations of the present. The continual rewriting of the history of gender assignments is necessary because the stories of gender hierarchy and bipolarity—the fundamental ideologies of what has produced us as "men" and "women"—remain so deeply ingrained in our day-to-day assumptions that we must ask repeatedly what alternatives stories have not been told us, or taken from us, and why, what different his- (and hers)tories we might construct from both what is apparently "there" in the records of our pasts and also what is not there.

My history of the sexual and textual relationships between Pembroke and Wroth, therefore, is also an account of the present, or at least of some aspects of the present to which their lives and relationships point—sometimes accusingly, sometimes encouragingly. The crisis of gender assignment in the early modern period is related to the crisis in our own time; it may, of course, be a permanent crisis of humanity, or at least of humanity organized under patriarchy. One of the dangerous seductions of psychoanalysis is that, like any theory of existence tempting one into foundationalism, it offers a model for explaining why nothing can be done about the human condition; one of the hopes it offers is that it may, however clumsily and tentatively, give us a way of linking the ideas and ideologies that swirl around us with the material and emotional details of our lives. It also affirms (perhaps the most profound thing it offers) that we are story-telling animals: we are continually telling and retelling, starting and trying to finish stories; continually finding that stories we started are being finished by other people, or being totally rewritten. Petrarch, who has played something of a villain's role in this book, gives us one of the most powerful metaphors for this sense of how our stories may be taken from us when he recounts his first meeting with Laura: from that moment, he states, his story was not his, it centered on the desired mutuality of his with another's desires, and he had perforce to divide not only his but the whole of history into two parts, before and after meeting her. Further, he had to tell and retell that story, teasing out its implications, under the shadow of many of which we still live.

The stories Pembroke and Wroth lived out were multiple and contradictory; some they shared, others show significant discrepancies of commitment or power that reveal much about the nature of their society and our history. Above all else, they were divided by the gender assignments that have characterized and distorted Western history. Cousins, members of the same extended family, they had their strivings for selfhood, what I have termed—greatly extending the frame of reference of Freud's phrase—their family romances, formed and given their initial shapes within their families. Their fantasies were, at the most general level, those of independence and autonomy, dreams generated within the family, thwarted and transferred there, and then projected upon the worlds into which they were thrust. What differentiates their fantasies, their dreams, their stories, is primarily gender. Pembroke's romances, lived out in his multiple career as a courtier, politician, patron, patriarch, husband, lover, son, father, are based on the assumptions of dominance, autonomy, secure changeableness, "sophisticate affection," and accessibility to the world outside the family which had nurtured him and had given him the raw material for his stories. Wroth's romances were predominantly those of subjection, limitation, envy, and anger. As a daughter, wife, court lady, mother, widow, and indebted family dependent, her stories are those of being "wached," primarily by the men who controlled and limited her access to the stories she acted out through her life. But not just "acted out": she also told stories, not only her own, but also those of other women, of her class and society and of women in patriarchal history. What distinguishes Wroth from her cousin is that one of the fantasies to which she returned obsessively was to put her strivings into language. Davis notes the ways in which a woman in early modern Europe "could reflect on and write about herself while retaining the image of the patriarchal family," and how even "a patriarchal family unit could stimulate people within its borders toward self-discovery and self-presentation."[3] Part of the importance of Wroth's

285

life—both her writing and her relationship with her cousin—is that it promised, and spasmodically articulated, more than that, both for her time and for ours.

In my opening chapter I argued that this history was in many untrivial, if indirect, ways, my history. Many of my family romances have parts in it, no doubt some I do not, or do not want to, recognize. But they are not, any more than Pembroke's or Wroth's were, "mine" in a naively subjective sense: what writing this history (or story) has brought home to me has been that the fantasies I act out or find myself caught up in have been, over and over, part of the history I share with Wroth and, especially, Pembroke. Such continuities force us to face not the naive matter of "identifying" with a person or fictional character, but rather the question of continuity and difference with the past and, even more important, the question of our own futures. In that tentative utopianism, this is unapologetically a book with an agenda, trying to provide a glimpse of past struggles in order to help create another world in which real people, not just abstract "human subjects," can play a multiplicity of roles with, in, and as one another, accepting and reveling in difference by making it more familiar. And yet, admittedly, contradictorily, this book also looks back and records a fascination with the otherness of these two long-dead people, a man and a woman who struggled to leave their marks on a world that is also long gone. That realisation may lead to nostalgia as easily as to determination; to fantasies of the past as readily as of the future. We must realise that however hard one stares at records, manuscripts, buildings, one can never capture the "reality" of their inner lives. So let the last words be Freud's challenge to those of us, whether cultural historians, poets, or ordinary men and women striving to make sense of our histories and futures, our gender assignments and the family romances they have generated for and through and despite us. We are all, in the stories we live out and tell, over and over, to ourselves and each others, tellers of tales:

> Up til now we have left it to the creative writer to depict for us the "necessary conditions for loving" which govern peoples' choice of an object, and the way in which they bring the demands of their imaginations into harmony with reality. The writer can indeed draw on certain conditions which fit him to carry out such a task: above all, a sensitivity that enables him to perceive the hidden impulses in the minds of other people, and the courage to let his own unconscious speak.[4]

NOTES

Chapter One

1. Sigmund Freud, "Family Romances," *The Standard Edition of the Works of Sigmund Freud*, ed. and trans. James Strachey et al. (London: Hogarth Press, 1952–66), IX, pp. 237–41; Louise Kaplan, *Female Perversions: The Temptations of Madame Bovary* (New York: Doubleday, 1991), p. 53.

2. Phyllis Greenacre, "The Family Romance of the Artist," *Psychological Study of the Child*, 13 (1958), 10; *The Complete Letters of Sigmund Freud to Wilhelm Fliess 1887–1904*, trans. and ed. Jeffrey Moussaieff Masson (Cambridge, Mass.: Harvard University Press, 1985), pp. 317–18; Freud, *Standard Edition* VII, p. 229. See also "A Special Type of Choice of Object Made by Men," *Standard Edition*, XI, pp. 171–72.

3. Harold Bloom, *The Anxiety of Influence: A Theory of Poetry* (New York: Seabury, 1973), p. 94. For "kissing cousins," see James B. Twitchell, *Forbidden Partners: The Incest Taboo in Modern Culture* (New York: Columbia University Press, 1987), pp. 8–9.

4. Although in recent years scholarly attention to Wroth has increased, neither her nor Pembroke's writings have ever been accorded "canonical" status. *Urania* has occasionally received a mention, sometimes a brief and often inaccurate paraphrase, in standard surveys of prose fiction before Richardson; my *English Poetry of the Sixteenth Century* (London: Longmans, second edition, 1993) is the only standard survey of the period's poetry to mention either cousin's poetry in any detail, and the volume in the same series on seventeenth-century poetry, where discussion of their poems would more properly belong, barely mentions Wroth and does not mention Pembroke at all.

5. Catherine Belsey, *John Milton: Language, Gender, Power* (London: Methuen, 1988), p. 8.

6. Stephen Greenblatt, *Shakespearean Negotiations* (Berkeley: University of California Press, 1988), p. 86.

7. Joan Wallach Scott, *Gender and the Politics of History* (New York: Columbia University Press, 1988), p. 25; Judith Newton, "Family Fortunes: 'New History' and 'New Historicism'," *Radical History Review*, 43 (1989), 15. See also *Freud to Fliess*, p. 257; Jessica Benjamin, *A Desire of One's Own: Psychoanalytic Feminism and Intersubjective Space* (University of Wisconsin-Milwaukee: Center for Twentieth Century Studies, Working Paper #2, 1985), p. 3; Kaplan, *Female Perversions*, p. 11; Ellen Ross, "Rethinking 'the Family'," *Radical History Review* 20. (Spring/ Summer, 1979), 78.

8. Julia Swindells and Lisa Jardine, *What's Left? Women in Culture and the Labour Movement* (London: Routledge, 1990), p. 71. Together, sometimes in conflict, sometimes as allies, new historicism, cultural materialism, and feminism have transformed the writing of literary and cultural history, especially in the early modern period: we can no longer speak of "the text" and its "historical background," or of "authors" with the confidence we could a generation, even a decade, ago. Nor, for that matter, I suggest—attempting to mark a distance from the current dominance of New Historicism and ally myself more closely with some aspects of the agenda of both Cultural Materialism and Feminism—can we speak of them as if we ourselves were uninvolved in their construction. Inevitably, we bring our historically constructed repertoires of questions and issues into our readings. In particular, adding one more term to what has become a cliché of criticism, not to mention popular journalism, the quaternity of *class, race, gender*, and (the term I wish to add to them) *agency*, invariably plays a crucial role not just in the writing of the texts we study but those we ourselves write. Three of these four certainly play a major part in this study: class, gender, and agency are sites of major struggle in the story of the Sidney family romance that I will unfold. And while race is less prominent in this book, it should not be forgotten that the early modern period marks the opening phase of the European colonization of the New World, an enterprise on the margins of which Pembroke exerted some financial influence, as I shall note in chapter two, nor that it was the cousins' great-uncle, Sir Henry Sidney, who was one of the instruments of the English occupation and brutalization of Ireland.

9. Jacqueline Rose, "Feminine Sexuality: Interview with Juliet Mitchell and Jacqueline Rose," *m/f*, 8 (1983), 7; Philip Greven, *The Protestant Temperament: Patterns of Child-Rearing, Religious Experience, and the Self in Early America* (New York: Knopf, 1977), p. 5.

10. Juliet Mitchell, *Psychoanalysis and Feminism* (London: Allen Lane, 1974), p.xxii; Juliet Mitchell, *Woman's Estate* (Harmondsworth: Penguin, 1971), p. 167; Gilles Deleuze and Felix Guattari, *Anti-Oedipus: Capitalism and Schizophrenia*, trans. Robert Hurley, Mark Seem, and Helen R. Lane (Minneapolis: University of Minnesota Press, 1983), chapter 17; John Brenkman, *Culture and Domination* (Ithaca: Cornell University Press, 1987), pp. 196, 143; Jane Gallop, *Thinking through the Body* (New York: Columbia University Press, 1988), p. 132.

11. Eli Zaretsky, *Capitalism, the Family, and Personal Life* (New York: Harper & Row, 1976), p.128; Richard Lichtman, *The Production of Desire* (New York: Free Press, 1981), pp. x, 174; Mark Poster, *Critical Theory of the Family* (New York: Pluto Press, 1978), p. 160.

12. Fredric Jameson, *The Political Unconscious* (Princeton: Princeton University Press, 1980), p. 9.

13. Lichtman, *Production of Desire*, p. 195; Mitchell, *Psychoanalysis and Feminism*, p. xvi.

14. Daniel Dervin, "Reading Freud and Returning to Lacan: An Essay Review," *The Psychoanalytic Review*, 78 (1991), 252.

15. Michael Rustin, *The Good Society and the Inner World: Psychoanalysis, Politics and Culture* (London: Verso, 1991), pp. 15, 179, 193.

16. David Leverenz, *Manhood and American Renaissance* (Ithaca: Cornell University Press, 1989), pp. 7–8; Gallop, *Thinking through the Body*, p. 7; Camille Paglia, *Sexual Personae: Art and Decadence from Nefertiti to Emily Dickinson* (New York: Vintage, 1991).

17. See e. g., Hannah S. Decker, *Freud, Dora and Vienna* (New York: Free Press, 1990; *In Dora's Case*, ed. Charles Bernheimer and Claire Kahane (New York: Columbia University Press, 1985); Riccardo Steiner, "Dora: 'La Belle Indifference', or 'Label(le) in Difference," in *Desire*, ed. Lisa Appignanesi (London: ICA), pp. 9–13.

18. George Herbert, "The Church Militant," *The Works of George Herbert*, ed. F.E. Hutchinson (Oxford: Clarendon Press, 1941), p. 196.

19. R. W. Connell, *Gender and Power: Society, the Person, and Sexual Politics* (Cambridge: Polity Press, 1987), p. xii.

20. Marguerite Waller, "Academic Tootsie: The Denial of Difference and the Difference it Makes," *Diacritics*, 17.1 (Spring, 1987), 5.

21. Carol Thomas Neely, "Constructing the Subject: Feminist Practice and the New Renaissance Discourses," *English Literary Renaissance*, 18 (1988), 5–18; Leverenz, *Manhood*, p. 2.

22. Klaus Theweleit, *Male Fantasies, Volume I: Women, Floods, Bodies, History*, trans. Stephen Conway; *Volume II: Male Bodies: Psychoanalyzing the White Terror*, trans. Erica Carter and Chris Turner (Minneapolis: University of Minnesota Press, 1988, 1989).

23. Kaplan, *Female Perversions*, p. 405.

24. Raymond Williams, *Keywords* (London: Oxford University Press, 1983); R. W. Connell, *Gender and Power: Society, the Person, and Sexual Politics* (Cambridge: Polity Press, 1987), p. xii. For recent work in family history, see e. g. Lawrence Stone, *Family, Sex and Marriage in England, 1500–1800* (1977); Alan MacFarlane, *Marriage and Love in England: Modes of Reproduction 1300–1840* (Oxford: Blackwell, 1986); Peter Laslett, Kaula Oosterveen, and Richard M. Smith, *Bastardy and Its Comparative History* (Cambridge, Mass: Harvard University Press, 1980). For "family," see Laurence Stone, "Family History in the 1980s," *Journal of Interdisciplinary History*, 12 (1981), 51–87; Peter Laslett, "The Character of Familial History, Its Limitations and the Conditions for Its Proper Pursuit," *Journal of Family History*, 12 (1987), 263–84.

25. A useful survey of recent developments in psychoanalysis is Maurice N. Eagle, *Recent Developments in Psychoanalysis* (New York: McGraw Hill,1984). For work in object relations, see e.g., D. W. Winnicott, *The Family and Individual Development* (New York: Basic Books, 1965). Alan Roland, "The Familial Self, the Individualized Self, and the Transcendent Self: Psychoanalytic Reflections on India and America," *Psychoanalytic Review*, 74 (1987), 237, takes what he terms a "comparative civilization approach" to the "familial" and "individualized" self; he argues that there has been a major shift in psychoanalytic practices, from orthodox Freudianism to a position that acknowledges the determinative effects of social construction in the belief that "psychic structures will develop in a somewhat different way and form different gestalts within highly differing sociocultural contexts and child-rearing." Different schools of psychoanalytical criticism focused on early modern literature are represented in, e.g., *Shakespeare's Personality*, ed. Norman N. Holland, Sidney Homan, and Bernard J. Paris (Berkeley: University of California Press, 1990) and *Representing Shakespeare: New Psychoanalytic Essays*, ed. Murray Schwartz and Coppélia Kahn (Baltimore: Johns Hopkins University Press, 1980).

26. Gayle Rubin, "The Traffic in Women: Notes on the 'Political Economy' of Sex," in *Toward an Anthropology of Women*, ed. Rayna R. Reiter (New York: Monthly Review Press, 1975), p. 166.

27. Stephen Heath, *The Sexual Fix* (New York: Schocken Books, 1984), p. 145; Poster, *Critical Theory of the Family*, p. 143.

28. Laslett, "The Character of Family History," p. 274; Keith Wrightson, "Household and Kinship in Sixteenth-century England," *History Workshop*, 12 (Autumn, 1981), 154; Carol Gilligan, *In a Different Voice: Psychological Theory and Women's Development* (Cambridge, Mass.: Harvard University Press, 1982); Nancy Chodorow, *The Reproduction of Mothering: Psychoanalysis and the Sociology of Gender* (New Haven: Yale University Press, 1978); Kaplan, *Female Perversions*.

29. Althusser, quoted in Swindells and Jardine, *What's Left?*, p. 79.

30. Theweleit, *Male Fantasies*, I, p. 204. Focusing on patterns of gender formation in the early modern family, even one so well documented as the Sidneys, necessarily

involves more speculation than in what Stanley Stewart recently praised as a "no-nonsense" approach to biography. See Stanley Stewart, "Recent Studies in the English Renaissance," *Studies in English Literature, 1500–1900*, 31 (1991), 196. An instance of Stewart's "no nonsense" school, Margaret Hannay's *Philip's Phoenix*, a biography of the countess of Pembroke, takes to task those critics who indulge in what she terms "biographical speculations about [the countess's] own experience of love," dismissing such matters as "tenuous at best." To the charge that the countess's relation with her brother was, as she rather melodramatically puts it, "tainted by incest," she sternly rejoins that "given the Sidneys' piety and their unembarrassed affection for all members of their family, the charge of incest is preposterous," a comment which simply misses the point. Those critics who wish to explore oedipal and related patterns of desire within (and beyond) the family structure are not overly concerned with any physical act (John Aubrey is perhaps the dishonorable exception), but rather wish to focus on questions of fantasy formation, gender assignment, authority, and rivalry within the family, matters that are clearly fundamental to understanding the Sidneys. See Margaret Hannay, *Philip's Phoenix: Mary Sidney Countess of Pembroke* (New York: Oxford University Press, 1990), pp. 109, 259. However more firmly grounded in "facts" the "no-nonsense" school of biography might appear, it runs the fatal risk of being irrelevant to all but the most archaically or nostalgically minded readers. I have commented on the issue in more detail in "Mother/Son, Father/Daughter, Brother/Sister, Cousins: the Sidney Family Romance," *Modern Philology*, 88 (1991), 401–14.

31. Scott, *Gender*, pp. 2, 25, 28; France Morrow, *Unleashing Our Unknown Selves: An Inquiry into the Future of Femininity and Masculinity* (New York: Praeger, 1991), p. 2; Nancy Armstrong, *Desire and Domestic Fiction: a Political History of the Novel* (New York: Oxford University Press, 1987), p. 24; Connell, *Gender and Power*, p. 84; Kaplan, *Female Perversions*, p. 487.

32. Coppélia Kahn, "The Absent Mother in King Lear," in *Rewriting the Renaissance*, ed. Margaret W. Ferguson, Maureen Quilligan, and Nancy J. Vickers (Chicago: University of Chicago Press, 1986), p. 38; Abigail J. Stewart, David G. Winter, and A. David Jones, "Coding for the Study of Child-Rearing from Historical Sources," *Journal of Interdisciplinary History*, 5 (1975), 687–701; Lawrence Stone, "Passionate Attachments in the West in Historical Perspective," in *Passionate Attachments: Thinking about Love*, ed. Willard Gaylin and Ethel Person (New York: Free Press, 1988), p. 16. For Filmer, see Gordon J. Schochet, *Patriarchalism in Political Thought: The Authoritarian Family and Political Speculation and Attitudes in Seventeenth-Century England* (New York: Basic Books, 1975), and R. W. K. Hinton, "Husbands, Fathers and Conquerors," *Political Studies*, 15–16 (1967, 1968), 291–300, 55–67. Filmer is also discussed in the context of the iconography of the Renaissance family portrait by Jonathan Goldberg, "Fatherly Authority: the Politics of Stuart Family Images," in *Rewriting the Renaissance*, pp. 3–5.

33. Benjamin, *Bonds of Love*, p. 18; for Margaret Mahler, see especially Margaret S. Mahler, Fred Pine, and Anni Bergman, *The Psychological Birth of the Human Infant: Symbiosis and Individuation* (New York: Basic Books, 1975).

34. Ruth Kelso, *Doctrine for the Lady of the Renaissance* (Urbana: University of Illinois Press, 1956); Kathleen McLuskie, *Renaissance Dramatists* (Atlantic Highlands, N. J.: Humanities Press International, 1989), p. 42. Thomas Laqueur's *Making Sex* (Cambridge, Mass.: Harvard University Press, 1990), further complicates our uses of these shifting signifiers, *man, woman, male, female.* "Sex," he argues, is not a neutral, biological drive that "civilization," Freud's seductive and ubiquitous term, directs and distorts in various ways, but a term pointing to the socially constructed ways by which the body and bodily experience have been organized. He notes, for instance, "the notion, so powerful after the eighteenth century, that there had to be something outside, inside, and throughout

the body which defines male as opposed to female and which provides the foundation for an attraction of opposites is entirely absent from classical or Renaissance medicine" (p. 22). What Laqueur terms the "one-sex body" provided the dominant anatomical model for sexual differentiation in the early modern period: there was only one sex, more perfectly exemplified by men, with women seen as imperfectly formed men. But as Jean Howard has commented, even if there were (apparently) no biological basis for sexual difference, the dominant ideology of the time certainly required "the idea of two genders, one subordinate to the other, to provide a key element in its hierarchical view of the social order and to buttress its gendered division of labor." See "Crossdressing, the Theatre, and Gender Struggle in Early Modern England," *Shakespeare Quarterly*, 39 (1989), 423.

35. Louis Althusser, "Ideological State Apparatuses," *Lenin and Philosophy and Other Essays*, trans. Ben Brewster (London: New Left Books, 1971), esp. pp. 127–86.

36. See, e.g., Janet Adelman, " 'Anger is My Meat': Feeding and Dependency in 'Coriolanus'," in Schwartz and Kahn, *Representing Shakespeare*, pp. 129–45; Robert J. Stoller, "Shakespearean Tragedy: Coriolanus," *Psychoanalytical Quarterly*, 35 (1966), 263–74.

37. Greven, *Protestant Temperament*, p. 12. For a contentious but influential argument on the dominance of a cold-hearted "personality type" in the period, see Stone, *Family, Sex and Marriage*, e. g., p. 99, and the long and highly critical review of Stone's book by Alan MacFarlane, *History and Theory*, 17/18 (1978/79), 103–26. For a discussion of the importance of skin contact and touching, see Ashley Montagu, *Touching: The Human Significance of the Skin* (San Francisco: Harper & Row, 1986).

38. Boyd M. Berry, "The First English Pediatricians and Tudor Attitudes toward Childhood," *Journal of the History of Ideas*, 35 (1974), 561–77; William Perkins, "Christian Oeconomie," *The Work of William Perkins*, ed. Ian Breward (Appleford: Sutton Courtenay Press, 1970), p. 431; Stone, *Family, Sex, and Marriage*, p. 4.

39. Gary Waller, "This Matching of Contraries: The influence of Calvin and Bruno on the Sidney Circle," *Neophilologus*, 56 (1972), 331–43; David Hunt, *Parents and Children in History: The Psychology of Family Life in Early Modern France* (New York: Basic Books, 1970), p. 134.

40. Hunt, *Parents and Children*, p. 138

41. Kaplan, *Female Perversions*, p. 485; Poster, *Critical Theory of the Family*, p. 181.

42. Nancy Hartsock, *Money, Sex, and Power: Toward a Feminist Historical Materialism* (London: Longmans, 1983), p. 238. My exposition at this point owes much, in both ideas and phrasing, to Benjamin's brilliant argument in *A Desire of One's Own*, pp. 9–11, which is elaborated in *The Bonds of Love: Psychoanalysis, Feminism, and the Problem of Domination* (New York: Pantheon), p. 102.

43. Doris Bernstein, "The Female Superego: a Different Perspective," *International Journal of Psychoanalysis*, 64 (1983), 192.

44. *Henry Howard Earl of Surrey: Poems*, ed. Emrys Jones (Oxford: Clarendon Press, 1964), p. 321; *The Penguin Book of Renaissance Verse 1609–1659*, ed. David Norbrook and H. R. Woodhuysen (Harmondsworth: Penguin, 1992), p. 17; Stone, *Sex, Love and Marriage*, p. 4.

45. For discussions of Deleuze and Guattari's re-reading of Freud on this point see Theweleit, *Male Fantasies*, I, p. 327, and Benjamin, *Bonds of Love*, p. 96. Russell Jacoby has argued that Freud's disciple Otto Fenichel came closer than Freud to detailing the social construction of family romances and other neuroses. Fenichel wrote: "Neuroses do not occur out of biological necessity, like aging . . . Neuroses are social diseases . . . the outcome of unfavorable and socially determined educational measures, corresponding to a given and historically developed social milieu." See Russell Jacoby, *The Repression of*

Psychoanalysis: Otto Fenichel and the Political Freudians (New York: Basic Books, 1983), p. 120.

46. Dollimore, *Sexual Dissidence*, pp. 27, 103–05; Kaplan, *Female Perversions*, pp. 9–11, 518.

47. *Freud to Fliess*, p. 257; Freud, "Creative Writing and Day-dreaming," *Standard Edition*, IX, p. 145.

48. Benjamin, *Bonds of Love*, p. 102; Freud, "Female Sexuality," *Standard Edition*, XXI, p. 231; Benjamin, *Desire of One's Own*, p. 3; Hartsock, Money, Sex, and Power, p. 242.

49. Benjamin, *Bonds of Love*, p. 75

50. Robert J. Stoller, *Perversion: The Erotic Form of Hatred* (London: Mansfield Library, 1975), p. 99.

51. Paglia, *Sexual Personae*, p. 287.

52. Benjamin, *Bonds of Love*, pp. 95, 47.

53. Kaplan, *Female Perversions*, p. 174, 88.

54. Benjamin, *Bonds of Love*, pp. 86, 60; Freud, " 'A child is being beaten': A Contribution to the Study of the Origin of Sexual Perversion," *Standard Edition*, XVII, pp. 175–204; Bernstein, "Female Superego," 192.

55. Nancy Chodorow, "Gender, Relations and Difference in Psychoanalytical Perspective," in *The Future of Difference*, ed. Hester Eisenstein and Alice Jardine (Boston: G. K. Hall. 1980), pp. 3–19.

56. Natalie Zemon Davis, "Boundaries and the Sense of Self in Sixteenth-Century France," in *Reconstructing Individualism*, ed. Thomas C. Heller, Morton Sosna, and David E. Welbury (Stanford: Stanford University Press, 1986), p. 63.

57. John Stevens, *Medieval Romance* (New York: Norton, 1974), pp. 16, 40.

58. Northrop Frye, *Anatomy of Criticism* (Princeton: Princeton University Press, 1957) and *A Natural Perspective: the Development of Shakespearean Comedy and Romance* (New York: Columbia University Press, 1965). For a recent feminist rereading of romance, see Tania Modleski, *Loving with a Vengeance: Mass-Produced Fantasies for Women* (London: Methuen, 1984).

59. Paglia, *Sexual Personae*, p. 4.

60. Gaston Bachelard, *The Poetics of Space*, trans. Maria Jolas (Boston: Beacon Press, 1969); Michel Foucault, "Of Other Spaces," Diacritics, 16 (1986), 22–27; Mark Girouard, *Life in an English Country House: A Social and Architectural History* (Harmondsworth: Penguin, 1980), p. 57. I owe some of the formulation in this paragraph to Scott Wilson, "Sir Philip Sidney and the Extraordinary Forms of Desire," *Assays*, 7 (1993), which I was privileged to read in typescript.

61. Raymond Williams, *The Country and the City* (London: Chatto and Windus, 1973), preface.

62. Nicholas Breton, *Wits Trenchmour* (London: N. Ling, 1597), p. 18; *The Pilgrimage to Paradise* (Oxford: J. Barnes, 1592), introduction; Williams, *Country and City*, p. 33.

63. Don Wayne, *Penshurst: The Semiotics of Place and the Poetics of History* (Milwaukee: University of Wisconsin Press, 1984); see also J. C. A. Rathmell, "Jonson, Lord Lisle, and Penshurst," *English Literary Renaissance*, 1 (1972), 250–60.

64. Michael G. Brennan, *Literary Patronage in the English Renaissance* (London: Routledge, 1988), pp. 33, 42.

Chapter Two

1. *HMC Salisbury*, XI, p. 340; Barbara Ehrenreich, "Introduction," *Male Fantasies*, I, p. xvi.

2. Stanley Kojnacki, "Comment: Blurring Genders," *Renaissance Quarterly*, 40 (1987), 746.

3. Paglia, *Sexual Personae*, pp. 268, 9.

4. There has been only one substantial biography of Pembroke published, that by Andreas Gebauer, *Von Macht und Mazenatentum: Leben und Werk William Herberts, der dritten Earls von Pembroke* (Heidelberg: Winter, 1987). Brennan's *Literary Patronage* has four valuable chapters on his career and influence. Over twenty years ago Dick Taylor, Jr., published a number of essays on Pembroke's career: "Clarendon and Ben Jonson as Witnesses for the Earl of Pembroke's Character," in Josephine W. Bennett, Oscar Cargill, and Vernon Hall, Jr., *Studies in the English Renaissance Drama* (London: Peter Owen, 1961); "The Third Earl of Pembroke as a Patron of Poetry," *Tulane Studies in English*, 5 (1955), 41–67; "The Masque and the Lance: the Earl of Pembroke in Jacobean Court Entertainments," *Tulane Studies in English*, 8 (1958), 21–53. There are also two exhaustively documented unpublished dissertations on Pembroke's career: J. R. Briley, "William Herbert, Third Earl of Pembroke" (University of Birmingham, 1961), and Brian O'Farrell, "Politician, Patron, Poet: William Herbert, Third Earl of Pembroke, 1580–1630" (U.C.L.A., 1966). For the family background, see Brennan, *Literary Patronage*, chapter one, and Narasingha P. Sil, *William Lord Herbert of Pembroke (c.1507–1570): Politique and Patriot* (Lewiston, N. Y.: Edwin Mellen, 1988).

5. *Aubrey's Brief Lives*, ed. O. L. Dick (Harmondsworth: Penguin, 1962), pp. 138–40; Rudolf Holzapfel, *Shakespeare's Secret* (Dublin: Dolmen Press, 1961), pp. xi-xii; John Dover Wilson, ed., *The Sonnets* (Cambridge: Cambridge University Press, 1969), pp. lxxxviii-cviii; John Padel, *New Poems by Shakespeare* (London: The Herbert Press, 1981); Stephen Booth, ed., *Shakespeare's Sonnets* (New Haven: Yale University Press, 1977), pp. 543–46. For examples of earlier scholars claiming Pembroke as either "W. H." and/or the "Fair Youth," see, e.g., *Shakespeare's Sonnets*, ed. Thomas Tyler (London: David Nutt, 1800); James Boaden, *On the Sonnets of Shakespeare* (London: Thomas Rodd, 1837).

6. [Mary Erskine,] *Memoirs Relating to the Queen of Bohemia By one of her ladies* (London: n. p., 1770), p. 62; for the Countess of Bedford's remark, see Gebauer, p. 126. Clarendon's shrewd five pages are the most substantial account of Pembroke until the contemporary studies by Briley, O'Farrell, Brennan, and Gebauer: see Edward Hyde, Earl of Clarendon, *The History of the Rebellion and Civil Wars in England* (Oxford: Clarendon Press, 1839), I, pp. 87–91; Clarendon's account is largely repeated by David Lloyd, *The Statesmen and Favourites of England Since the Reformation* (London: Samuel Speed, 1665), pp. 687–89. Gardner's nineteenth-century account is more hostile: see note 61 below.

7. Coppélia Kahn, *Man's Estate: Masculine Identity in Shakespeare* (Berkeley: University of California Press, 1981), pp. 55, 12, 20.

8. As Linda Pollock usefully remarks, in reconstructing a personality profile, especially one that stresses the effects of childhood experiences on later behavioral and attitudinal patterns, we should remind ourselves that there is inevitably a gap between expert child rearing manuals of our own time, like those of Benjamin Spock or Penelope Leach, and our own various experiences as parents and children. We need to realize how more complex and over determined individual experiences inevitably are than the pattern typified in any handbook or manual. See *Forgotten Children: Parent-Child Relations from 1500 to 1900* (Cambridge: Cambridge University Press, 1981).

9. Greven, *The Protestant Temperament*, p. 3.

10. Mary Ellen Lamb, *Gender and Authorship in the Sidney Circle* (Madison: University of Wisconsin Press, 1990), chapter 1.

11. Walter Sweeper, *A Briefe Treatise Declaring the True Noble-man, and the Base Worldling* (1623), sigs. A3[r]-A4.[v]

12. Gary Waller, *Mary Sidney, Countess of Pembroke: A Critical Study of her Writings and Literary Milieu* (Salzburg: Universitat Salzburg, 1979), chapter three; Waller, Mother/Son," 404–09.

13. Breton, *Wits Trenchmour*, p. 18; *Pilgrimage to Paradise*, introduction.

14. Abraham Fraunce, *The Third Part of the Countesses of Pembrokes Ivychurch* (1592), sig A2ʳ; *The Countess of Pembrokes Ivychurch* (1591), sigs. B2ᵛ, E1ᵛ, E2ᵛ. For the Countess of Pembroke's support of militant Protestant policies, see Hannay, *Philip's Phoenix*, chapter 4.

15. Mary Ellen Lamb, "Effeminizing Fictions in *Macbeth, The Winter's Tale,* and *The Tempest*," paper presented at the Shakespeare Association of America, Kansas City, April, 1992; Briley, "William Herbert," p. 190. For the discussion of Elyot, I am indebted to Mary Ellen Lamb's unpublished paper, "Apologizing for Pleasure in Sidney's *Apology for Poetry*."

16. Briley, "William Herbert," p. 323.

17. See also Thomas Moffet, *Nobilis* (1594), preface, where the young William Herbert is described to Sidney's shade as "your second self (unless the growing shoot deceives me)."

18. *Nobilis*, pp. 95, 107. For a discussion of some of the tributes to Pembroke, see Taylor, "Pembroke as a Patron," 41–67.

19. Margot Heinemann, *Puritanism and Theatre* (Cambridge: Cambridge University Press, 1980), p. 214; Philip Massinger, *The Bondman*, ed. B. T. Spenser (Princeton: Princeton University Press, 1932).

20. Paglia, *Sexual Personae*, p. 7; Freud, "Civilisation and its Discontents," *Standard Edition*, XXI, pp. 114, 111, 112. For an alternative view to Freud's, see Richard E. Leakey, *The Making of Mankind* (New York: E. P. Dutton, 1981).

21. Theweleit, *Male Fantasies*, I, p. 276; II, p. 9.

22. Ehrenreich, "Introduction," *Male Fantasies*, I, p. xii.

23. See e.g., Roy Strong, *Splendor at Court* (Boston: Houghton Mifflin, 1973), esp. chs. 2, 6; Frances Yates, "Elizabethan Chivalry: the Romance of the Accession Day Tilts," *Astraea: The Imperial Theme in the Sixteenth Century* (London: Routledge and Kegan Paul, 1975), pp. 88–111.

24. Richard C. McCoy, *The Rites of Knighthood: the Literature and Politics of Elizabethan Chivalry* (Berkeley: University of California Press, 1989), pp. 23–24; William Segar, *The Booke of Honor and Armes*, ed. Diane Bornstein (Delmar, N.Y.: Scholars' Facsimiles and Reprints, 1975), pp. 89–90; John Nichols, *The Progresses, Processions, and Magnificent Festivities, of King James the First* (New York: B. Franklin, 1968), III, pp. 392–93.

25. Robert Barret, *The Theorike and Practike of Modern Wars* (1598; rpt. New York: Da Capo Press, 1969), preface, p. 3.

26. Jonathan Goldberg, "Fatherly Authority," p. 8.

27. Maureen Quilligan, "Lady Mary Wroth: Female Authority and the Family Romance," in *Unfolded Tales: Essays on the Renaissance Romance*, ed. Gordon M. Logan and Gordon Teskey, (Ithaca: Cornell University Press, 1989), pp. 274–78; Paglia, *Sexual Personae*, p. 173. For portraits of Pembroke, see A. M. Hind, *Engraving in England* (Cambridge: Cambridge University Press), plate 157; Ellis Waterhouse, *Painting in Britain 1530 to 1790* (Harmondsworth: Penguin, 1969) p. 58; Roy Strong, *The English Icon* (London: Routledge Kegan Paul, 1969), p. 287. For an account of the portraits of Pembroke at Wilton House, see [Herbert] Sidney, *A Catalogue of the Paintings and Drawings in the Collection at Wilton House* (London: Phaeton, 1968).

28. Quilligan, "Female Authority," p. 276; Theweleit, *Male Fantasies*, II, p. 150; Benjamin, *Bonds of Love*, p. 50.

29. Mark Roskill, "Van Dyck at the English Court: the Relations of Portrait and Allegory," *Critical Inquiry*, 14 (1987), 199.

30. Bernstein, "The Female Superego," p. 192.

31. Stoller, *Perversion*, p. 99; Theweleit, *Male Fantasies*, I, p. 213; Benjamin, *Bonds of Love*, p. 135.

32. Theweleit, *Male Fantasies*, I, p. 222; Kahn, *Man's Estate*, p. 55; Kaplan, *Female Perversions*, p. 103.

33. Jonathan Dollimore, *Sexual Dissidence: Augustine to Wilde, Freud to Foucault* (Oxford: Clarendon Press, 1991), p. 305; Benjamin, *Bonds of Love*, p. 164; Kaplan, *Female Perversions*, p. 107. I owe the references to Machiavelli to Kay Stanton's paper at the 1992 Shakespeare Association meeting at Kansas City, "*The Prince* versus the 'The Princess': Machiavellian 'Masculinity' and Subversion by the Fortune of 'Femininity' in *Henry V*." Hannay, *Philip's Phoenix*, p. 50, notes that Pembroke was so appreciative of the care of his nurse that he later rewarded her husband, Edward Williams, with the bailiwick of Llantrissent.

34. Paglia, *Sexual Personae*, pp. 173, 19, 10; Judith Butler, *Gender Trouble: Feminism and the Subversion of Identity* (London: Routledge, 1990), p. 122.

35. Dollimore, *Sexual Deviance*; Freud, "On the Universal Tendency to Debasement in Love," *Standard Edition*, XI, pp. 181, 189. See also W. Ralph Leyland, "The Use of a Mistress and the Internalized Sexual Mother," *International Journal of Psychoanalysis*, 65 (1984), 323–30.

36. *The Latin Poetry of George Herbert: A Bilingual Edition*, trans. Mark McCloskey and Paul R. Murphy (Athens, Ohio.: Ohio University Press, 1985), pp. 123–55. I owe these observations to Deborah Rubin's paper on "Representing Women's Lives and Voices," at the 1990 conference at the University of Maryland, "Attending to Women in Early Modern England."

37. Freud, "Leonardo da Vinci and a Memory of his Childhood," *Standard Edition*, XI, p. 108.

38. Julia Kristeva, *Tales of Love*, trans. Leon S. Roudiez (New York: Columbia University Press, 1987), p. 202. See also Joseph H. Smith, "Evening the Score," *Modern Language Notes*, 104 (1989), 1050–65. Paglia, *Sexual Personae*, p. 339, comes close to acknowledging her description of men as inherently aggressive and women as the embodiment of the irresistible chtnonian forces of nature as "ideological" rather than "inherent" when she notes: "That the penis is power is one of the social lies men tell themselves to overcome their fear of the daemonism of sex." She then resumes her astounding essentialism by asserting: "That women can drain and paralyze is part of the latent vampirism in female physiology. The archetype of the femme fatale began in prehistory and will live forever."

39. Edmund Lodge, *Illustrations of British History* (1791), III, p. 243; Hannay, *Philip's Phoenix*, p. 155; Arthur Collins, *Letters and Memorials of State* (1746), II, pp. 43, 118, 122. Whyte was at Christ Church, Oxford, at the same time as Robert Sidney, and was working for him by 1589, when he was clerk of the ordnance at Flushing. He lived at Baynard's Castle and, although primarily employed by Sidney, accompanied Pembroke on some progresses. See Lodge, III, pp. 102–05, and Millicent Hay, *The Life of Robert Sidney* (Washington, D.C.: Folger Library, 1984), pp. 153–57.

40. *HMC Salisbury*, XI, pp. 340, 361.

41. Clarendon, *History*, I, pp. 5, 10; Waller, *English Poetry*, pp. 13–31; *Life and Letters of John Donne*, ed. Edmund Gosse (Gloucester, Mass.: Peter Smith, 1959), II, p. 190. For Holles's remark, see *HMC Portland*, IX, p. 129.

42. Collins, *Letters and Memorials*, II, pp. 216, 220.

43. *HMC Salisbury*, XI, p. 340; John Donne, "To Sir Henry Wotton, at his Going

NOTES TO CHAPTER TWO

Ambassador to Venice," *The Complete English Poems*, ed. A. J. Smith (Harmondsworth: Penguin, 1971), p. 217; Donne, *Life and Letters*, I, p. 168.

44. Donne, *Life and Letters*, I, p. 190.

45. *HMC Salisbury*, XI, p. 340; Collins, *Letters and Memorials*, II, pp. 113, 115, 118, 165; Steven R. Brown, "Child Raising and Melancholia in Tudor England," *Journal of Psychohistory*, 5 (1978), 58, 69; Otto F. Kernburg, *Borderline Conditions and Pathological Narcissism* (New York: Jason Aronson, 1975), is uncannily relevant here, especially pp. 17, 233–36, 264; Kristeva, *Tales of Love*, p. 193.

46. Briley, "William Herbert," p. 323; Collins, *Letters and Memorials*, II, pp. 122, 139, 144.

47. Hannay, *Philip's Phoenix*, pp. 167, 168; Berry, "The First English Pediatricians," 561–77.

48. *Freud to Fliess*, p. 317; see also Paglia, *Sexual Personae*, p. 258. For the sibling sexuality studies, see Stephen P. Bank and Michael D. Kahn, *The Sibling Bond* (New York: Basic Books, 1982), chapter 7.

49. Freud, "Special Type of Choice," pp. 165–73; Heath, *Sexual Fix*, p. 25; Paglia, *Sexual Personae*, p. 27.

50. *Letters from Sir Robert Cecil to Sir George Carew*, ed. John Maclean (London: Camden Society, 1864), p. 65; *HMC Salisbury*, XI, pp. 201, 340, 361; Lady Newdigate-Newdigate, *Gossip from a Muniment Room* (London: David Nutt, 1897), pp. 42, 37; PRO SP15/34/38, quoted in Gebauer, *Von Macht*, p. 43; *HMC Carew Manuscripts*, IV, p. 20; *HMC Salisbury*, XI, p. 340.

51. Kaplan, *Female Perversions*, p. 405; *HMC Salisbury*, XI, p. 464; Briley, "William Herbert," p. 466.

52. John Davies, *Microcosmos: The Discovery of the Little World, with the Government thereof* (Oxford: J. Barnes, 1603), p. 14; Briley, "William Herbert," pp. 409, 410; *HMC Salisbury*, XI, pp. 464, 40.

53. Hannay, *Philip's Phoenix* mentions only in passing, pp. 171, 173, 184, the quarrel between Pembroke and his mother. See *Talbot Collection* M, fol. 259; *HMC De L'Isle and Dudley*, III, p. 312; Briley, "William Herbert," 466. Briley, "William Herbert," chapter 10 has the fullest documentation of the long and tortuous attempts by Herbert's parents to get him married, and of his own marriage negotiations. See also Gebauer, *Von Macht*, pp. 22–23, 29, 31–32, 34.

54. *HMC De L'Isle and Dudley*, II, p. 478; Clarendon, *History*, I, p. 289.

55. *HMC Salisbury*, XVI, p. 383; Lodge, *Illustrations*, III, pp. 124, 138–39, 148–54, 161; Gebauer, pp. 71–74, reprints the letters from the Talbot Papers. See also *HMC Shrewsbury and Talbot*, II, pp. 240, 242, 249.

56. Thomas Birch, *The Court and Times of James the First* (London: Thomas Colburn, 1848), p. 190; *HMC Salisbury*, XI, p. 40; R. Malcolm Smuts, *Court Culture and the Origins of a Royalist Tradition in Early Stuart England* (Philadelphia: University of Pennsylvania Press, 1987), p. 59; *The Life and Letters of Sir Henry Wotton*, ed. Logan Pearsall Smith (Oxford: Clarendon, 1907), II, pp. 16–17; *HMC Bath*, p. 128.

57. *CSP Venice, 1623–25*, p. 216; Sir Francis Bacon, *The Essayes or Counsels, Civill and Morall*, ed. Michael Kiernan (Cambridge, Mass.: Harvard University Press, 1985), p. 33.

58. Freud, "Group Psychology," *Standard Edition*, XVIII, pp. 122–23; "Totem and Taboo," *Standard Edition*, XIII, pp. 125–26, 141–46.

59. Nichols, *Progresses*, I, p. 472; *HMC Bath* V, p. 128.

60. For the quarrel with Wharton, see Nichols, *Progresses*, III, pp. 241–45.

61. Samuel R. Gardner, *History of England from the Accession of James I to the Outbreak of the Civil War 1603–1642* (London: Longman, Green, 1883), VI, p. 133; Briley, "William Herbert," Appendix.

62. Robert C. Evans, "Literature as Equipment for Living: Ben Jonson and the Politics of Patronage," *College Literature Association Journal*, 30 (1987), pp. 379–80; Donne, *Life and Letters*, 1, p. 190.

63. Thomas Nashe, *Pierce Pennilesse*, in *Works*, ed. E. D. McKerrow (New York: Barnes and Noble, 1958), I, p. 159. Brennan, *Literary Patronage*, chapter six, summarizes Pembroke's literary connections and patronage in detail.

64. Ben Jonson, *Conversations with William Drummond of Hawthornden*, ed. G. B. Harrison (New York: Barnes and Noble, 1966), p. 14.

65. Daniel Featley, *The Grand Sacrilege of the Church of Rome* (1630), dedication; *CSP Venice 1623–30*, XIV, p. 245. For Pembroke's part in the staging of *A Game at Chesse*, see Heinemann, *Puritanism and Theatre*, pp. 166ff., 268, 269; for references to him in *The Bondman*, see Jerzy Limon, *Dangerous Matter: English Drama and Politics in 1623/4* (Cambridge: Cambridge University Press, 1986), pp. 64–76.

66. For detailed discussion of the family's wealth in the period, see O'Farrell, "Politician, Patron, Poet," chapter 1.

67. *CSP Venice 1603–7*, X, p. 77.

68. *The Letters of John Chamberlain*, ed. Norman E. McClure (Westport, Conn.: Greenwood Press, 1979), II, p. 144; *CSP Domestic 1611–18*, p. 144; O'Farrell, "Politician, Patron, Poet," chapter four, has a painstakingly detailed account of Pembroke's accumulation of parliamentary support. See also Robert E. Ruigh, *The Parliament of 1624* (Cambridge, Mass.: Harvard University Press, 1971), esp. pp. 36, 126–31.

69. Briley, "William Herbert," p. 580; Freud, "Group Psychology," *Standard Edition*, XVIII, p. 122. For James's letter, see *Letters of the Kings of England*, ed. J. O. Halliwell (London: n.p., 1848), II, 126–32.

70. Briley, "William Herbert," pp. 595–96.

71. David Harris Willson, *The Privy Councillors in the House of Commons 1604–1629* (New York: Octagon Books, 1971), p. 38; "Summoning and Dissolving Parliament, 1603–1625," *American History Review*, 45 (1940), 297. Pembroke's sentiments were expressed in almost the same words in 1621: see British Library Add. MS 34324, fol. 149, and Robert Zaller, *The Parliament of 1621: A Study in Constitutional Conflict* (Berkeley: University of California Press, 1971), p. 185.

72. O'Farrell, "Politician, Patron, Poet," p. 181, nn. 40, 44; p. 185, n. 88.

73. Samuel R. Gardner, "Notes by Sir James Bagg on the Parliament of 1626," *Notes and Queries*, 4th series (1872), 325–26.

74. *CSP Dom. MSS Add. 1625–49*, p. 295.

75. *CSP Dom. MSS Add. 1625–49*, p. 290; see the discussion in Roger Lockyer, *Buckingham* (London: Longman, 1981), p. 333.

76. *CSP Venice 1629–32*, p. 329; Sir Thomas Herbert, "Herbertorum Prosapia," Cardiff Central Library Phillipps MS 5.7, 93. For an account of the prophecies of Pembroke's death, see Briley, "William Herbert," chapter 18 and Gebauer, pp. 162–64. For detailed accounts of Pembroke's death, see Birch, *Life and Times*, I, pp. 123–32; Gebauer, pp. 158–60; Briley, "William Herbert," p. 409.

77. T[homas] C[haffinger], *The Just Mans Memorial* (London: Elizabeth Allde, 1630), sigs. A3^{r-v}, A4^{r}.

Chapter Three

1. [Samuel Dugard,] *The Marriages of Cousin Germans, Vindicated from the Censures of Unlawfulnesse, and Inexpediency* (London: n. p., 1673), pp. 106, 8; Kaplan, *Female Perversions*, p. 182.

2. Kaplan, *Female Perversions*, p. 505.

3. Sara Heller Mendelson, *The Mental World of Stuart Women* (Brighton: Harvester, 1987), pp. 10–11.

NOTES TO CHAPTER THREE

4. Benjamin, *Bonds of Love*, pp. 116, 122–23.

5. Hélène Deutsch, *The Psychology of Women* (London: Research Books, 1946), p. 195; Benjamin, *Desire of One's Own*, p. 7; see also Kaplan, *Female Perversions*, pp. 184, 454.

6. Hartsock, *Money, Sex, and Power*, p. 2; Margaret Hannay, " 'Your vertuous and learned Aunt': The Countess of Pembroke as a Mentor to Mary Wroth," in *Reading Mary Wroth: Representing Alternatives in Early Modern England*, ed. Naomi J. Miller and Gary Waller (Knoxville: University of Tennessee Press, 1991), pp. 15–34; Sheila Rowbotham, quoted in Swindells and Jardine, *What's Left?*, p. 88. Again, Paglia's *Sexual Personae* articulates—more blatantly than most men, at least today, would want (or dare) to do—the patriarchal assumption that men are somehow inherently more able to be artists than women who embody, in their very nature, the "chthonian black magic" with which the artist struggles. See e. g., pp. 28–29, and the following, on pp. 295–96: "In *A Room of One's Own*, Virginia Woolf satirically describes her perplexity at the bulging card catalog of the British Museum: why, she asks, are there so many books written by men about women but none by women about men? The answer to her question is that from the beginning of time men have been struggling with the threat of women's dominance. The flood of books was prompted not by woman's weakness but by her strength, her complexity and impenetrability, her dreadful omniscience."

7. Ann Shaver, "Outspoken Women in Book I of Lady Mary Wroth's *Urania*," *Sidney Newsletter*, 10.1 (1990), 89; Donne, *Complete Poems*, pp. 84–85.

8. R. Johnston, *Historia Rerum Britannicarum* (Amsterdam: Sumtibes J. Roses-teysii, 1655), p. 443. For a somewhat melodramatic but lively account of Penelope's life, see Sylvia Freedman, *Poor Penelope* (Abbotsbrook: The Kensal Press, 1983).

9. Dollimore, *Sexual Dissidence*, pp. 119–20; Simon Shepherd, *Amazons and Warrior Women: Varieties of Feminism in Seventeenth-century Drama* (Brighton: Harvester, 1981), pp. 1, 107–28; Louis A. Montrose, "The Work of Gender in the Discourse of Discovery," *Representations*, 33 (1991), 25–27; Lynda E. Boose, "The Father's House and the Daughter in It: the Structures of Western Culture's Daughter-Father Relationship," in *Daughters and Fathers*, ed. Lynda E. Boose and Betty S. Flowers (Baltimore: Johns Hopkins University Press, 1989), p. 34.

10. Freud, "The Neuroses of Defence: A Christmas Fairy Tale," *Standard Edition*, I, pp. 224–25; Alison M. Jaggar, *Feminist Politics and Human Nature* (Totowa, N.J.: Rowman and Allanheld, 1983).

11. Constance Jordan, *Renaissance Feminism: Literary Texts and Political Models* (Ithaca: Cornell University Press, 1990), p. 221.

12. *The Kristeva Reader*, ed. Toril Moi (New York: Columbia University Press, 1986), p. 242; Benjamin, *Bonds of Love*, p. 128; Donna Bassin, "Woman's Images of Inner Space: Data Towards Expanded Interpretive Categories," *International Review of Psychoanalysis*, 9 (1982), 195,196,198; Paglia, *Sexual Personae*, p. 23. See also D. W. Winnicott, "Transitional Objects and Transitional Phenomena" and "The Location of Cultural Experience," in *Playing and Reality* (London: Methuen, 1971), and the discussion in Claire Kahane, "Questioning the Maternal Voice," *Genders*, 3 (1986), 89–90.

13. Joan [Kelly-]Gadol, "Notes on Women in the Renaissance and Renaissance Historiography," *Conceptual Frameworks for Studying Women's History*, ed. Marylin Arthur et al. (Lawrence: University of Kansas, 1975), pp. 4–7; Kristeva, *Tales of Love*, p. 112; Benjamin, *Desire of One's Own*, p. 18.

14. Lamb, *Gender and Authorship*, p. 88.

15. Miranda Chaytor, "Household and Kinship: Ryton in the late 16th and early 17th Centuries," *History Workshop Journal*, 10 (1980), 49; *The Lady Falkland, Her Life*, ed. Richard I. Simpson (London: Catholic Publishing and Bookselling Co., 1861), p. 132.

16. Kristeva, "Stabat Mater," *Tales of Love*, p. 234; Haunami-Kay Trask, *Eros and Power: the Promise of Feminist Theory* (Philadelphia: University of Pennsylvania Press, 1986), p. x; Benjamin, *Bonds of Love*, pp. 93, 206.

17. Benjamin, *Bonds of Love*, p. 116; Laqueur, *Making Sex*, e.g., pp. 65, 149.

18. Edward Shorter, "On Writing the History of Rape," *Signs*, 3 (1977–78), 474; Hunt, *Parents and Children in History*, p. 80.

19. Chamberlain to Carleton, 20 February, 1619, *Chamberlain Letters*, II, p. 216. See Ruth Kelso, *Doctrine for the Lady of the Renaissance* (Urbana: University of Illinois Press, 1956). For the woman controversy, see Sandra Clark, "*Hic Mulier, Haec Vir*, and the Controversy over Masculine Women," *Studies in Philology*, 82 (1985), 157–83.

20. Ann Rosalind Jones, "Surprising Fame: Renaissance Gender Ideologies and Women's Lyric," in *The Politics of Gender*, ed. Nancy Miller (New York: Columbia University Press, 1986), p. 79.

21. E. g. *Urania*, p. 409; Denise Riley, *"Am I that Name": Feminism and the Category of "Women" in History* (Minneapolis: University of Minnesota Press, 1988), p. 105; Peter Stallybrass, "Patriarchal Territories: The Body Enclosed," in *Rewriting the Renaissance*, p. 129.

22. Lamb, *Gender and Authorship*, pp. 26, 25.

23. Benjamin, Bonds of Love, p. 116; *CSP Domestic 1619–23*, pp. 37, 40; *HMC De L'Isle and Dudley*, II, p. 233; 4, pp. 40, 44, 53, 134.

24. *HMC De L'Isle and Dudley*, II, pp. 2, 4, 44; Margaret McLaren [Witten-Hannah], "Lady Mary Wroth's *Urania*: The Work and the Tradition," (unpub. diss., University of Auckland, 1978), 19.

25. Collins, *Letters and Memorials*, II, p. 81; *HMC De L'Isle and Dudley*, II, pp. 488, 100; Collins, *Letters and Memorials*, II, pp. 41–42, 152. The fullest survey of Wroth's life is McLaren's, in "*Urania*," chapters 1–2. See also Roberts, *Poems*, pp. 6–40; Hannay, "Countess of Pembroke as Mentor" and Waller, "Family Romance," in Miller and Waller, *Reading Mary Wroth*, pp. 14–63.

26. *HMC De L'Isle and Dudley*, II, p. 176.

27. Collins, *Letters and Memorials*, II, p. 81; *HMC De L'Isle and Dudley*, II, pp. 191, 261.

28. *HMC de L'Isle and Dudley*, II, p. 420.

29. Kahn "The Absent Mother in 'King Lear,'" p. 33; Kahane, "Questioning the Maternal Voice," p. 82; *HMC De L'Isle, and Dudley* II, pp. 268, 618–19.

30. For the Wroth family, see William Chapman Waller, "An Extinct County Family: Wroth of Loughton Hall," *Transactions of the Essex Archaeological Society*, n.s. 8 (1903), 145–80, and D. O. Pam, *Protestant Gentlemen: The Wroths of Durants Arbour, Enfield and Loughton, Essex* (Edmonton, Essex: Edmonton Hundred Historical Society, Occasional Paper, n.s. 25, 1973).

31. Waller, "Extinct County Family," 155–56.

32. Waller, "Extinct County Family," 155–56; Daniel Lysons, *The Environs of London* (London: L. P., 1792–96), II, pp. 299–301.

33. *HMC De L'Isle and Dudley*, III, pp. 127–28, 130, 134, 139, 140; McLaren, "*Urania*," pp. 21–25; Josephine A. Roberts, "The Knott Never to Bee Untide': The Controversy Regarding Marriage in Mary Wroth's *Urania*," in *Reading Mary Wroth*, pp. 121–23; Jonson, *Conversations*, p. 15.

34. *HMC De L'Isle and Dudley*, III, pp. 139, 140, 127–28, 134. McLaren, "*Urania*," pp. 47–49, 64, comments on the closeness between Wroth and the Countess of Montgomery.

35. Roberts, *Poems*, pp. 11, 14–22

36. Paul A. Cubeta, "A Jonsonian Ideal: 'To Penshurst'," *Philological Quarterly*, 42

(1963), 187; *The Complete Poetry of Ben Jonson*, ed. William B. Hunter, Jr. (New York: New York University Press, 1963), pp. 48, 49, 50, 57, 77–84, 93, 110–11, 166.

37. Jonson, *Poetry*, pp. 81–84.

38. Williams, *Country and the City*, p. 17.

39. David Norbrook, *Poetry and Politics in the English Renaissance* (London: Routledge and Kegan Paul, 1984), pp. 190, 192; Roberts, *Poems*, p. 23.

40. Rathmell, "Jonson," pp. 250–260; Jonson, *Conversations*, p. 14.

41. Hunt, *Parents and Children in History*, p. 83

42. *CSP Domestic 1611–18*, p. 227; Waller, "Extinct County Family," p. 165; *HMC De L'Isle and Dudley*, V, pp. 298–301.

43. Christianne Klapisch-Zuber, *Women, Family, and Ritual in Renaissance Italy*, trans, Lydia Cochrane (Chicago: University of Chicago Press, 1985), p. 119.

44. *HMC De L'Isle and Dudley*, V, pp. 414, 422. For the connections with the Herberts, see Amy M. Charles, *A Life of George Herbert* (Ithaca: Cornell University Press, 1977), p. 120.

45. Waller, "Extinct County Family," pp. 167, 174, 176, 167, 173, 174, 176, 178. Roberts, *Poems*, pp. 59–60. See, e.g., *CSP Domestic 1619–23*, pp. 596, 599.

46. M. A. Beese, "A Critical Edition of the Poems Printed by John Donne the Younger in 1660, As Written by William Herbert, Earl of Pembroke, and Sir Benjamin Ruddier," unpub. B.Litt. diss. (Oxford University, 1935), pp. 98–99. For an account of the reliability of the Herbert family records, see Norman H. McKenzie, "Sir Thomas Herbert of Tintern: A Parliamentary 'Royalist,' " *Bulletin of the Institute of Historical Research*, 29 (1956), 32–86.

47. *The Diary of the Lady Anne Clifford*, introd. V. Sackville-West (London: Heinemann, 1923), pp. 16–17; *Letters from Sir Robert Cecil to Sir George Carew*, ed. John Maclean (Camden Society, 1864), p. 65; John Updike, *Couples* (London: André Deutsch, 1968), p. 429.

48. Shorter, "History of Rape," p. 494; Chaytor, "Household and Kinship," p. 44.

49. *Marriages of Cousin Germans*, p. 5.

50. Kaplan, *Female Perversions*, pp. 128, 105.

51. Boose, *Fathers and Daughters*, p. 441.

52. Benjamin, *Bonds of Love*, pp. 62, 45.

53. Roberts, " 'The Knott Never to Bee Untide,' " in *Reading Mary Wroth*, pp. 109–32; Susan Brownmiller, *Against their Will: Men, Women, and Rape* (New York: Simon and Schuster, 1975); Shorter, "History of Rape," p. 494.

54. Ivy Pinchbeck and Margaret Hewitt, *Children in English Society Vol I: From Tudor Times to the Eighteenth Century* (London: Routledge Kegan Paul, 1969), p. 203.

55. *Poems English and Latin of Edward, Lord Herbert of Cherbury*, ed. G. C. Moore Smith (Oxford: Clarendon Press, 1923), p. 42. For the references to Pembroke and Wroth's two children, see Beese, "Poems," pp. 98–99, Roberts, *Poems*, pp. 24–25, and Brennan, *Literary Patronage*, p. 232.

56. "Old Herbert Papers at Powis Castle and in the British Museum," *Collections Historical & Archaeological Relating to Montgomeryshire*, II (1886), 121. For the connections with Behn, I am indebted to Sharon Valiant, of New York City, who gave me a copy of her paper, "Sidney's Sister, Pembroke's Mother . . . and Aphra Behn's Great-Grandmother?," delivered at the American Society for Eighteenth Century Studies conference, New Orleans, 1989.

57. Alice Jardine, "Death Sentences: Writing Couples and Ideology," in *The Female Body in Western Culture*, ed. Susan Rubin Suleiman (Cambridge, Mass.: Harvard University Press, 1986), p. 86; Hélène Cixous, "Castration or Decapitation?," *Signs* 7 (1981), 44.

58. *Urania*, p. 31; Roberts, *Poems*, p. 115; and see Roberts, "The Biographical Problem of Pamphilia to Amphilanthus," *Tulsa Studies in Women's Literature*, 1 (1983), 43–53.

59. Anna Clark, *Women's Silence Men's Violence: Sexual Assault in England 1770–1845* (London: Routledge Kegan Paul, 1987), p. 6.

60. *HMC Rutland, Appendix*, IV. i, p. 520.

61. For the sources quoted here, and a useful account of the controversy, see Roberts, *Poems*, pp. 31–36, and "An Unpublished Literary Quarrel Concerning the Suppression of Mary Wroth's "Urania" (1621)," *Notes and Queries*, 222 (December, 1977), 532–35, where the documents cited are printed. For Briley's suggestion, see "William Herbert," p. 503.

62. Chaffinger, *Just Mans's Memoriall*, sig A4r; *CSP Domestic 1625–49, Addenda*, p. 675; Waller, "Extinct County Family," p. 180.

63. Raymond Williams, *Marxism and Literature* (London: Oxford University Press, 1977), p. 126; Theweleit, *Male Fantasies*, I, p. 308.

Chapter Four

1. Jane Anger, "Her Protection for Women," in *First Feminists*, ed. Moira Ferguson (Bloomington: Indiana University Press, 1985), pp. 59, 60, 70; Freud, "Three Essays on Sexuality," *Standard Edition*, VII, p. 171.

2. *Tottel's Miscellany*, ed. Hyder Edward Rollins, rev. ed. (Cambridge, Mass.: Harvard University Press, 1965), p. 28; Charles Trinkaus, *The Poet as Philosopher* (New Haven: Yale University Press, 1979), p. 2.

3. See Gordon Braden, "Love and Fame: The Petrarchan Career," in *Pragmatism's Freud: The Moral Disposition of Psychoanalysis*, ed. Joseph H. Smith and William Kerrigan (Baltimore: Johns Hopkins University Press, 1986), pp. 126–29.

4. Helen Carr, "Donne's Masculine Persuasive Force," in *Jacobean Poetry and Prose: Rhetoric, Representation and the Popular Imagination*, ed. Clive Bloom (New York: St. Martin's, 1988), p. 101; Malcolm Evans, " 'In Love with Curious Words': Signification and Sexuality in English Petrarchism," in *Jacobean Poetry and Prose*, pp. 119–150.

5. Leonard Forster, *The Icy Fire* (Cambridge: Cambridge University Press, 1969), pp. 4, 5, 22.

6. Greenblatt, *Renaissance Self-Fashioning* (Chicago: University of Chicago Press, 1980); Eugene Vance, "Love's Concordance: The Poetics of Desire and Joy of the Text," *Diacritics*, 5 (Spring 1975), 49.

7. Germaine Warkentin, " 'The Meeting of the Muses': Sidney and the Mid-Tudor Poets," in *Sir Philip Sidney and the Interpretation of Renaissance Culture*, ed. Gary F. Waller and Michael D. Moore (London: Croom Helm 1984), p. 18; Carol Thomas Neely, "The Structure of English Renaissance Sonnet Sequences," *ELH*, 45 (1978), 359–89; Germaine Warkentin. " 'Love's Sweetest Part, Variety': Petrarch and the Curious Frame of the Renaissance Sonnet Sequences," *Renaissance and Reformation*, 11 (1975), 14–23.

8. Samuel Daniel, "A Defence of Rhyme," in *Elizabethan Critical Essays*, ed. G. Gregory Smith (Oxford: Clarendon, 1904), p. 366.

9. Sir John Harington, quoted in A. C. Hamilton, *Sir Philip Sidney* (Cambridge: Cambridge University Press 1977), p. 86. For the Countess of Pembroke's poetry, see Waller, *English Poetry*, chapters 5, 9; Hannay, *Philip's Phoenix*, chapters 3, 4.

10. Hamilton, *Sidney*, p. 86. Quotations from Philip Sidney's poetry are taken from *Poems of Sir Philip Sidney*, ed. William A. Ringler (Oxford: Clarendon, 1963).

11. Alan Sinfield, "Sidney and Astrophil," *Studies in English Literature*, 20 (1980), 35.

12. *HMC, De Lisle and Dudley*, II. p. 145; see also II. pp. 160, 164. Quotations

from the poems are taken from *The Poems of Robert Sidney*, ed. P. J. Croft (Oxford: Clarendon, 1984).

13. For the Countess of Pembroke's revisions, see Waller, *Triumph of Death*, pp. 19–36.

14. Stoller, *Observing the Erotic Imagination* (New Haven: Yale University Press, 1985), pp. 31–32.

15. Paglia, *Sexual Personae*, p. 189.

16. Kaplan, *Female Perversions*, p. 40.

17. Freud, "Three Essays on Sexuality," *Standard Edition*, VII, p. 171.

18. See, e.g., Forster, *Icy Fire*, Appendix 1; Theweleit, *Male Fantasies*, I, p. 284.

19. Raquel Zak de Goldstein, "The Dark Continent and its Enigmas," *International Journal of Psychoanalysis*, 65 (1984), 187.

20. Freud, "Three Essays," *Standard Edition*, VII, p. 156; Paglia, *Sexual Personae*, p. 242; Stoller, *Perversion*, pp. 99, 105. See also Charles W. Socarides, "The Demonified Mother: A Study of Voyeurism and Sexual Sadism," *International Review of Psycho-Analysis*, 1 (1974), 192–93 and David W. Allen, *The Fear of Looking or Scopophilic-Exhibitionist Conflicts* (Bristol: John Wright and Sons, 1974), especially pp. 40–41.

21. Nancy S. Vickers, "Diana Described: Scattered Woman and Scattered Rhyme," *Critical Inquiry*, 8 (1981–2), 265. For the remarks by the Duchess of Newcastle, see MacFarlane, Marriage and Love, p. 53.

22. Rosalind Coward, "Sexual Violence and Sexuality," *Feminist Review*, 11 (June, 1982), 17; Kaplan, *Female Perversions*, p. 125.

23. Kaplan, *Female Perversions*, pp. 35. 54. See also Freud, "Three Essays on Sexuality," *Standard Edition*, VII, p. 171.

24. Tony Bennett, "Texts in History," *Journal of the Midwest Modern Language Association*, 18:1 (1985), 1–18.

25. Sidney, *Defence*, in *Assorted Prose*, pp. 92, 81, 91.

26. Ralph Lever, *The Arte of Reason* (1573), foreword; Richard Mulcaster, *The First Part of the Elementarie*, ed. E. T. Campagnac (Oxford: Clarendon, 1925), p. 172.

27. Roland Barthes, *S/Z*, trans. Richard Miller (New York: Hill and Wang, 1974), pp. 15–16; Bernard Sharratt, *Reading Relations* (Brighton: Harvester, 1983), pp. 16–24.

Chapter Five

1. Kaplan, *Female Perversions*, p. 146; Benjamin, *Bonds of Love*, p. 135.

2. *Poems, Written by the Right Honorable William Earl of Pembroke, Lord Steward of his Majesties Household, Whereof Many of Which Are Answered by Way of Repartee, by Sir Benjamin Ruddier*, henceforth cited as *1660*, with page references incorporated into the text.

3. *Ben Jonson: The Complete Masques*, ed. Stephen Orgel (New Haven: Yale University Press, 1969), pp. 338–39.

4. Nashe, *Pierce Pennilesse*, *Works*, I, p. 159. For Davidson's and other contemporary tributes to Pembroke's poetry, see Taylor, "Patron," pp. 45–47.

5. For additional information on the early printing of Pembroke's lyrics, see Diana Poulton, *John Dowland* (London: Faber: rev. ed., 1962), pp. 277–78; *Lyrics from English Airs 1596–1622*, ed. Edward Doughtie (Cambridge, Mass.: Harvard University Press, 1970), pp. 514, 525, 602, 607.

6. Beese, "Critical Edition," I, pp. 11–14.

7. *Poems of William Herbert, third Earl of Pembroke, K.G. and Sir Benjamin Rudyerd*, ed. Sir Egerton Brydges (London: Bensley and Son, 1817), p. xxiii.

8. Brydges, *Poems*; Beese, "Critical Edition;" Robert Krueger, "The Poems of William Herbert, Third Earl of Pembroke," unpub. B.Litt. diss., Oxford University, 1961;

Memoirs of Sir Benjamin Rudyerd (1840), ed. A. J. Manning (London: n.p., 1840); *Poems Written by the Earl of Pembroke (1660)*, ed. Gaby Onderwyzer. (Los Angeles: Augustan Reprint Society, 1959).

9. Beese, "Critical Edition," I, pp. 14, 18; R. C. Bald, *John Donne: A Life* (Oxford: Oxford University Press, 1970), p. 3.

10. In assessing the authorship of the poems in *1660*, my count differs from those of both Beese and Krueger. It should be noted that they omit some (different) poems without presenting convincing evidence they are not by Pembroke and accept without question Pembroke's authorship of Drayton's "If that you needs must go." See *The Poems of Michael Drayton*, ed. John Buxton (London: Routledge and Kegan Paul, 1953), II, p. 127. Other poems probably by Pembroke have been attributed to Townshend and Donne; still others are found in manuscripts at the British Library, the National Library of Scotland, Chetham Library, Manchester, the Bodleian, Cambridge University Library, and elsewhere. In *John Donne: Poems* (Oxford: Oxford University Press, 1912), II, p. xc, H. J. C. Grierson warned that seventeenth-century printed miscellanies "inspire little confidence" and that "an editor would be rash to adopt a reading from them without some external evidence of reliability." Much the same can be said about most of the manuscript miscellanies. What they do help establish is something of the nature of the copy text Donne provided the printer. Krueger ("Poems," p. xxxi), showed that the poems written by Pembroke with Rudyerd tend to occur together in the manuscripts. He also suggested that with some of the lyrics—most notably "Can you suspect a change in me," and "Disdain me still"—attributions in miscellanies suggest that they are Pembroke's, and it is possible that these poems were obtained by Donne from the countess of Devonshire. Another closely connected group of manuscripts contains, with fairly consistent attribution to Pembroke, another dozen or so of the poems in *1660*, which confirms that they, too, are his.

11. For the 1647/8 fire, see Brennan, *Literary Patronage*, pp. xiii, 146–47, 200–01.

12. Brydges, *Poems*, p. xxiii; Clarendon, History, I, 89.

13. See *The Poems of Sir Walter Ralegh*, ed. Agnes Latham (London: Routledge and Kegan Paul, 1952), p. 4.

14. Krueger, "Poems," p. xix. For Pembroke's masquing activities, see Taylor, "The Masque and the Lance," p. 53; for Wroth's contemporary reputation as a poet, see Roberts, *Poems*, pp. 16–19.

15. George Puttenham, *The Arte of English Poesie*, ed. Gladys Doidge Willcock and Alice Walker (Cambridge: Cambridge University Press, 1936), p. 61.

16. Lewis, *English Literature*, p. 519; Richard Newton, "Jonson and the (Re-)Invention of the Book," in *Classic and Cavalier: Essays on Jonson and the Sons of Ben* (Pittsburgh: University of Pittsburgh Press, 1982), p. 32; Arthur Marotti, *John Donne, Coterie Poet* (Madison: University of Wisconsin Press, 1986), p. 19; Arthur Marotti, "Shakespeare's Sonnets as Literary Property," in *Soliciting Interpretation*, pp. 149–51. For the connections between Pembroke and Drummond, see *Poems of William Drummond of Hawthornden*, ed. L. E. Kastner (Manchester: Manchester University Press, 1913), II, pp. 187–88, 390.

17. Jameson, *Political Unconscious*, p. 85. Other poems set by Lawes found in *1660* include "Since every man I come upon," attributed to Rudyerd, but probably by John Grange; "Not that I wish my Mistress more or less," and "Be not proud, cause fair and trim," both also probably by Grange; and Neville's "Till now I never did behave." Outside the Lawes collections, there is one further musical setting of a poem probably by Pembroke: "Chloris sighted and sang and wept" (*1660*, p. 104) is found in at least twenty other printed and manuscript sources, many of which attribute it to him. One manuscript (British Library Add. 11608) has a musical setting by "Mr. Bales," who may be Richard (or Alphonso) Bales, or Balls, who was associated with the King's Men and who died in 1622.

18. Wotton, *Elements*, p. 6.

19. John Stevens, *Music and Poetry in the Early Tudor Court* (London: Chatto and Windus, 1961), p. 160; Lewis, *English Literature*, p. 230.

20. Graham Parry, *The Seventeenth Century: the Intellectual and Cultural Context of English Literature 1603-1700* (London: Longman, 1989), p. 59. Robert Sidney was godfather to John Dowland's son, Robert, who also became a musician, dedicating *A Musicall Banquett* (1602) to Sidney. That collection starts with a galliard by John Dowland for Sidney, and it also includes one of Sidney's poems. It is possible that Dowland had some connection with Pembroke since he printed Pembroke's "Disdaine Me Still" in *A Booke of Ayres* (1611) and again in 1612 in *A Pilgrimes Solace*.

21. For a discussion of the settings of some of Pembroke's poems in early seventeenth-century anthologies and songbooks, see Doughtie, *Lyrics*, pp. 514, 525, 602, 607.

22. Macdonald P. Emslie, "Nicholas Lanier's Innovations in English Song," *Music & Letters*, 51 (1961), 111–26. See also Willa McClung Evans, *Henry Lawes: Musician and Friend of Poets* (New York: Modern Language Association, 1941), p. 58; Murray Lefkowitz, *William Lawes* (London: Routledge and Kegan Paul, 1960), p. 177; Pamela J. Willetts, *The Henry Lawes Manuscripts* (London: British Museum, 1969); Peter Walls, " 'Music and Sweet Poetry'? Verse for English Lute Song and Continuo Song," *Music & Letters*, 65 (1984), 237–54.

23. Louise Schleiner, *The Living Lyre in English Verse from Elizabeth through the Restoration* (Columbia: University of Missouri Press, 1984), pp. 8–9.

24. Macdonald Emslie, "The Relationship between Words and Music in the English Secular Song 1622–1700." unpub. diss., (University of Cambridge, 1957), 3.2.3213 [sic].

25. The poem has been printed in *The Dr Farmer Chetham MS, Being a Commonplace Book*, ed. A. B. Grosart (Manchester: Chetham Society, 1883), II, p. 188.

26. Robert Sidney, *Poems*, pp. 81–88.

27. Newdigate-Newdigate, *Gossip*, pp. 13–15.

28. Roberts, *Poems*, pp. 217–18.

29. Ralegh, *Poems*, p. 11.

30. Lawrence Venuti, *Our Halcyon Dayes* (Madison: University of Wisconsin Press, 1989), p. 242.

31. Kaplan, *Female Perversions*, p. 103.

32. Kaplan, *Female Perversions*, pp. 34, 116.

33. Kaplan, *Female Perversions*, p. 124.

34. Kaplan, *Female Perversions*, pp. 25, 28

35. Evans, "Curious Words," pp. 135–36.

36. Kaplan, *Female Perversions*, pp. 74, 125.

Chapter Six

1. Benjamin, *Desire of One's Own*, pp. 19–20; Marion Glastonbury, "At the Mercy of Men's Dreams," *New Statesman*, 102, no. 2042 (6 November, 1981), 18.

2. An annotated bibliography of studies of Wroth through 1990 may be found in *Reading Mary Wroth*, ed. Miller and Waller, pp. 229–34.

3. Roberts, *Poems*, p. 19.

4. Roberts, *Poems*, pp. 47–48.

5. The Folger text is a puzzling one and—even if Jeff Masten's suggestion that it does not necessarily pre-date the 1621 edition is wrong—it does not look as if it is designed for circulation, but rather for working over in private. It was not used as the copytext for *1621*, so one or more intermediary copies must also have existed. *1621* is substantially rearranged, with some poems dropped and some placed into the text of *Urania*; as Josephine Roberts notes, despite the large number of printer's accidentals

in 1621, such revisions are "clearly not the kind of change likely to have been made independently by a compositor or typesetter." See Jeff Masten, " 'Shall I turne Blabb?': Circulation, Gender, and Subjectivity in Mary Wroth's Sonnets," in *Reading Mary Wroth*, ed. Miller and Waller, pp. 67–69; Roberts, *Poems*, pp. 62–63.

6. Roger Kuin, "*Astrophil and Stella* (the early Quartos): The Text as Desiring-Machine," *Sidney Newsletter*, 9.1 (1988), 68–69.

7. Lester Beaurline, "Dudley North's Criticism of Metaphysical Poetry," *Huntington Library Quarterly*, 35 (1935), 304; Robert Cleaver, *A Godly Form of Household Government* (London: T. Man, 1630), p. 32.

8. Warkentin, " 'Love's Sweetest Part," pp. 14–23.

9. For different versions of the structure of *Pamphilia to Amphilanthus*, see: Masten, " 'Shall I turne Blabb?',", pp. 68–69; May Nelson Pauliessen, *The Love Sonnets of Lady Mary Wroth: a Critical Introduction* (Salzburg: Institut für Anglistik und Amerikanistik, 1982), pp. iv-v; Roberts, *Poems*, pp. 44–46; McLaren, "Urania," p. 143; Elaine Beilin, *Redeeming Eve: Women Writers in the Renaissance* (Princeton: Princeton University Press, 1987), p. 234.

10. Vance, "Love's Concordance," p. 49; Forster, *Icy Fire*, pp. 3–4.

11. Kristeva, *Tales of Love*, pp. 11, 225.

12. Pauliessen, *Love Sonnets*, pp. 140–41. Pauliessen's was the first extended discussion of the references to Pembroke in the poems: see esp. pp. 44, 66–67, 139–41.

13. Roberts, *Poems*, p. 115.

14. J. B. Broadbent, *Poetic Love* (London: Chatto and Windus, 1964), p. 143; Pauliessen, *Love Sonnets*, pp. 139–40.

15. Kaplan, *Female Perversions*, pp. 285, 295, 296.

16. Kaplan, *Female Perversions*, p. 443; Clark, *Women's Silence*, p. 6.

17. Benjamin, *Bonds of Love*, p. 73.

18. Stallybrass, "Patriarchal Territories," p. 129.

19. Freud, "Three Essays on Sexuality," *Standard Edition*, VII, p. 159; Mitchell, *Psychoanalysis and Feminism*, p. 413; Kaplan, *Female Perversions*, p. 518.

20. Kaplan, *Female Perversions*, p. 238.

21. Donne, *Complete English Poems*, p. 85; Fulke Greville, *Selected Poems*, ed. Thom Gunn (London: Methuen, 1968), pp. 76–77.

22. Benjamin, *Bonds of Love*, p. 78.

23. Benjamin, *Bonds of Love*, p. 61; Benjamin, p. 61, n. 11, quotes Masud R. Khan, *Alienation in Perversions* (New York: International Universities Press, 1979).

24. Beilin, *Redeeming Eve*, p. 241.

25. Freud, "Mourning and Melancholia," *Standard Edition*, XIV, p. 244; "Three Essays on Sexuality," *Standard Edition*, VII, p.157.

26. Kaplan, *Female Perversions*, pp. 105, 258.

27. Penley is quoted by Stephen Heath, "Difference," *Screen*, 19 (1978), 97. See also Laura Mulvey, *Visual and Other Pleasures* (Bloomington: Indiana University Press, 1988), pp. 361–73; Gaylyn Studlar, *In the Realm of Pleasure: Von Sternberg, Dietrich, and the Masochistic Aesthetic* (Urbana: University of Illinois Press, 1988).

28. Stoller, *Perversion*, p. 90.

29. Stoller, *Perversion*, p. 90; Kaplan, Female Perversions, p. 257.

30. Roland Barthes, "Theory of the Text," in *Untying the Text*, ed. Robert Young (London: Routledge and Kegan Paul, 1981), p. 42.

31. Francis Barker, *The Tremulous Private Body: Essays on Subjection* (London: Methuen, 1984), pp. 31, 36; Catherine Belsey, *The Subject of Tragedy: Identity and Difference in Renaissance Drama* (London: Methuen, 1985), both cited in Masten, " 'Shall I turne Blabb?',", pp. 80–81.

32. Freud, "Beyond the Pleasure Principle," *Standard Edition*, XXIV, pp. 14–17. See also Kaplan, *Female Perversions*, pp. 218, 220.

33. Mary E. Hazard, "Absent Presence and Present Absence: Cross-Couple Convention in Elizabethan Culture," *Texas Studies in Language and Literature*, 29 (1987), 4.

34. Masten, " 'Shall I turne Blabb?'," pp. 82–85.

35. See, e. g., Freud, "A Special Type of Object Choice Made by Men. (Contributions to the Psychology of Love I)," *Standard Edition*, XI, p. 140.

36. Wilson, "Extraordinary Forms."

37. Roberts, *Poems*, p. 45; Beilin, *Redeeming Eve*, pp. 238–40.

38. Naomi J. Miller, "Ancient Fictions and True Forms: the Role of the Lady in Lady Mary Wroth's Pamphilia to Amphilanthus," unpub. paper, 8; Lamb, *Gender and Authorship*, p. 141.

39. Erik H. Erikson, *Life History and the Historical Moment* (New York: Norton, 1975), p. 227.

Chapter Seven

1. Chaffinger, *Just Man's Memoriall*, sig. A3r; Pamela White Hadas, *Beside Herself: Pocahontas to Patty Hearst* (New York: Alfred A. Knopf, 1983), p. 5.

2. Puttenham, *Arte*, p. 24.

3. Jonathan Dollimore, *Radical Tragedy* (Chicago: University of Chicago Press, 1984), presents an account of the socially dislocative impact of Jacobean theatrical practices; he also comments usefully, pp. 17–19, 25–27, 59–69, on the value of an Althusserian symptomatic reading for analyzing the Jacobean theater. See also Graham Holderness, Nick Potter, and John Turner, *Shakespeare: Out of Court—Dramatizations of Court Society* (New York: St. Martin's Press, 1990).

4. Sidney, *Apology*, pp. 74–80, 17; for further discussion of the tension between Sidney and Greville on the attractions and dangers of unconstrained reading, see Waller, *English Poetry*, chapter 2. I borrow the term *homo seriosus* from Richard Lanham, *Motives of Eloquence* (New Haven: Yale University Press, 1976), p. 4.

5. Joan Rees, *Samuel Daniel* (Liverpool: Liverpool University Press, 1964), p. 46. For discussion of her translation, see Waller, *Mary Sidney*, chapter 4.

6. Hannay, *Philip's Phoenix*, p. 121.

7. E. K. Chambers, *The Elizabethan Stage* (Oxford: Clarendon Press, 1923), II, p. 128. For material on Pembroke's Men, see Brennan, *Literary Patronage*, pp. 92–96; Chambers, *Elizabethan Stage*, II, pp. 128–34; K. P. Wentersdorf, "The Origin and Personnel of the Pembroke Company," *Theatre Research International*, 5–6 (1979–81), 45–68.

8. Michael G. Brennan, " 'We have the man Shakespeare with us': Wilton House and *As You Like It*," *Wiltshire Archaeological Magazine*, 80 (1986), 225–27; Brennan, *Literary Patronage*, p. 105.

9. Richard Dutton, "Patronage, Politics, and the Master of the Revels, 1622–1640: the Case of Sir John Astley," *English Literary Renaissance*, 20 (1990), 287–319. For the office of Lord Chamberlain, see G. R. Elton, *The Tudor Revolution in Government: Administrative Changes in the Reign of Henry VIII* (Cambridge: Cambridge University Press 1953), p. 371; G. E. Aylmer, *The King's Servants; The Civil Service of Charles I, 1625–1642* (New York: Columbia University Press, 1961), pp. 27, 206, 250, 473.

10. British Library, Egerton MS 2592, fol. 81; Chambers, *Elizabethan Theatre*, II, p. 308.

11. Bacon, *Essayes*, pp. 117–18; Wotton, *Elements*, p. 6.

12. Louis Althusser, *Reading Capital*, trans. Ben Brewster (London: Verso, 1970), pp. 15–16.

13. *HMC De L'Isle and Dudley*, II, pp. 618–19.

14. *The Theatre of the Stuart Court*, ed. Stephen Orgel and Roy Strong, (Berkeley: University of California Press, 1973), I, p. 90; Sir Ralph Winwood, *Memorials of State in the Reigns of Q. Elizabeth and K. James* (London: n. p., 1725), II, p. 44; Roberts, *Poems*, p. 13; Antimo Galli, *Rime di Antimo Galli all'Illustrissima Signora Elizabetta Talbot-Grey* (London: M. Bradwood, 1609), pp. 23, 24.

15. Drummond, *Conversations*, p. 17; Margaret Anne McLaren, "An Unknown Continent: Lady Mary Wroth's Forgotten Pastoral Drama, 'Loves Victorie'," in *The Renaissance Englishwoman in Print*, ed. Anne M. Haselkorn and Betty Travitsky (Amherst: University of Massachusetts Press, 1990), p. 283; McLaren, "*Urania*," pp. 171–79.

16. Taylor, "Patron," p. 22; Brennan, *Literary Patronage*, pp. 109–11, 114, 130.

17. Chambers, *Elizabethan Stage*, III, p. 279; Winwood, *Memorials*, I, p. 243.

18. *CSP Domestic 1603–10*, p. 319; William Drummond, *The Works (1711)* (Hildesheim: Georg Olms Verlag, 1970), pp. 231–32; Wotton, Life and Letters, II, pp. 16–17.

19. *Ben Jonson*, ed. C. H. Herford and Percy Simpson (Oxford: Clarendon, 1937), VII, p. 395.

20. Margot Heinemann, *Puritanism and Theatre*, pp. 265, 166. See also Paul Yachnin, "*A Game at Chess*: Thomas Middleton's "Praise of Folly," *Modern Language Quarterly* 48 (1987), 107–23; and Thomas Cogswell, "Thomas Middleton and the Court, 1624: *A Game at Chess* in Context," *Huntington Library Quarterly* 47 (1984), 273–88.

21. Miller, "Engendering Discourse," pp. 154–72; McLaren, "Urania," p. 179.

22. Bacon, *Essays*, p. 118.

23. Greenblatt, *Renaissance Self-Fashioning*, p. 162.

24. Heather L. Weidemann, "Theatricality and Female Identity in Mary Wroth's *Urania*," in *Reading Mary Wroth*, pp. 206–7.

25. Suzanne Grossett, " 'Man-maid, begone!': Women in Masques," *English Literary Renaissance* 18 (1988), 96–113.

26. *Jonson*, I, pp. 243, 245.

27. Weidemann, "Theatricality," p. 200; Lamb, *Gender and Authorship*, p. 25.

28. Weidemann, "Theatricality," p. 202.

29. Josephine A. Roberts, "The Huntington Manuscript of Lady Mary Wroth's Play, *Loves Victorie*," *Huntington Library Quarterly*, 46 (1983), 163–66; Barbara K. Lewalski, "Mary Wroth's *Love's Victory* and Pastoral Tragicomedy," in *Reading Mary Wroth*, p. 88.

30. Lewalski, "*Love's Victory*," pp. 88–108.

31. *Jonson*, VII, p. 7.

32. Sara Jayne Steen, "Fashioning an Acceptable Self: Lady Arbella Stuart," *English Literary Renaissance*, 18 (1988), 84.

33. Lewalski, "*Love's Victory*," p. 96.

Chapter Eight

1. Robert S. Wallerstein, "Psychoanalysis as a Science: A Response to the New Challenges," *Pychoanalytical Quarterly*, 55 (1986), 422; Benjamin, *Bonds of Love*, p. 111.

2. McLaren, "Urania," p. 202.

3. For details of the publication, see McLaren, "*Urania*," chapter 3.

4. cf. Lamb, *Gender and Authorship*, pp. 143–44: "The rejection of perspective or unity of form is essential to the aesthetics of organizing, or refusing to organize, *Urania*."

5. Shaver, "Outspoken Women," p. 89.

6. Frye, *Anatomy*, p. 193.

7. Frye, *The Secular Scripture: a Study of the Structure of Romance* (Cambridge, Mass.: Harvard University Press, 1976), p. 161.

8. Sara Heller Mendelson, "Reply," *Past and Present*, 85 (1979), 130; James to Charles and Buckingham, British Library Harleian MS 6287, fol. 13; Sidney, *Defence*, p. 15.

9. Rosemary Jackson, *Fantasy: the Literature of Subversion* (London: Methuen, 1981), p. 8.

10. Quilligan, "Female Authority," p. 267; Carolyn Ruth Swift, "Feminine Identity in Lady Mary Wroth's Romance *Urania*," *English Literary Renaissance*, 14 (1984), 338.

11. Quilligan, "Female Authority," p. 271.

12. Swift, "Feminine Identity," p. 338; Lamb, *Gender and Authorship*, p. 183; McLaren, "*Urania*," p. 214. The pioneering work on the autobiographical references in *Urania* was done by Roberts; see especially "Biographical Problem," "An Unpublished Literary Quarrel," and *Poems*, pp. 28–37. See also Lamb, *Gender and Authorship*, pp. 185–88.

13. On the lost children, see McLaren, "*Urania*," chapter 5, esp. 201–2; Lamb, *Gender and Authorship*, pp. 144, 147–48.

14. Kaplan, *Female Perversions*, p. 238.

15. Nancy K. Miller, "Emphasis Added: Plots and Plausibilities in Women's Fiction," *PMLA* ,96 (1981), 36–47.

16. Frye, *Anatomy*, p. 193.

17. Benjamin, *Bonds of Love*, p. 72; Kaplan, *Female Perversions*, p. 230.

18. Roberts, " 'The Knott Never to Bee Untide'," pp. 109–32.

19. Frye, *Secular Scripture*, p. 57.

20. Graham Parry, "Lady Mary Wroth's *Urania*," *Proceedings of the Leeds Philosophical and Literary Society*, 16 (1975), 68; Barret, *Theorike and Practike*.

21. Theweleit, *Male Fantasies*, I, pp. 162, 166, 192.

22. Kaplan, *Female Perversions*, pp. 223, 527.

23. Beilin, *Redeeming Eve*, pp. 212, 215, 208.

24. Benjamin, *Bonds of Love*, pp. 78–79.

25. Masten, " 'Shall I turne blabb?' " p. 78; Roberts, " 'The Knott Never to Bee Untide," pp. 121–23.

26. Shaver, "Outspoken Women," p. 89.

27. Shaver, "Outspoken Women," p. 89; Swift, "Feminine Identity," p. 343.

28. McLaren, " *Urania*," p. 198.

29. Theweleit, *Male Fantasies*, I, pp. 216, 276.

30. Benjamin, *Bonds of Love*, pp. 62, 83.

31. Benjamin, *Bonds of Love*, p. 88.

32. John Frosch, "Transference Derivatives of the Family Romance," *American Psychoanalytic Association Journal*, 7 (1959), 518–19.

33. Greenblatt, *Renaissance Self-Fashioning*, p. 141.

Chapter Nine

1. Sigmund Freud, "Fragment of an Analysis of a Case of Hysteria," *Standard Edition*, III, p. 50; Raymond Williams, *The English Novel from Dickens to Lawrence* (London: Chatto & Windus, 1974), p. 54.

2. Kristeva, "Histoires d'Amour," p. 19.

3. Davis, "Sense of Self," pp. 58–59.

4. Freud, "On the Universal Tendency to Debasement in the Sphere of Love," *Standard Edition*, XIV, pp. 188–89.

SELECT BIBLIOGRAPHY

1. Primary Texts

Bacon, Sir Francis. *The Essayes or Counsels, Civill and Morall*, ed. Michael Kiernan. Cambridge, Mass.: Harvard University Press, 1985.

Barret, Robert. *The Theorike and Practike of Modern Wars*. 1598; rpt. New York: Da Capo Press, 1969.

Bodleian Library
 MS. Eng. poet. f. 9

Breton, Nicholas. *The Pilgrimage to Paradise*. Oxford: Joseph Barnes, 1592.

———. *Wits Trenchmour*. London: N. Ling, 1597.

British Library
 Egerton MS 2592.
 Add. MS 34324.
 Add. MS 11608.
 Harleian MS 6287.

Cambridge University Library
 MS Add. 4138.

Carleton, Dudley. *Dudley Carleton to John Chamberlain, 1603–1624: Jacobean Letters*, ed. Maurice Lee, Jr. New Brunswick, N.J.: Rutgers University Press, 1972.

Cecil, Sir Robert. *Letters from Sir Robert Cecil to Sir George Carew*, ed. John Maclean. London: Camden Society, 1864.

C[haffinger], T[homas]. *The Just Mans Memorial*. London: Elizabeth Allde, 1630.

Chamberlain, John. *The Letters of John Chamberlain*, ed. Norman E. McClure. Westport, Conn.: Greenwood Press, 1979.

Cleaver, Robert. *A Godly Form of Household Government*. London: T. Man, 1630.

Clifford, Anne. *The Diary of the Lady Anne Clifford*, introd. V. Sackville-West. London: Heinemann, 1923.

Collins, Arthur. *Letters and Memorials of State*. London: T. Osborne, 1746.

Daniel, Samuel. *Complete Works*, ed. Alexander B. Grosart. New York: Russell and Russell, 1963.

Davies, John. *Microcosmos: The Discovery of the Little World, with the Government Thereof*. Oxford: J. Barnes, 1603.

De L'Isle and Dudley Papers, Kent County Archives.

D'Ewes, Sir Simonds. *A Compleat Journal of . . . the House of Lords and House of Commons, throughout the Whole reign of Elizabeth. . . .* London: J. S., 1708.

Dick, O. L., ed. *Aubrey's Brief Lives.* Harmondsworth: Penguin, 1962.

Donne, John. *Poems,* ed. H. J. C. Grierson. Oxford: Oxford University Press, 1912.

———. *Life and Letters of John Donne,* ed. Edmund Gosse. Gloucester, Mass.: Peter Smith, 1959.

———. *The Complete English Poems,* ed. A. J. Smith. Harmondsworth: Penguin, 1971.

Doughtie, Edward, ed. *Lyrics from English Airs 1596–1622.* Cambridge, Mass.: Harvard University Press, 1970.

Drayton, Michael. *The Poems of Michael Drayton,* ed. John Buxton. London: Routledge and Kegan Paul, 1953.

Drummond of Hawthornden, William. *Poems of William Drummond of Hawthornden,* ed. L. E. Kastner. Manchester: Manchester University Press, 1913.

———. *The Works (1711).* Hildesheim: Georg Olms Verlag, 1970.

[Dugard, Samuel]. *The Marriages of Cousin Germans, Vindicated from the Censures of Unlawfulnesse, and Inexpediency.* London: Thomas Bowman, 1673.

Earle, John. *Microcosmographie.* London: White and Cochrane, 1811.

[Erskine, Frances]. *Memoirs Relating to the Queen of Bohemia By one of her Ladies.* London, 1772.

Featley, Daniel. *The Grand Sacrilege of the Church of Rome.* London: Robert Milburne, 1630.

Ferguson, Moira, ed. *First Feminists.* Bloomington: Indiana University Press, 1985.

Ford, John. *Honour Triumphant.* London: Shakespeare Society, 1843.

Fraunce, Abraham. *The Countess of Pembrokes Ivychurch.* London: William Ponsonby, 1591.

———. *The Third Part of the Countesses of Pembrokes Ivychurch.* London: Thomas Woodcocke, 1592.

Galli, Antimo. *Rime di Antimo Galli all'Illustrissima Signora Elizabetta Talbot-Grey.* London: M. Bradwood, 1609.

Greville, Fulke. *Selected Poems,* ed. Thom Gunn. London: Methuen, 1968.

———. *The Prose Works of Fulke Greville, Lord Brooke,* ed. John Gouws. Oxford: Clarendon Press, 1986.

Grosart, A. B., ed. *The Dr Farmer Chetham MS, Being a Commonplace Book.* Manchester: Chetham Society, 1883.

Halliwell. J. O., ed. *Letters of the Kings of England.* London; H. Colburn, 1848.

Herbert of Cherbury, Lord Edward. *The Autobiography of Edward, Lord Herbert of Cherbury,* ed. Sidney Lee. London: Routledge, 1906.

———. *Poems English and Latin.* ed. G. C. Moore Smith. Oxford: Clarendon Press, 1923.

Herbert, George. *The Works of George Herbert,* ed. F. E. Hutchinson. Oxford: Clarendon Press, 1941.

———. *The Latin Poetry of George Herbert,* trans. Mark McCloskey and Paul R. Murphy. Athens, Ohio: Ohio University Press, 1985.

Herbert, Sir Thomas. "Herbertorum Prosapia." Cardiff Central Library Phillipps MS 5.7.

Historical Manuscripts Commission: H. M. Stationery Office.
> *Bath.*
> *Carew.*
> *De L'Isle, and Dudley.*
> *Portland.*
> *Rutland, Appendix.*
> *Salisbury.*

Hyde, Edward, Earl of Clarendon, *The History of the Rebellion and Civil Wars in England*. Oxford: Clarendon Press, 1839.

Johnston, R. *Historia Rerum Britannicarum*. Amsterdam: Sumptibes J. Rosesteysii, 1655.

Jonson, Ben. *Ben Jonson*, ed. C. H. Herford and Percy Simpson. Oxford: Clarendon Press, 1925–52.

———. *The Complete Poetry of Ben Jonson*, ed. William B. Hunter, Jr. New York: New York University Press, 1963.

———. *Conversations with William Drummond of Hawthornden*, ed. G. B. Harrison. New York: Barnes and Noble, 1966.

———. *The Complete Masques*, ed. Stephen Orgel. New Haven: Yale University Press, 1969.

Lloyd, David. *The Statesmen and Favourites of England Since the Reformation*. London: Samuel Speed, 1665.

Lodge, Edmund. *Illustrations of British History*. London: John Chidley, 1838.

Maclean, John, ed. *Letters from Sir Robert Cecil to Sir George Carew*. London: Camden Society, 1864.

Massinger, Philip. *The Bondman*, ed. B. T. Spencer. Princeton: Princeton University Press, 1932.

Moffet, Thomas. *Nobilis*, ed. Virgil B. Heltzel and Hoyt H. Hudson. San Marino, Calif.: Huntington Library, 1940.

Mulcaster, Richard. *The First Part of the Elementarie*, ed. E. T. Campagnac. Oxford: Clarendon Press, 1925.

Nashe, Thomas. *Works*, ed. E. D. McKerrow. New York: Barnes and Noble, 1958.

Newdigate-Newdigate, Lady, ed. *Gossip from a Muniment Room*. London: David Nutt, 1897.

Nichols, John. *The Progresses, Processions, and Magnificent Festivities, of King James the First*. New York: B. Franklin, 1968.

"Old Herbert Papers at Powis Castle and in the British Museum," *Collections Historical & Archaeological Relating to Montgomeryshire*. London: British Museum, 1886.

Orgel, Stephen, and Roy Strong, eds. *The Theatre of the Stuart Court*. Berkeley: University of California Press, 1973.

Pembroke, William Herbert, third Earl of. *Poems, Written by the Right Honorable William Earl of Pembroke, Lord Steward of his Majesties Household, Whereof Many of Which Are Answered by Way of Repartee, by Sir Benjamin Ruddier*. London: Matthew Inman, 1660.

———. *Poems of William Herbert, third Earl of Pembroke, K.G., and Sir Benjamin Ruddier* ed. Sir Egerton Brydges. London: Bensley and Son, 1817.

———. "A Critical Edition of the Poems Printed by John Donne the Younger in 1660, As Written by William Herbert, Earl of Pembroke, and Sir Benjamin Ruddier," ed. M. A. Beese. Unpub. B.Litt. diss., Oxford University, 1935.

———. *Poems Written by the Earl of Pembroke (1660)*, ed. Gaby Onderwyzer. Los Angeles: Augustan Reprint Society, 1959.

———. "The Poems of William Herbert, Third Earl of Pembroke," ed. Robert Krueger. Unpub. B.Litt. diss., Oxford University, 1961.

Perkins, Williams. *The Work of William Perkins*, ed. Ian Breward. Appleford: Sutton Courtenay Press, 1970.

Public Record Office. H. M. Stationery Office.

    Calendar of State Papers Domestic 1603–10.

    Calendar of State Papers: Domestic 1611–18.

    Calendar of State Papers Domestic 1619–23.

    Calendar of State Papers Dom. MSS Add. 1625–49.

Calendar of State Papers Venice 1603–7.

Calendar of State Papers Venice, 1623–25.

Calendar of State Papers Venice 1623–30.

Calendar of State Papers Venice 1629–32.

Puttenham, [George]. *The Arte of English Poesie*, ed. Gladys Doidge Willcock and Alice Walker. Cambridge: Cambridge University Press, 1936.

Ralegh, Sir Walter. *The Poems of Sir Walter Ralegh*, ed. Agnes Latham. London: Routledge and Kegan Paul, 1952.

Rollins, Hyder Edward, ed. *Tottel's Miscellany*. Cambridge, Mass.: Harvard University Press, 1965.

Rudyerd, Sir Benjamin. *Memoirs of Sir Benjamin Rudyerd*. ed. A. J. Manning. London: T. and W. Boone, 1840.

Segar, William. *The Booke of Honor and Armes*, ed. Diane Bornstein. Delmar, N. Y.: Scholars' Facsimiles and Reprints, 1975.

Shakespeare, William. *Shakespeare's Sonnets*, ed. Thomas Tyler. London: David Nutt, 1800.

———. *The Sonnets*, ed. John Dover Wilson. Cambridge: Cambridge University Press, 1969.

———. *Shakespeare's Sonnets*, ed. Stephen Booth. New Haven: Yale University Press, 1977.

Sidney, Mary, Countess of Pembroke. *The Countess of Pembroke's Antonie*, ed. Alice Luce. Weimar: Verlag von Emil Felber, 1897.

———. *The Triumph of Death and Other Unpublished and Uncollected Poems*, ed. Gary Waller. Salzburg: Institut für Anglistik und Amerikanistik, 1979.

Sidney, Sir Philip. *The Poems of Sir Philip Sidney*, ed. William A. Ringler. Oxford: Clarendon Press, 1963.

———. *Miscellaneous Prose*, ed Katherine Duncan-Jones and Jan van Dorsten. Oxford: Clarendon Press, 1973.

———. *The Countess of Pembrokes Arcadia [the Old Arcadia]*, ed. Jean Robertson. Oxford: Clarendon Press, 1973.

———. *The Countess of Pembroke's Arcadia [the New Arcadia]*, ed. Victor Skretkowicz. Oxford: Clarendon Press, 1987.

Sidney, Robert. *The Poems of Robert Sidney*, ed. P. J. Croft. Oxford: Clarendon Press, 1984.

Smith, G. Gregory, ed. *Elizabethan Critical Essays*. Oxford: Oxford University Press, 1904.

Sweeper, Walter. *A Briefe Treatise Declaring the True Noble-man, and the Base Worldling*. London: William Jones, 1623.

Winwood, Sir Ralph. *Memorials of State in the Reigns of Q. Elizabeth and K. James*. London, n. p., 1725.

Wotton, Sir Henry. *The Life and Letters of Sir Henry Wotton*, ed. Logan Pearsall Smith. Oxford: Clarendon Press, 1907.

Wroth, Lady Mary. *The Countess of Mountgomeries Urania*. London: John Marriott and John Grismand, 1621.

———. *Pamphilia to Amphilanthus*, ed. Gary Waller. Salzburg: Institut für Anglistik und Amerikanistik, 1977.

———. *The Poems of Lady Mary Wroth*, ed. Josephine A. Roberts. Baton Rouge: Louisiana State University Press, 1983.

———. *Lady Mary Wroth's Loves Victory: The Penshurst Manuscript*, ed. Michael Brennan. London: Roxburghe Club, 1988.

———. *The Countess of Mongomery's Urania*, ed. Josephine A. Roberts. New York: English Renaissance Text Society, forthcoming.

————. "The Second Part of the Countess of Montgomerys Urania." Newberry Library Case MS fY 1565. W 95.

2. Modern Studies

Aarons, Z. Alexander. "Fetish, Fact and Fantasy: A Clinical Study of the Problem of Fetishism." *International Review of Psychoanalysis*, 2 (1975), 199–230.

Adams, Parveen, and Elizabeth Cowie. "Feminine Sexuality: Interview with Juliet Mitchell and Jacqueline Rose," *m/f*, 8 (1983), 3–16.

Allen, David W. *The Fear of Looking or Scopophilic-Exhibitionist Conflicts*. Bristol: John Wright and Sons, 1974.

Althusser, Louis. *Reading Capital*, trans. Ben Brewster. London: Verso, 1970.

————. *Lenin and Philosophy and Other Essays*, trans. Ben Brewster. London: New Left Books, 1971.

Amussen, Susan. *An Ordered Society: Gender and Class in Early Modern England*. Oxford: Blackwell, 1988.

Appignanesi, Lisa, ed. *Desire*. London: ICA, 1985.

Armstrong, Nancy. *Desire and Domestic Fiction: a Political History of the Novel*. New York: Oxford University Press, 1987.

Ashplant, T. G. "Psychoanalysis in Historical Writing," *History Workshop*, 26 (1988), 102–19.

Aylmer, G. E. *The King's Servants; The Civil Service of Charles I, 1625–1642*. New York: Columbia University Press, 1961.

Bachelard, Gaston. *The Poetics of Space*, trans. Maria Jolas. Boston: Beacon Press, 1969.

Bak, Robert C. "Being in Love and Object Loss," *International Journal of Psycho-Analysis*, 54 (1973), 1–8.

Bald, R. C. *John Donne: A Life*. London: Oxford University Press, 1970.

Bank, Stephen P., and Michael D. Kahn. *The Sibling Bond*. New York: Basic Books, 1982.

Barker, Francis. *The Tremulous Private Body: Essays on Subjection*. London: Methuen, 1984.

Barthes, Roland. *S/Z*, trans. Richard Miller. New York: Hill and Wang, 1974.

————. "Theory of the Text," in *Untying the Text*, edited by Robert Young. Boston: Routledge & Kegan Paul, 1981.

Bassin, Donna. "Woman's Images of Inner Space: Data Towards Expanded Interpretive Categories," *International Review of Psychoanalysis*, 9 (1982), 191–203.

Beaurline, Lester. "Dudley North's Criticism of Metaphysical Poetry," *Huntington Library Quarterly*, 35 (1935), 299–313.

Beilin, Elaine. *Redeeming Eve: Women Writers in the Renaissance*. Princeton: Princeton University Press, 1987.

Belsey, Catherine. *The Subject of Tragedy: Identity and Difference in Renaissance Drama*. London: Methuen, 1985.

————. *John Milton: Language, Gender, Power*. Oxford: Blackwell, 1988.

Benjamin, Jessica. *A Desire of One's Own: Psychoanalytic Feminism and Intersubjective Space*. University of Wisconsin-Milwaukee: Center for Twentieth Century Studies, Working Paper #2. 1985.

————. *The Bonds of Love: Psychoanalysis, Feminism, and the Problem of Domination*. New York: Pantheon, 1988.

Bennett, Tony. "Reading in History," *Journal of the Midwest Modern Language Association*, 18.1 (1985), 1–10.

Bernheimer, Charles and Claire Kahane, eds. *In Dora's Case: Freud-Hysteria-Feminism*. New York: Columbia University Press, 1985.

Bernstein, Doris. "The Female Superego: a Different Perspective," *International Journal of Psychoanalysis*, 64 (1983), 187–201.

Berry, Boyd M. "The First English Pediatricians and Tudor Attitudes toward Childhood," *Journal of the History of Ideas*, 35 (1974), 561–77.

Birch, Thomas. *The Court and Times of James the First*. London: H. Colburn, 1848.

Bloom, Clive, ed. *Jacobean Poetry and Prose: Rhetoric, Representation, and the Popular Imagination*. New York: St. Martin's Press, 1988.

Bloom, Harold. *The Anxiety of Influence: A Theory of Poetry*. New York: Seabury, 1973.

Boaden, James. *On the Sonnets of Shakespeare*. London: Thomas Rodd, 1837.

Boose, Lynda E., and Betty S. Flowers, eds. *Daughters and Fathers*. Baltimore: Johns Hopkins University Press, 1989.

Bradlow, Paul A., and Stanley J. Koon. "Mirror Masturbation." *Psychoanalytical Quarterly*, 53 (1984), 267–85.

Brenkman, John. *Culture and Domination*. Ithaca: Cornell University Press, 1987.

Brennan, Michael G. " 'We have the man Shakespeare with us': Wilton House and *As You Like It*," *Wiltshire Archaeological Magazine*, 80 (1986), 225–27.

———. *Literary Patronage in the English Renaissance: the Pembroke Family*. London: Routledge, 1988.

Briley, J. R. "William Herbert, Third Earl of Pembroke." unpub. doct. diss., University of Birmingham, 1961.

Broadbent, J. B. *Poetic Love*. London: Chatto and Windus, 1964.

Brown, Steven R. "Child Raising and Melancholia in Tudor England." *Journal of Psychohistory*, 5 (1978), 67–92.

Brownmiller, Susan. *Against Their Will: Men, Women, and Rape*. New York: Simon and Schuster, 1975.

Butler, Judith. *Gender Trouble: Feminism and the Subversion of Identity*. London: Routledge, 1990.

Buxton, John. *Sir Philp Sidney and the English Renaissance*. London: Macmillan, 1954.

Carlton, Charles. "Towards a Psychobiography of Charles I," *Journal of Psychohistory*, 11 (1984), 517–32.

Chalkin, C. W. *Seventeenth-Century Kent*. London: Longmans, Green, 1965.

Chambers, E. K. *The Elizabethan Stage*. Oxford: Clarendon Press, 1923.

Charles, Amy M. *A Life of George Herbert*. Ithaca: Cornell University Press, 1977.

Chasseguet-Smirgel, Janine. *Creativity and Perversion*. London: Free Association Books, 1985.

———. *Sexuality and Mind*. New York: New York University Press, 1986.

Chaytor, Miranda. "Household and Kinship: Ryton in the late 16th and early 17th Centuries," *History Workshop Journal*, 10 (1980), 26–51.

Chodorow, Nancy. *The Reproduction of Mothering: Psychoanalysis and the Sociology of Gender*. New Haven: Yale University Press, 1978.

Cixous, Hélène. "Castration or Decapitation?", *Signs* 7 (1981), 41–55.

Clark, Anna. *Women's Silence Men's Violence: Sexual Assault in England 1770–1845* London: Routledge Kegan Paul, 1987.

Clark, Sandra. "*Hic Mulier*, Haec Vir, and the Controversy over Masculine Women," *Studies in Philology*, 82 (1985), 157–83.

Cloward, Richard A., and Frances Fox Piven. "Hidden Protest: the Channelling of Female Personification and Resistance," *Signs* 4 (1979), 651–69.

Cogswell, Thomas. "Thomas Middleton and the Court, 1624: *A Game at Chess* in Context," *Huntington Library Quarterly*, 47 (1984), 273–88.

Connell, R. W. *Gender and Power: Society, the Person, and Sexual Politics* Cambridge: Polity Press, 1987.

Coward, Rosalind. "Sexual Violence and Sexuality," *Feminist Review*, 11 (June, 1982), 9–22.

———. *Patriachal Precedents*. London: Routledge Kegan Paul, 1985.

Cubeta, Paul A. "A Jonsonian Ideal: 'To Penshurst'," *Philological Quarterly*, 42 (1963), 14–24.

Davis, Natalie Zemon. *Society and Culture in Early Modern France*. Stanford: Stanford University Press, 1975.

Decker, Hannah S. *Freud, Dora and Vienna*. New York: Free Press, 1990.

Deleuze, Gilles. *Masochism: An Interpretation of Coldness and Cruelty*. trans. Jean Mc-Neil. New York: Braziller, 1971.

———. *Masochism: Coldness and Cruelty* [with] Sacher-Masoch, Leopold von. *Venus in Furs*. New York: Zone Books, 1989.

Deluze, Gilles and Felix Guattari. *Anti-Oedipus: Capitalism and Schizophrenia*, trans. Robert Hurley, Mark Seem, and Helen R. Lane. Minneapolis: University of Minnesota Press, 1983.

Dervin, Daniel. "Reading Freud and Returning to Lacan: An Essay Review," *The Psychoanalytic Review*, 78 (1991), 237–66.

Deutsch, Hélène. *The Psychology of Women*. London: Research Books, 1946.

Dollimore, Jonathan. *Radical Tragedy*. Chicago: University of Chicago Press, 1984.

———. *Sexual Dissidence: Augustine to Wilde, Freud to Foucault*. Oxford, Clarendon Press, 1991.

Dutton, Richard. "Patronage, Politics, and the Master of the Revels, 1622–1640: the Case of Sir John Astley," *English Literary Renaissance*, 20 (1990), 287–319.

Eagle, Maurice N. *Recent Developments in Psychoanalysis*. New York, McGraw Hill, 1984.

Eisenstein, Hester, and Alice Jardine, eds. *The Future of Difference*. Boston: G. K. Hall, 1980.

Elton, G. R. *The Tudor Revolution in Government: Administrative Changes in the Reign of Henry VIII*. Cambridge: Cambridge University Press, 1953.

Emslie, Macdonald P. "The Relationship between Words and Music in the English Secular Song 1622–1700." Unpub. doct. diss., University of Cambridge, 1957.

———. "Nicholas Lanier's Innovations in English Song," *Music & Letters* 51 (1961), 111–26.

Erikson, Erik H. *Life History and the Historical Moment*. New York: Norton, 1975.

Evans, Robert C. "Literature as Equipment for Living: Ben Jonson and the Politics of Patronage." *College Literature Association Journal*, 30 (1987), 379–94.

———. *Ben Jonson and the Poetics of Patronage*. Lewisburg: Bucknell University Press, 1989.

Evans, Willa McClung. *Henry Lawes: Musician and Friend of Poets*. New York: Modern Language Association, 1941.

Fenichel, Otto. *The Collected Papers of Otto Fenichel*. ed. Hanna Fenichel and David Rapoport. London: Routledge and Kegan Paul, 1954.

Ferguson, Margaret W., Maureen Quilligan, and Nancy J. Vickers, eds. *Rewriting the Renaissance*. Chicago: University of Chicago Press, 1986.

Ferry, Anne. *The 'Inward' Language: Sonnets of Wyatt, Sidney, Shakespeare, Donne*. Chicago: University of Chicago Press, 1983.

Forster, Leonard. *The Icy Fire*. Cambridge: Cambridge University Press, 1969.

Foucault, Michel. "Of Other Spaces," *Diacritics*, 16 (1986), 22–27.

Freccero, John. "The Fig Tree and the Laurel: Petrarch's Poetics." *Diacritics*, 5 (Spring 1975), 34–40.

Freedman, Sylvia. *Poor Penelope*. Abbotsbrook: Kensal Press, 1983.

Freud, Sigmund. *The Standard Edition of the Works of Sigmund Freud*, ed. and trans. James Strachey et. al. London: Hogarth Press, 1952–66.

———. *The Complete Letters of Sigmund Freud to Wilhelm Fliess 1887–1904*, trans. and ed. Jeffrey Moussaieff Masson. Cambridge, Mass.: Harvard University Press, 1985.

Frosch, John. "Transference Derivatives of the Family Romance," *American Psychoanalytic Association Journal*, 7 (1959), 503–22.

Frye, Northrop. *Anatomy of Criticism*. Princeton: Princeton University Press, 1957.

———. *A Natural Perspective: the Development of Shakespearean Comedy and Romance*. New York: Columbia University Press, 1965.

———. *The Secular Scripture: a Study of the Structure of Romance*. Cambridge, Mass.: Harvard University Press, 1976.

Gallop, Jane. *Thinking through the Body*. New York: Columbia University Press, 1988.

Gardner, Samuel R. "Notes by Sir James Bagg on the Parliament of 1626." *Notes and Queries*, 4th series (1872), 325–26.

———. *History of England from the Accession of James I to the Outbreak of the Civil War 1603–1642*. London: Longman, Green and Co., 1883.

Gaylin, Willard, and Ethel Person, eds. *Passionate Attachments: Thinking about Love*. New York: Free Press, 1988.

Gebauer, Andreas. *Von Macht und Mazenatentum: Leben und Werk William Herberts, der dritten Earls von Pembroke*. Heidelberg: Carl Winter, 1987.

George, David. "Shakespeare and Pembroke's Men," *Shakespeare Quarterly*, 32 (1981), 305–23.

Gilligan, Carol. *In a Different Voice: Psychological Theory and Women's Development*. Cambridge, Mass.: Harvard University Press, 1982.

Girouard, Mark. *Life in an English Country House: A Social and Architectural History*. Harmondsworth: Penguin, 1980.

Glastonbury, Marion. "At the Mercy of Men's Dreams," *New Statesman*, 102, no. 2042 (6 November 1981), 18–19.

Goldstein, Raquel Zak de. "The Dark Continent and its Enigmas." *International Journal of Psychoanalysis*, 65 (1984), 179–89.

Greenacre, Phyllis. "The Family Romance of the Artist," *Psychological Study of the Child*, 13 (1958), 136–49.

Greenblatt, Stephen. *Renaissance Self-Fashioning*. Chicago: University of Chicago Press, 1980.

———. *Shakespearean Negotiations*. Berkeley: University of California Press, 1988.

———. *Learning to Curse*. London: Routledge, 1990.

Greven, Philip. *The Protestant Temperament: Patterns of Child-Rearing Religious Experience, and the Self in Early America*. New York: Knopf, 1977.

Grossett, Suzanne. " 'Man-maid, begone!': Women in Masques," *English Literary Renaissance*, 18 (1988), 96–113.

Guntrip, Harry. *Personality Structure and Human Interaction*. London: Hogarth, 1961.

Hadas, Pamela White. *Beside Herself: Pocohontas to Patty Hearst*. New York: Knopf, 1983.

Hamilton, A. C. *Sir Philip Sidney*. Cambridge: Cambridge University Press, 1977.

Hannay, Margaret, ed., *"Silent But for the Word" : Tudor Women as Patrons, Translators, and Writers of Religious Works*. Kent, Ohio: Kent State University Press, 1985.

———. *Philip's Phoenix: Mary Sidney Countess of Pembroke*. New York: Oxford University Press, 1990.

Hartsock, Nancy. *Money, Sex, and Power: Toward a Feminist Historical Materialism*. London: Longmans, 1983.

Hay, Millicent. *The Life of Robert Sidney*. Washington, D.C.: Folger Shakespeare Library, 1984.

Hazard, Mary E. "Absent Presence and Present Absence: Cross-Couple Convention in Elizabethan Culture," *Texas Studies in Language and Literature*, 29 (1987), 1–27.

Heath, Stephen. *The Sexual Fix*. London: Macmillan, 1984.

Heinemann, Margot. *Puritanism and Theatre: Thomas Middleton and Oppositional Drama under the Early Stuarts*. Cambridge: Cambridge University Press, 1980.

Heller, Thomas C., Morton Sosna, and David E. Welbury. *Reconstructing Individualism*. Stanford: Stanford University Press, 1986.

Hind, A. M. *Engraving in England*. Cambridge: Cambridge University Press, 1954.

Hinton, R. W. K. "Husbands, Fathers and Conquerors," *Political Studies*, 15–16 (1967–8), 291–300, 55–67.

Holderness, Graham, Nick Potter, and John Turner. *Shakespeare: Out of Court—Dramatizations of Court Society*. New York: St. Martin's Press, 1990.

Holland, Norman N., Sidney Homan, and Bernard J. Paris, eds. *Shakespeare's Personality*. Berkeley: University of California Press, 1990.

Holzapfel, Rudolf. *Shakespeare's Secret*. Dublin: Dolmen Press, 1961.

Horney, Karen. "The Problem of Feminine Masochism." *Psychoanalytic Review*, 22 (1935), 241–57.

Hotson, Leslie. *The First Night of Twelfth Night*. London: Rupert Hart-Davis, 1954.

Howard, Jean. "Crossdressing, the Theatre, and Gender Struggle in Early Modern England," *Shakespeare Quarterly*, 39 (1989), 418–40.

Hunt, David. *Parents and Children in History: The Psychology of Family Life in Early Modern France*. New York: Basic Books, 1970.

Hussey, Christopher. "Wilton House, Wiltshire," *Country Life*, 9 May, 1963, 1044–48.

Jackson, Rosemary. *Fantasy: the Literature of Subversion*. London: Methuen, 1981.

Jacoby, Russell. *The Repression of Psychoanalysis: Otto Fenichel and the Political Freudians*. New York: Basic Books, 1983.

Jaggar, Alison M. *Feminist Politics and Human Nature*. Totowa, N.J.: Rowman and Allanheld, 1983.

Jameson, Fredric. *The Political Unconscious*. Princeton: Princeton University Press, 1980.

Janeway, Elizabeth. "On the Power of the Weak," *Signs*, 1 (1975), 103–09.

Jones, Ann Rosalind. "The Lyric Sequence: Poetic Performance as Plot." Unpub. doct. diss., Cornell University, 1976.

Jordan, Constance. *Renaissance Feminism: Literary Texts and Political Models*. Ithaca: Cornell University Press, 1990.

Kahane, Claire. "Questioning the Maternal Voice," *Genders*, 3 (1986), 82–91.

Kahn, Coppélia. *Man's Estate: Masculine Identity in Shakespeare*. Berkeley: University of California Press, 1981.

Kaplan, Louise. *Female Perversions: The Temptations of Emma Bovary* New York: Doubleday, 1991.

[Kelly-] Gadol, Joan. "Notes on Women in the Renaissance and Renaissance Historiography," *Conceptual Frameworks for Studying Women's History*, ed. Marylin Arthur et. al. Lawrence: University of Kansas, 1975. Reprinted in *Becoming Visible: Women in European History*. Ed. Renate Bridenthal and Claudia Koonz. Boston: Houghton Mifflin, 1977.

Kelso, Ruth. *Doctrine for the Lady of the Renaissance*. Urbana: University of Illinois Press, 1956.

Kernburg, Otto F. *Borderline Conditions and Pathological Narcissism*. New York: Jason Aronson, 1975.

Khan, M. Masud R. *Alienation in Perversions*. London: Hogarth Press, 1979.

Klapisch-Zuber, Christianne. *Women, Family, and Ritual in Renaissance Italy*, trans. Lydia Cochrane. Chicago: University of Chicago Press, 1985.

317

Kohon, Gregorio. "Fetishism Revisited," *International Journal of Psycho-Analysis* 68 (1987), 213–28.

Kojnacki, Stanley. "Comment: Blurring Genders," *Renaissance Quarterly*, 40 (1987), 743–51.

Krafft-Ebing, R. von. *Psychopathia Sexualis*. Trans. Charles Chadock. Philadelphia: F. A. Davis, 1893.

Kristeva, Julia. *The Kristeva Reader*, ed. Toril Moi. New York: Columbia University Press, 1986.

———. *Tales of Love*, trans. Leon S. Roudiez. New York: Columbia University Press, 1987.

Kuin, Roger. "*Astrophil and Stella* (the early Quartos): The Text as Desiring-Machine," *Sidney Newsletter*, 9.1 (1988), 68–69.

Lacan, Jacques. *Feminine Sexuality: Jacques Lacan and the École freudienne*, trans. Jacqueline Rose and Juliet Mitchell. London: Macmillan, 1982.

Lamb, Mary Ellen. *Gender and Authorship in the Sidney Circle*. Madison: University of Wisconsin Press, 1990.

———. "Apologizing for Pleasure in Sidney's *Apology for Poetry*." unpub. paper.

———. "Effeminizing Fictions in *Macbeth, The Winter's Tale*, and *The Tempest*." unpub. paper.

Lanham, Richard. *Motives of Eloquence*. New Haven: Yale University Press, 1976.

Laqueur, Thomas. *Making Sex*. Cambridge, Mass.: Harvard University Press, 1990.

Laslett, Peter, Kaula Oosterveen, and Richard M. Smith, *Bastardy and its Comparative History*. Cambridge, Mass.: Harvard University Press, 1980.

———. The Character of Familial History, its Limitations and the Conditions for its Proper Pursuit," *Journal of Family History*, 12 (1987), 263–84.

Leakey, Richard E. *The Making of Mankind*. New York: E. P. Dutton, 1981.

Lefkowitz, Murray. *William Lawes*. London: Routledge and Kegan Paul, 1960.

Leonard, Peter. *Personality and Ideology: Towards a Materialist Understanding of the Individual*. London: Macmillan, 1984.

Lever, Tresham. *The Herberts of Wilton*. London: John Murray, 1907.

Leverenz, David. *Manhood and American Renaissance*. Ithaca: Cornell University Press, 1989.

Lewis, C. S. *English Literature of the Sixteenth Century Excluding Drama*. Oxford: Clarendon Press, 1954.

Leyland, W. Ralph. "The Use of a Mistress and the Internalized Sexual Mother," *International Journal of Psychoanalysis*, 65 (1984), 323–30.

Lichtman, Richard. *The Production of Desire*. New York: Free Press, 1981.

Limon, Jerzy. *Dangerous Matter: English Drama and Politics in 1623/4*. Cambridge: Cambridge University Press, 1986.

Lockyer, Roger. *Buckingham*. London: Longman, 1981.

Lorand, Sandor, and Michael Balint, eds. *Perversions*. London: Ortolan Press, 1965.

Lysons, Daniel. *The Environs of London*. London: L. P., 1792–96.

MacFarlane, Alan. Review of Stone, *Family, Sex and Marriage, History and Theory*, 17/18 (1978/79), 103–26.

———. *Marriage and Love in England: Modes of Reproduction 1300–1840*. Oxford: Blackwell, 1986.

Mahler, Margaret S., Fred Pine, and Anni Bergman, *The Psychological Birth of the Human Infant: Symbiosis and Individuation*. New York: Basic Books, 1975.

Marotti, Arthur. *John Donne, Coterie Poet*. Madison: University of Wisconsin Press, 1986.

———. "Shakespeare's Sonnets as Literary Property," in *Soliciting Interpretation: Literary Theory and Seventeenth-Century English Poetry*, ed. Elizabeth D. Harvey and Katharine Eisaman Maus. Chicago: University of Chicago Press, 1990.

McCoy, Richard C. *The Rites of Knighthood: the Literature and Politics of Elizabethan Chivalry*. Berkeley: University of California Press, 1989.

McKenzie, Norman H. "Sir Thomas Herbert of Tintern: A Parliamentary 'Royalist'," *Bulletin of the Institute of Historical Research*, 29 (1956), 32–86.

McLaren [Witten-Hannah], Margaret, "Lady Mary Wroth's *Urania*: The Work and the Tradition." Unpub. doct. diss., University of Auckland, 1978.

———. "An Unknown Continent: Lady Mary Wroth's Forgotten Pastoral Drama, 'Loves Victorie'," in *The Renaissance Englishwoman in Print*, ed. Anne M. Haselkorn and Betty Travitsky. Amherst: University of Massachusetts Press, 1990.

McLuskie, Kathleen. *Renaissance Dramatists*. Atlantic Highlands, N.J.: Humanities Press International, 1989.

Meares, Russell. "Inner Space: Its Construction in Anxiety States and Narcissistic Personality," *Psychiatry*, 49 (1984), 162–71.

Mendelson, Sara Heller. "Reply," *Past and Present* 85 (1979), 130.

———. *The Mental World of Stuart Women*. Brighton: Harvester, 1987.

Miller, Nancy K. "Emphasis Added: Plots and Plausibilities in Women's Fiction," *PMLA*, 96 (1981), 36–47.

———, ed. *The Politics of Gender*. New York: Columbia University Press, 1986.

Miller, Naomi J., and Gary Waller, ed. *Reading Mary Wroth: Representing Alternatives in Early Modern England*. Knoxville: University of Tennessee Press, 1991.

———. "Ancient Fictions and True Forms: the Role of the Lady in Lady Mary Wroth's *Pamphilia to Amphilanthus*." Unpub. paper.

Mitchell, Juliet. *Woman's Estate*. Harmondsworth: Penguin, 1971.

———. *Psychoanalysis and Feminism*. London: Allen Lane, 1974.

Modleski, Tania. *Loving with a Vengeance: Mass- Produced Fantasies for Women*. London: Methuen, 1984.

Montagu, Ashley. *Touching: The Human Significance of the Skin*. San Francisco: Harper & Row, 1986.

Montrose, Louis A. "The Work of Gender in the Discourse of Discovery," *Representations*, 33 (1991), 1–41.

Morrow, France. *Unleashing Our Unknown Selves: An Inquiry into the Future of Femininity and Masculinity*. New York: Praeger, 1991.

Mulvey, Laura. *Visual and Other Pleasures*. Bloomington: Indiana University Press, 1988.

Neely, Carol Thomas. "The Structure of English Renaissance Sonnet Sequences," *ELH*, 45 (1978), 359–89.

———. "Constructing the Subject: Feminist Practice and the New Renaissance Discourses," *English Literary Renaissance*, 18 (1988), 5–18.

Newton, Judith. "Family Fortunes: 'New History' and 'New Historicism'," *Radical History Review*, 43 (1989), 5–22.

———. Mary P. Ryan, and Judith R. Walkowitz, eds. *Sex and Class in Women's History*. London: Routledge and Kegan Paul, 1983.

Newton, Richard. "Jonson and the (Re-)Invention of the Book," in *Classic and Cavalier: Essays on Jonson and the Sons of Ben*. Pittsburgh: University of Pittsburgh Press, 1982.

Norbrook, David. *Poetry and Politics in the English Renaissance*. London: Routledge and Kegan Paul, 1984.

North, Maurice. *The Outer Fringe of Sex: A Study in Sexual Fetishism*. London: Odyssey Press, 1970.

O'Farrell, Brian. "Politician, Patron, Poet: William Herbert, Third Earl of Pembroke, 1580–1630." Unpub. doct. diss., U.C.L.A., 1966.

Padel, John. *New Poems by Shakespeare*. London: The Herbert Press, 1981.

Paglia, Camille. *Sexual Personae: Art and Decadence from Nefertiti to Emily Dickinson.* New York: Vintage, 1991.

Pam, D. O. *Protestant Gentlemen: The Wroths of Durants Arbour, Enfield and Loughton, Essex.* Edmonton Hundred Historical Society, Occasional Paper, n.s. 25, 1973.

Parry, Graham. "Lady Mary Wroth's *Urania,*" *Proceedings of the Leeds Philosophical and Literary Society,* 16 (1975), 51–70.

———. *The Seventeenth Century: the Intellectual and Cultural Context of English Literature 1603–1700.* London: Longman, 1989.

Pauliessen, May Nelson. *The Love Sonnets of Lady Mary Wroth: a Critical Introduction.* Salzburg: Institut für Anglistik und Amerikanistik, 1982.

Person, Ethel S. "The Erotic Transference in Women and Men: Differences and Consequences," *Journal of the American Academy of Psychoanalysis,* 13.2 (1985), 159–80.

Pinchbeck, Ivy, and Margaret Hewitt. *Children in English Society, Vol 1: From Tudor Times to the Eighteenth Century.* London: Routledge and Kegan Paul, 1969.

Pollock, Linda. *Forgotten Children: Parent-Child Relations from 1500 to 1900.* Cambridge: Cambridge University Press, 1981.

Poster, Mark. *Critical Theory of the Family.* New York: Pluto Press, 1978.

Poulton, Diana. *John Dowland.* London: Faber, 1962.

Quilligan, Maureen. "Lady Mary Wroth: Female Authority and the Family Romance," in *Unfolded Tales: Essays on the Renaissance Romance,* ed. Gordon M. Logan and Gordon Teskey. Ithaca: Cornell University Press, 1989.

———. "The Constant Subject: Instability and Female Authority in Wroth's Urania Poems," in *Soliciting Interpretation: Literary Theory and Seventeenth-Century Poetry,* ed. Elizabeth D. Maus and Katherine Eisaman Maus. Chicago: University of Chicago Press, 1990.

Rathmell, J. C. A., "Jonson, Lord Lisle, and Penshurst," *English Literary Renaissance,* 1 (1972), 250–260.

Rees, Joan. *Samuel Daniel.* Liverpool: Liverpool University Press, 1964.

Riley, Denise. *"Am I that Name": Feminism and the Category of "Women" in History.* Minneapolis: University of Minnesota Press, 1988.

Roberts, Josephine A. "An Unpublished Literary Quarrel Concerning the Suppression of Mary Wroth's 'Urania' (1621)," *Notes and Queries,* 222 (December, 1977), 532–35.

———. "Lady Mary Wroth's Sonnets: A Labyrinth of the Mind," *Journal of Women's Studies in Literature,* 1 (1979), 319–29.

———. "The Biographical Problem of Pamphilia to Amphilanthus," *Tulsa Studies in Women's Literature,* 1 (1983), 43–53.

———. "The Huntington Manuscript of Lady Mary Wroth's Play, *Loves Victorie,*" *Huntington Library Quarterly,* 46 (1983), 156–74.

Roland, Alan. "The Familial Self, the Individualized Self, and the Transcendent Self: Psychoanalytic Reflections on India and America," *Psychoanalytic Review,* 74 (1987), 236–50.

Roskill, Mark. "Van Dyck at the English Court: the Relations of Portrait and Allegory," *Critical Inquiry* 14 (1987), 173–99.

Ross, Ellen. "Rethinking 'the Family'," *Radical History Review,* 20 (Spring/ Summer, 1979), 76–84.

Rowe, Violet A. "The Influence of the Earls of Pembroke on Parliamentary Elections, 1625–41." *English Historical Review,* 50 (1935), 242–56.

Rubin, Gayle. "The Traffic in Women: Notes on the 'Political Economy' of Sex," in *Toward an Anthropology of Women,* ed. Rayna R. Reiter. New York: Monthly Review Press, 1975.

Ruigh, Robert E. *The Parliament of 1624.* Cambridge, Mass.: Harvard University Press, 1971.

Russell, Conrad. *The Crisis of Parliaments*. London: Oxford University Press, 1971.

Rustin, Michael. *The Good Society and the Inner World*. London: Verso, 1991.

Sacher-Masoch, Leopold von. *Venus in Furs*. See Deleuze, Gilles.

Sayers, Janet. *Sexual Contradictions: Psychology, Psychoanalysis, and Feminism*. London: Tavistock, 1986.

Schleiner, Louise. *The Living Lyre in English Verse from Elizabeth through the Restoration*. Columbia, Mo.: University of Missouri Press, 1984.

Schochet, Gordon J. *Patriarchalism in Political Thought: The Authoritarian Family and Political Speculation and Attitudes in Sevententh-Century England*. New York: Basic Books, 1975

Schwartz, Murray, and Coppélia Kahn. *Representing Shakespeare: New Psychoanalytic Essays*. Baltimore: Johns Hopkins University Press, 1980.

Scott, Joan Wallach. *Gender and the Politics of History*. New York: Columbia University Press, 1988.

Sharratt, Bernard. *Reading Relations*. Brighton: Harvester, 1982.

Shaver, Ann. "Outspoken Women in Book I of Lady Mary Wroth's *Urania*," *Sidney Newsletter*, 10.1 (1990), 89.

Shepherd, Simon. *Amazons and Warrior Women: Varieties of Feminism in Seventeenth-century Drama*. Brighton: Harvester, 1981.

Shorter, Edward. "On Writing the History of Rape," *Signs*, 3 (1977–78), 471–82.

Shullenburger, William. "Lacan and the Play of Desire in Poetry," *Massachusetts Studies in English*, 7 (1978), 33–40.

Sidney, [Herbert]. *A Catalogue of the Paintings and Drawings in the Collection at Wilton House*. London: Phaeton, 1968.

Sil, Narasingha P. *William Lord Herbert of Pembroke (c.1507–1570): Politique and Patriot*. Lewiston, N.Y.: Edwin Mellen, 1988.

Simpson, Richard I. *The Lady Falkland, Her Life*. London: Catholic Publishing and Bookselling Co., 1861.

Sinfield, Alan. "Sidney and Astrophil." *Studies in English Literature*, 20 (1980), 25–41.

———. *Literature in Protestant England*. London: Croom Helm, 1983.

Slater, Miriam. *Family Life in the Seventeenth Century: the Verneys of Slater House*. London: Routledge and Kegan Paul, 1984.

Smirnoff, Victor N. "The Masochistic Contract," *International Journal of Psycho-Analysis*, 50 (1969), 665–70.

Smith, Joseph H., and William Kerrigan, ed. *Pragmatism's Freud: The Moral Disposition of Psychoanalysis*. Baltimore: Johns Hopkins University Press, 1986.

———. "Evening the Score," *Modern Language Notes*, 104 (1989), 1050–65.

Smuts, R. Malcolm. *Court Culture and the Origins of a Royalist Tradition in Early Stuart England*. Philadelphia: University of Pennsylvania Press, 1987.

Socarides, Charles W. "The Demonified Mother: A Study of Voyeurism and Sexual Sadism," *International Review of Psycho-Analysis*, 1 (1974), 187–95.

Steen, Sara Jayne. "Fashioning an Acceptable Self: Lady Arbella Stuart," *English Literary Renaissance*, 18 (1988), 76–94.

Stevens, John. *Music and Poetry in the Early Tudor Court*. London: Chatto and Windus, 1961.

———. *Medieval Romance*. New York: Norton, 1974.

Stewart, Abigail J., David G. Winter, and A. David Jones, "Coding for the Study of Child-Rearing from Historical Sources," *Journal of Interdisciplinary History*, 5 (1975), 687–701.

Stewart, Stanley. "Recent Studies in the English Renaissance," *Studies in English Literature, 1500–1900*, 31 (1991), 179–222.

Stoller, Robert J. "Shakespearean Tragedy: Coriolanus," *Psychoanalytical Quarterly*, 35 (1966), 263–74.

———. *Perversion: The Erotic Form of Hatred*. London: Mansfield Library, 1975.

———. *Observing the Erotic Imagination*. New Haven: Yale University Press, 1985.

Stone, Lawrence. *The Crisis of the Aristocracy, 1558–1641*. Oxford: Clarendon Press, 1965.

———. *The Family, Sex and Marriage in England, 1500–1800*. New York: Harper and Row, 1977.

———. "Family History in the 1980s," *Journal of Interdisciplinary History*, 12 (1981), 51–87.

Strong, Roy. *The English Icon*. London: Routledge Kegan Paul, 1969.

———. *Splendor at Court*. Boston: Houghton Mifflin, 1973.

Studlar, Gaylyn. *In the Realm of Pleasure: Von Sternberg, Dietrich, and the Masochistic Aesthetic*. Urbana: University of Illinois Press, 1988.

Suleiman, Susan Rubin, ed. *The Female Body in Western Culture*. Cambridge, Mass.: Harvard University Press, 1986.

Swift, Carolyn Ruth. "Feminine Identity in Lady Mary Wroth's Romance *Urania*," *English Literary Renaissance*, 14 (1984), 328–46.

Swindells, Julia, and Lisa Jardine. *What's Left? Women in Culture and the Labour Movement*. London: Routledge, 1990.

Taylor, Dick, Jr. "The Third Earl of Pembroke as a Patron of Poetry," *Tulane Studies in English*, 5 (1955), 41–67.

———. "The Masque and the Lance: the Earl of Pembroke in Jacobean Court Entertainments," *Tulane Studies in English*, 8 (1958), 21–53.

———. "The Earl of Pembroke and the Youth of Shakespeare's Sonnets: An Essay in Rehabilitation." *Studies in Philology*, 56 (1959), 26–54.

———. "Clarendon and Ben Jonson as Witnesses for the Earl of Pembroke's Character," in Josephine W. Bennett, Oscar Cargill, and Vernon Hall, Jr., eds., *Studies in the English Renaissance Drama*. London: Peter Owen, 1961.

Theweleit, Klaus. *Male Fantasies, Volume I: Women, Floods, Bodies, History*, trans. Stephen Conway; *Volume II: Male Bodies: Psychoanalyzing the White Terror*, trans. Erica Carter and Chris Turner. Minneapolis: University of Minnesota Press, 1988, 1989.

Thorpe, Thomas. *Catalogue of Manuscripts*. London: Thomas Thorpe, 1833.

Tiger, Lionel, and Robin Fox. *The Imperial Animal*. Holt Rinehart and Winston. 1971.

Trask, Haunami-Kay. *Eros and Power: the Promise of Feminist Theory*. Philadelphia: University of Pennsylvania Press, 1986.

Trinkaus, Charles. *The Poet as Philosopher*. New Haven: Yale University Press, 1979.

Tuve, Rosemund. *Selected Essays*. Princeton: Princeton University Press, 1980.

Twitchell, James B. *Forbidden Partners: the Incest Taboo in Modern Culture*. New York: Columbia University Press, 1987.

Updike, John. *Couples*. London: André Deutsch, 1968.

Vance, Eugene. "Love's Concordance: The Poetics of Desire and Joy of the Text," *Diacritics*, 5 (Spring 1975), 40–52.

Venuti, Lawrence. *Our Halcyon Dayes*. Madison: University of Wisconsin Press, 1989.

Vickers, Nancy J. "Diana Described: Scattered Woman and Scattered Rhyme." *Critical Inquiry*, 8 (1981–2), 265–79.

Waller, Gary. "This Matching of Contraries: the influence of Calvin and Bruno on the Sidney Circle," *Neophilologus*, 56 (1972), 331–43.

———. *Mary Sidney, Countess of Pembroke: A Critical Study of her Study of her Writings and Literary Milieu*. Salzburg: Institut für Anglistik und Amerikanistik 1979.

——. *English Poetry of the Sixteenth Century*. London: Longman, 1986; second edition, 1993.

——. "Mother/Son, Father/Daughter, Brother/Sister, Cousins: the Sidney Family Romance," *Modern Philology*, 88 (1991), 401–14.

Waller, Gary, and Michael D. Moore, eds. *Sir Philip Sidney and the Interpretation of Renaissance Culture*. London: Croom Helm, 1984.

Waller, Marguerite. "Academic Tootsie: The Denial of Difference and the Difference it Makes," *Diacritics*, 17.1 (Spring, 1987), 2–20.

Waller, William Chapman. "An Extinct County Family: Wroth of Loughton Hall," *Transactions of the Essex Archaeological Society*, n.s. 8 (1903), 145–80.

Wallerstein, Robert S. "Psychoanalysis as a Science: A Response to the New Challenges," *Pychoanalytical Quarterly*, 55 (1986), 414–51.

Walls, Peter. "Music and Sweet Poetry? Verse for English Lute Song and Continuo Song," *Music & Letters*, 65 (1984), 237–54.

Warkentin, Germaine. " 'Love's Sweetest Part, Variety': Petrarch and the Curious Frame of the Renaissance Sonnet Sequence," *Ren. and Ref.*, 11 (1975), 14–23.

Waterhouse, Ellis. *Painting in Britain 1530 to 1790*. Harmondsworth: Penguin, 1969.

Wayne, Don. *Penshurst: The Semiotics of Place and the Poetics of History*. Milwaukee: University of Wisconsin Press, 1984.

Weeks, Jeffrey. *Sexuality*. Chichester: Ellis Harwood, 1986.

Welldon, Estella V. *Mother, Madonna, Whore: The Idealization and Denigration of Motherhood*. Free Association Books, 1988.

Wentersdorf, K. P. "The Origin and Personnel of the Pembroke Company," *Theatre Research International*, 5–6 (1979–81), 45–68.

Willetts, Pamela J. *The Henry Lawes Manuscripts*. London: British Museum, 1969.

Williams, Raymond. *The Country and the City*. London: Chatto and Windus, 1973.

——. *The English Novel from Dickens to Lawrence*. London: Chatto and Windus, 1974.

——. *Marxism and Literature*. London: Oxford University Press, 1977.

——. *Keywords*. London: Oxford University Press, 1983.

——. *What I Came to Say*, ed. Neil Belton, Francis Mulhern, and Jenny Taylor. London: Hutchinson Radius, 1989.

Willson, D. H. *The Privy Councillors in the House of Commons 1604–1629*. New York: Octagon Books, 1971.

Wilson, Scott. "Sir Philip Sidney and the Extraordinary Forms of Desire," *Assays*, 7 (1993).

Winnicott, D. W. *The Family and Individual Development*. New York: Basic Books, 1965.

——. *Playing and Reality*. London: Methuen, 1971.

Wrightson, Keith. "Household and Kinship in Sixteenth-century England," *History Workshop*, 12 (Autumn, 1981), 151–58.

Yachnin, Paul. "*A Game at Chess*: Thomas Middleton's "Praise of Folly," *Modern Language Quarterly*, 48 (1987), 107–23.

Yates, Frances. *Astraea: The Imperial Theme in the Sixteenth Century*. London: Routledge and Kegan Paul, 1975.

Zaller, Robert. *The Parliament of 1621: A Study in Constitutional Conflict*. Berkeley: University of California Press, 1971.

Zaretsky, Eli. *Capitalism, the Family, and Personal Life*. New York: Harper & Row, 1976.

Zavitzianos, George. "Fetishism and Exhibitionism in the Female and their Relationship to Psychopathy and Kleptomania," *International Journal of Psycho-Analysis*, 52 (1971), 297–305.

——. "The Object in Fetishism, Homovestism and Transvestism." *International Journal of Psycho-Analysis*, 58 (1977), 487–95.

Index

Donne, John, the younger, 18, 159,
162–64, 169
Dowland, John, 165, 169, 171, 186,
304n.5
Drayton, Michael, 136, 143, 163, 164
Drummond of Hawthornden, William,
165, 166–67
Durance, 49, 115, 117–19

Elizabeth I, Queen, 34, 74, 78, 91, 138,
252, 271
Erikson, Eric, 57, 103, 219
Evans, Malcolm, 84, 85, 187

Family, 17–18, 22, 23–24, 29–36, 39–40,
48, 56, 70, 95, 104–6, 285
Family Romance, 17–18, 39, 42–47,
96–100, 109, 124, 218, 250, 252–55,
260–61, 285
Feminism, 21, 24, 27–34, 46, 53, 98–110,
217–19, 262–63, 284, 288n.8,
292n.58
Fitton, Mary, 58, 73, 78–79, 87, 100, 122,
177, 225, 237
Ford, John, 61, 166, 229
Fraunce, Abraham, 60
Freud, Sigmund, 16–18, 19, 21, 22, 23,
25–27, 30, 34, 37, 39, 40, 41–44,
46, 62, 70, 71, 77–78, 82–84, 95–96,
98–99, 102, 123, 128, 130–31, 132,
146, 147, 148, 152, 206–7, 211, 215,
252–54, 282, 286, 291–92n.45
Frye, Northrop, 46, 250–51, 261

Gallop, Jane, 24, 25
Gebauer, Andreas, 5, 57, 85
Gender, 29, 32–40, 42, 43, 50, 53, 56–57,
68, 82, 165, 169, 179, 197–98,
233–45, 266
Greenblatt, Stephen, 25, 74, 135, 232, 282
Greven, Philip, 22, 32, 35, 59
Greville, Fulke, Lord Brooke, 139, 140,
141, 156, 194, 207–8, 224

Hamilton, A. C., 11, 138
Hannay, Margaret, 79, 225, 290n.30,
295n.30, 296n.53

Harington, Sir John, the younger, 137, 140
Hartsock, Nancy, 37, 42, 98
Henrietta Maria, Queen, 65, 233, 239
Herbert, George, 27, 70–72, 72
Herbert, Sir Henry, 226, 230
Herbert of Cherbury, Lord, 126
Héroard, Jean, 36, 38
Hickes, Sir Michael, 113
Hunt, David, 32, 36, 119

Ivychurch, 49–50, 54–55, 60

James VI, King of Scotland (James I of
England), 18, 33, 49, 81–83, 87,
88–90, 110, 119, 121, 163, 166, 225,
232, 233, 252, 279
Jones, Inigo, 86, 114, 229
Jonson, Ben, 50, 85–86, 116–19, 161, 172,
192, 195, 221, 225, 228, 229, 230,
233, 234, 239, 267

Kahn, Coppélia, 33, 57, 60, 68, 111, 208
Kahn, Michael, 77
Kaplan, Louise, 12, 16, 24, 29, 32, 40, 41,
44, 68, 78, 94, 95, 124, 147, 150–51,
158, 181, 185, 187, 203, 211, 214,
263, 269
Kelly-Gadol, Joan, 102
Knollys, Sir Francis, 78–79
Kristeva, Julia, 72, 75, 102, 104–5, 199
Krueger, Robert, 162, 172, 303n.10
Kuin, Roger, 194

Lacan, Jacques, 24, 98
Lamb, Mary Ellen, 13, 59, 60, 104, 108,
219, 234, 256
Lawes, Henry, 163–64, 169–72, 182–84
Lawes, William, 163–64, 169–71, 182
Leverenz, David, 25, 28
Lewalski, Barbara, 237–38
Lewis, C. S., 166, 169
"Literature," 19, 20, 47, 191, 221
Loughton, 82, 108–9, 113, 115, 117–21,
130, 150

Sidney, Sir Philip, 36, 50, 54–55, 59, 64, 65, 75, 85, 100, 102, 104, 135, 137–40, 144, 153, 154–55, 161, 165, 173, 175, 198, 221, 223–24, 227, 237, 240, 247, 250, 252, 270, 277, 290n.30
Sidney, Sir Robert, Earl of Leicester, 35, 39, 50, 61, 65, 75–76, 80, 89, 96, 108, 110–12, 114, 120, 121, 141–45, 165, 176, 194, 198, 304n.20
Spenser, Edmund, 46, 134, 141, 146, 156, 252, 264, 270, 276
Stevens, John, 46, 169
Stoller, Robert, 24, 145–46, 149, 150, 212, 213
Stone, Laurence, 39, 291n.37

Theater, 85, 86, 89, 92, 108, 119, 120, 221–25
Theweleit, Klaus, 12, 29, 32, 62–65, 67–68, 70–71, 267, 269, 274, 281

Waller, Gary, 11, 36, 194, 287n.4, 306n.4
Weidemann, Heather, 234, 235
Whyte, Rowland, 72–76, 80–81, 110, 111, 227, 295n.39
Williams, Raymond, 25, 29, 49, 50, 118, 282
Wilton House, 49–50, 54, 58, 62, 65, 86, 122, 164, 169, 225
Wood, Anthony à, 58, 161
Wotton, Sir Henry, 74, 164, 169, 217, 227
Writing, 79, 99, 109–11, 122, 127–30, 304–5, 159, 165–66, 176, 179, 192, 204–5, 215–17, 227–29, 242, 278–80
[Wroth], Catherine, 126

Wroth, Lady Mary, 11, 20, 46, 48, 49, 51, 95–131, 191–219, 247–81; early life, 38, 47, 76, 96–98, 110–12, 150–51; in Jacobean court, 108–9, 112, 115–19, 227–28, 231, 233–35, 252, 254, 266; *Love's Victory*, 128–29, 223, 237–45; marriage, 106, 112–19, 151, 242, 254–55, 267; *Pamphilia to Amphilanthus*, 102, 127, 156–57, 173, 191–219, 240, 242, 245, 247, 304–5n.5; relationship with cousin William, 18, 44, 47, 48, 76–77, 92, 107–9, 114–15, 119, 121, 122–31, 140–41, 153, 157, 159, 176–78, 183, 192, 199–203, 249–50, 254, 255, 257–60, 261–63, 264–67, 284–85; *Urania*, 44, 65, 88, 102–3, 105, 109–10, 127, 128–30, 177–78, 191, 192, 213–15, 231–33, 236–37, 239–40, 242, 245, 247–81; widowhood and later life, 119–22, 125, 130–31, 163; as woman, 28, 38, 43–44, 102–6, 124–31, 147, 153, 156–57, 181, 188, 194, 195–99, 203–19, 253–60, 261–81; as writer, 45, 71, 85, 99, 109, 127–30, 140–41, 147, 154, 156, 179, 192, 194, 216–17, 260–64
Wroth, Sir Robert, 19, 49, 82, 112–15, 117–19, 238, 240, 242–43, 254–55, 267
[Wroth,] William, 108, 122, 125
Wyatt, Sir Thomas, 133, 136, 155

Zagorin, Perez, 164
Zumthor, Paul, 32, 79, 97